D1116359

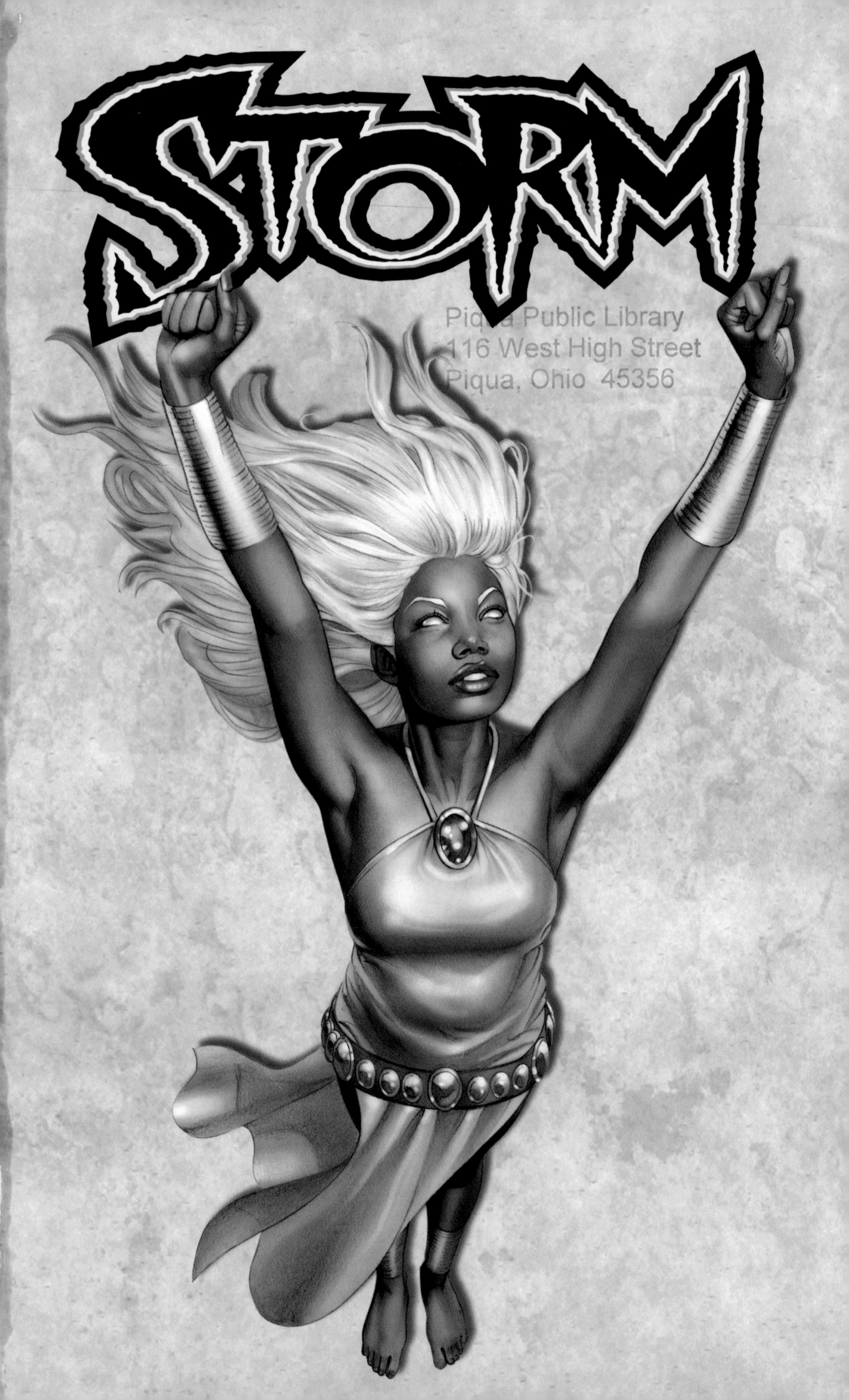
STORM

Writer: Eric Jerome Dickey
Pencilers: David Yardin & Lan Medina
Inkers: Jay Leisten with Sean Parsons

Colorist: Matt Milla
Letterer: Virtual Calligraphy's Randy Gentile
Cover Art: Mike Mayhew
Assistant Editor: Daniel Ketchum
Associate Editor: Cory Sedlmeier
Editor: Axel Alonso

Collection Editor: Jennifer Grünwald
Assistant Editor: Michael Short
Associate Editor: Mark D. Beazley
Senior Editor, Special Projects: Jeff Youngquist
Vice President of Sales: David Gabriel
Book Designer: Carrie Beadle
Vice President of Creative: Tom Marvelli

Editor in Chief: Joe Quesada
Publisher: Dan Buckley

STORM. Contains material originally published in magazine form as STORM #1-6. First printing 2007. ISBN# 0-7851-2283-4. Published by MARVEL PUBLISHING, INC., a subsidiary of MARVEL ENTERTAINMENT, INC. OFFICE OF PUBLICATION: 417 5th Avenue, New York, NY 10016. Copyright © 2006 and 2007 Marvel Characters, Inc. All rights reserved. $19.99 per copy in the U.S. and $32.00 in Canada (GST #R127032852); Canadian Agreement #40668537. All characters featured in this issue and the distinctive names and likenesses thereof, and all related indicia are trademarks of Marvel Characters, Inc. No similarity between any of the names, characters, persons, and/or institutions in this magazine with those of any living or dead person or institution is intended, and any such similarity which may exist is purely coincidental. **Printed in the U.S.A.** ALAN FINE, President & CEO Of Marvel Toys and Marvel Publishing, Inc.; DAVID BOGART, VP Of Publishing Operations; DAN CARR, Executive Director of Publishing Technology; JUSTIN F. GABRIE, Managing Editor; STAN LEE, Chairman Emeritus. For information regarding advertising in Marvel Comics or on Marvel.com, please contact Joe Maimone, Advertising Director, at jmaimone@marvel.com or 212-576-8534.

10 9 8 7 6 5 4 3 2 1

Issue #1

AUG 2006

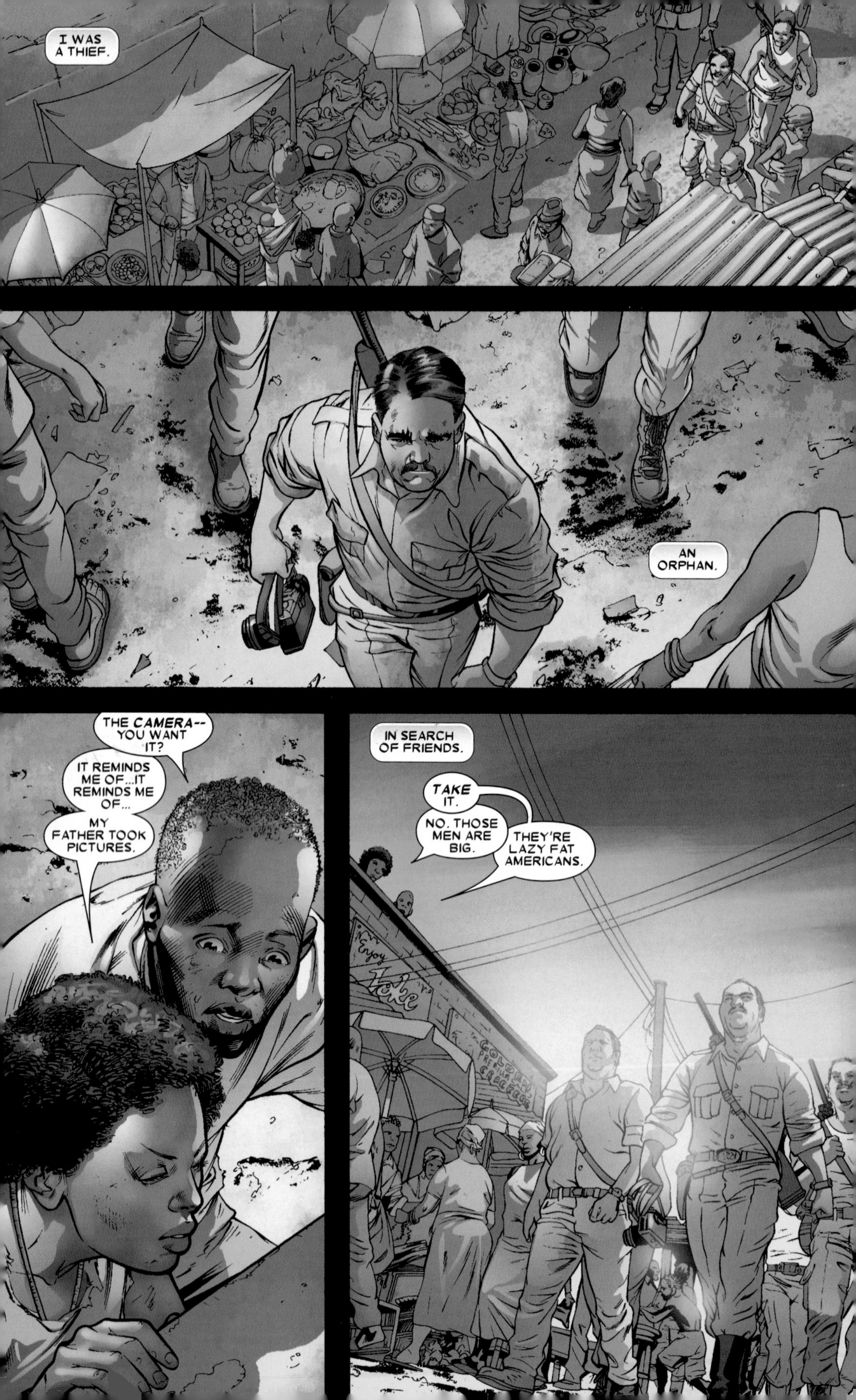
I WAS A THIEF.
AN ORPHAN.
THE *CAMERA*-- YOU WANT IT?
IT REMINDS ME OF... IT REMINDS ME OF...
MY FATHER TOOK PICTURES.
IN SEARCH OF FRIENDS.
TAKE IT.
NO. THOSE MEN ARE BIG.
THEY'RE LAZY FAT AMERICANS.

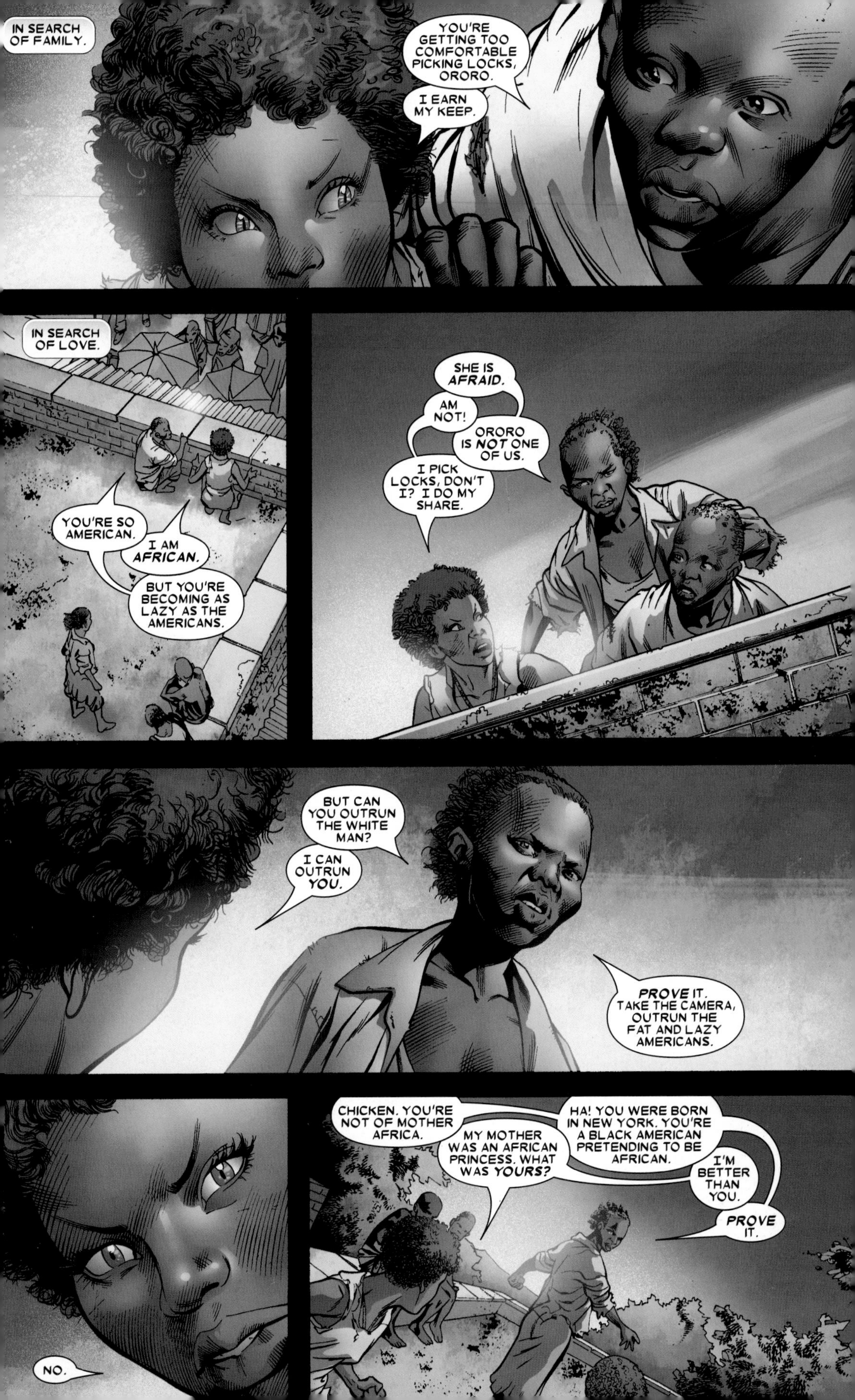
IN SEARCH OF FAMILY.
YOU'RE GETTING TOO COMFORTABLE PICKING LOCKS, ORORO.
I EARN MY KEEP.
IN SEARCH OF LOVE.
YOU'RE SO AMERICAN.
I AM AFRICAN.
BUT YOU'RE BECOMING AS LAZY AS THE AMERICANS.
SHE IS AFRAID.
AM NOT!
ORORO IS NOT ONE OF US.
I PICK LOCKS, DON'T I? I DO MY SHARE.
BUT CAN YOU OUTRUN THE WHITE MAN?
I CAN OUTRUN YOU.
PROVE IT. TAKE THE CAMERA, OUTRUN THE FAT AND LAZY AMERICANS.
NO.
CHICKEN. YOU'RE NOT OF MOTHER AFRICA.
MY MOTHER WAS AN AFRICAN PRINCESS. WHAT WAS YOURS?
HA! YOU WERE BORN IN NEW YORK. YOU'RE A BLACK AMERICAN PRETENDING TO BE AFRICAN.
I'M BETTER THAN YOU.
PROVE IT.

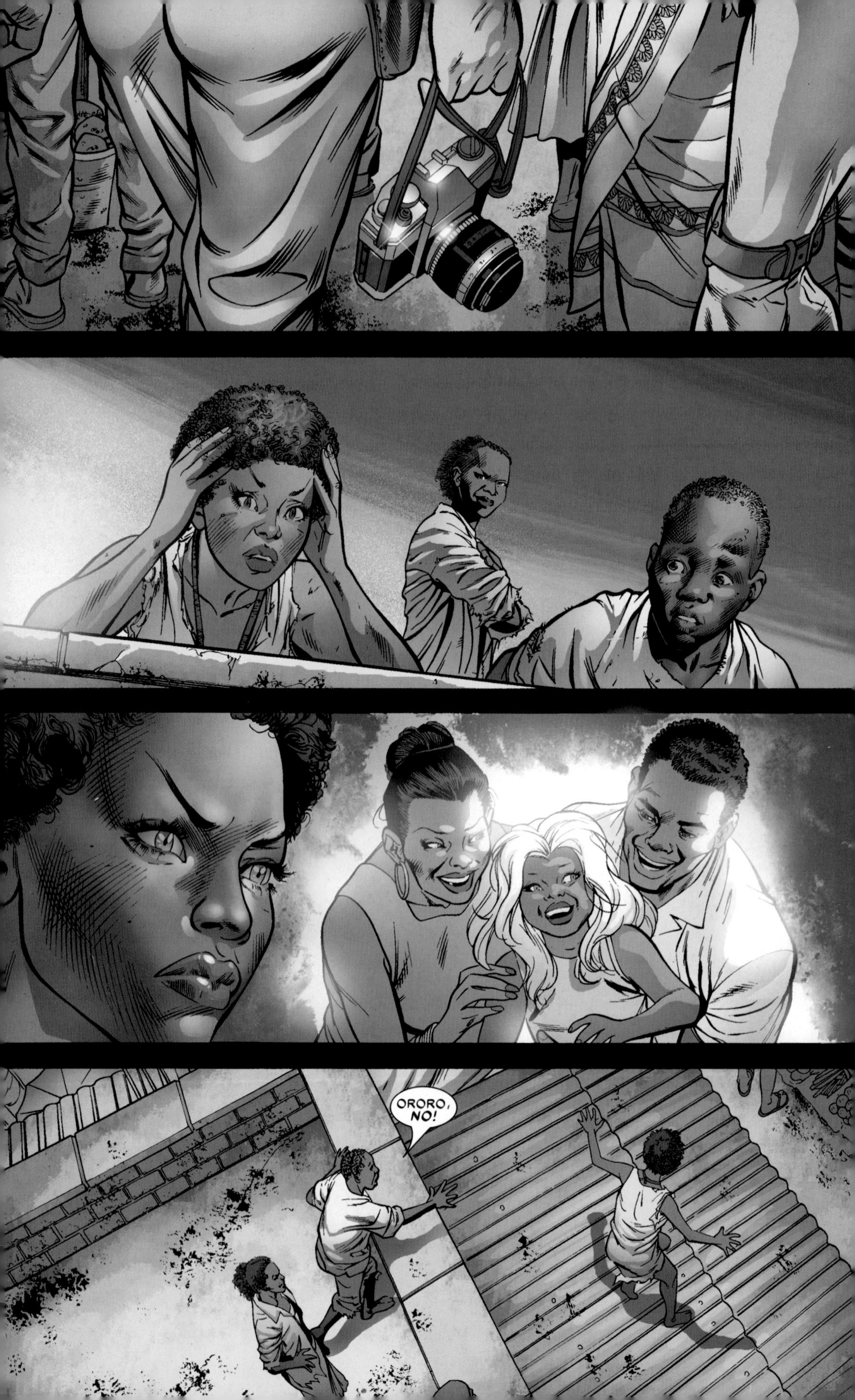
ORORO, NO!

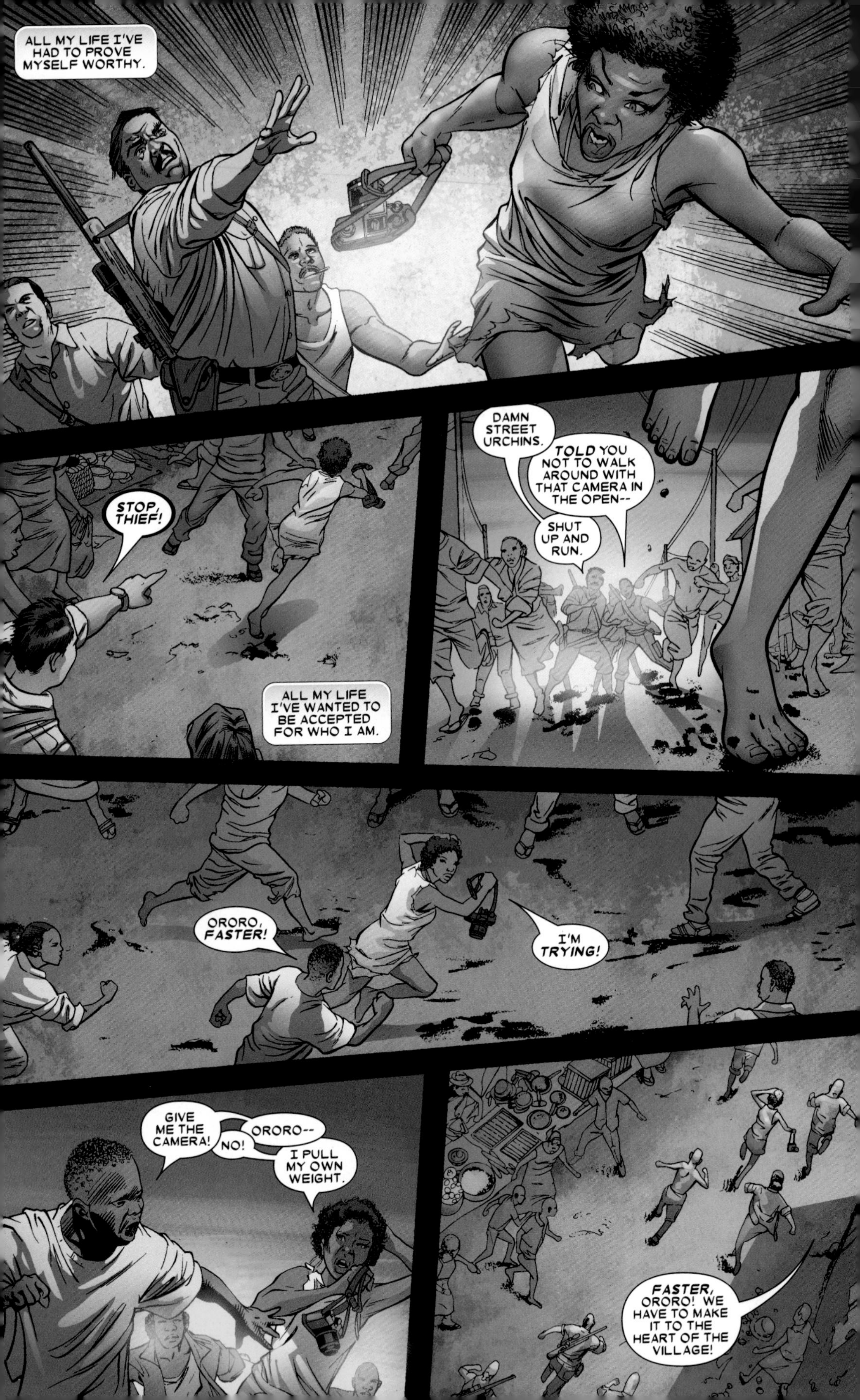
ALL MY LIFE I'VE HAD TO PROVE MYSELF WORTHY.
STOP, THIEF!
ALL MY LIFE I'VE WANTED TO BE ACCEPTED FOR WHO I AM.
DAMN STREET URCHINS.
TOLD YOU NOT TO WALK AROUND WITH THAT CAMERA IN THE OPEN--
SHUT UP AND RUN.
ORORO, FASTER!
I'M TRYING!
GIVE ME THE CAMERA!
ORORO--
NO!
I PULL MY OWN WEIGHT.
FASTER, ORORO! WE HAVE TO MAKE IT TO THE HEART OF THE VILLAGE!

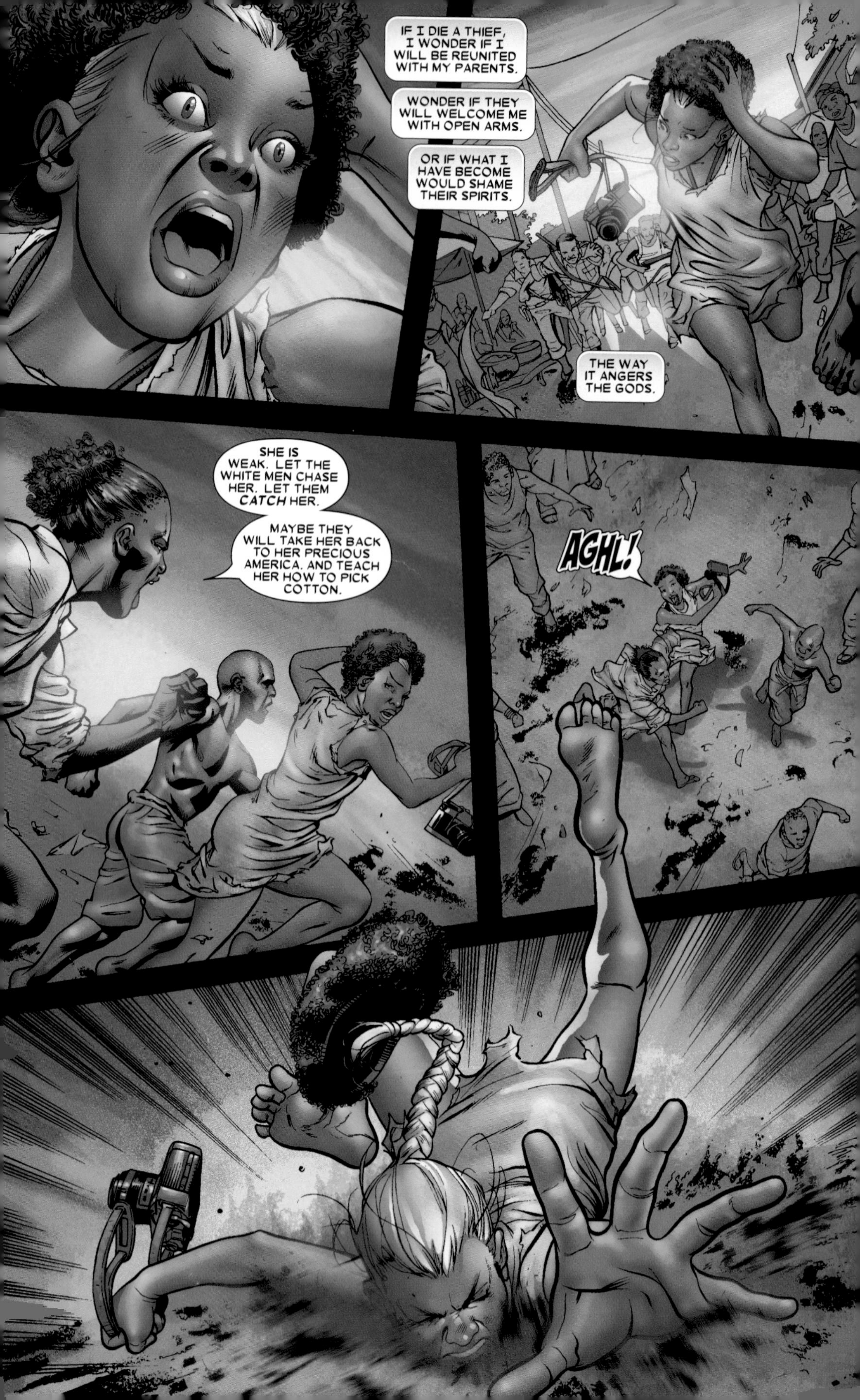

IF I DIE A THIEF, I WONDER IF I WILL BE REUNITED WITH MY PARENTS.
WONDER IF THEY WILL WELCOME ME WITH OPEN ARMS.
OR IF WHAT I HAVE BECOME WOULD SHAME THEIR SPIRITS.
THE WAY IT ANGERS THE GODS.
SHE IS WEAK. LET THE WHITE MEN CHASE HER. LET THEM *CATCH* HER.
MAYBE THEY WILL TAKE HER BACK TO HER PRECIOUS AMERICA, AND TEACH HER HOW TO PICK COTTON.
AGHL!

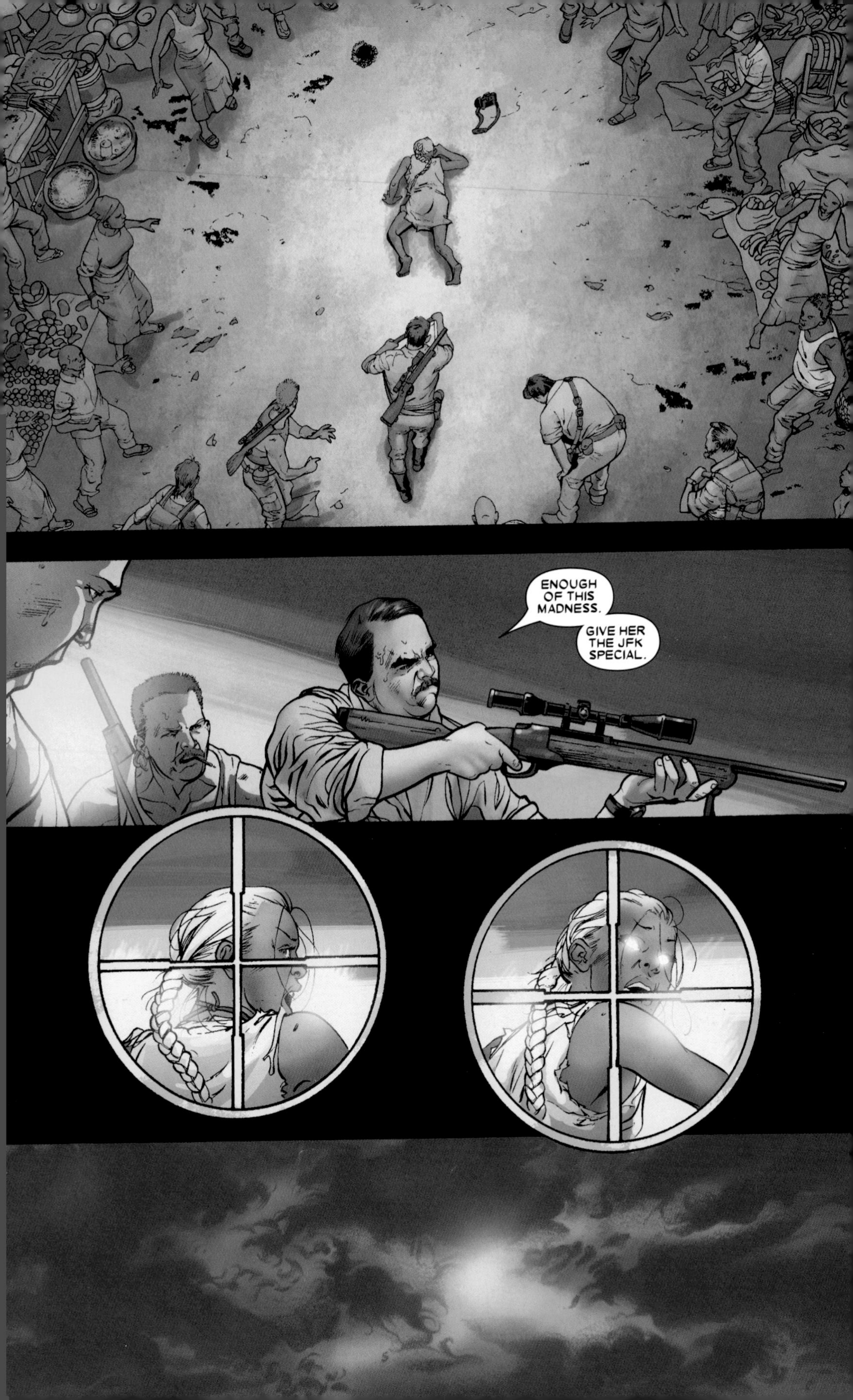
ENOUGH OF THIS MADNESS.
GIVE HER THE JFK SPECIAL.

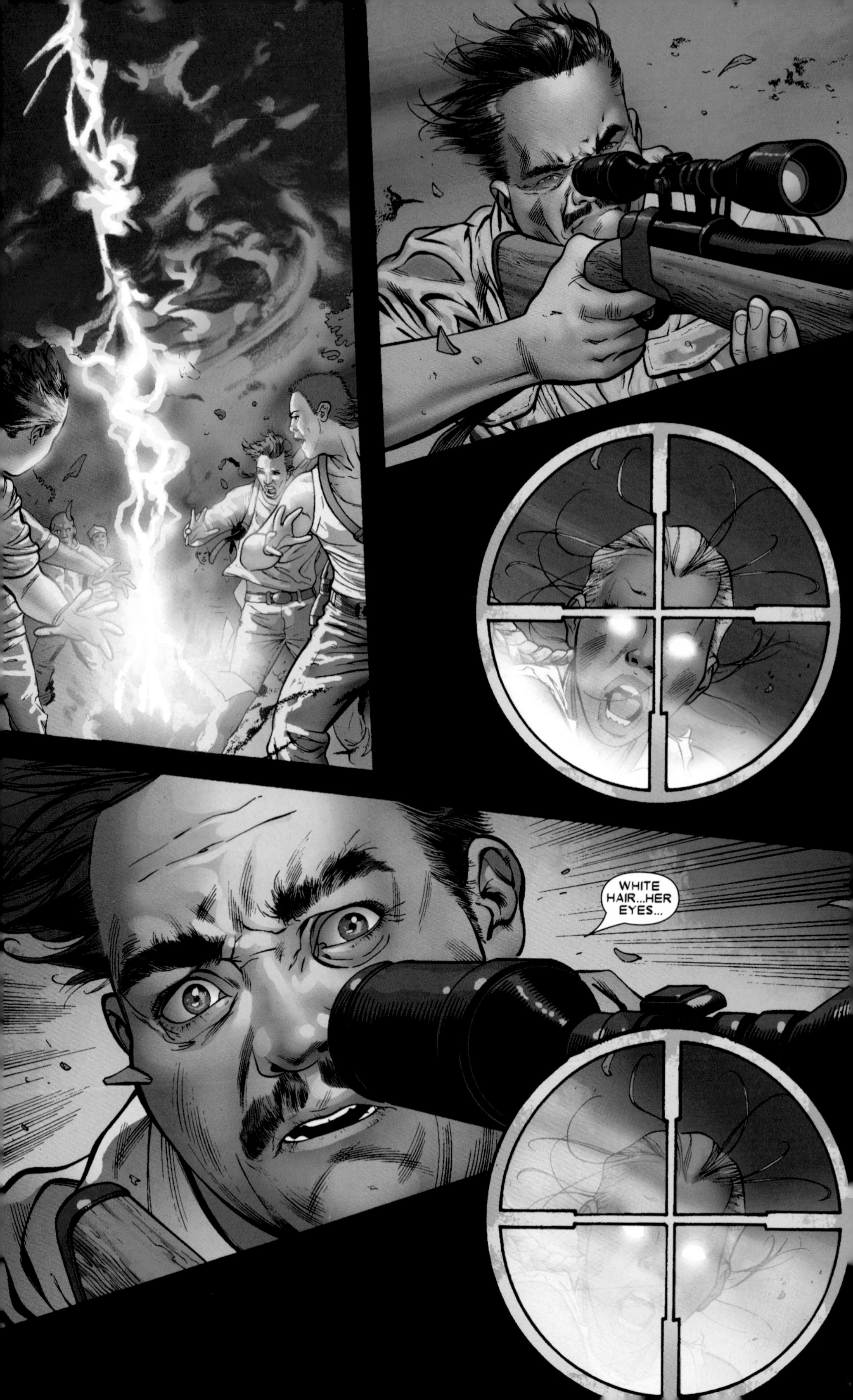
WHITE HAIR...HER EYES...

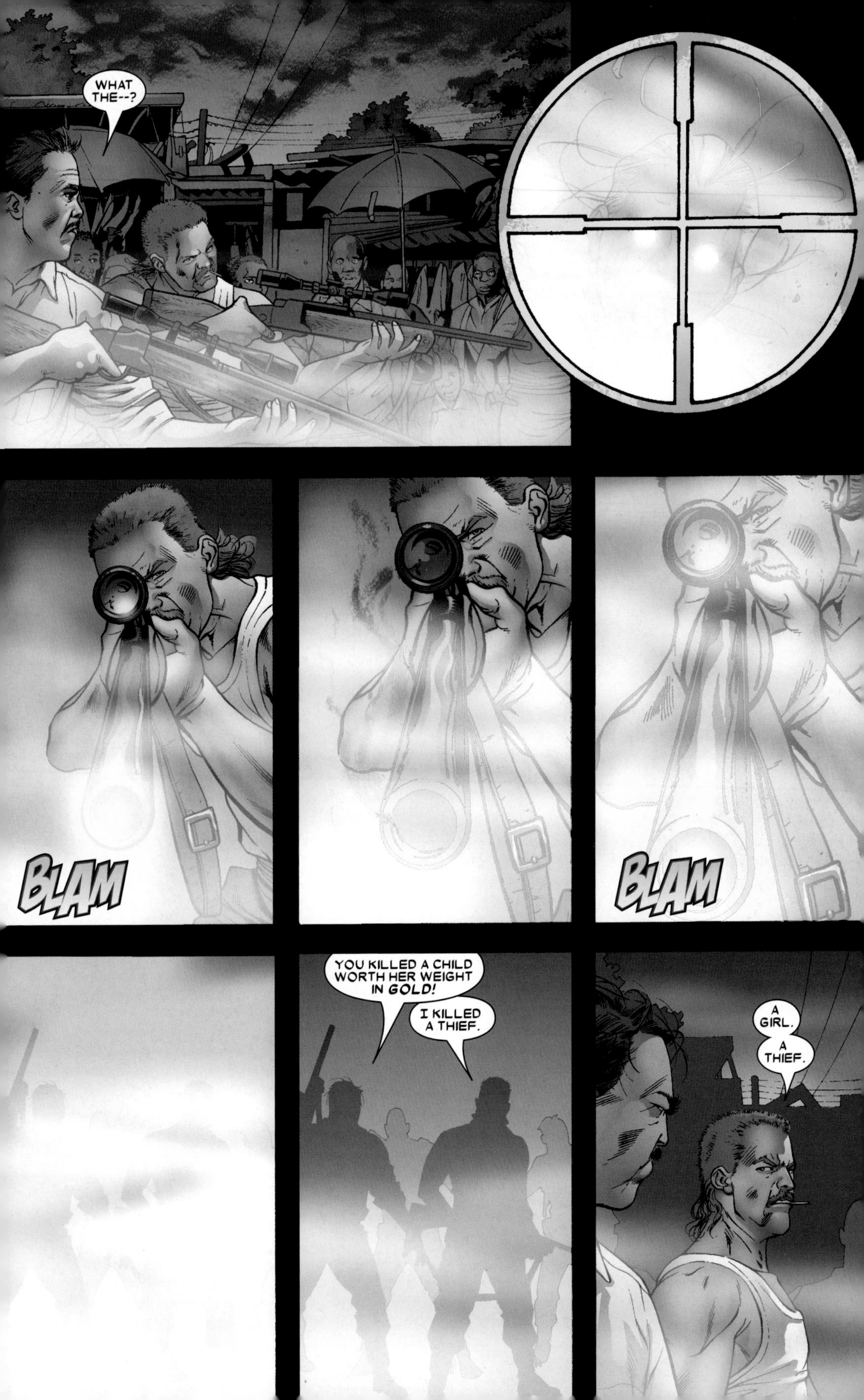
WHAT THE--?
BLAM
BLAM
YOU KILLED A CHILD WORTH HER WEIGHT IN GOLD!
I KILLED A THIEF.
A GIRL.
A THIEF.

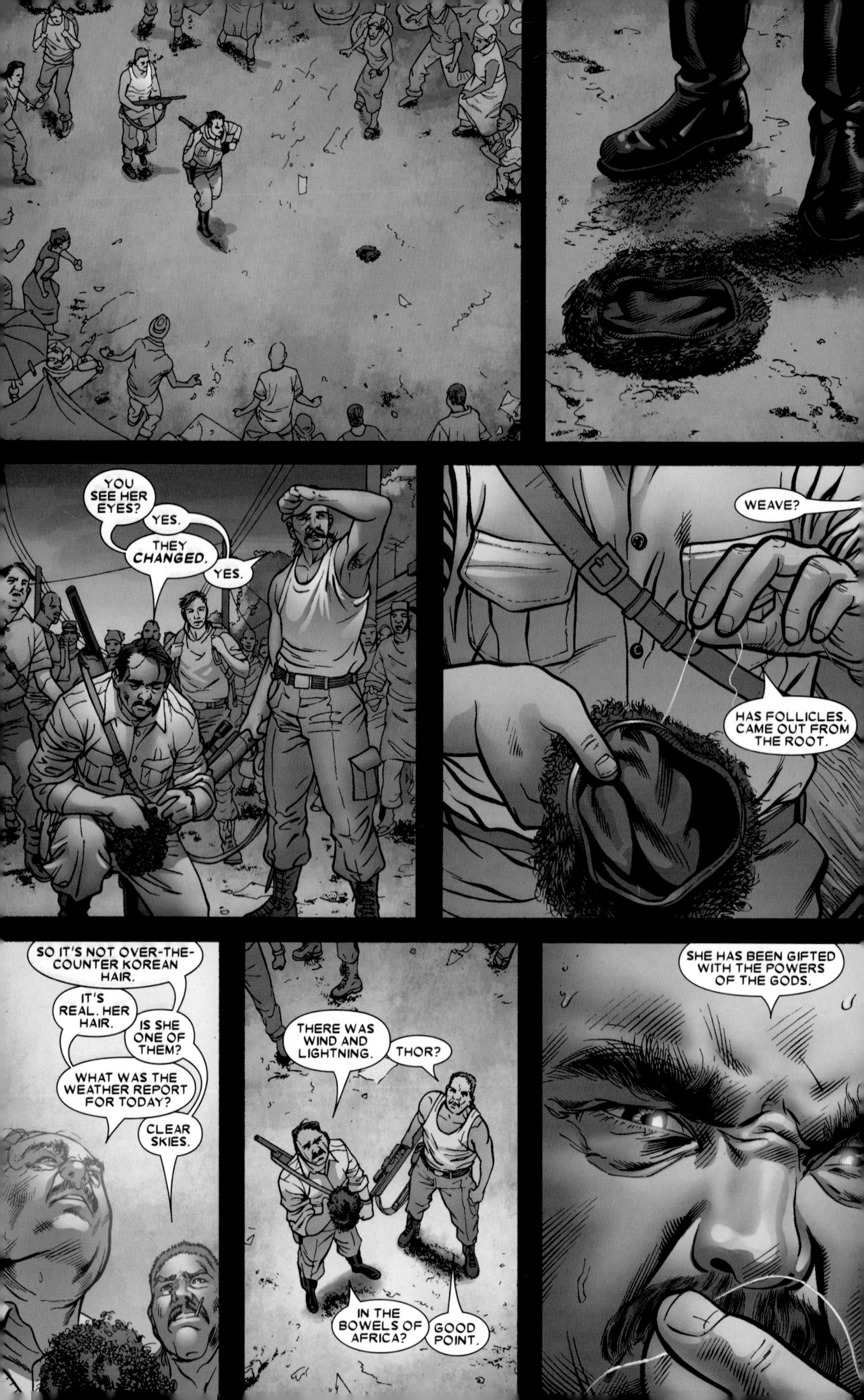
YOU SEE HER EYES?
YES.
THEY *CHANGED.*
YES.
WEAVE?
HAS FOLLICLES. CAME OUT FROM THE ROOT.
SO IT'S NOT OVER-THE-COUNTER KOREAN HAIR.
IT'S REAL. HER HAIR.
IS SHE ONE OF THEM?
WHAT WAS THE WEATHER REPORT FOR TODAY?
CLEAR SKIES.
THERE WAS WIND AND LIGHTNING.
THOR?
IN THE BOWELS OF AFRICA?
GOOD POINT.
SHE HAS BEEN GIFTED WITH THE POWERS OF THE GODS.

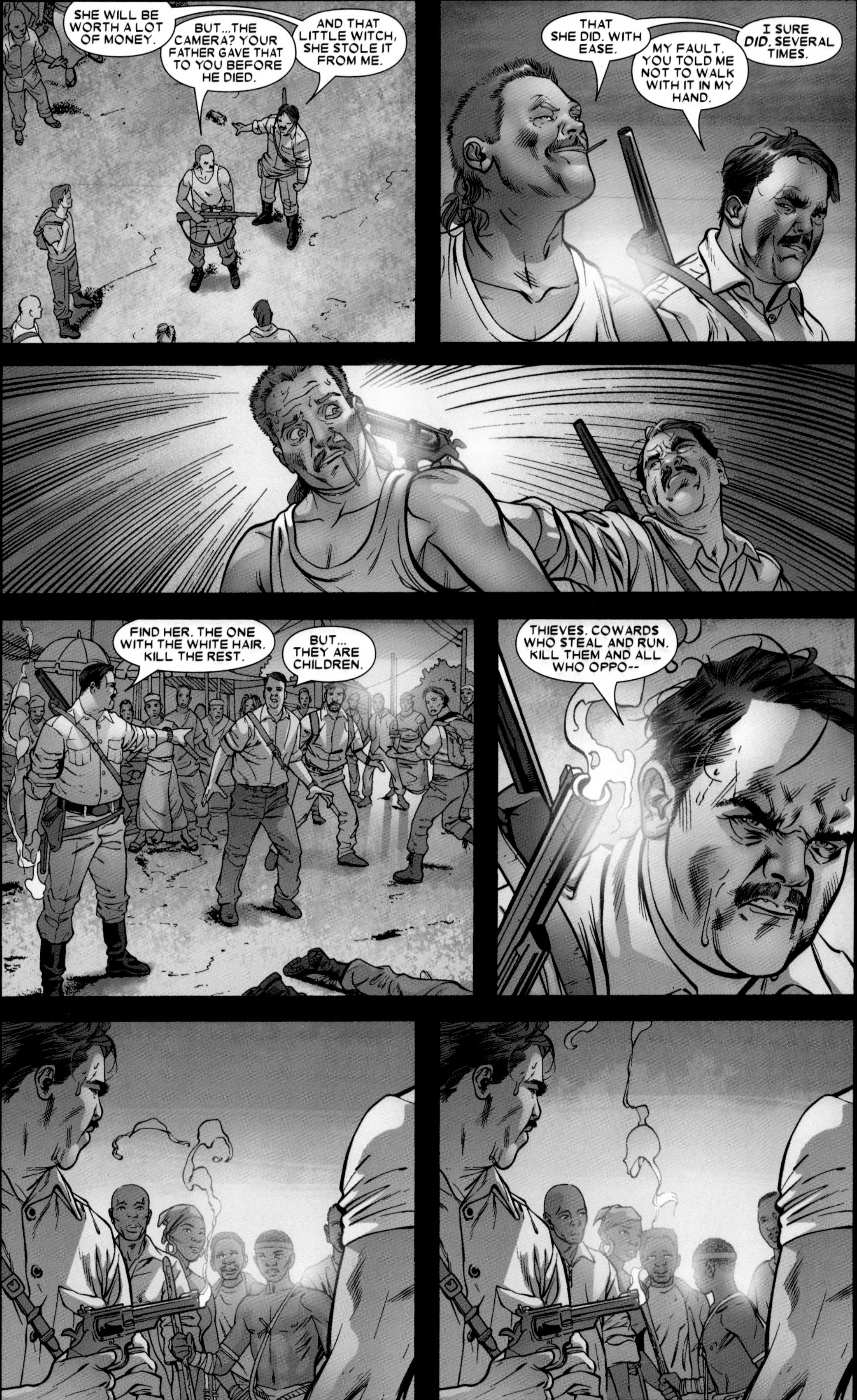
SHE WILL BE WORTH A LOT OF MONEY.
BUT...THE CAMERA? YOUR FATHER GAVE THAT TO YOU BEFORE HE DIED.
AND THAT LITTLE WITCH, SHE STOLE IT FROM ME.
THAT SHE DID. WITH EASE.
MY FAULT. YOU TOLD ME NOT TO WALK WITH IT IN MY HAND.
I SURE *DID*. SEVERAL TIMES.
FIND HER. THE ONE WITH THE WHITE HAIR. KILL THE REST.
BUT... THEY ARE CHILDREN.
THIEVES. COWARDS WHO STEAL AND RUN. KILL THEM AND ALL WHO OPPO--

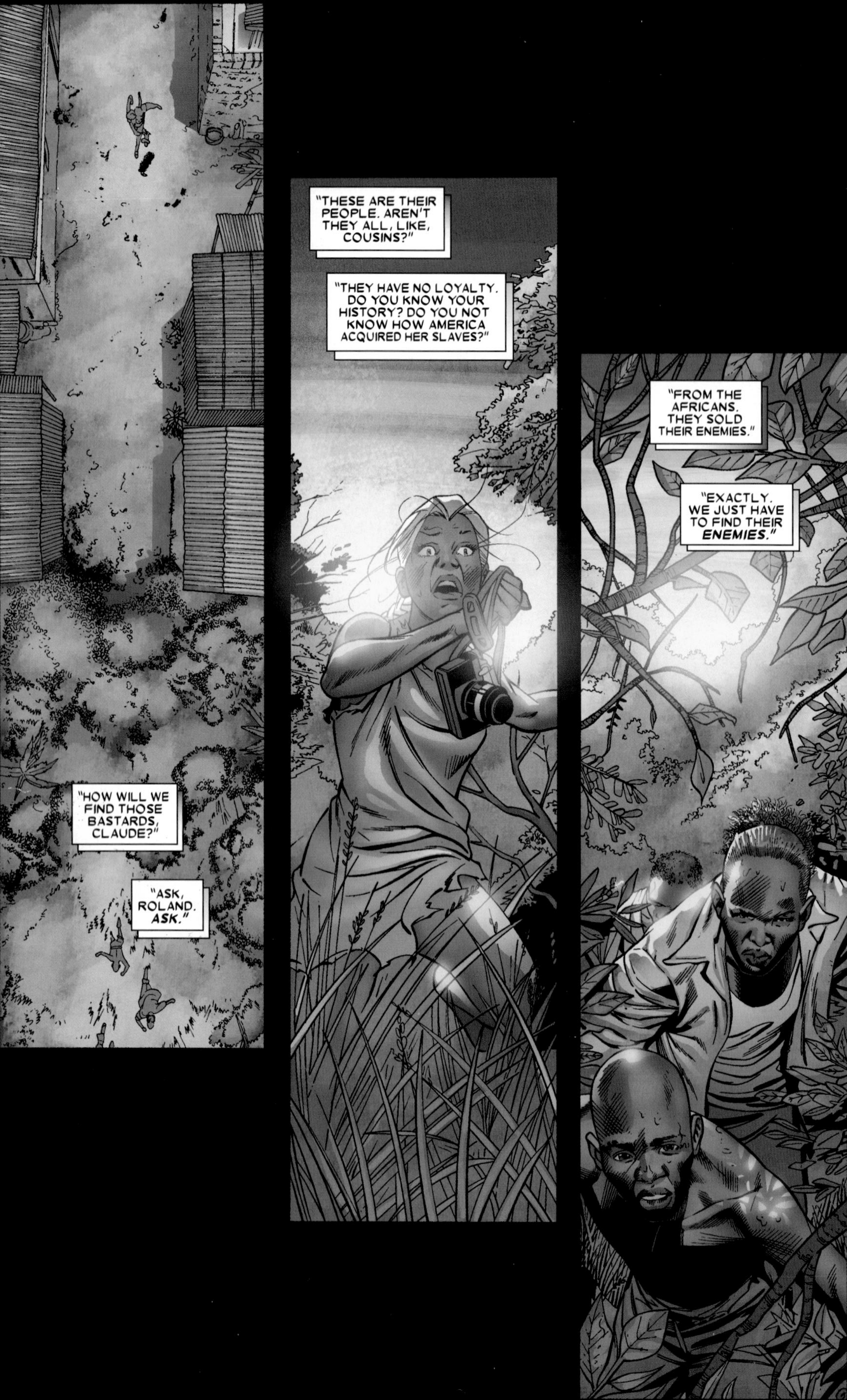
"HOW WILL WE FIND THOSE BASTARDS, CLAUDE?"
"ASK, ROLAND. ASK."
"THESE ARE THEIR PEOPLE. AREN'T THEY ALL, LIKE, COUSINS?"
"THEY HAVE NO LOYALTY. DO YOU KNOW YOUR HISTORY? DO YOU NOT KNOW HOW AMERICA ACQUIRED HER SLAVES?"
"FROM THE AFRICANS. THEY SOLD THEIR ENEMIES."
"EXACTLY. WE JUST HAVE TO FIND THEIR ENEMIES."

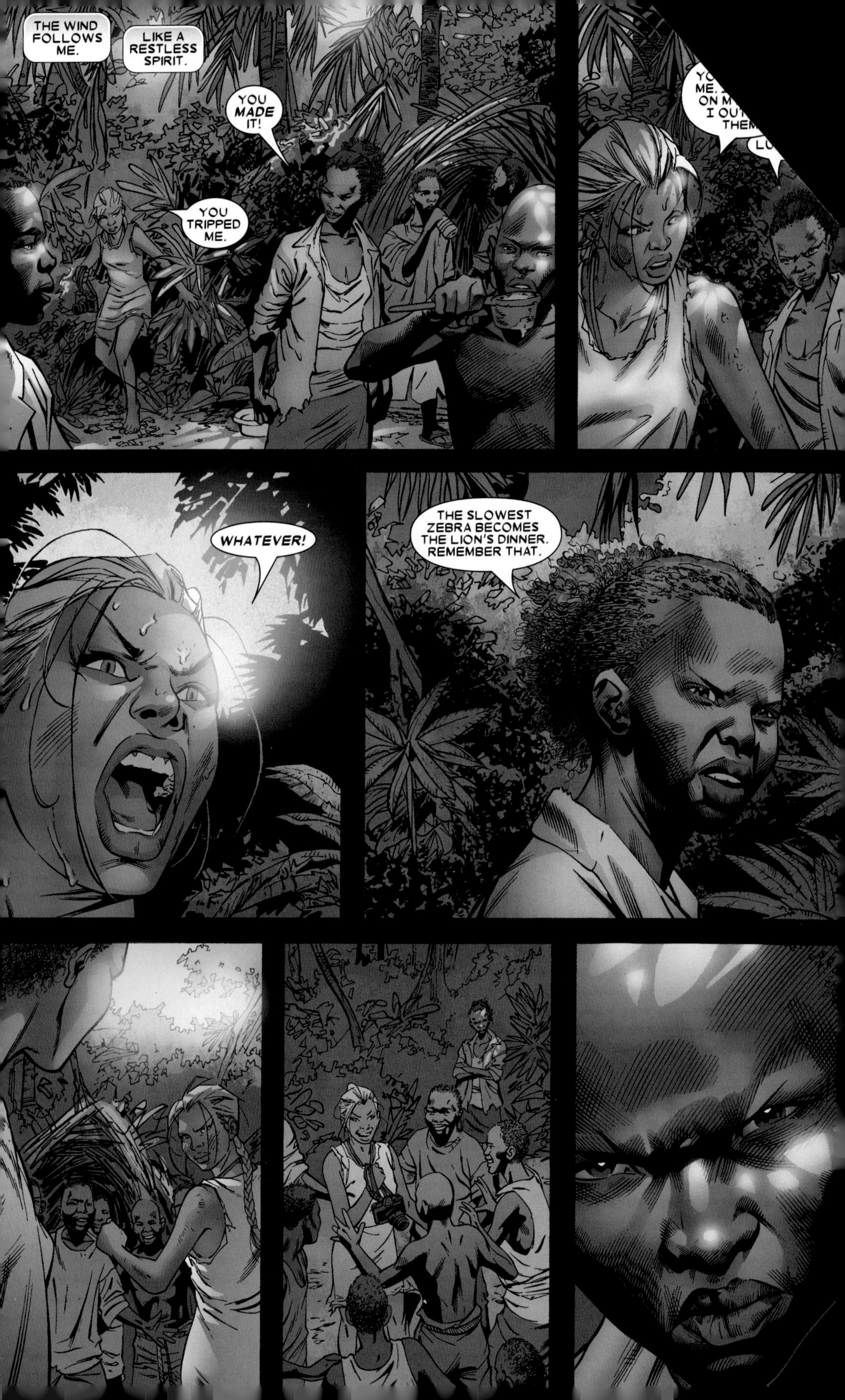
THE WIND FOLLOWS ME.
LIKE A RESTLESS SPIRIT.
YOU *MADE* IT!
YOU TRIPPED ME.
WHATEVER!
THE SLOWEST ZEBRA BECOMES THE LION'S DINNER. REMEMBER THAT.

DON'T BLAME THOSE BIG FEET ON ME.

...U TRIPPED ...AT MADE IT ...OWN. ...RAN ...CKY.

...N I WAS IN CAIRO, ...--ALONE, HUNGRY-- ...ER THIEF, ACHMED ...AR, TRAINED ME, ...DID ALL OF THE ...STREET URCHINS.

...TREET URCHINS. THAT WAS WHAT ...THEY CALLED US. BUT WE WERE ...CHILDREN. ABANDONED BY OUR PARENTS. ORPHANED BY THE GODS. LEFT WITH NOTHING. NO ONE. SOME OF US ABUSED IN WAYS UNIMAGINABLE AND UNFORGIVABLE.

NOW I AM IN A DIFFERENT LAND, WITH OTHER STREET URCHINS. ONCE AGAIN ALONE. AN ORPHAN AMONGST ORPHANS. STRUGGLING TO SURVIVE THE ONLY WAY WE KNOW HOW.

NO ONE HAS A MOTHER. NO ONE HAS A FATHER.

ALL WE HAVE IS EACH OTHER.

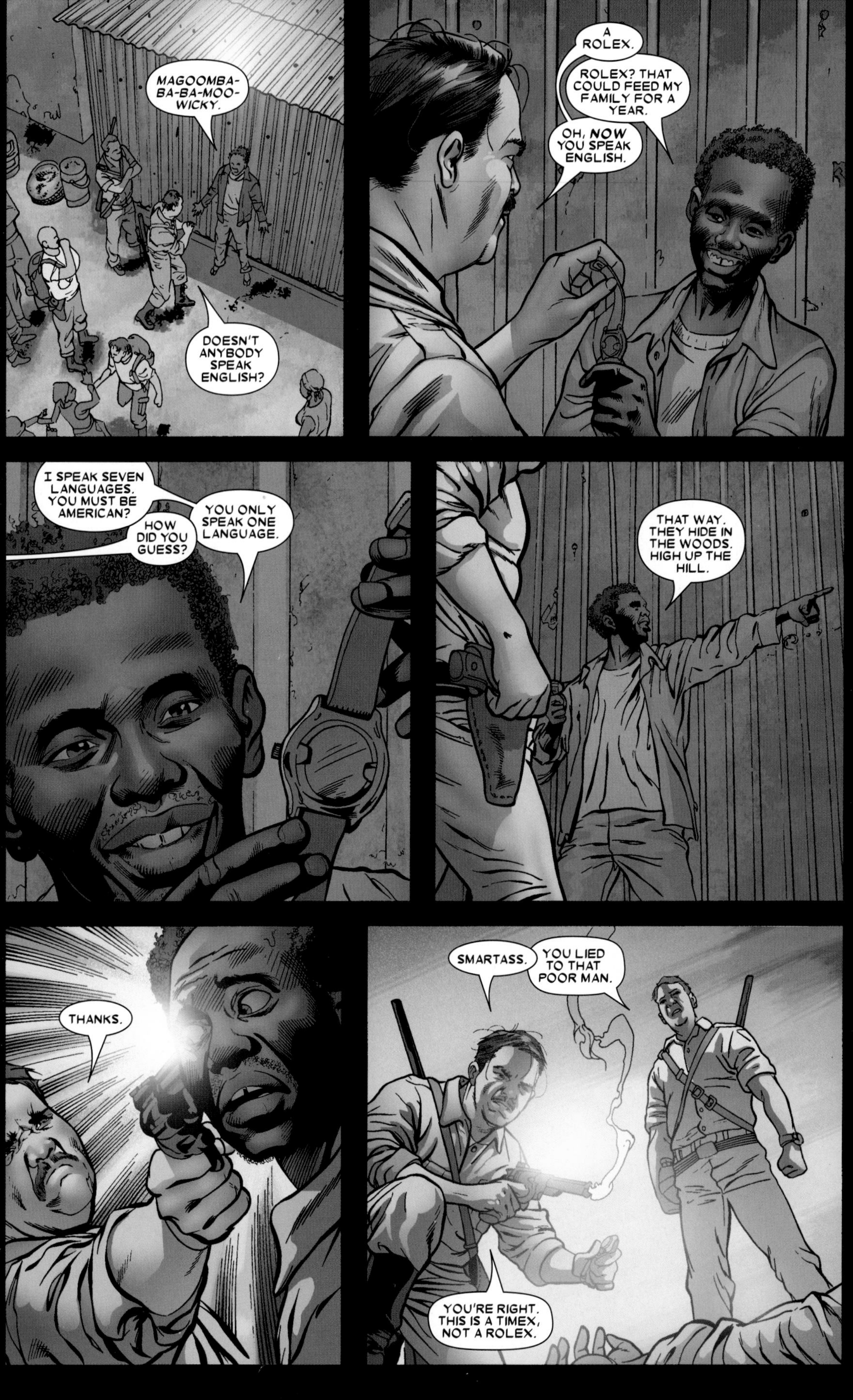
MAGOOMBA-BA-BA-MOO-WICKY.
DOESN'T ANYBODY SPEAK ENGLISH?
A ROLEX.
ROLEX? THAT COULD FEED MY FAMILY FOR A YEAR.
OH, NOW YOU SPEAK ENGLISH.
I SPEAK SEVEN LANGUAGES. YOU MUST BE AMERICAN?
HOW DID YOU GUESS?
YOU ONLY SPEAK ONE LANGUAGE.
THAT WAY. THEY HIDE IN THE WOODS. HIGH UP THE HILL.
THANKS.
SMARTASS.
YOU LIED TO THAT POOR MAN.
YOU'RE RIGHT. THIS IS A TIMEX, NOT A ROLEX.

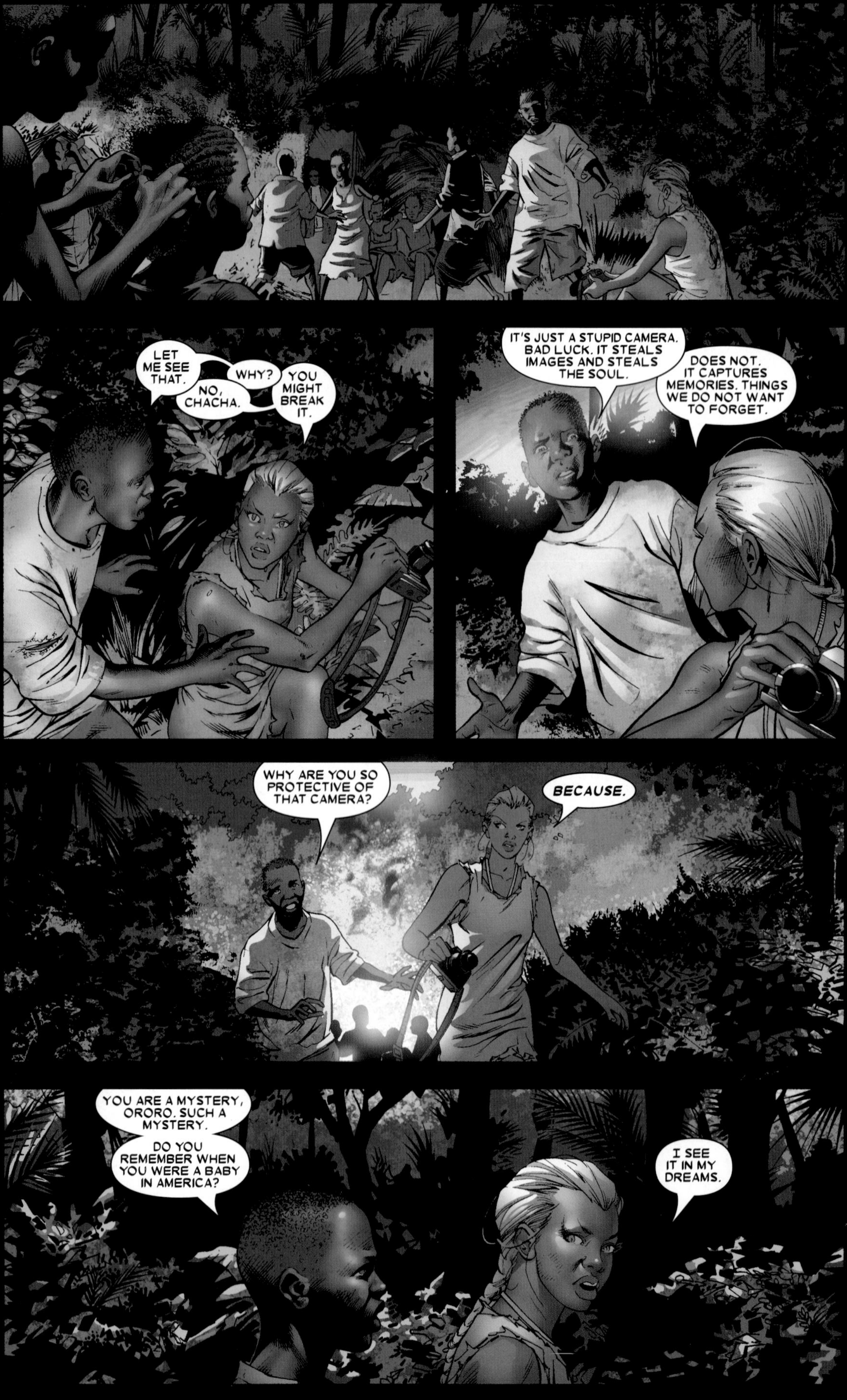
LET ME SEE THAT.
NO, CHACHA.
WHY?
YOU MIGHT BREAK IT.
IT'S JUST A STUPID CAMERA. BAD LUCK. IT STEALS IMAGES AND STEALS THE SOUL.
DOES NOT. IT CAPTURES MEMORIES. THINGS WE DO NOT WANT TO FORGET.
WHY ARE YOU SO PROTECTIVE OF THAT CAMERA?
BECAUSE.
YOU ARE A MYSTERY, ORORO. SUCH A MYSTERY.
DO YOU REMEMBER WHEN YOU WERE A BABY IN AMERICA?
I SEE IT IN MY DREAMS.

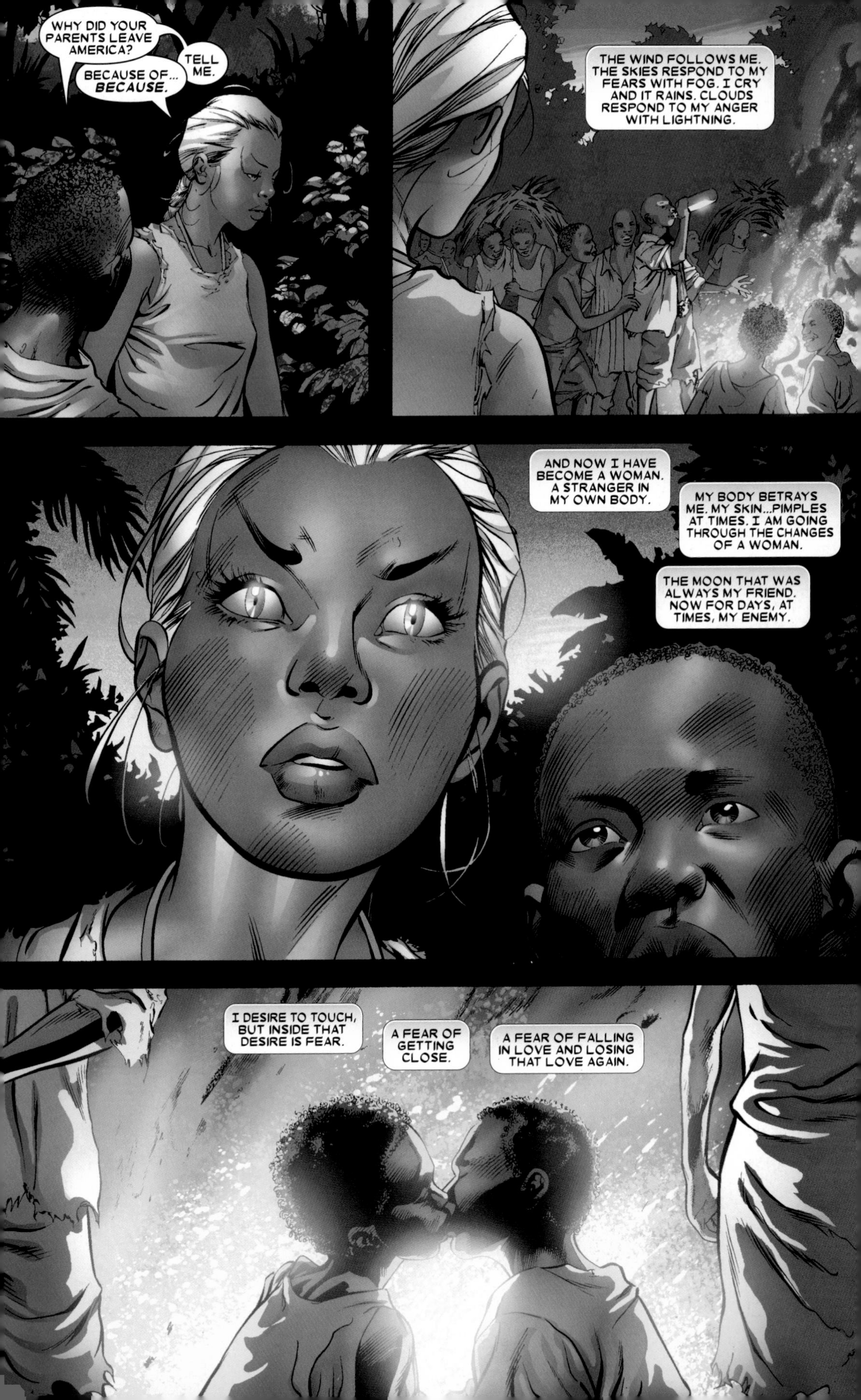
WHY DID YOUR PARENTS LEAVE AMERICA?
BECAUSE OF... *BECAUSE.*
TELL ME.
THE WIND FOLLOWS ME. THE SKIES RESPOND TO MY FEARS WITH FOG. I CRY AND IT RAINS. CLOUDS RESPOND TO MY ANGER WITH LIGHTNING.
AND NOW I HAVE BECOME A WOMAN. A STRANGER IN MY OWN BODY.
MY BODY BETRAYS ME. MY SKIN...PIMPLES AT TIMES. I AM GOING THROUGH THE CHANGES OF A WOMAN.
THE MOON THAT WAS ALWAYS MY FRIEND. NOW FOR DAYS, AT TIMES, MY ENEMY.
I DESIRE TO TOUCH, BUT INSIDE THAT DESIRE IS FEAR.
A FEAR OF GETTING CLOSE.
A FEAR OF FALLING IN LOVE AND LOSING THAT LOVE AGAIN.

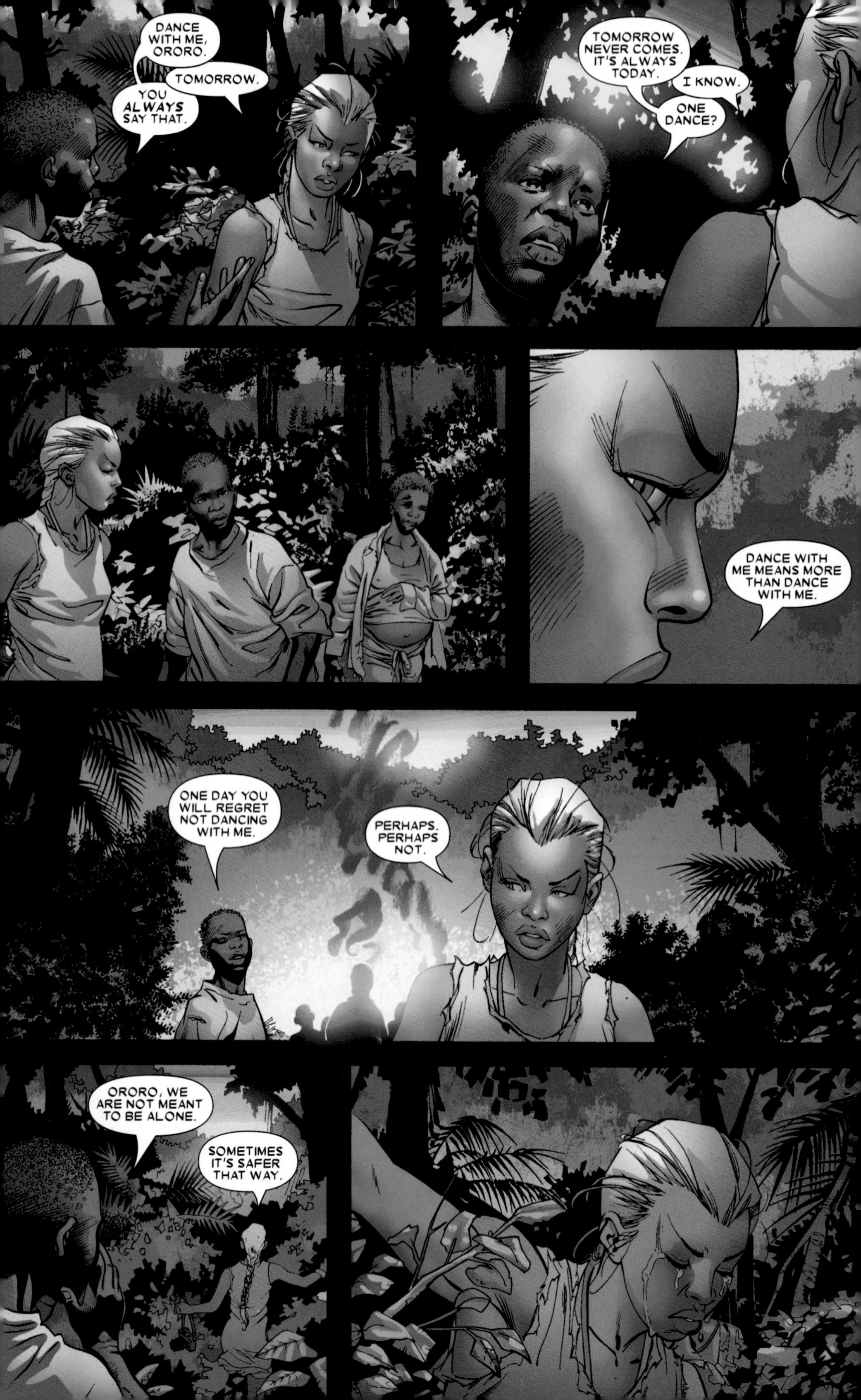
DANCE WITH ME, ORORO.
TOMORROW.
YOU ALWAYS SAY THAT.
TOMORROW NEVER COMES. IT'S ALWAYS TODAY.
I KNOW.
ONE DANCE?
DANCE WITH ME MEANS MORE THAN DANCE WITH ME.
ONE DAY YOU WILL REGRET NOT DANCING WITH ME.
PERHAPS. PERHAPS NOT.
ORORO, WE ARE NOT MEANT TO BE ALONE.
SOMETIMES IT'S SAFER THAT WAY.

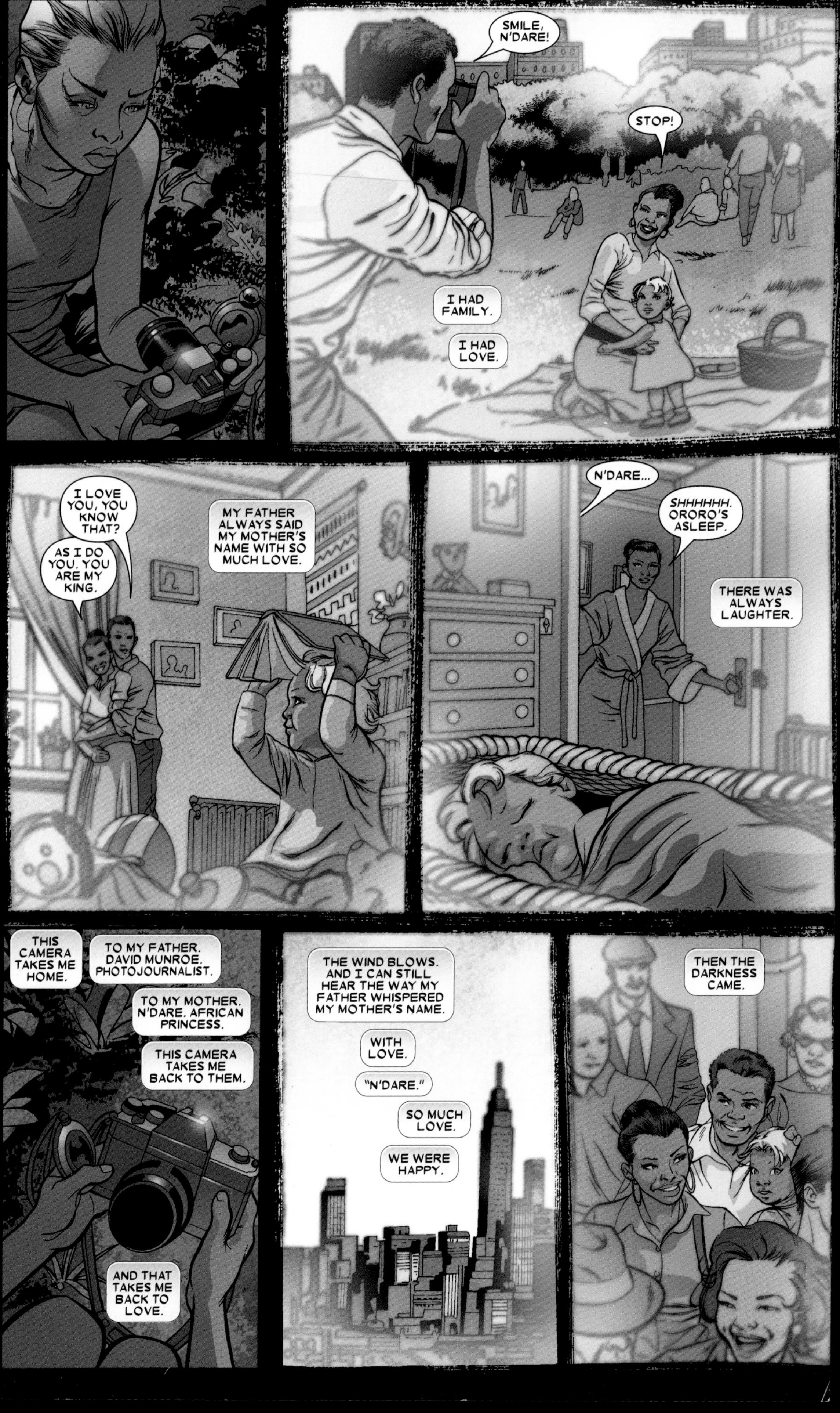
SMILE, N'DARE!
STOP!
I HAD FAMILY.
I HAD LOVE.
I LOVE YOU, YOU KNOW THAT?
AS I DO YOU. YOU ARE MY KING.
MY FATHER ALWAYS SAID MY MOTHER'S NAME WITH SO MUCH LOVE.
N'DARE...
SHHHHHH. ORORO'S ASLEEP.
THERE WAS ALWAYS LAUGHTER.
THIS CAMERA TAKES ME HOME.
TO MY FATHER. DAVID MUNROE. PHOTOJOURNALIST.
TO MY MOTHER. N'DARE. AFRICAN PRINCESS.
THIS CAMERA TAKES ME BACK TO THEM.
AND THAT TAKES ME BACK TO LOVE.
THE WIND BLOWS. AND I CAN STILL HEAR THE WAY MY FATHER WHISPERED MY MOTHER'S NAME.
WITH LOVE.
"N'DARE."
SO MUCH LOVE.
WE WERE HAPPY.
THEN THE DARKNESS CAME.

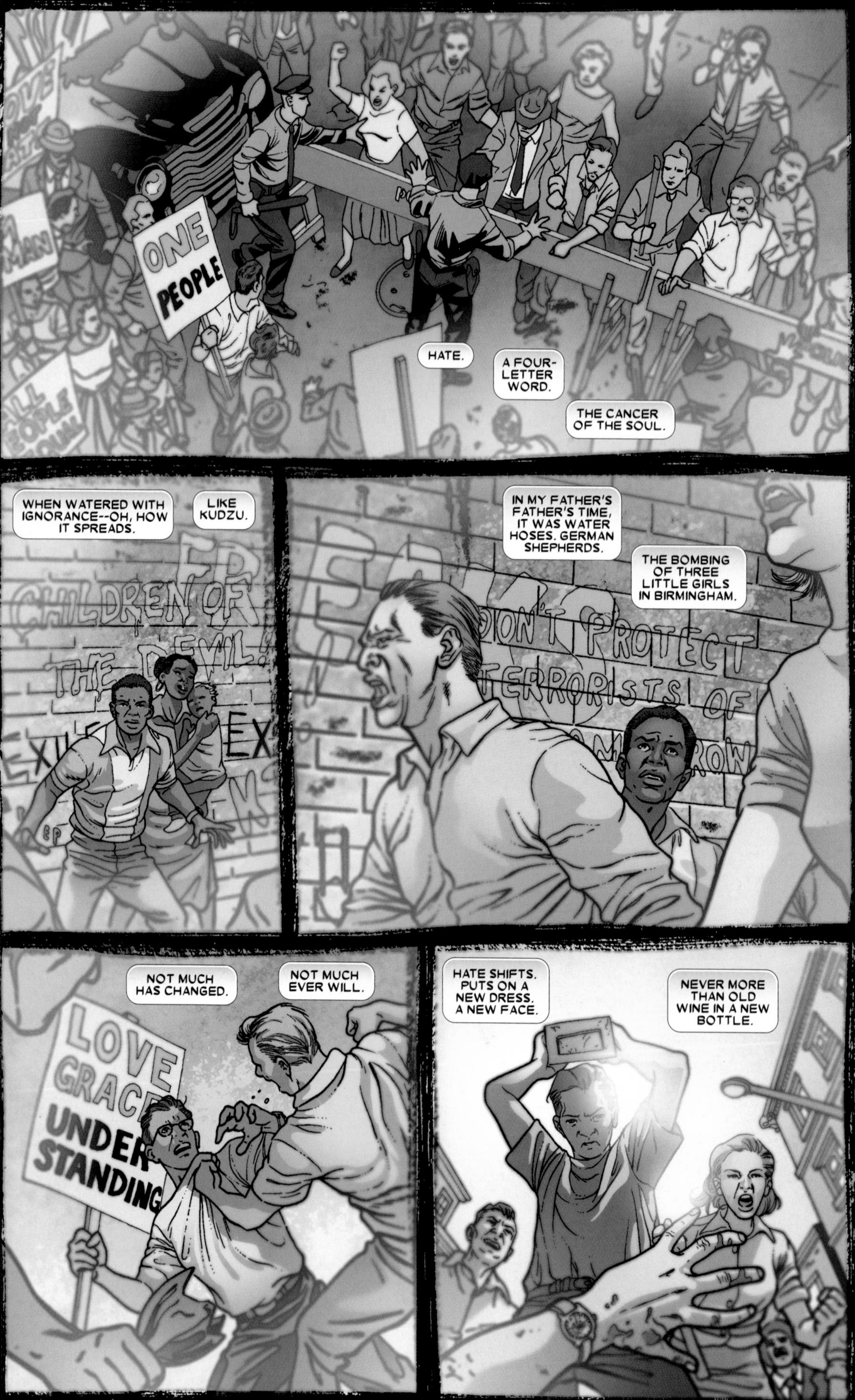
ONE PEOPLE
HATE.
A FOUR-LETTER WORD.
THE CANCER OF THE SOUL.
WHEN WATERED WITH IGNORANCE--OH, HOW IT SPREADS.
LIKE KUDZU.
CHILDREN OF THE DEVIL!
IN MY FATHER'S FATHER'S TIME, IT WAS WATER HOSES. GERMAN SHEPHERDS.
THE BOMBING OF THREE LITTLE GIRLS IN BIRMINGHAM.
DON'T PROTECT TERRORISTS OF
NOT MUCH HAS CHANGED.
NOT MUCH EVER WILL.
LOVE
UNDER STANDING
HATE SHIFTS. PUTS ON A NEW DRESS. A NEW FACE.
NEVER MORE THAN OLD WINE IN A NEW BOTTLE.

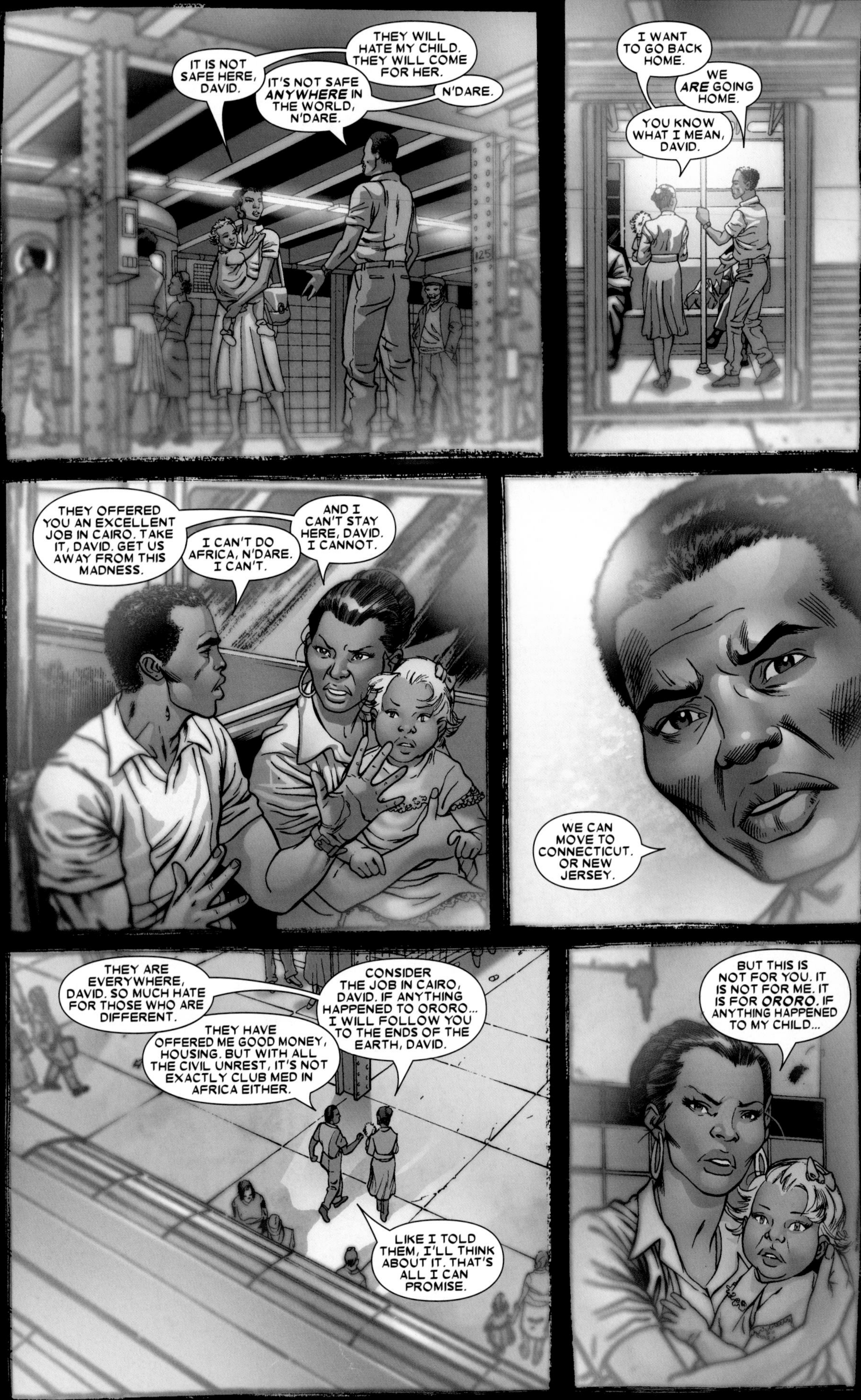
IT IS NOT SAFE HERE, DAVID.
THEY WILL HATE MY CHILD. THEY WILL COME FOR HER.
IT'S NOT SAFE *ANYWHERE* IN THE WORLD, N'DARE.
N'DARE.
I WANT TO GO BACK HOME.
WE *ARE* GOING HOME.
YOU KNOW WHAT I MEAN, DAVID.
THEY OFFERED YOU AN EXCELLENT JOB IN CAIRO. TAKE IT, DAVID. GET US AWAY FROM THIS MADNESS.
I CAN'T DO AFRICA, N'DARE. I CAN'T.
AND I CAN'T STAY HERE, DAVID. I CANNOT.
WE CAN MOVE TO CONNECTICUT. OR NEW JERSEY.
THEY ARE EVERYWHERE, DAVID. SO MUCH HATE FOR THOSE WHO ARE DIFFERENT.
THEY HAVE OFFERED ME GOOD MONEY, HOUSING. BUT WITH ALL THE CIVIL UNREST, IT'S NOT EXACTLY CLUB MED IN AFRICA EITHER.
CONSIDER THE JOB IN CAIRO, DAVID. IF ANYTHING HAPPENED TO ORORO... I WILL FOLLOW YOU TO THE ENDS OF THE EARTH, DAVID.
LIKE I TOLD THEM, I'LL THINK ABOUT IT. THAT'S ALL I CAN PROMISE.
BUT THIS IS NOT FOR YOU. IT IS NOT FOR ME. IT IS FOR *ORORO*. IF ANYTHING HAPPENED TO MY CHILD...

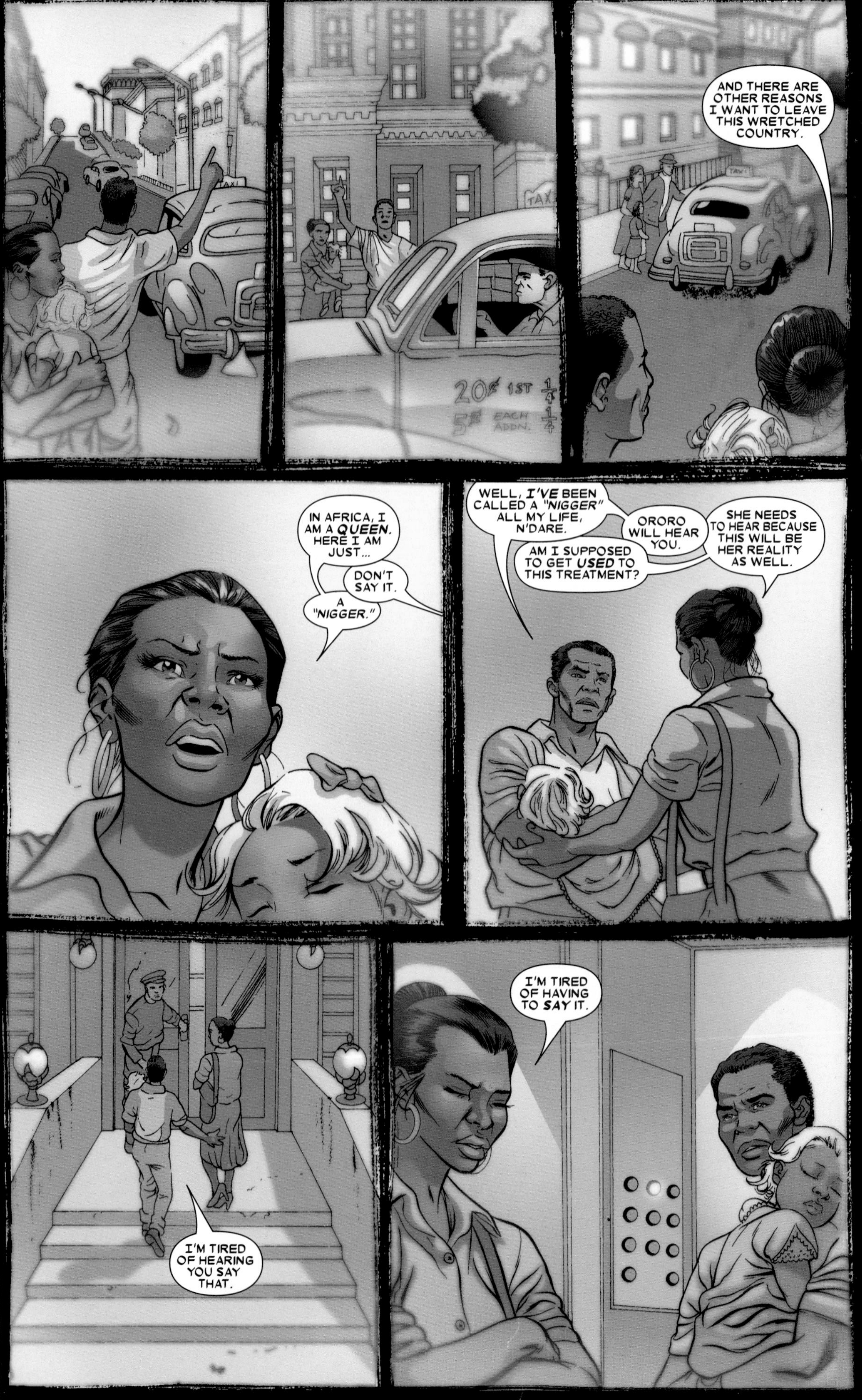
TAXI
20¢ 1ST 1/4
5¢ EACH ADDN. 1/4
AND THERE ARE OTHER REASONS I WANT TO LEAVE THIS WRETCHED COUNTRY.
IN AFRICA, I AM A **QUEEN**. HERE I AM JUST...
DON'T SAY IT.
A "**NIGGER**."
WELL, ***I'VE*** BEEN CALLED A "***NIGGER***" ALL MY LIFE, N'DARE.
ORORO WILL HEAR YOU.
AM I SUPPOSED TO GET ***USED*** TO THIS TREATMENT?
SHE NEEDS TO HEAR BECAUSE THIS WILL BE HER REALITY AS WELL.
I'M TIRED OF HEARING YOU SAY THAT.
I'M TIRED OF HAVING TO ***SAY*** IT.

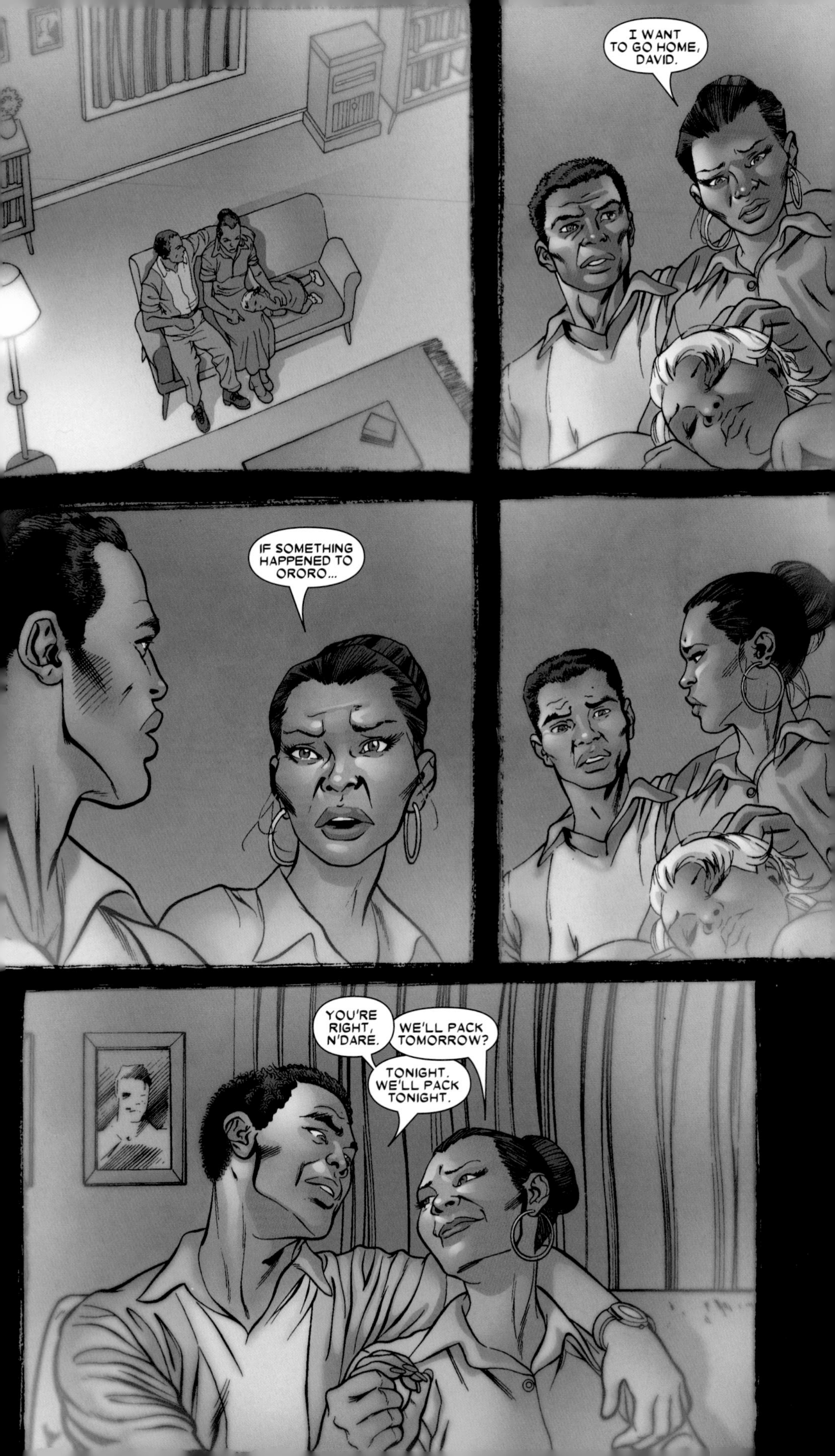
I WANT TO GO HOME, DAVID.
IF SOMETHING HAPPENED TO ORORO...
YOU'RE RIGHT, N'DARE.
WE'LL PACK TOMORROW?
TONIGHT. WE'LL PACK TONIGHT.

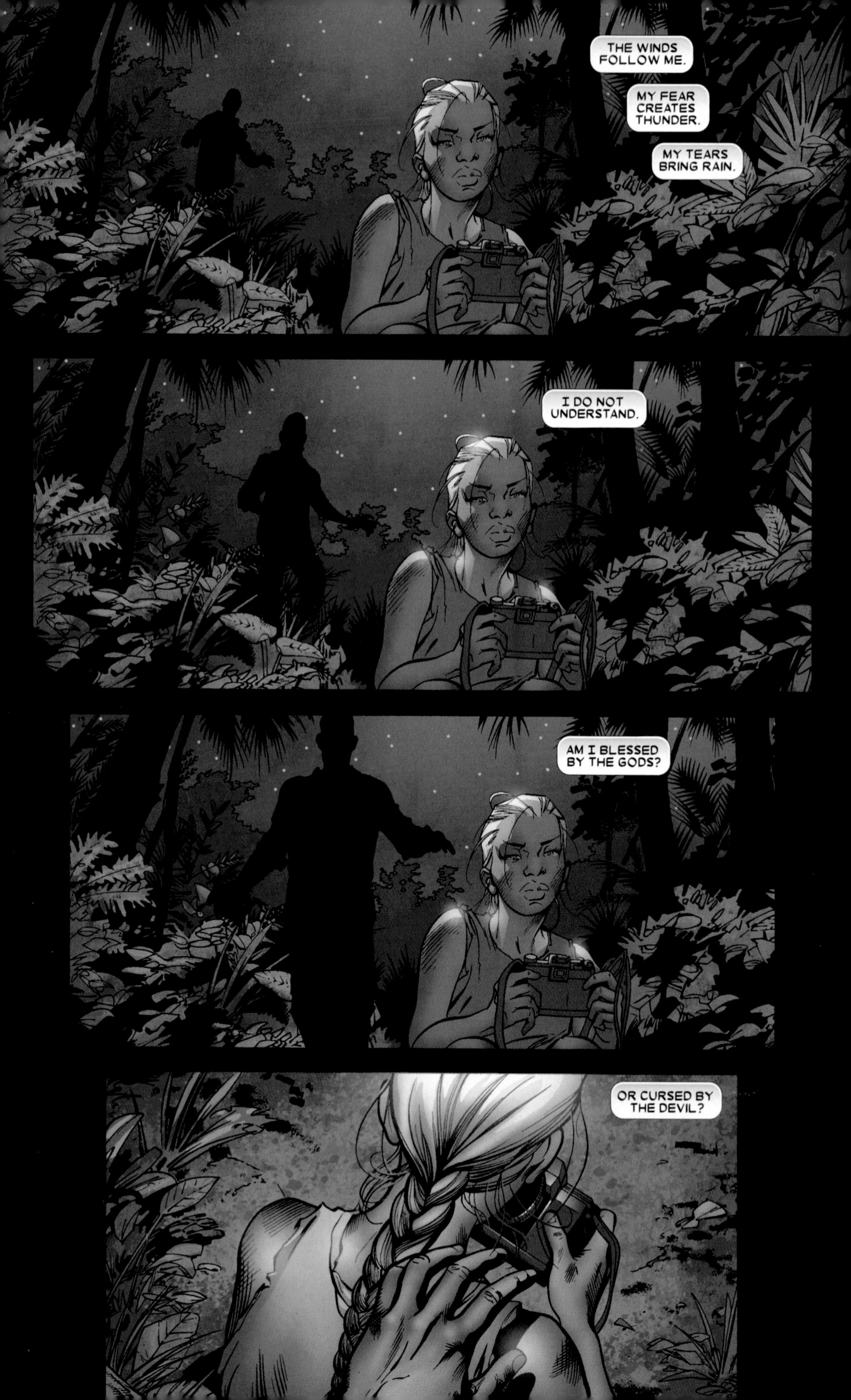
THE WINDS FOLLOW ME.
MY FEAR CREATES THUNDER.
MY TEARS BRING RAIN.
I DO NOT UNDERSTAND.
AM I BLESSED BY THE GODS?
OR CURSED BY THE DEVIL?

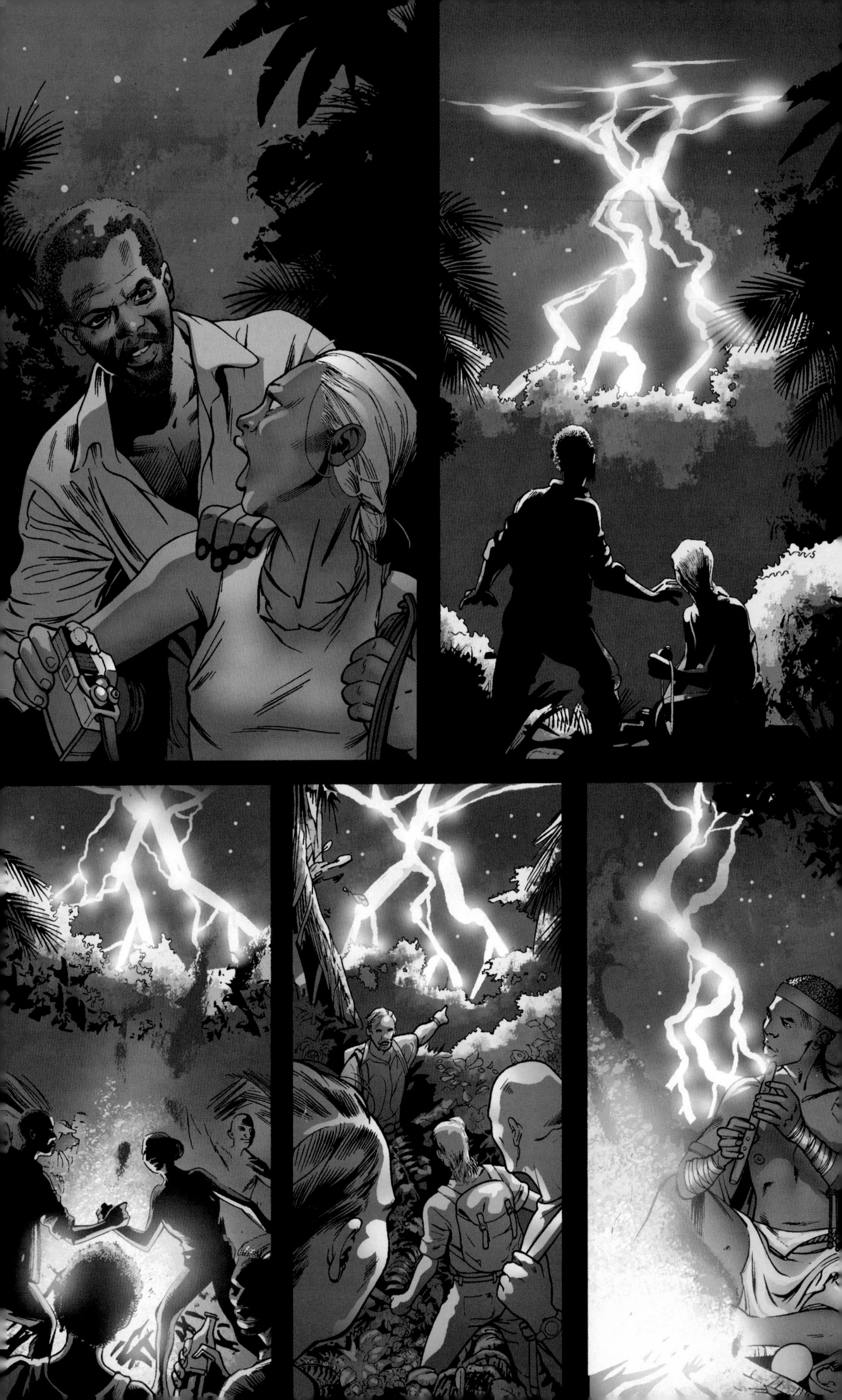

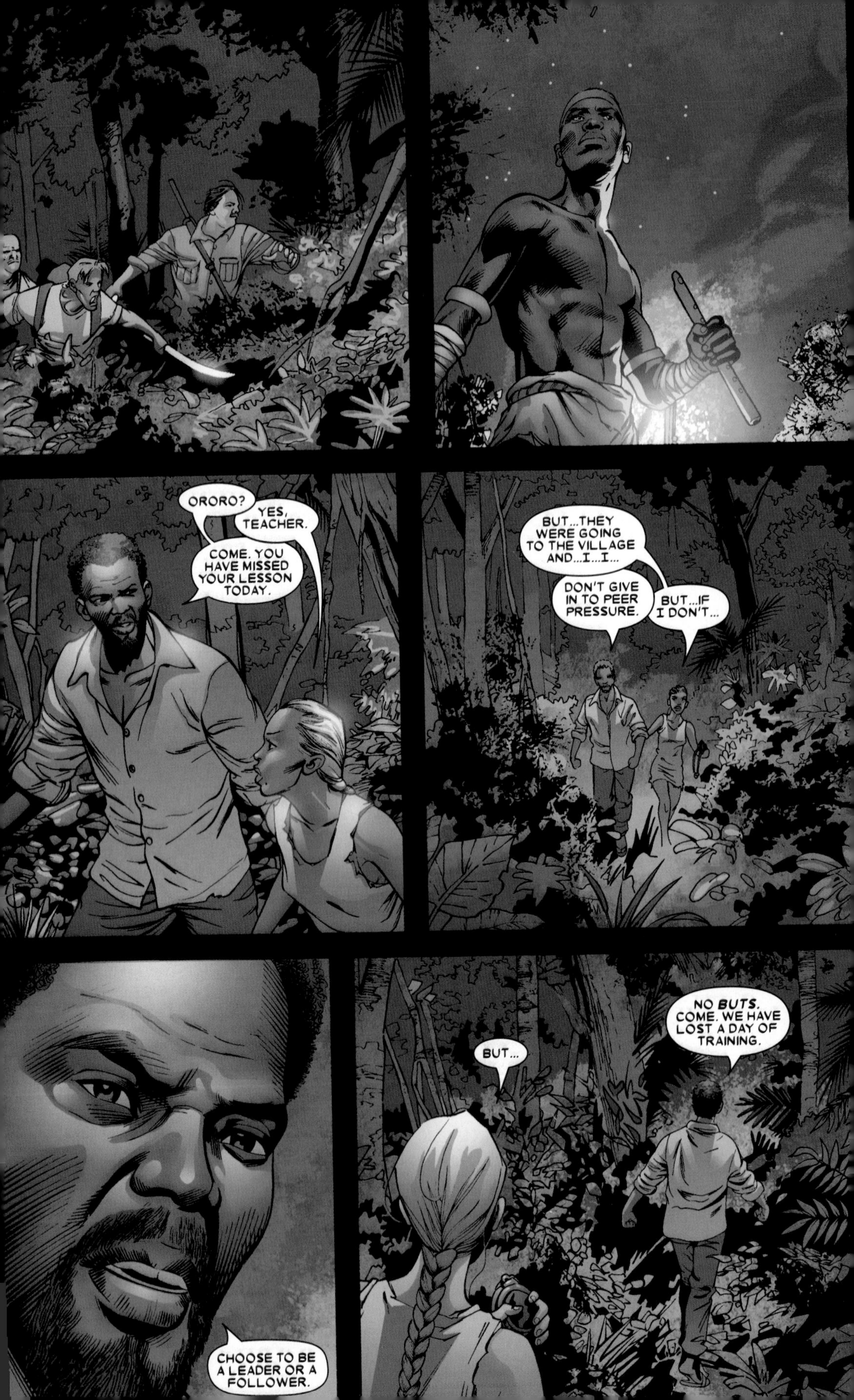
ORORO?
YES, TEACHER.
COME. YOU HAVE MISSED YOUR LESSON TODAY.
BUT...THEY WERE GOING TO THE VILLAGE AND...I...I...
DON'T GIVE IN TO PEER PRESSURE.
BUT...IF I DON'T...
CHOOSE TO BE A LEADER OR A FOLLOWER.
BUT...
NO *BUTS*. COME. WE HAVE LOST A DAY OF TRAINING.

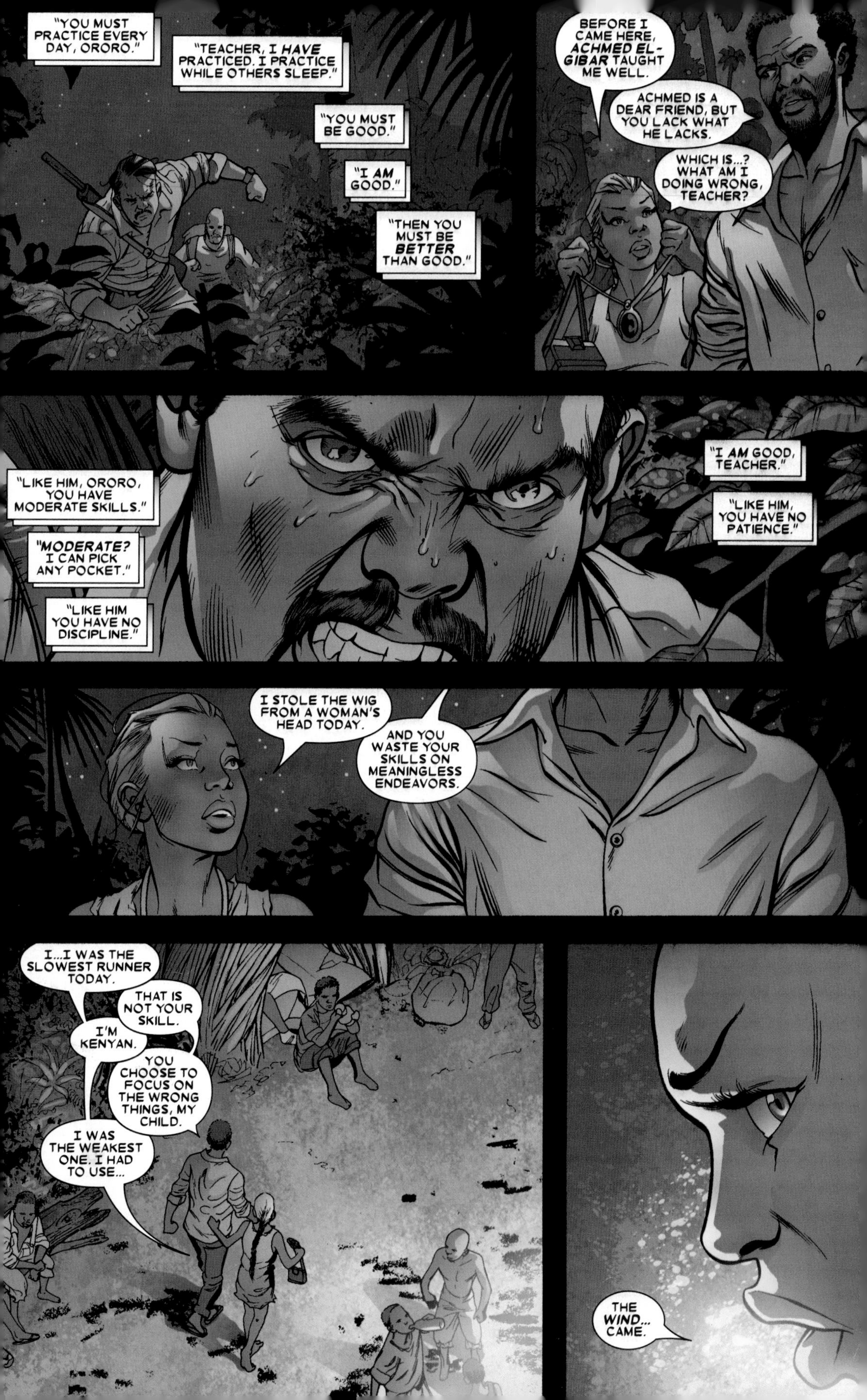
"YOU MUST PRACTICE EVERY DAY, ORORO."
"TEACHER, I *HAVE* PRACTICED. I PRACTICE WHILE OTHERS SLEEP."
"YOU MUST BE GOOD."
"I *AM* GOOD."
"THEN YOU MUST BE *BETTER* THAN GOOD."
BEFORE I CAME HERE, *ACHMED EL-GIBAR* TAUGHT ME WELL.
ACHMED IS A DEAR FRIEND, BUT YOU LACK WHAT HE LACKS.
WHICH IS...? WHAT AM I DOING WRONG, TEACHER?
"LIKE HIM, ORORO, YOU HAVE MODERATE SKILLS."
"*MODERATE?* I CAN PICK ANY POCKET."
"LIKE HIM YOU HAVE NO DISCIPLINE."
"I *AM* GOOD, TEACHER."
"LIKE HIM, YOU HAVE NO PATIENCE."
I STOLE THE WIG FROM A WOMAN'S HEAD TODAY.
AND YOU WASTE YOUR SKILLS ON MEANINGLESS ENDEAVORS.
I...I WAS THE SLOWEST RUNNER TODAY.
THAT IS NOT YOUR SKILL.
I'M KENYAN.
YOU CHOOSE TO FOCUS ON THE WRONG THINGS, MY CHILD.
I WAS THE WEAKEST ONE. I HAD TO USE...
THE *WIND*... CAME.

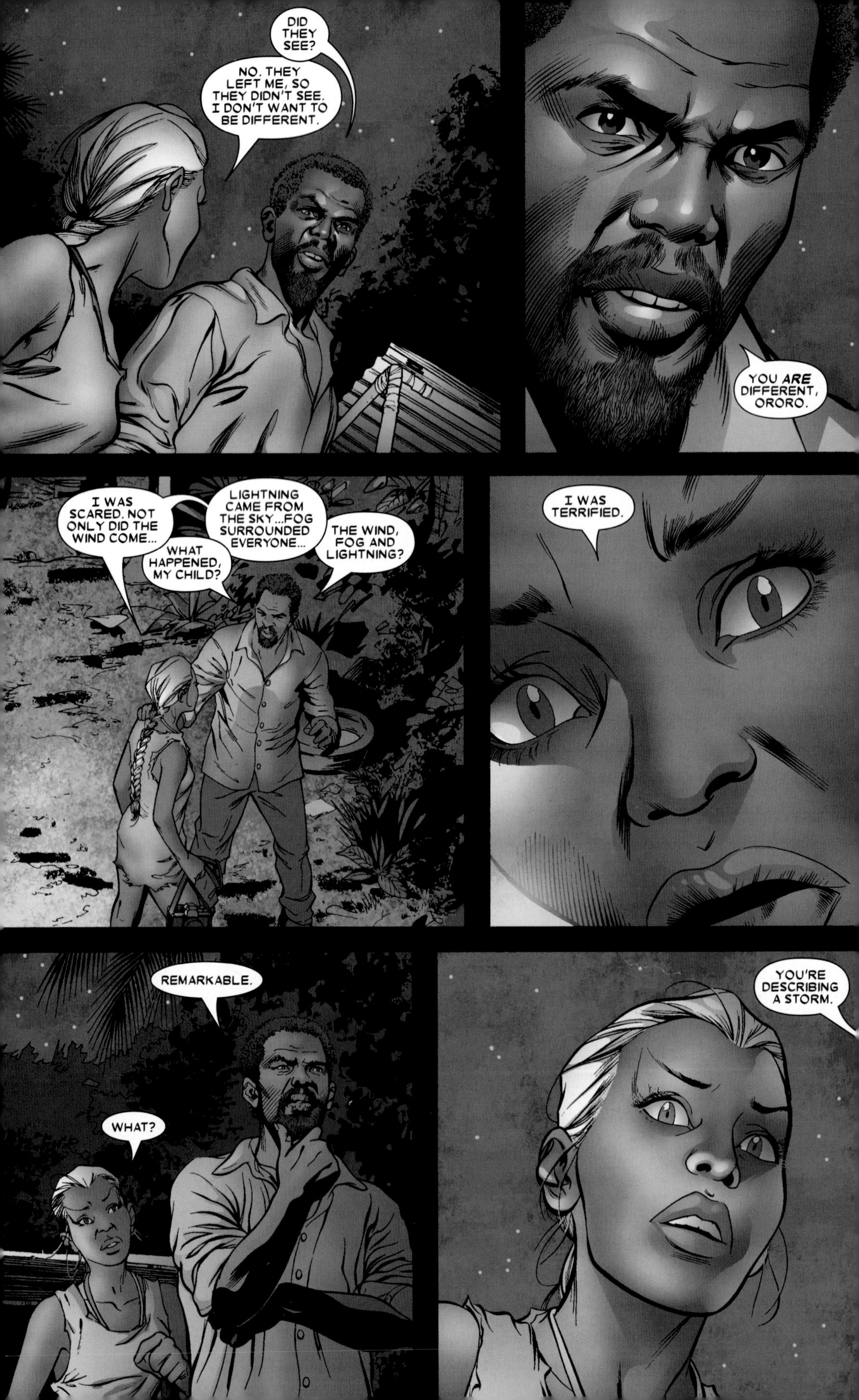

DID THEY SEE?
NO. THEY LEFT ME, SO THEY DIDN'T SEE. I DON'T WANT TO BE DIFFERENT.
YOU *ARE* DIFFERENT, ORORO.
I WAS SCARED. NOT ONLY DID THE WIND COME...
LIGHTNING CAME FROM THE SKY...FOG SURROUNDED EVERYONE...
WHAT HAPPENED, MY CHILD?
THE WIND, FOG AND LIGHTNING?
I WAS TERRIFIED.
REMARKABLE.
WHAT?
YOU'RE DESCRIBING A STORM.

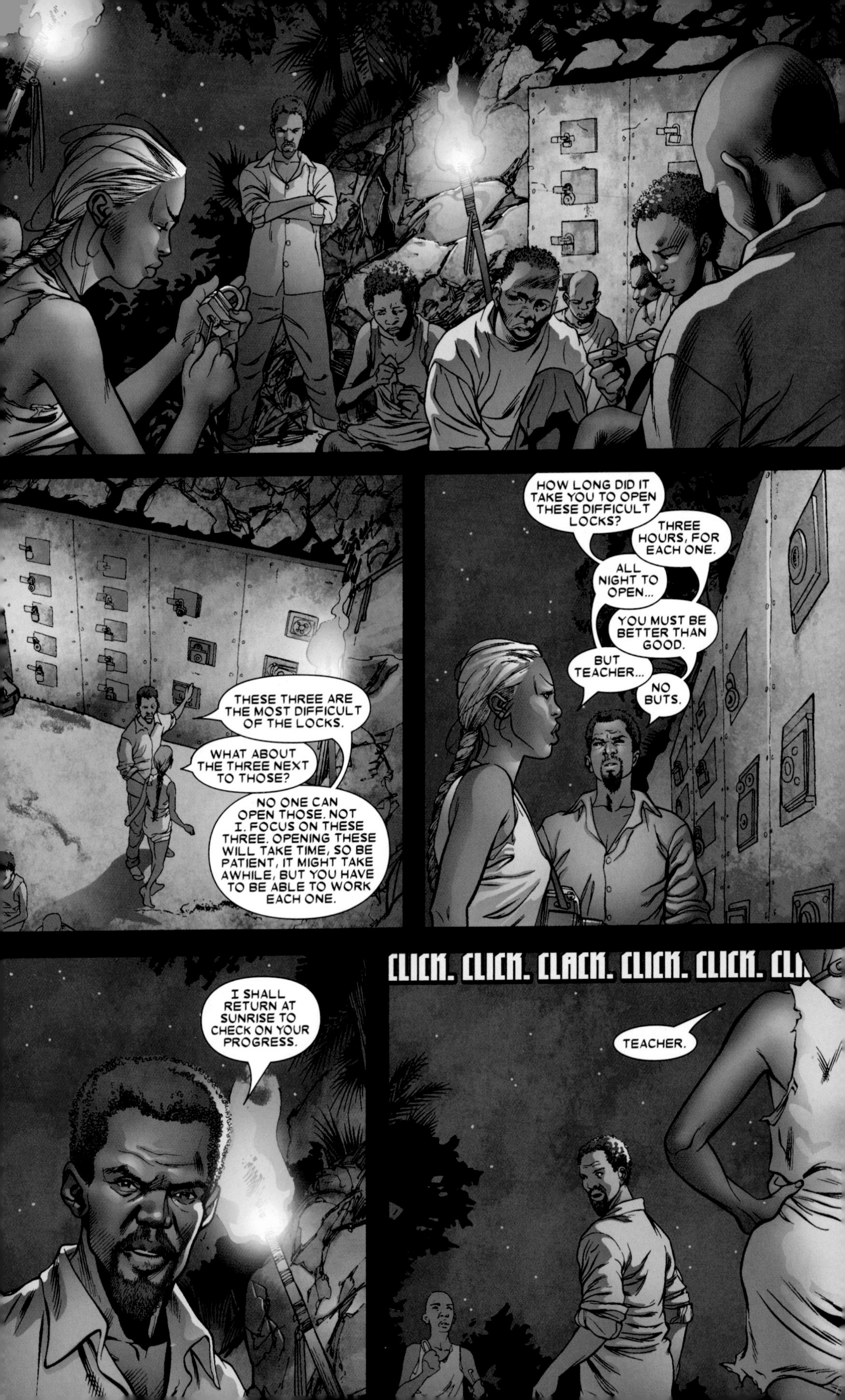
THESE THREE ARE THE MOST DIFFICULT OF THE LOCKS.
WHAT ABOUT THE THREE NEXT TO THOSE?
NO ONE CAN OPEN THOSE. NOT I. FOCUS ON THESE THREE. OPENING THESE WILL TAKE TIME, SO BE PATIENT, IT MIGHT TAKE AWHILE, BUT YOU HAVE TO BE ABLE TO WORK EACH ONE.
HOW LONG DID IT TAKE YOU TO OPEN THESE DIFFICULT LOCKS?
THREE HOURS, FOR EACH ONE.
ALL NIGHT TO OPEN...
YOU MUST BE BETTER THAN GOOD.
BUT TEACHER...
NO BUTS.
I SHALL RETURN AT SUNRISE TO CHECK ON YOUR PROGRESS.
CLICK. CLICK. CLACK. CLICK. CLICK.
TEACHER.

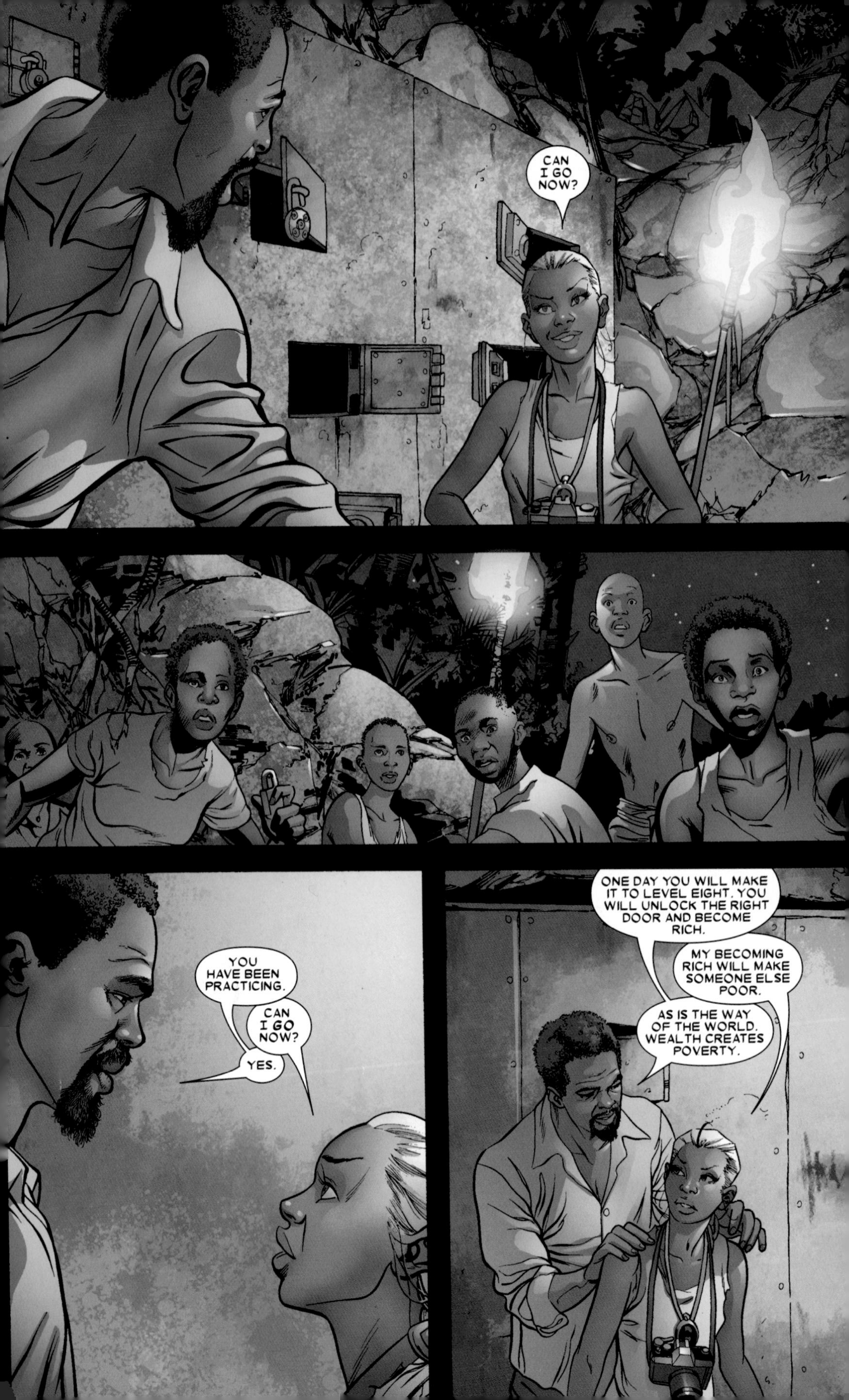
CAN I GO NOW?
YOU HAVE BEEN PRACTICING.
CAN I GO NOW?
YES.
ONE DAY YOU WILL MAKE IT TO LEVEL EIGHT. YOU WILL UNLOCK THE RIGHT DOOR AND BECOME RICH.
MY BECOMING RICH WILL MAKE SOMEONE ELSE POOR.
AS IS THE WAY OF THE WORLD. WEALTH CREATES POVERTY.

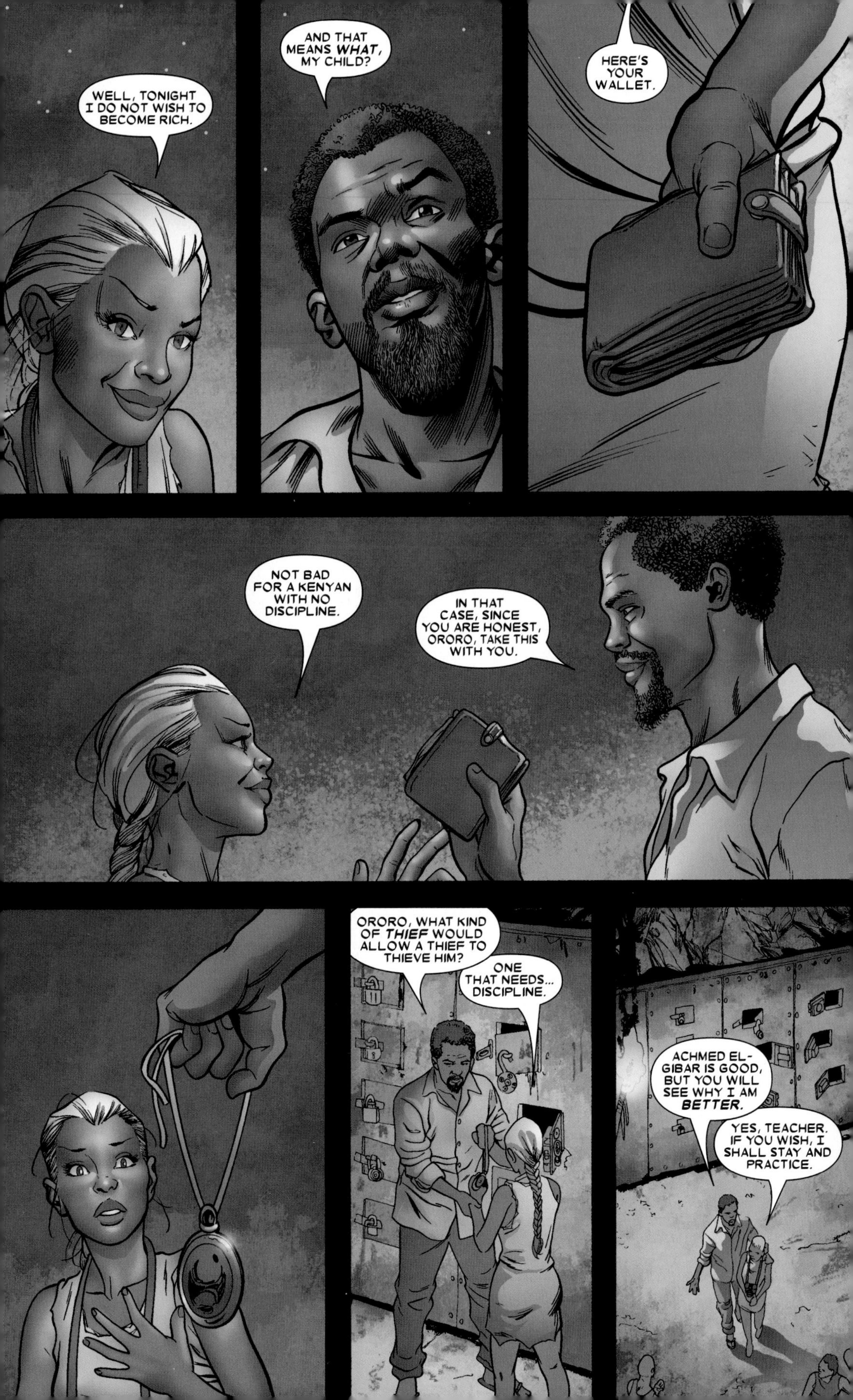
WELL, TONIGHT I DO NOT WISH TO BECOME RICH.
AND THAT MEANS *WHAT*, MY CHILD?
HERE'S YOUR WALLET.
NOT BAD FOR A KENYAN WITH NO DISCIPLINE.
IN THAT CASE, SINCE YOU ARE HONEST, ORORO, TAKE THIS WITH YOU.
ORORO, WHAT KIND OF *THIEF* WOULD ALLOW A THIEF TO THIEVE HIM?
ONE THAT NEEDS... DISCIPLINE.
ACHMED EL-GIBAR IS GOOD, BUT YOU WILL SEE WHY I AM *BETTER*.
YES, TEACHER. IF YOU WISH, I SHALL STAY AND PRACTICE.

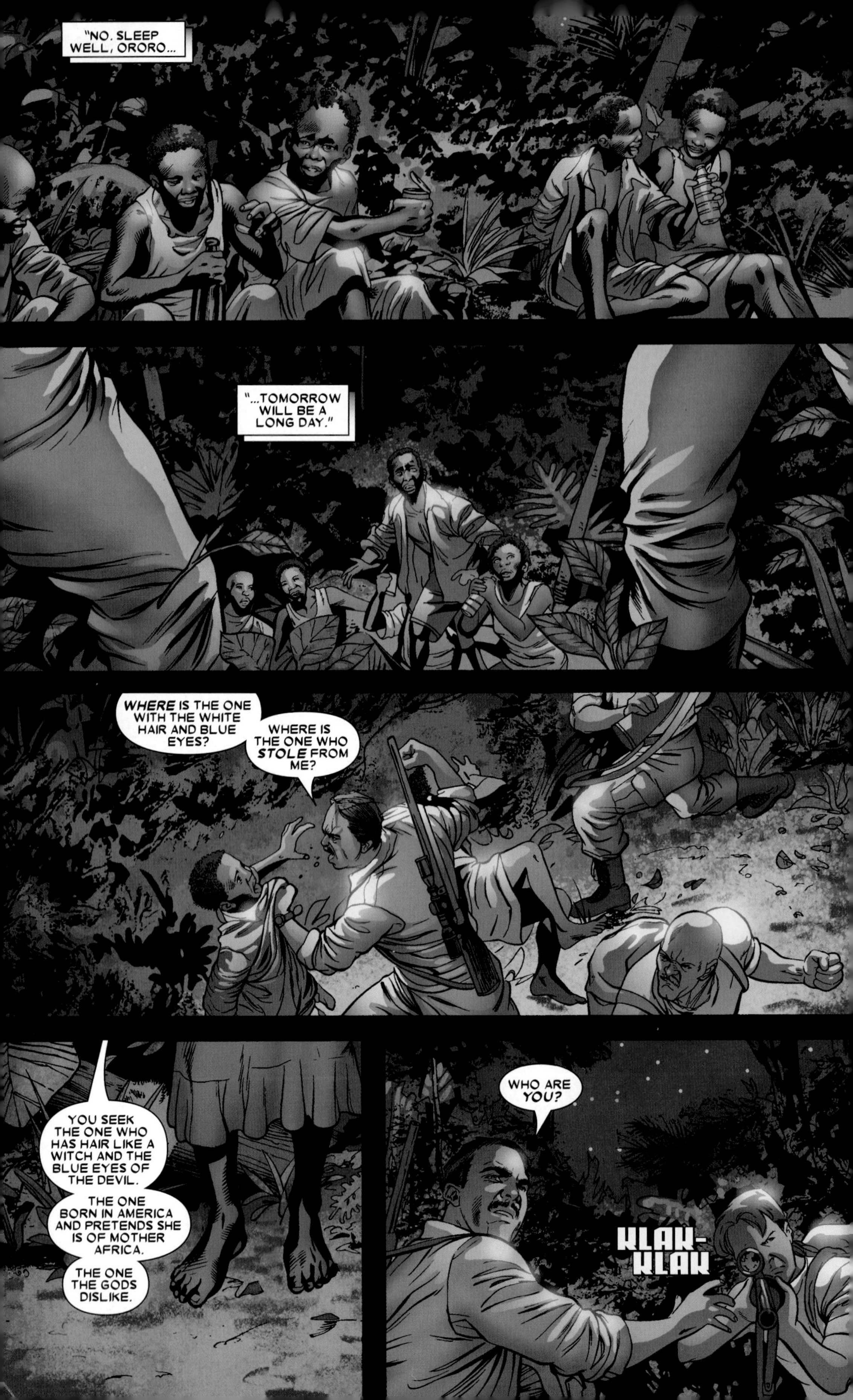
"NO. SLEEP WELL, ORORO...
"...TOMORROW WILL BE A LONG DAY."
WHERE IS THE ONE WITH THE WHITE HAIR AND BLUE EYES?
WHERE IS THE ONE WHO *STOLE* FROM ME?
YOU SEEK THE ONE WHO HAS HAIR LIKE A WITCH AND THE BLUE EYES OF THE DEVIL.
THE ONE BORN IN AMERICA AND PRETENDS SHE IS OF MOTHER AFRICA.
THE ONE THE GODS DISLIKE.
WHO ARE *YOU*?
KLAK-KLAK

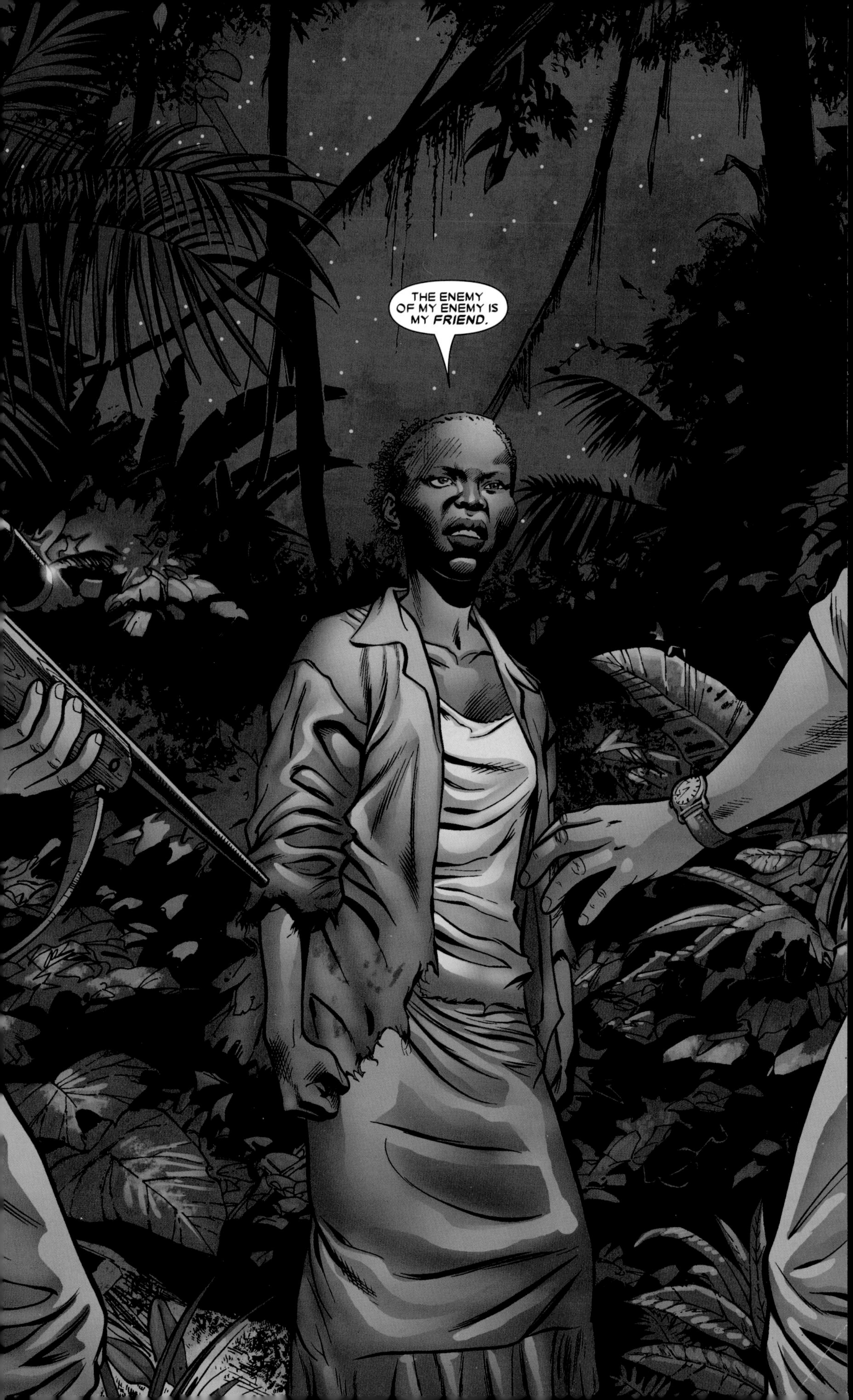
THE ENEMY OF MY ENEMY IS MY FRIEND.

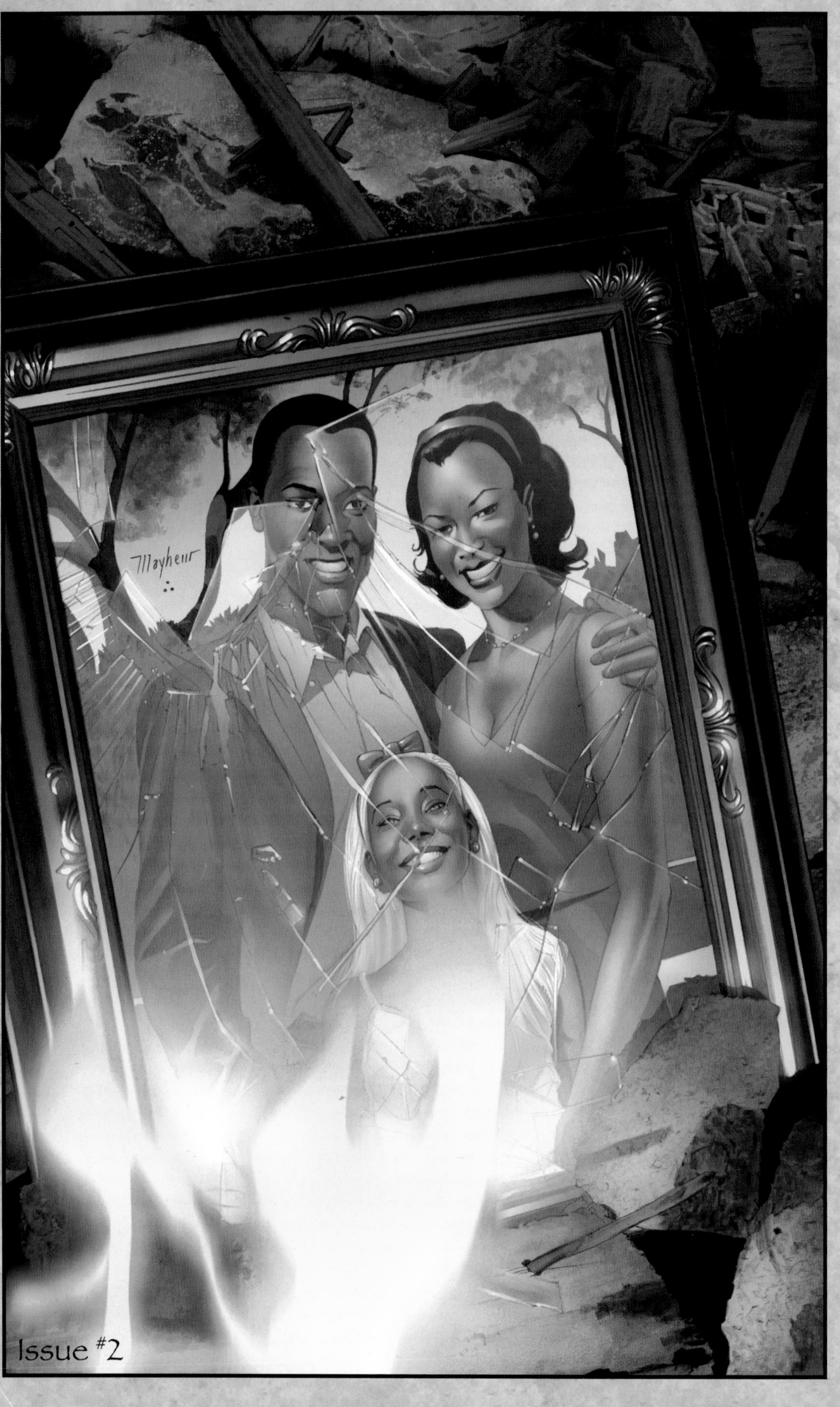
Mayhew
Issue #2

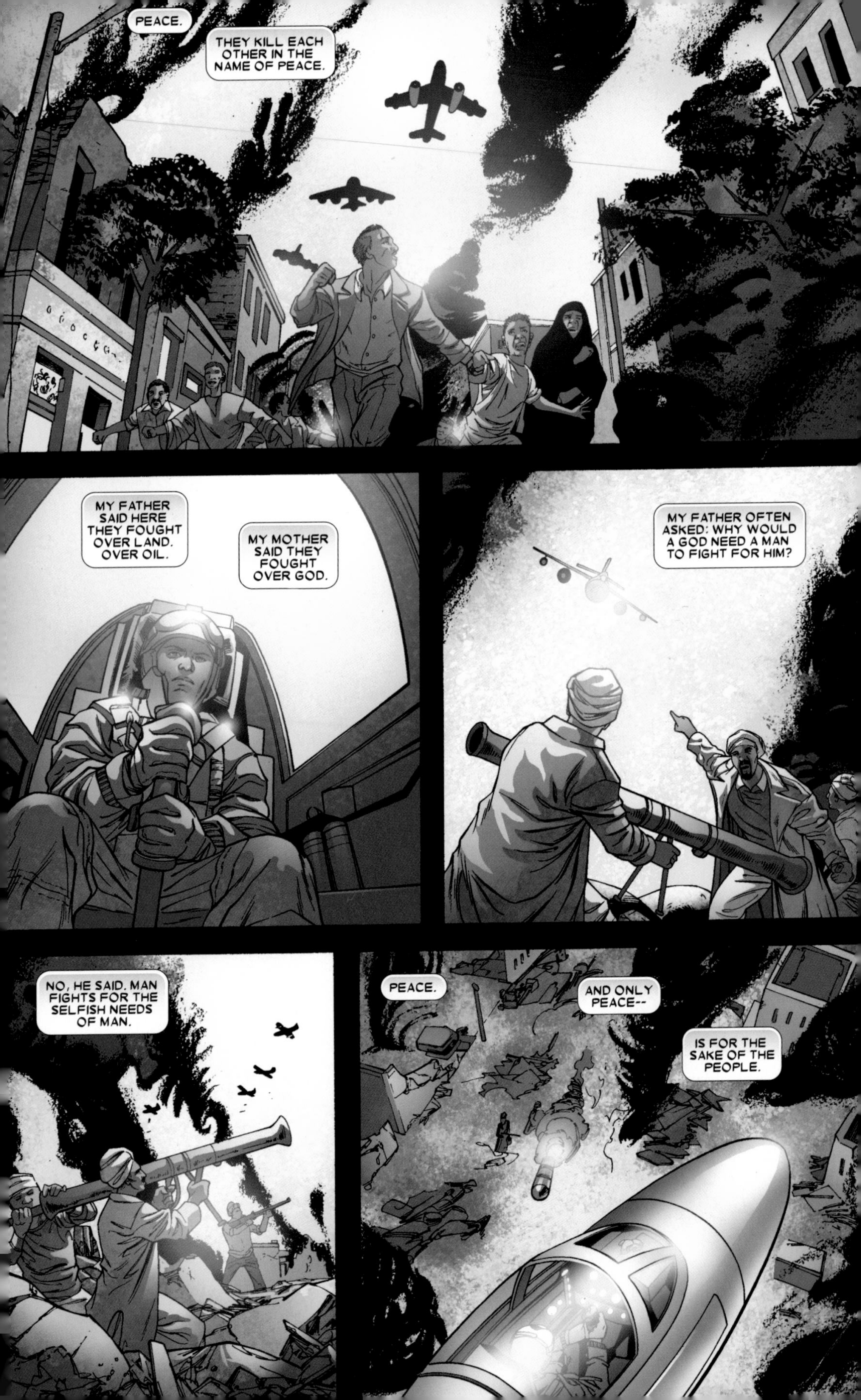
PEACE.
THEY KILL EACH OTHER IN THE NAME OF PEACE.
MY FATHER SAID HERE THEY FOUGHT OVER LAND. OVER OIL.
MY MOTHER SAID THEY FOUGHT OVER GOD.
MY FATHER OFTEN ASKED: WHY WOULD A GOD NEED A MAN TO FIGHT FOR HIM?
NO, HE SAID. MAN FIGHTS FOR THE SELFISH NEEDS OF MAN.
PEACE.
AND ONLY PEACE--
IS FOR THE SAKE OF THE PEOPLE.

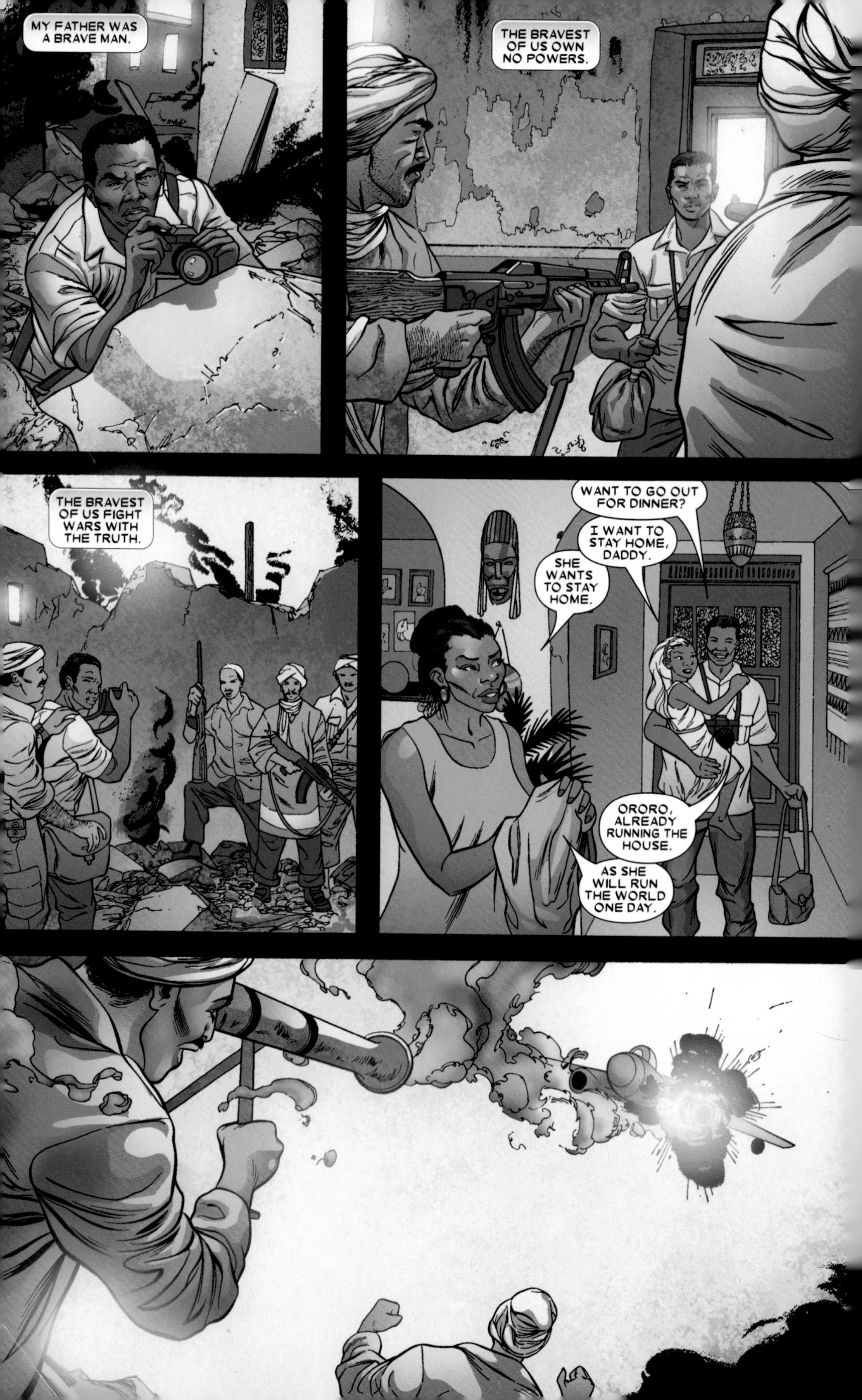
MY FATHER WAS A BRAVE MAN.
THE BRAVEST OF US OWN NO POWERS.
THE BRAVEST OF US FIGHT WARS WITH THE TRUTH.
WANT TO GO OUT FOR DINNER?
I WANT TO STAY HOME, DADDY.
SHE WANTS TO STAY HOME.
ORORO, ALREADY RUNNING THE HOUSE.
AS SHE WILL RUN THE WORLD ONE DAY.

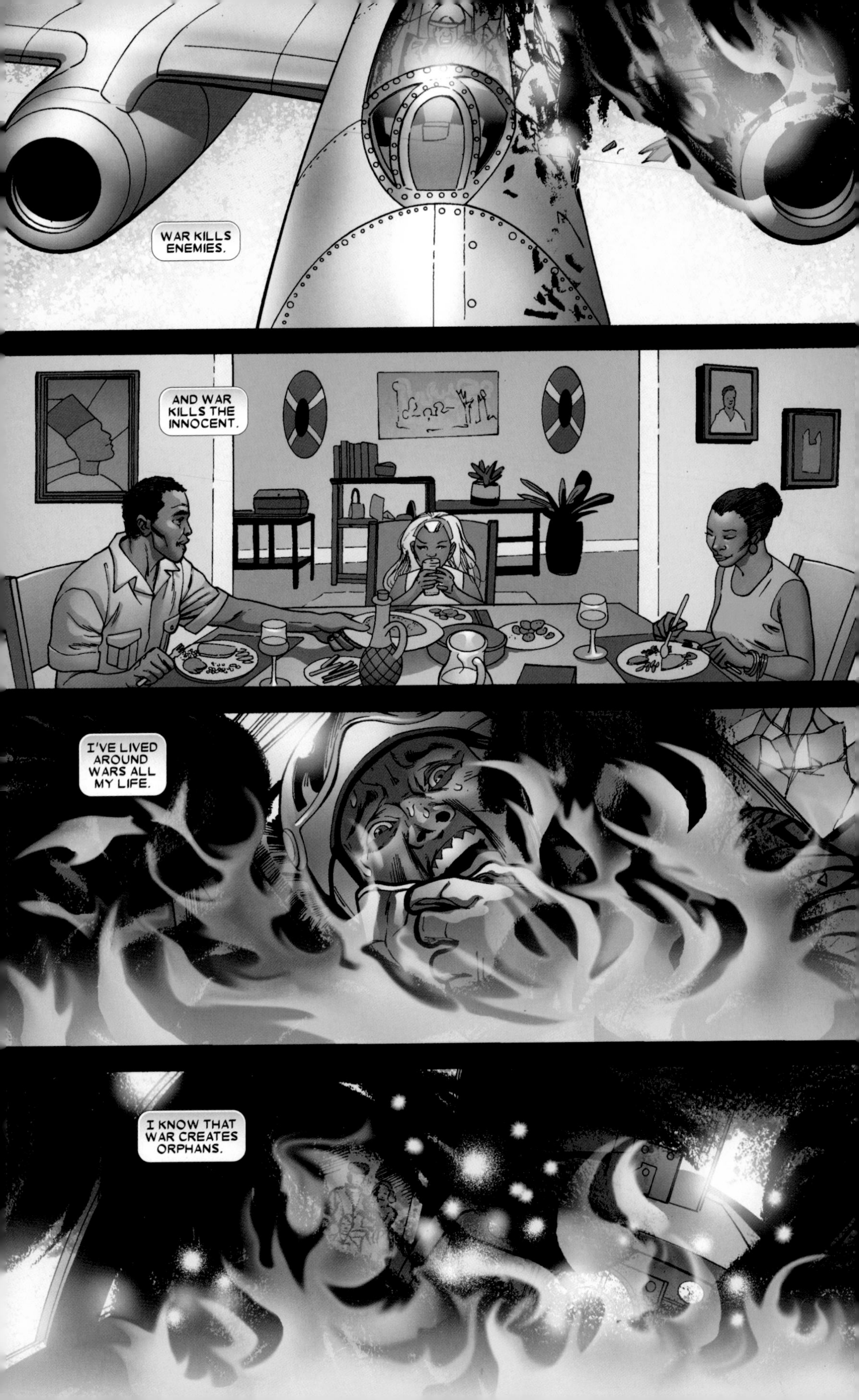
WAR KILLS ENEMIES.
AND WAR KILLS THE INNOCENT.
I'VE LIVED AROUND WARS ALL MY LIFE.
I KNOW THAT WAR CREATES ORPHANS.

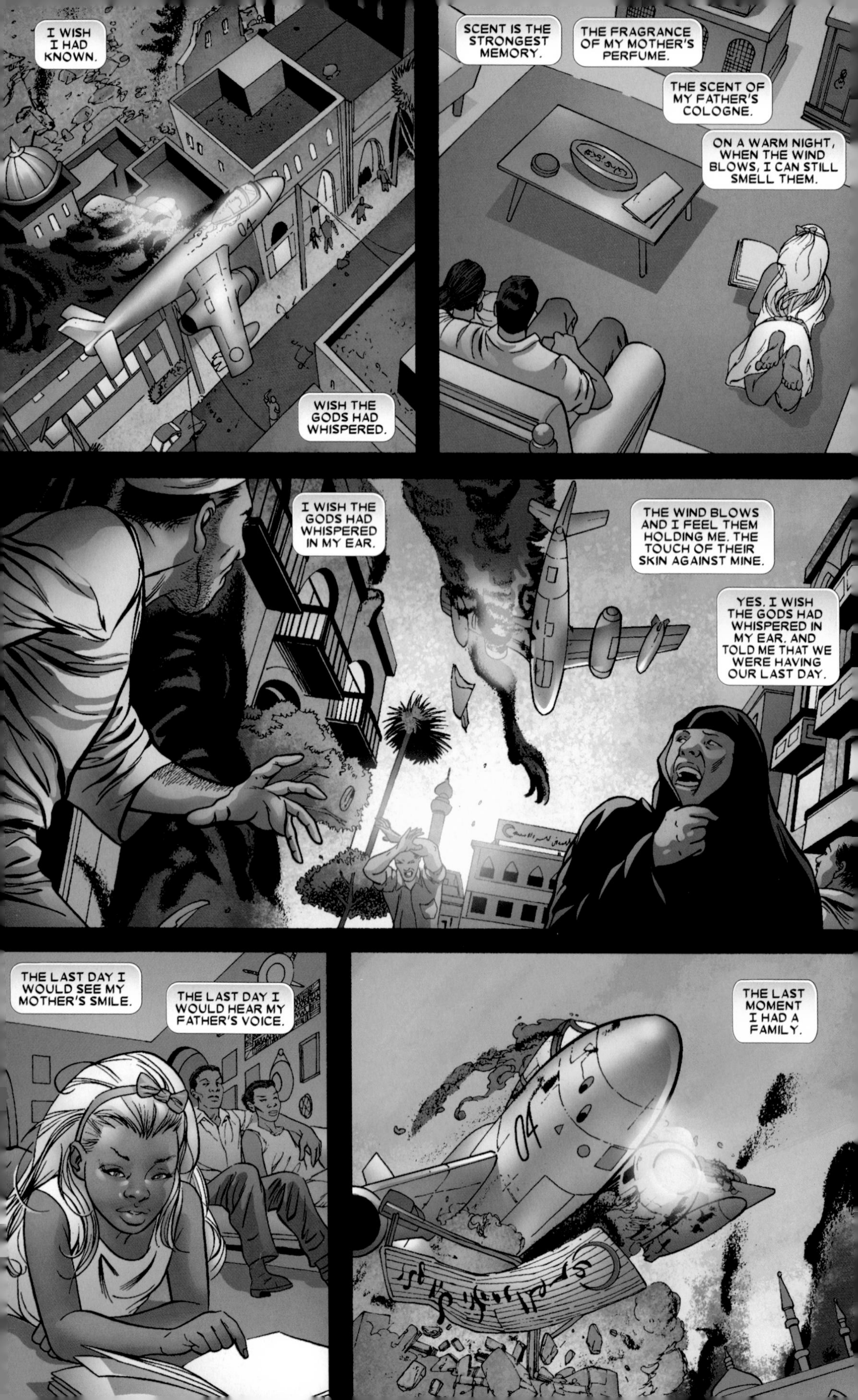
I WISH I HAD KNOWN.
WISH THE GODS HAD WHISPERED.
SCENT IS THE STRONGEST MEMORY.
THE FRAGRANCE OF MY MOTHER'S PERFUME.
THE SCENT OF MY FATHER'S COLOGNE.
ON A WARM NIGHT, WHEN THE WIND BLOWS, I CAN STILL SMELL THEM.
I WISH THE GODS HAD WHISPERED IN MY EAR.
THE WIND BLOWS AND I FEEL THEM HOLDING ME. THE TOUCH OF THEIR SKIN AGAINST MINE.
YES. I WISH THE GODS HAD WHISPERED IN MY EAR. AND TOLD ME THAT WE WERE HAVING OUR LAST DAY.
THE LAST DAY I WOULD SEE MY MOTHER'S SMILE.
THE LAST DAY I WOULD HEAR MY FATHER'S VOICE.
THE LAST MOMENT I HAD A FAMILY.

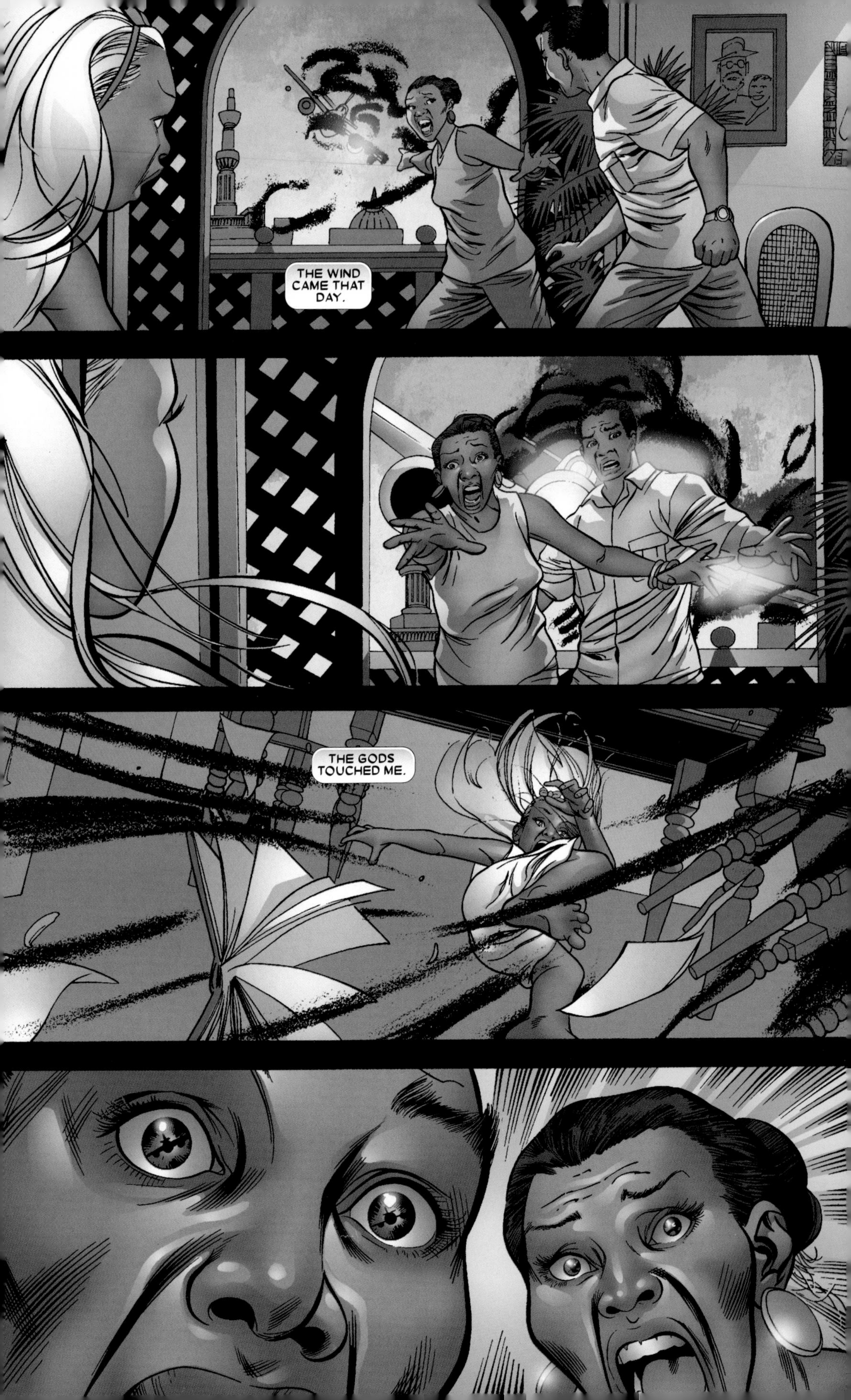
THE WIND CAME THAT DAY.
THE GODS TOUCHED ME.

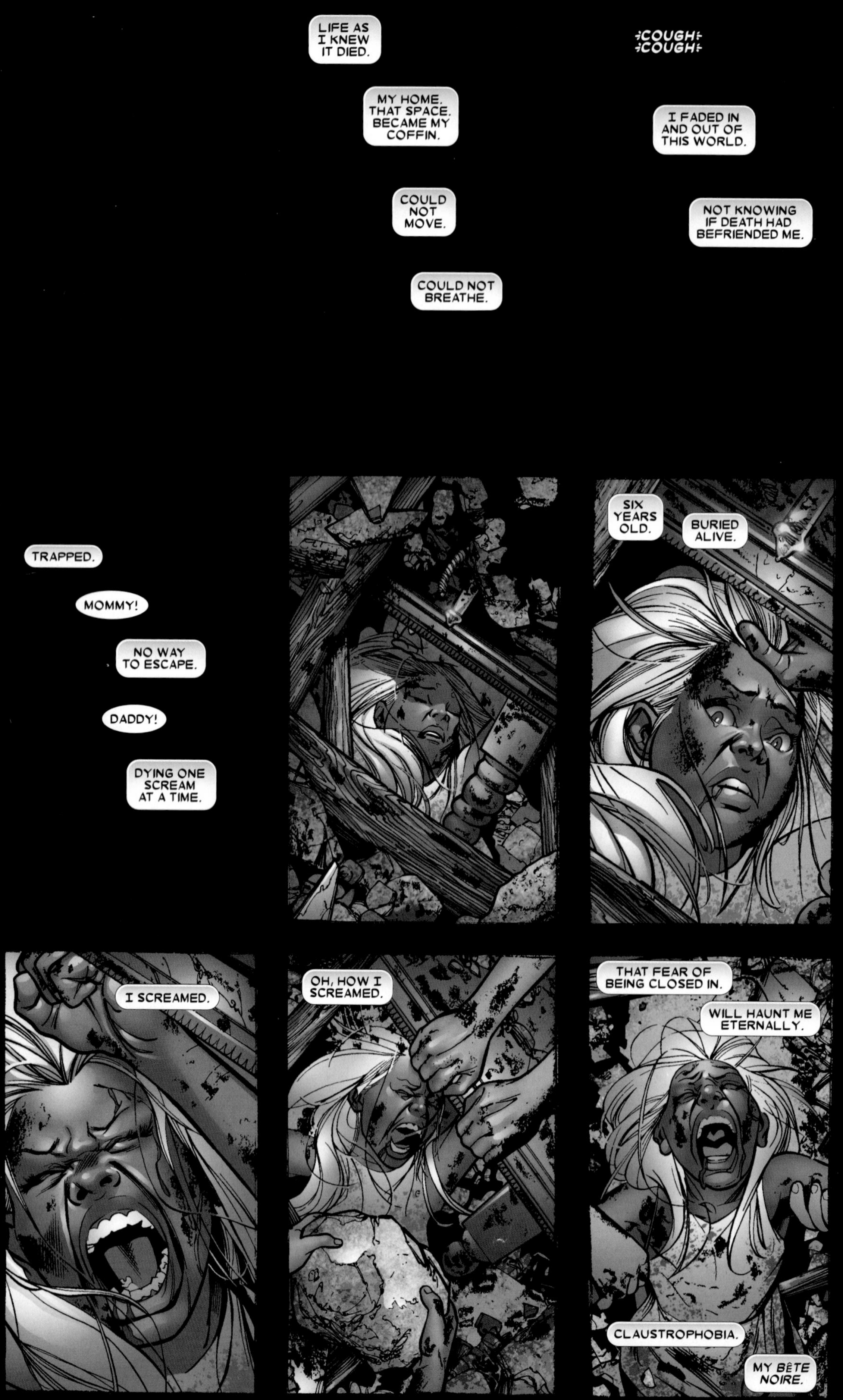
LIFE AS I KNEW IT DIED.
MY HOME. THAT SPACE. BECAME MY COFFIN.
COULD NOT MOVE.
COULD NOT BREATHE.
COUGH *COUGH*
I FADED IN AND OUT OF THIS WORLD.
NOT KNOWING IF DEATH HAD BEFRIENDED ME.
TRAPPED.
MOMMY!
NO WAY TO ESCAPE.
DADDY!
DYING ONE SCREAM AT A TIME.
SIX YEARS OLD.
BURIED ALIVE.
I SCREAMED.
OH, HOW I SCREAMED.
THAT FEAR OF BEING CLOSED IN.
WILL HAUNT ME ETERNALLY.
CLAUSTROPHOBIA.
MY BÊTE NOIRE.

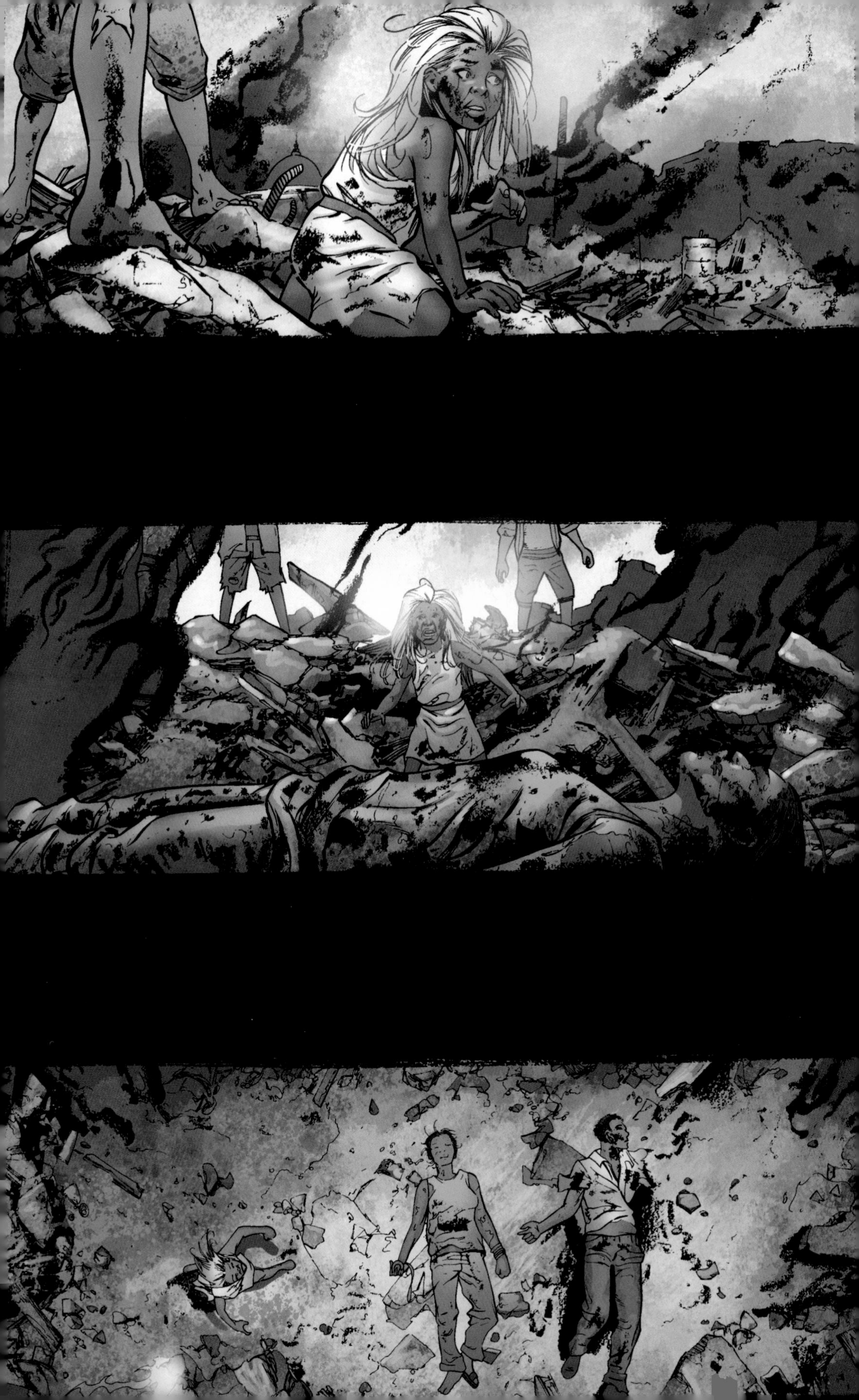

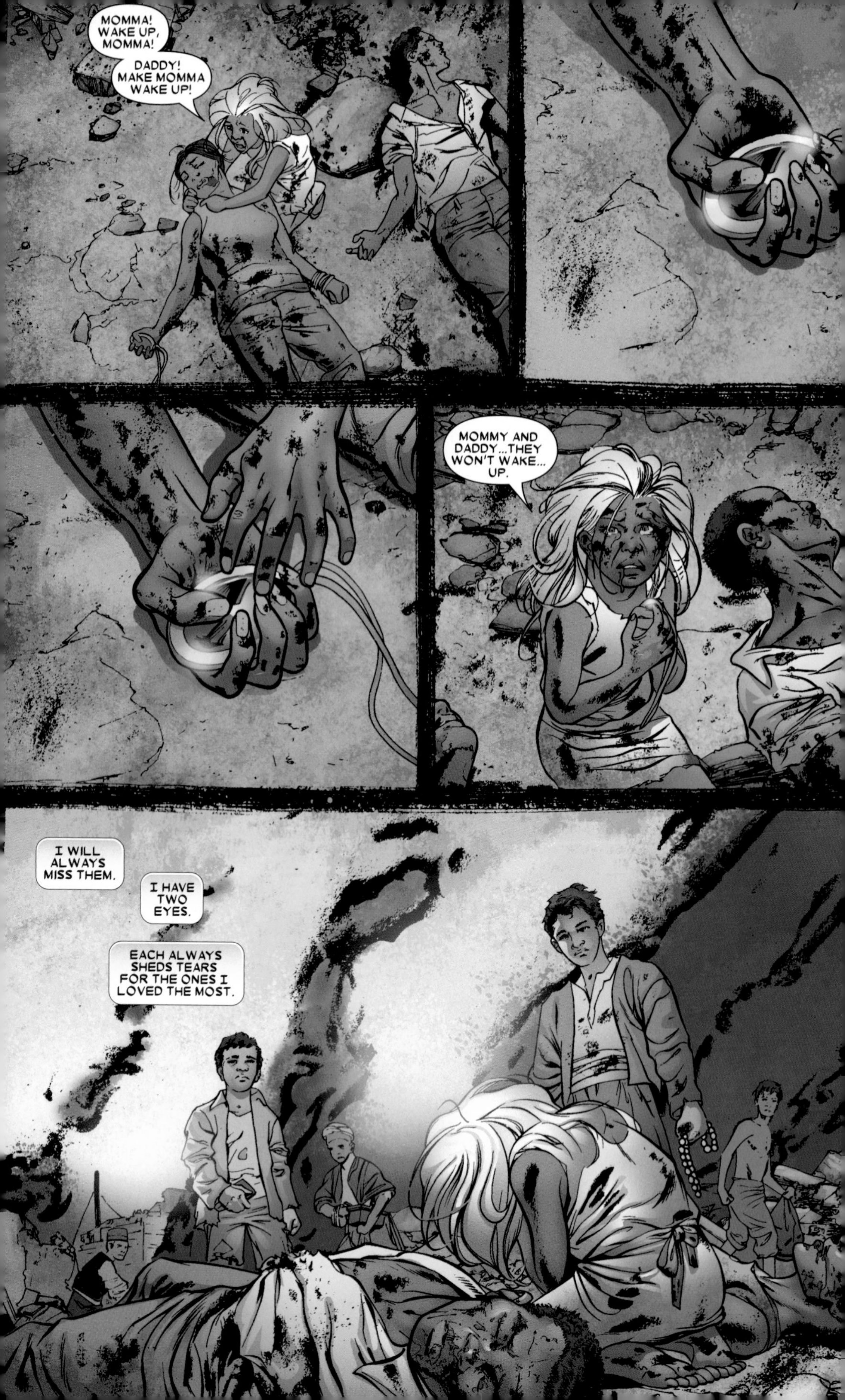
MOMMA! WAKE UP, MOMMA!
DADDY! MAKE MOMMA WAKE UP!
MOMMY AND DADDY...THEY WON'T WAKE... UP.
I WILL ALWAYS MISS THEM.
I HAVE TWO EYES.
EACH ALWAYS SHEDS TEARS FOR THE ONES I LOVED THE MOST.

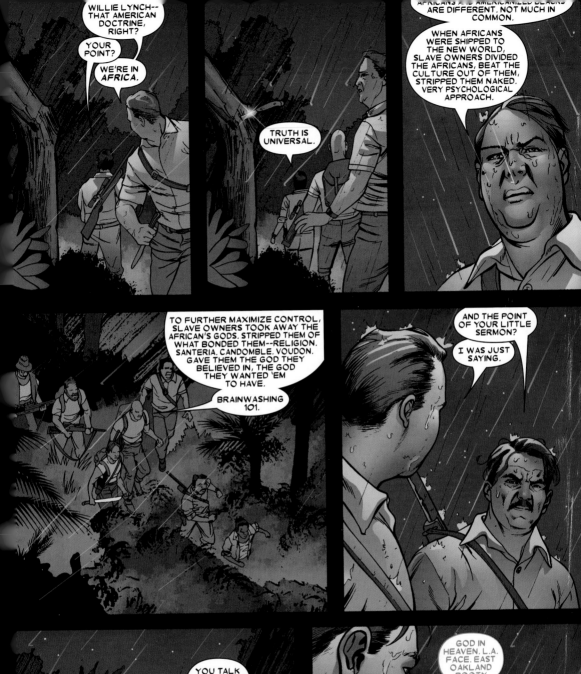

WILLIE LYNCH-- THAT AMERICAN DOCTRINE, RIGHT?

YOUR POINT?

WE'RE IN AFRICA.

TRUTH IS UNIVERSAL.

AFRICANS AND AMERICANIZED BLACKS ARE DIFFERENT. NOT MUCH IN COMMON.

WHEN AFRICANS WERE SHIPPED TO THE NEW WORLD, SLAVE OWNERS DIVIDED THE AFRICANS, BEAT THE CULTURE OUT OF THEM, STRIPPED THEM NAKED. VERY PSYCHOLOGICAL APPROACH.

TO FURTHER MAXIMIZE CONTROL, SLAVE OWNERS TOOK AWAY THE AFRICAN'S GODS. STRIPPED THEM OF WHAT BONDED THEM--RELIGION. SANTERIA. CANDOMBLE. VOUDON. GAVE THEM THE GOD THEY BELIEVED IN, THE GOD THEY WANTED 'EM TO HAVE.

BRAINWASHING 101.

AND THE POINT OF YOUR LITTLE SERMON?

I WAS JUST SAYING.

YOU TALK TOO DAMN MUCH, YOU KNOW THAT?

GOD IN HEAVEN. L.A. FACE. EAST OAKLAND BOOTY.

BEEN SO LONG SINCE I SAW A GIRL LIKE THAT.

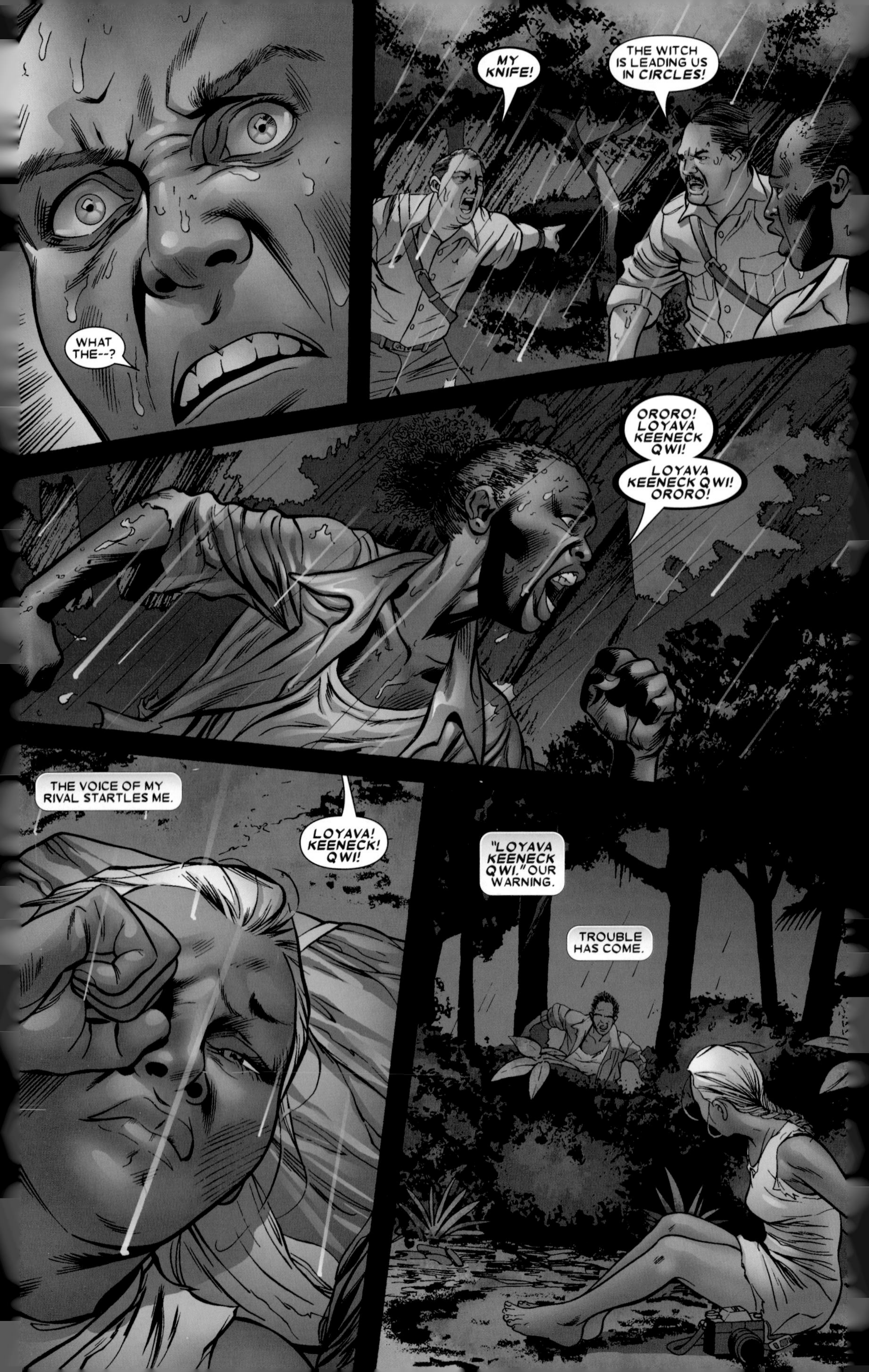
WHAT THE--?
MY KNIFE!
THE WITCH IS LEADING US IN CIRCLES!
ORORO! LOYAVA KEENECK QWI!
LOYAVA KEENECK QWI! ORORO!
THE VOICE OF MY RIVAL STARTLES ME.
LOYAVA! KEENECK! QWI!
"LOYAVA KEENECK QWI." OUR WARNING.
TROUBLE HAS COME.

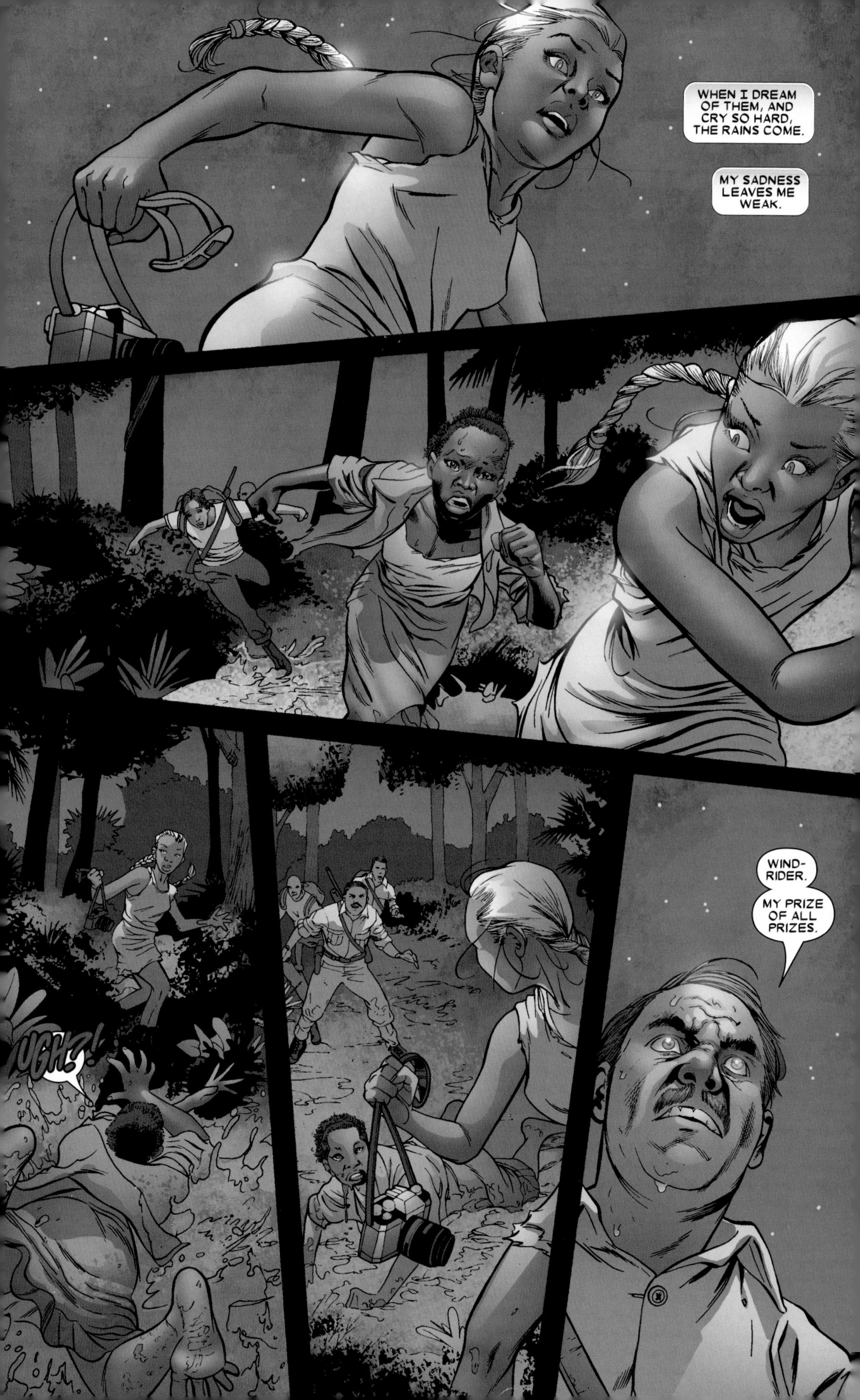
WHEN I DREAM OF THEM, AND CRY SO HARD, THE RAINS COME.
MY SADNESS LEAVES ME WEAK.
UGH!
WIND-RIDER.
MY PRIZE OF ALL PRIZES.

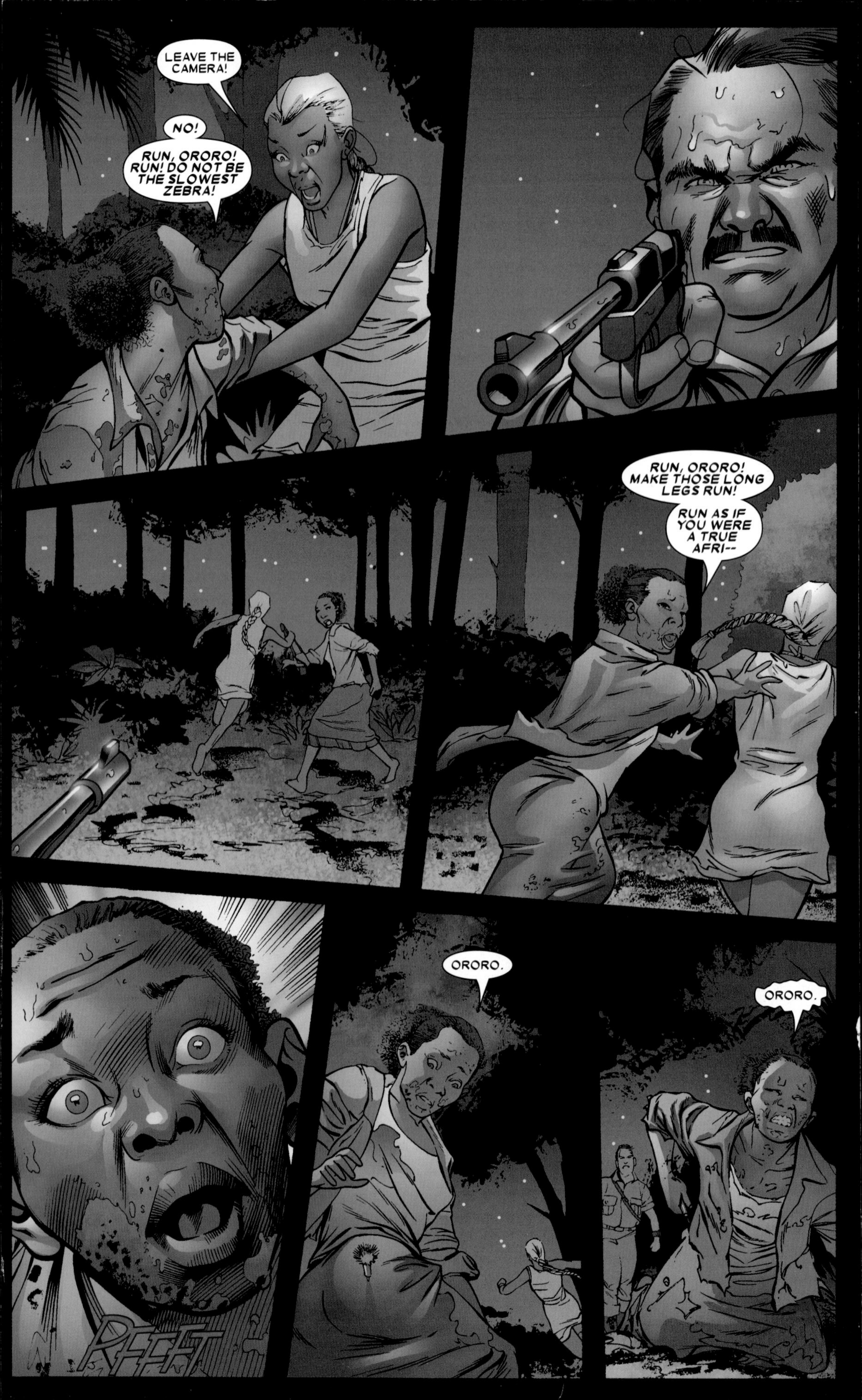

LEAVE THE CAMERA!
NO!
RUN, ORORO! RUN! DO NOT BE THE SLOWEST ZEBRA!
RUN, ORORO! MAKE THOSE LONG LEGS RUN!
RUN AS IF YOU WERE A TRUE AFRI--
PFFFT
ORORO.
ORORO.

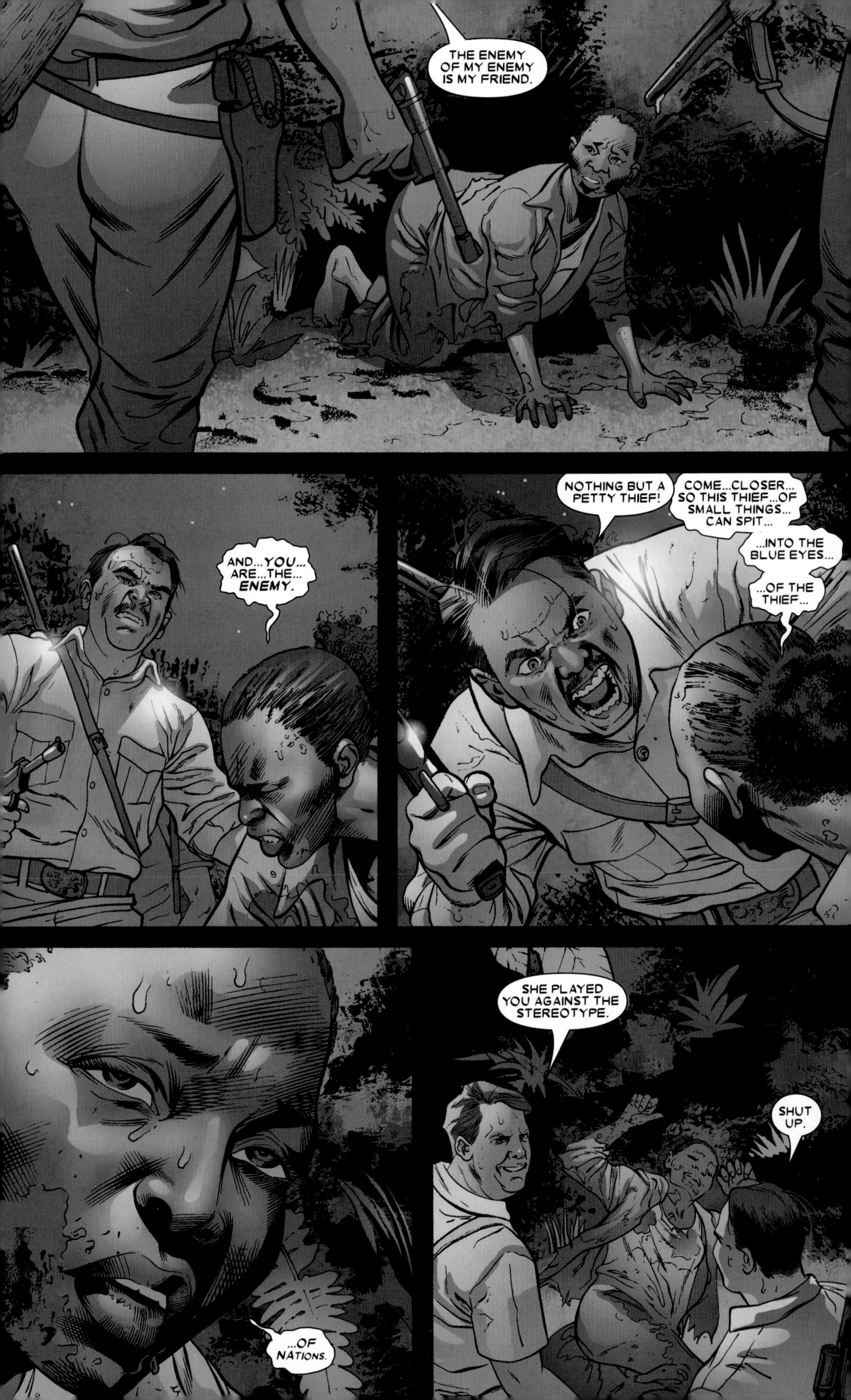
THE ENEMY OF MY ENEMY IS MY FRIEND.
AND...YOU... ARE...THE... ENEMY.
NOTHING BUT A PETTY THIEF!
COME...CLOSER... SO THIS THIEF...OF SMALL THINGS... CAN SPIT...
...INTO THE BLUE EYES...
...OF THE THIEF...
...OF NATIONS.
SHE PLAYED YOU AGAINST THE STEREOTYPE.
SHUT UP.

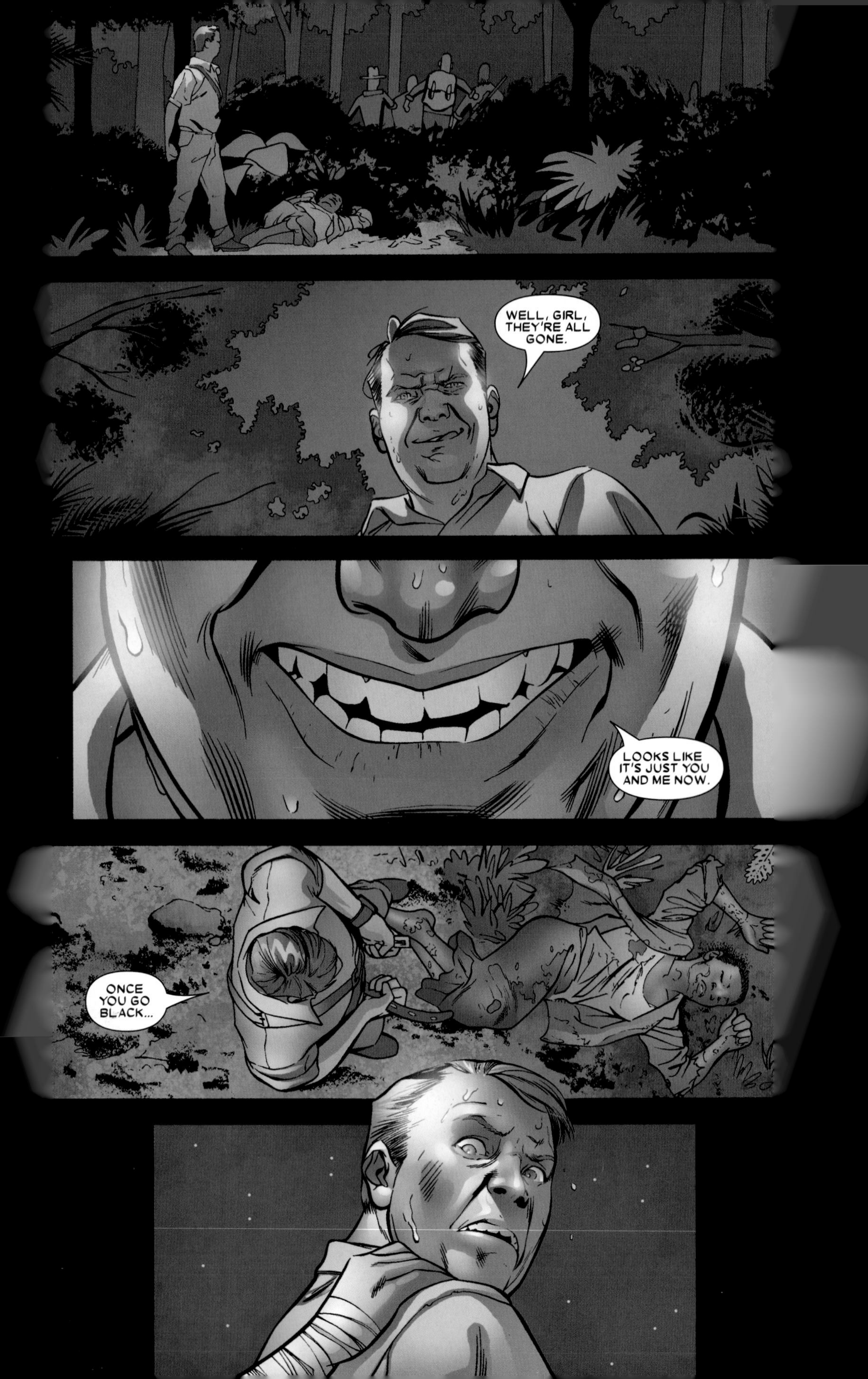
WELL, GIRL, THEY'RE ALL GONE.
LOOKS LIKE IT'S JUST YOU AND ME NOW.
ONCE YOU GO BLACK...

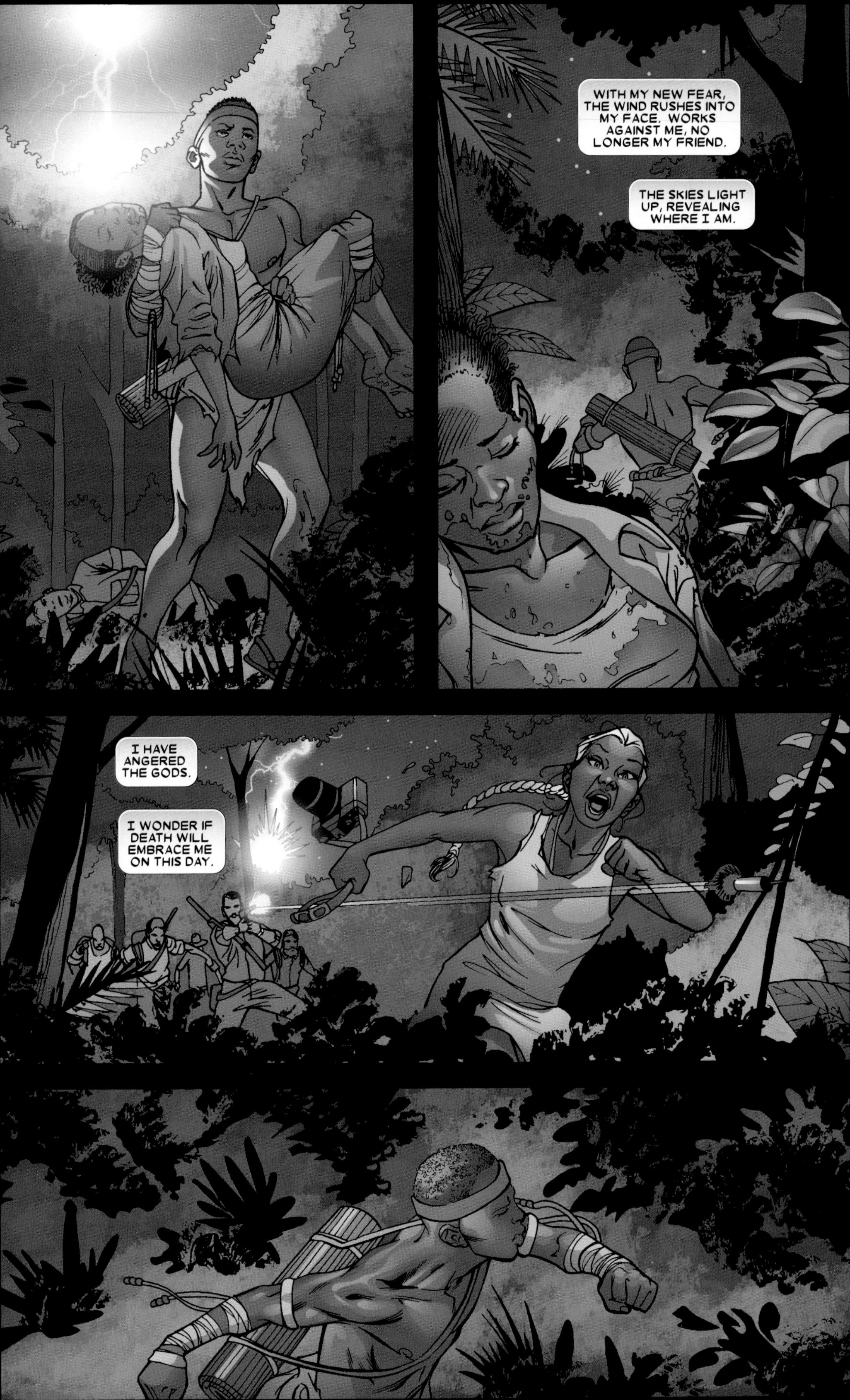

WITH MY NEW FEAR, THE WIND RUSHES INTO MY FACE. WORKS AGAINST ME, NO LONGER MY FRIEND.
THE SKIES LIGHT UP, REVEALING WHERE I AM.
I HAVE ANGERED THE GODS.
I WONDER IF DEATH WILL EMBRACE ME ON THIS DAY.

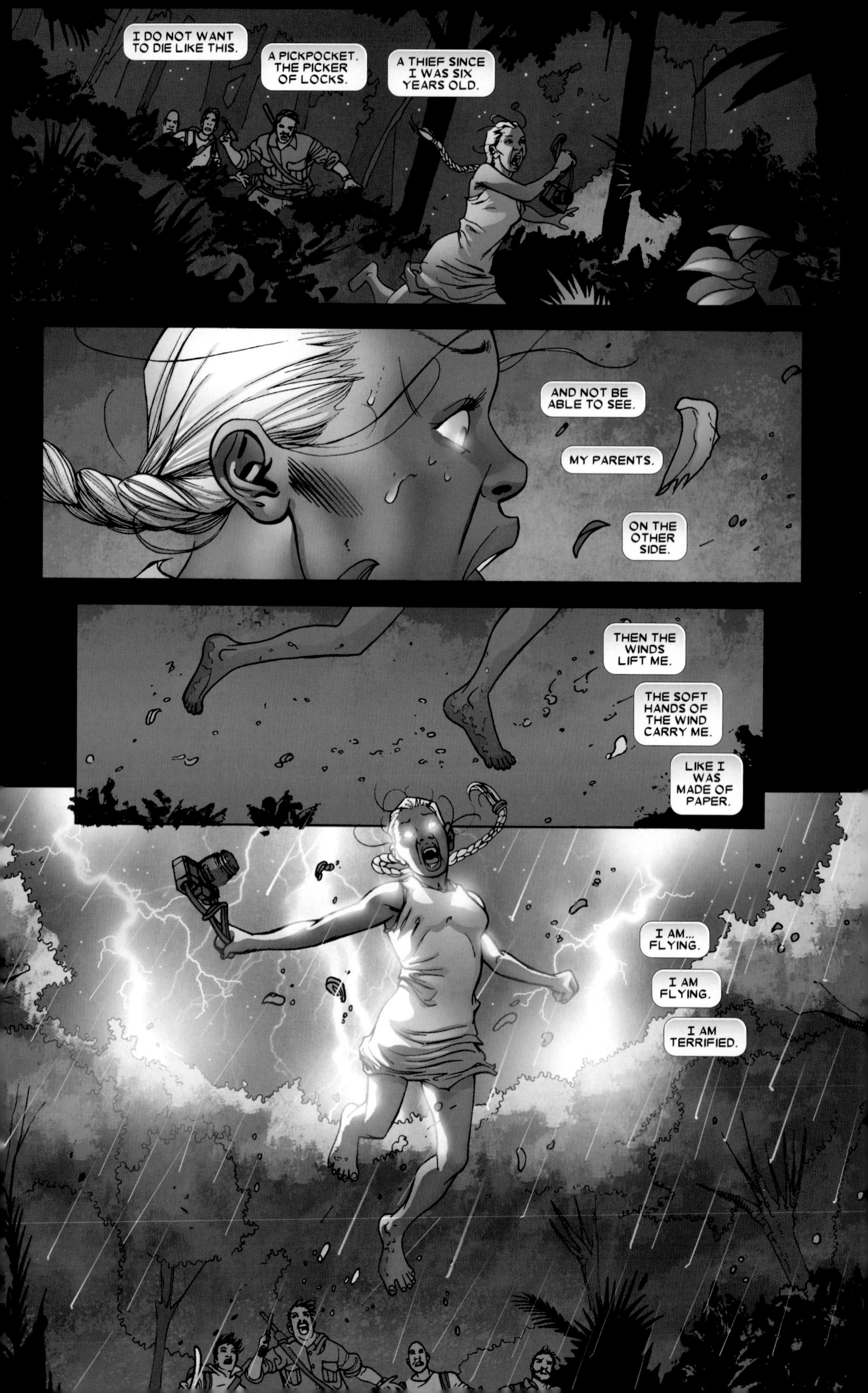
I DO NOT WANT TO DIE LIKE THIS.
A PICKPOCKET. THE PICKER OF LOCKS.
A THIEF SINCE I WAS SIX YEARS OLD.
AND NOT BE ABLE TO SEE.
MY PARENTS.
ON THE OTHER SIDE.
THEN THE WINDS LIFT ME.
THE SOFT HANDS OF THE WIND CARRY ME.
LIKE I WAS MADE OF PAPER.
I AM... FLYING.
I AM FLYING.
I AM TERRIFIED.

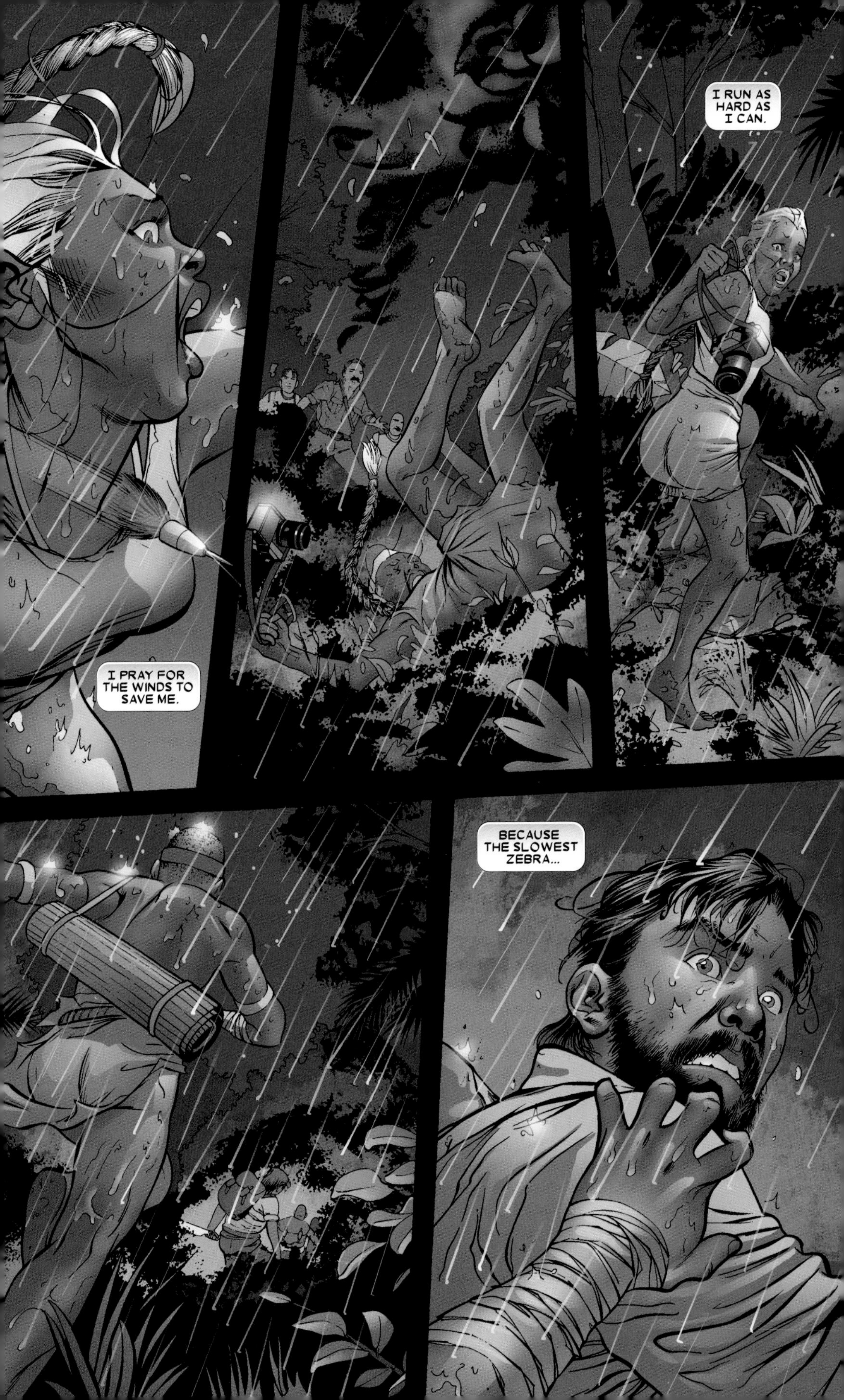
I PRAY FOR THE WINDS TO SAVE ME.
I RUN AS HARD AS I CAN.
BECAUSE THE SLOWEST ZEBRA...

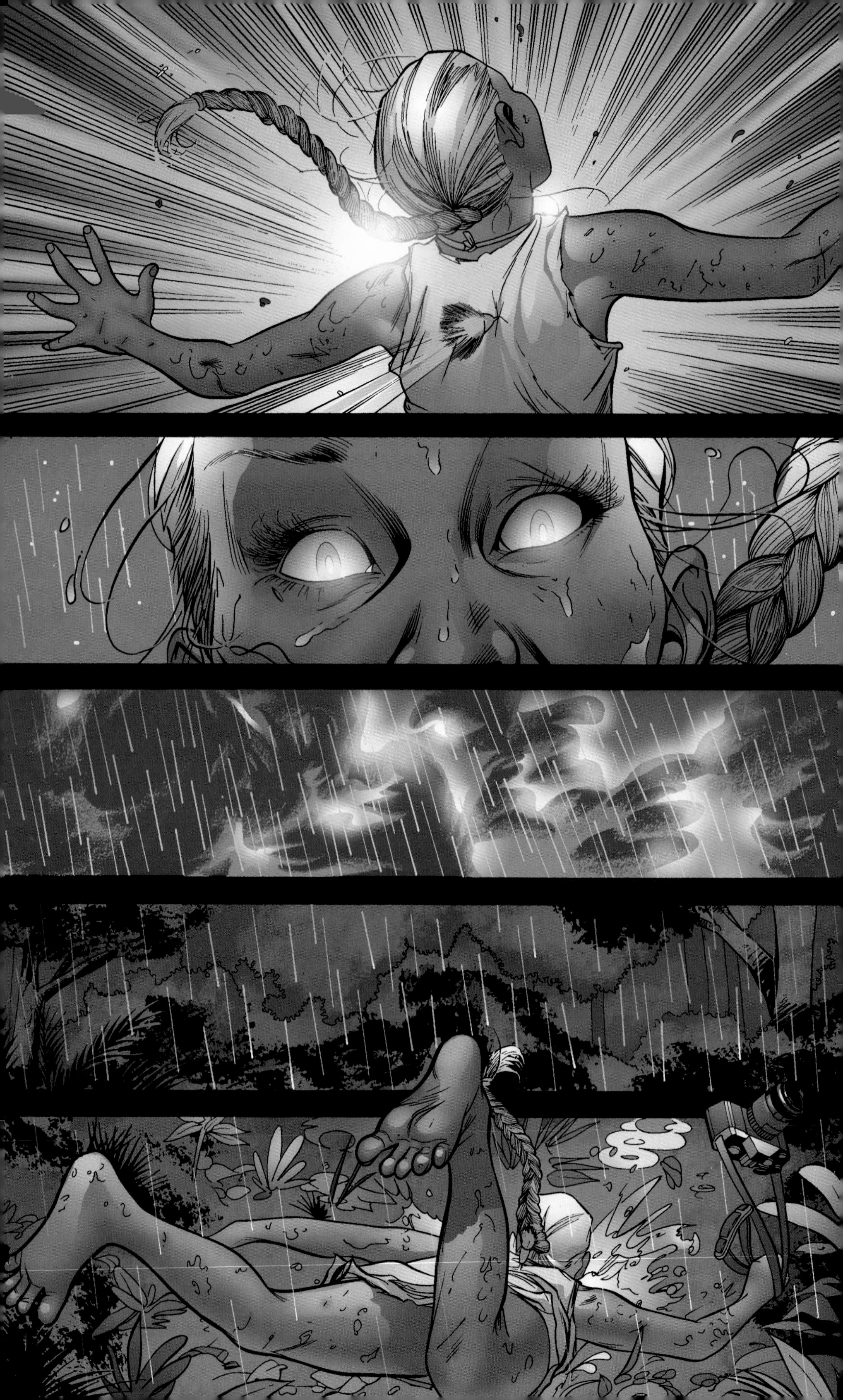

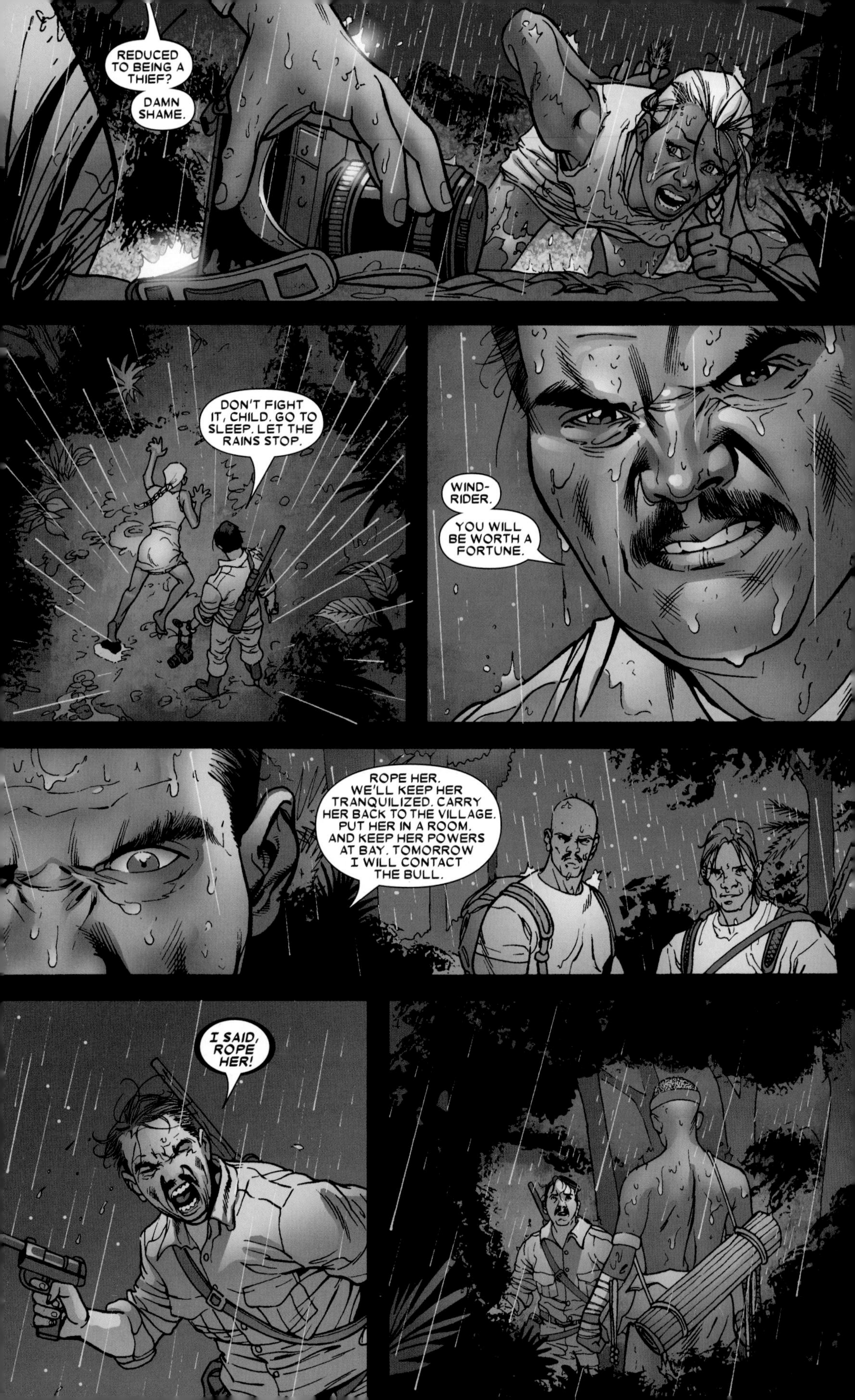
REDUCED TO BEING A THIEF?
DAMN SHAME.
DON'T FIGHT IT, CHILD. GO TO SLEEP. LET THE RAINS STOP.
WIND-RIDER.
YOU WILL BE WORTH A FORTUNE.
ROPE HER. WE'LL KEEP HER TRANQUILIZED. CARRY HER BACK TO THE VILLAGE. PUT HER IN A ROOM. AND KEEP HER POWERS AT BAY. TOMORROW I WILL CONTACT THE BULL.
I SAID, ROPE HER!

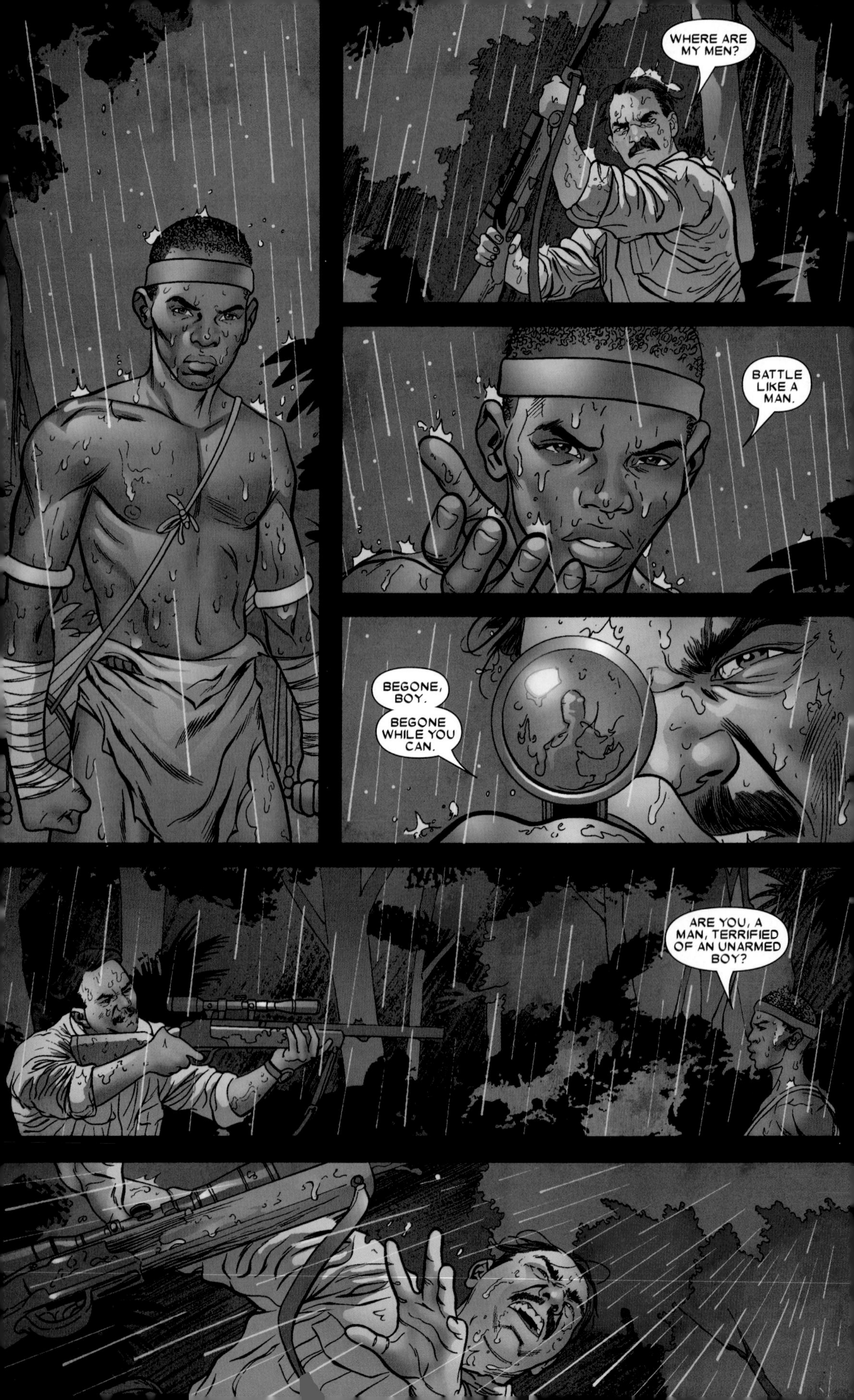
WHERE ARE MY MEN?
BATTLE LIKE A MAN.
BEGONE, BOY.
BEGONE WHILE YOU CAN.
ARE YOU, A MAN, TERRIFIED OF AN UNARMED BOY?

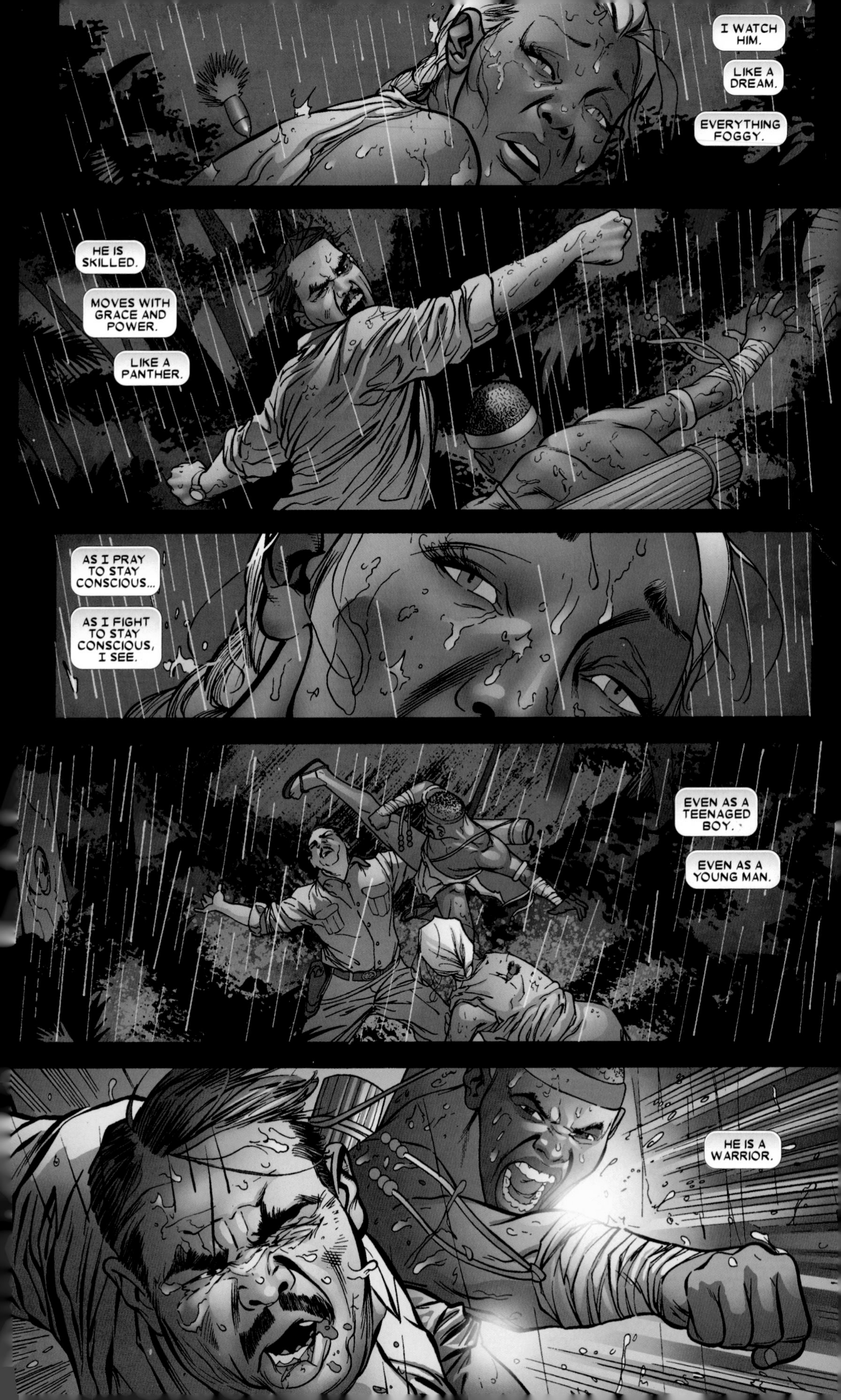
I WATCH HIM.
LIKE A DREAM.
EVERYTHING FOGGY.
HE IS SKILLED.
MOVES WITH GRACE AND POWER.
LIKE A PANTHER.
AS I PRAY TO STAY CONSCIOUS...
AS I FIGHT TO STAY CONSCIOUS, I SEE.
EVEN AS A TEENAGED BOY.
EVEN AS A YOUNG MAN.
HE IS A WARRIOR.

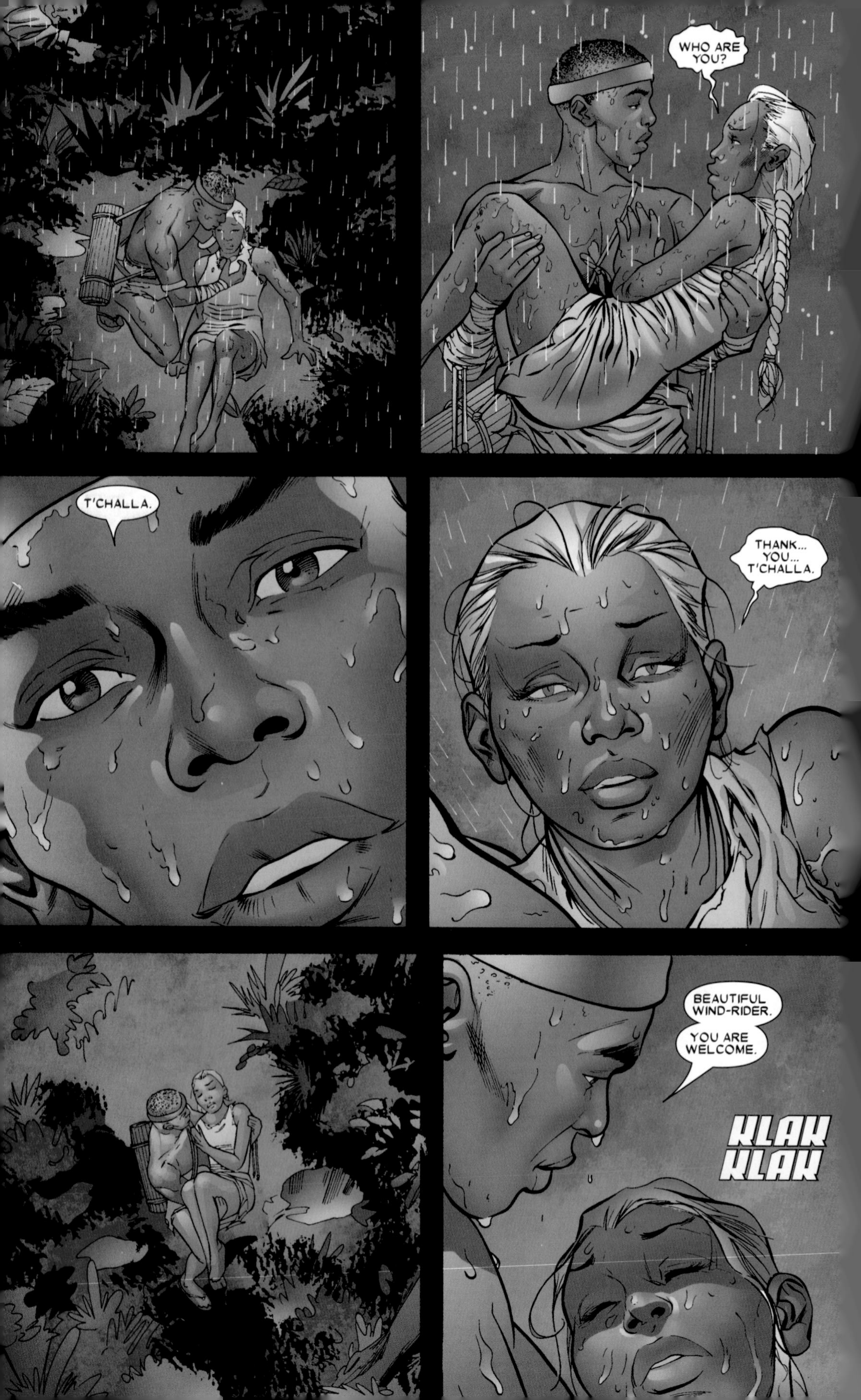
WHO ARE YOU?
T'CHALLA.
THANK... YOU... T'CHALLA.
BEAUTIFUL WIND-RIDER.
YOU ARE WELCOME.
KLAK KLAK

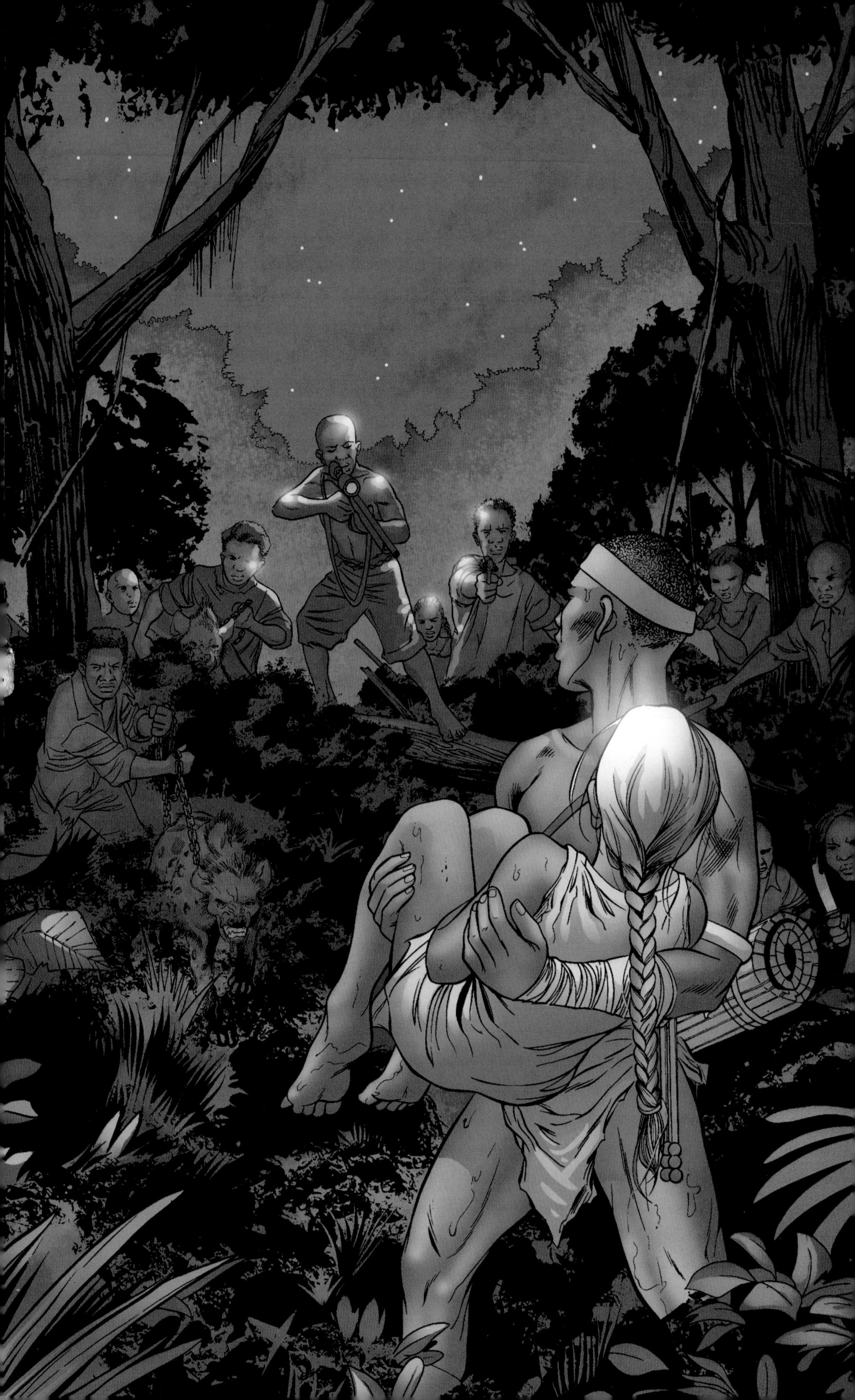

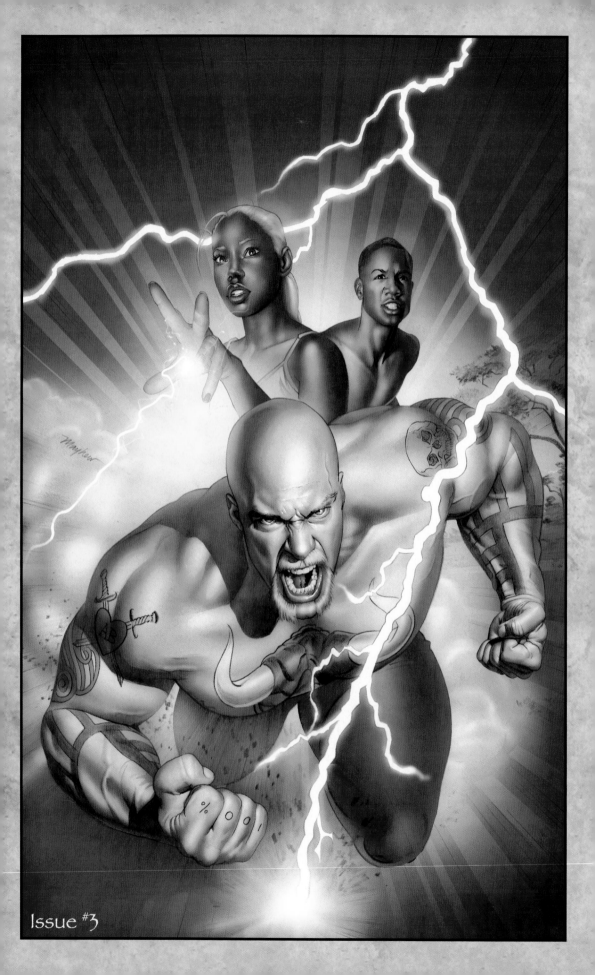

Issue #3

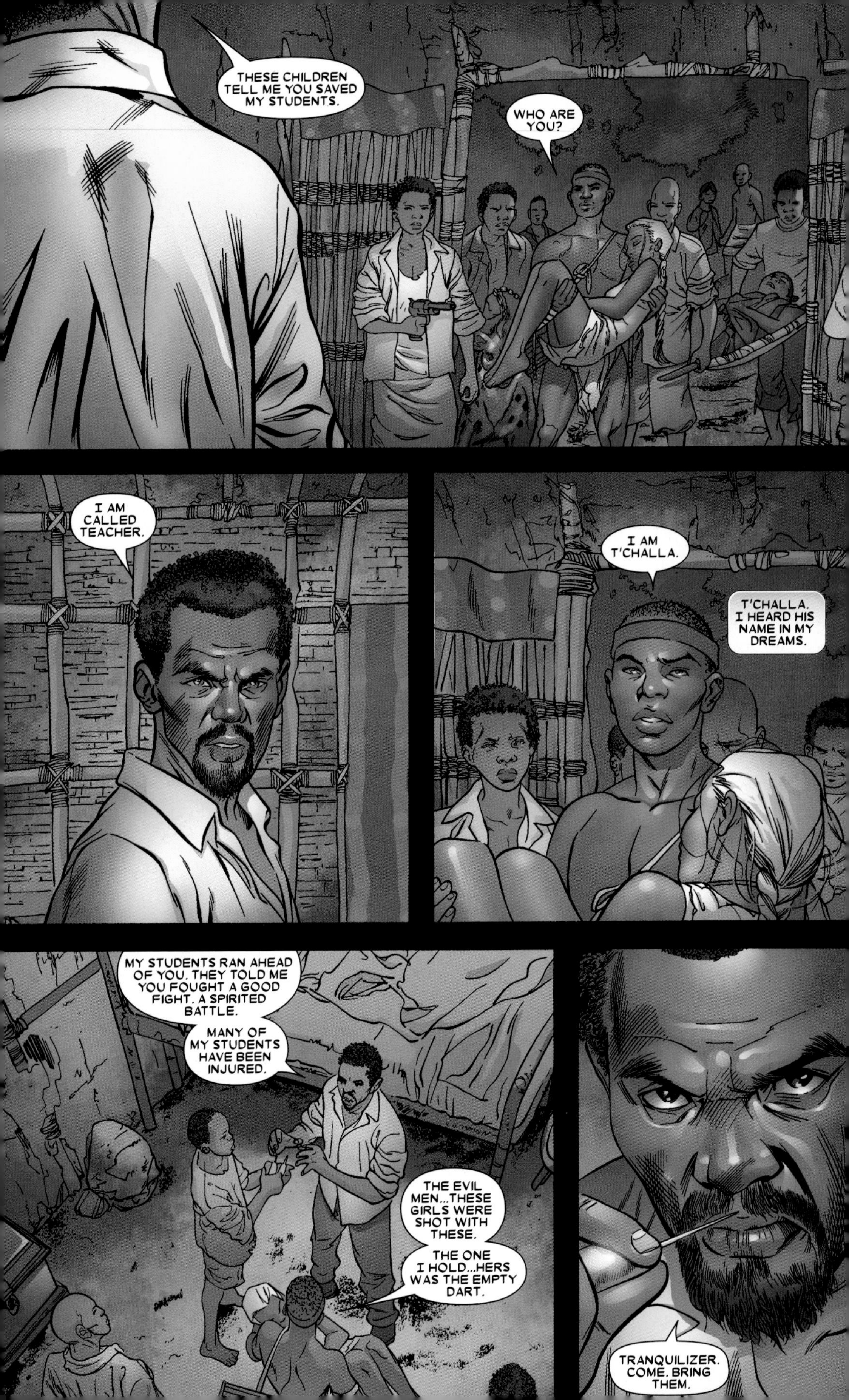
THESE CHILDREN TELL ME YOU SAVED MY STUDENTS.
WHO ARE YOU?
I AM CALLED TEACHER.
I AM T'CHALLA.
T'CHALLA. I HEARD HIS NAME IN MY DREAMS.
MY STUDENTS RAN AHEAD OF YOU. THEY TOLD ME YOU FOUGHT A GOOD FIGHT. A SPIRITED BATTLE.
MANY OF MY STUDENTS HAVE BEEN INJURED.
THE EVIL MEN...THESE GIRLS WERE SHOT WITH THESE.
THE ONE I HOLD...HERS WAS THE EMPTY DART.
TRANQUILIZER. COME. BRING THEM.

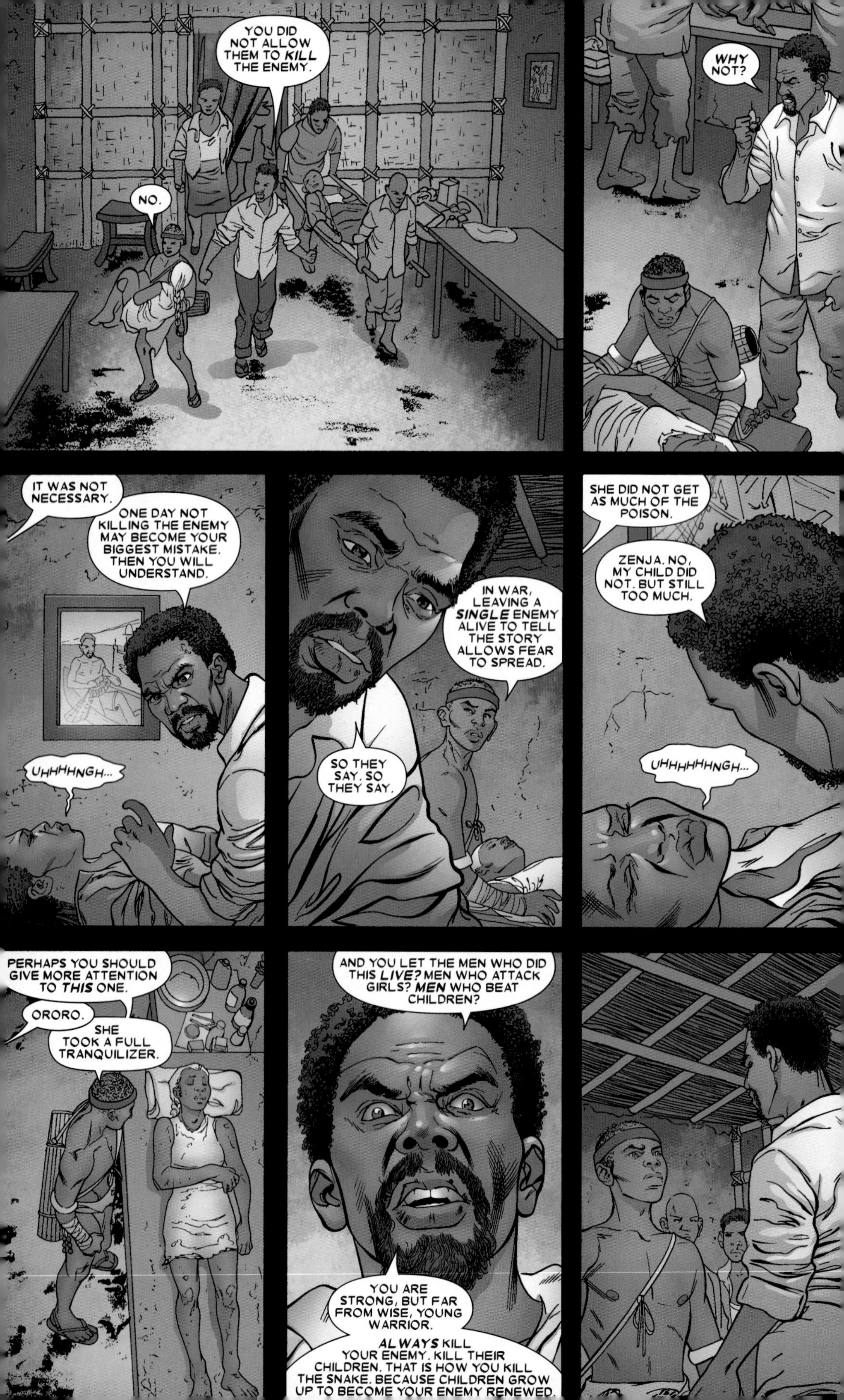
YOU DID NOT ALLOW THEM TO KILL THE ENEMY.
NO.
WHY NOT?
IT WAS NOT NECESSARY.
ONE DAY NOT KILLING THE ENEMY MAY BECOME YOUR BIGGEST MISTAKE. THEN YOU WILL UNDERSTAND.
UHHHHNGH...
IN WAR, LEAVING A SINGLE ENEMY ALIVE TO TELL THE STORY ALLOWS FEAR TO SPREAD.
SO THEY SAY. SO THEY SAY.
SHE DID NOT GET AS MUCH OF THE POISON.
ZENJA, NO, MY CHILD DID NOT. BUT STILL TOO MUCH.
UHHHHHHHNGH...
PERHAPS YOU SHOULD GIVE MORE ATTENTION TO THIS ONE.
ORORO.
SHE TOOK A FULL TRANQUILIZER.
AND YOU LET THE MEN WHO DID THIS LIVE? MEN WHO ATTACK GIRLS? MEN WHO BEAT CHILDREN?
YOU ARE STRONG, BUT FAR FROM WISE, YOUNG WARRIOR.
ALWAYS KILL YOUR ENEMY. KILL THEIR CHILDREN. THAT IS HOW YOU KILL THE SNAKE. BECAUSE CHILDREN GROW UP TO BECOME YOUR ENEMY RENEWED.

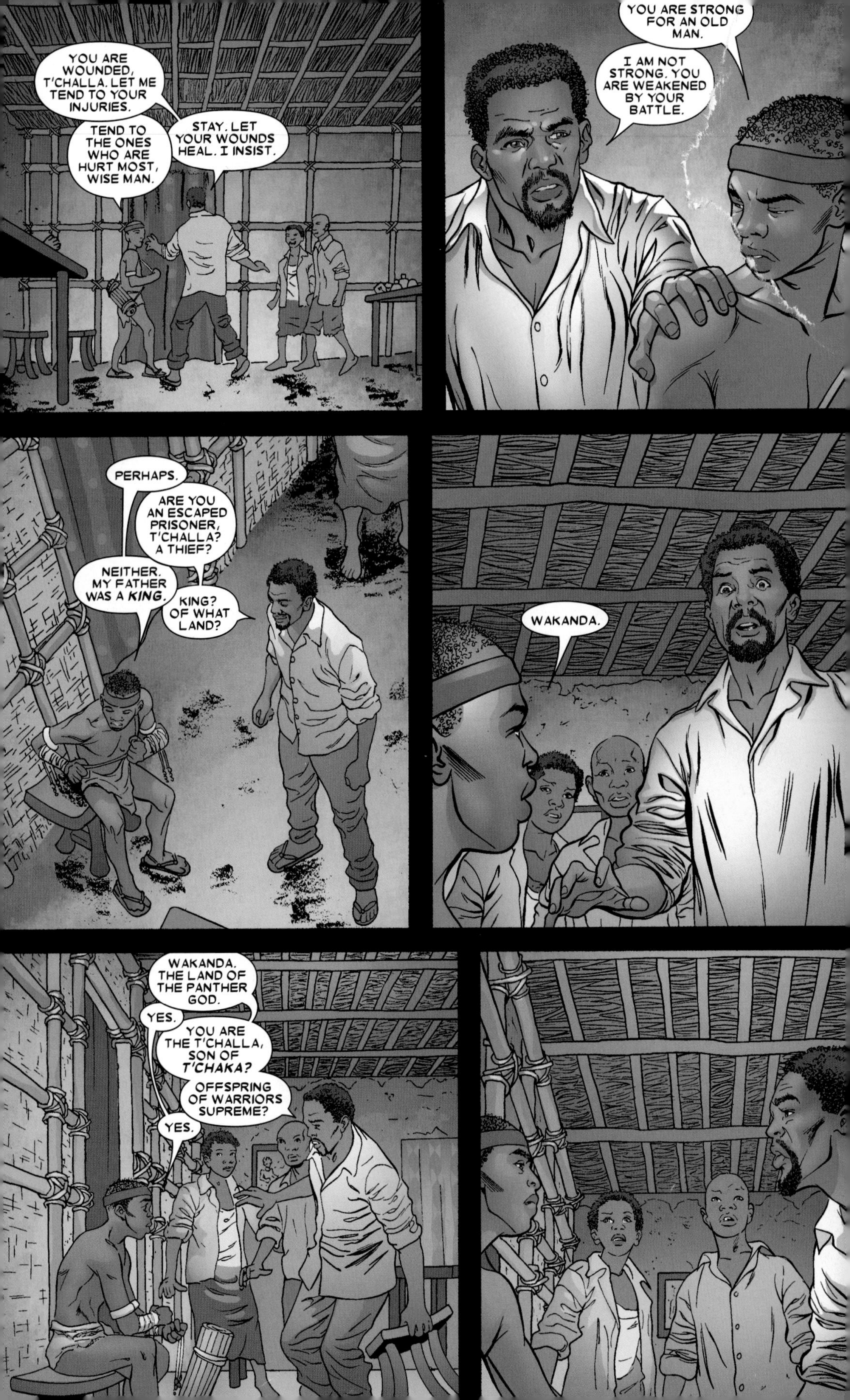
YOU ARE WOUNDED, T'CHALLA. LET ME TEND TO YOUR INJURIES.
TEND TO THE ONES WHO ARE HURT MOST, WISE MAN.
STAY. LET YOUR WOUNDS HEAL. I INSIST.
YOU ARE STRONG FOR AN OLD MAN.
I AM NOT STRONG. YOU ARE WEAKENED BY YOUR BATTLE.
PERHAPS.
ARE YOU AN ESCAPED PRISONER, T'CHALLA? A THIEF?
NEITHER. MY FATHER WAS A KING.
KING? OF WHAT LAND?
WAKANDA.
WAKANDA. THE LAND OF THE PANTHER GOD.
YES.
YOU ARE THE T'CHALLA, SON OF T'CHAKA?
OFFSPRING OF WARRIORS SUPREME?
YES.

"ALWAYS KILL YOUR ENEMY, T'CHALLA."

THIS ISN'T OVER.

THAT YOUNG BOY HANDED *YOU* YOUR BUTT.

YOURS AS WELL. DON'T FORGET THAT.

HE CAUGHT ME BY SURPRISE... MET YOU FACE-TO-FACE.

BACK AT THE TRUCK... WILL CALL...MY BROTHER...

I WILL HAVE THE WIND RIDER. I WILL CAPTURE THE LEGEND.

AS SOON AS WE GET TO THE TRUCK, I WILL RADIO DE RUYTER. WE'LL TELL HIM ABOUT THE WIND RIDER. NOW HE WILL BELIEVE ME.

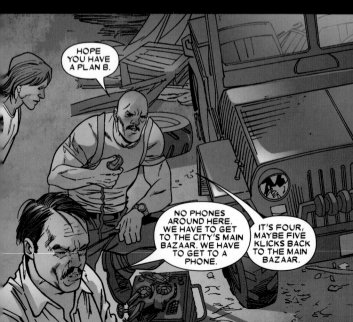

HOPE YOU HAVE A PLAN B.

NO PHONES AROUND HERE. WE HAVE TO GET TO THE CITY'S MAIN BAZAAR. WE HAVE TO GET TO A PHONE.

IT'S FOUR, MAYBE FIVE KLICKS BACK TO THE MAIN BAZAAR.

START WALKING.

"T'CHALLA, LEGEND HAS IT YOUR FATHER DEFEATED CAPTAIN AMERICA IN HAND-TO-HAND COMBAT."

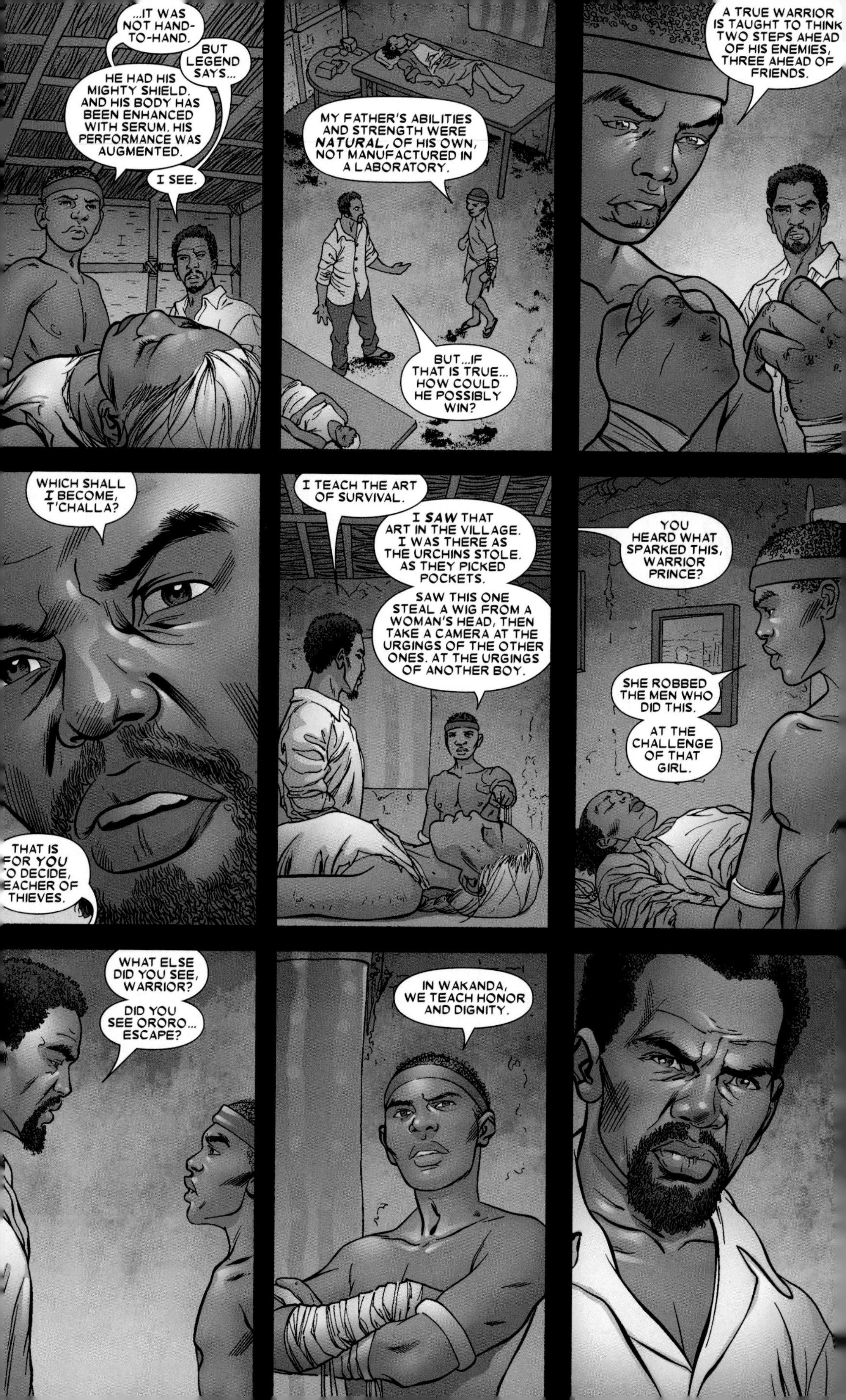
...IT WAS NOT HAND-TO-HAND.
BUT LEGEND SAYS...
HE HAD HIS MIGHTY SHIELD. AND HIS BODY HAS BEEN ENHANCED WITH SERUM. HIS PERFORMANCE WAS AUGMENTED.
I SEE.
MY FATHER'S ABILITIES AND STRENGTH WERE NATURAL, OF HIS OWN, NOT MANUFACTURED IN A LABORATORY.
BUT...IF THAT IS TRUE... HOW COULD HE POSSIBLY WIN?
A TRUE WARRIOR IS TAUGHT TO THINK TWO STEPS AHEAD OF HIS ENEMIES, THREE AHEAD OF FRIENDS.
WHICH SHALL I BECOME, T'CHALLA?
THAT IS FOR YOU 'O DECIDE, 'EACHER OF THIEVES.
I TEACH THE ART OF SURVIVAL.
I SAW THAT ART IN THE VILLAGE. I WAS THERE AS THE URCHINS STOLE. AS THEY PICKED POCKETS.
SAW THIS ONE STEAL A WIG FROM A WOMAN'S HEAD, THEN TAKE A CAMERA AT THE URGINGS OF THE OTHER ONES. AT THE URGINGS OF ANOTHER BOY.
YOU HEARD WHAT SPARKED THIS, WARRIOR PRINCE?
SHE ROBBED THE MEN WHO DID THIS.
AT THE CHALLENGE OF THAT GIRL.
WHAT ELSE DID YOU SEE, WARRIOR?
DID YOU SEE ORORO... ESCAPE?
IN WAKANDA, WE TEACH HONOR AND DIGNITY.

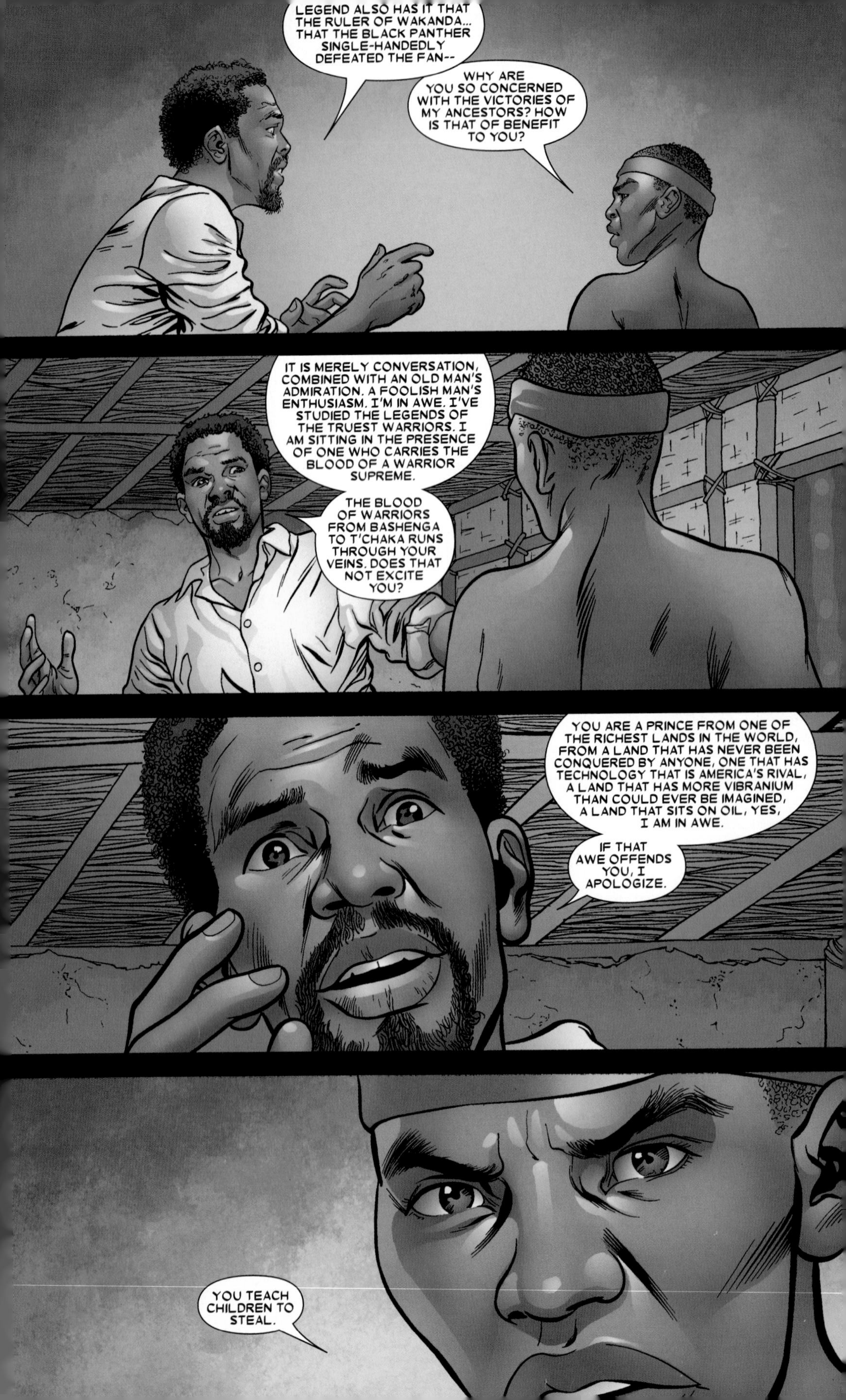
LEGEND ALSO HAS IT THAT THE RULER OF WAKANDA... THAT THE BLACK PANTHER SINGLE-HANDEDLY DEFEATED THE FAN--
WHY ARE YOU SO CONCERNED WITH THE VICTORIES OF MY ANCESTORS? HOW IS THAT OF BENEFIT TO YOU?
IT IS MERELY CONVERSATION, COMBINED WITH AN OLD MAN'S ADMIRATION. A FOOLISH MAN'S ENTHUSIASM. I'M IN AWE. I'VE STUDIED THE LEGENDS OF THE TRUEST WARRIORS. I AM SITTING IN THE PRESENCE OF ONE WHO CARRIES THE BLOOD OF A WARRIOR SUPREME.
THE BLOOD OF WARRIORS FROM BASHENGA TO T'CHAKA RUNS THROUGH YOUR VEINS. DOES THAT NOT EXCITE YOU?
YOU ARE A PRINCE FROM ONE OF THE RICHEST LANDS IN THE WORLD, FROM A LAND THAT HAS NEVER BEEN CONQUERED BY ANYONE, ONE THAT HAS TECHNOLOGY THAT IS AMERICA'S RIVAL, A LAND THAT HAS MORE VIBRANIUM THAN COULD EVER BE IMAGINED, A LAND THAT SITS ON OIL, YES, I AM IN AWE.
IF THAT AWE OFFENDS YOU, I APOLOGIZE.
YOU TEACH CHILDREN TO STEAL.

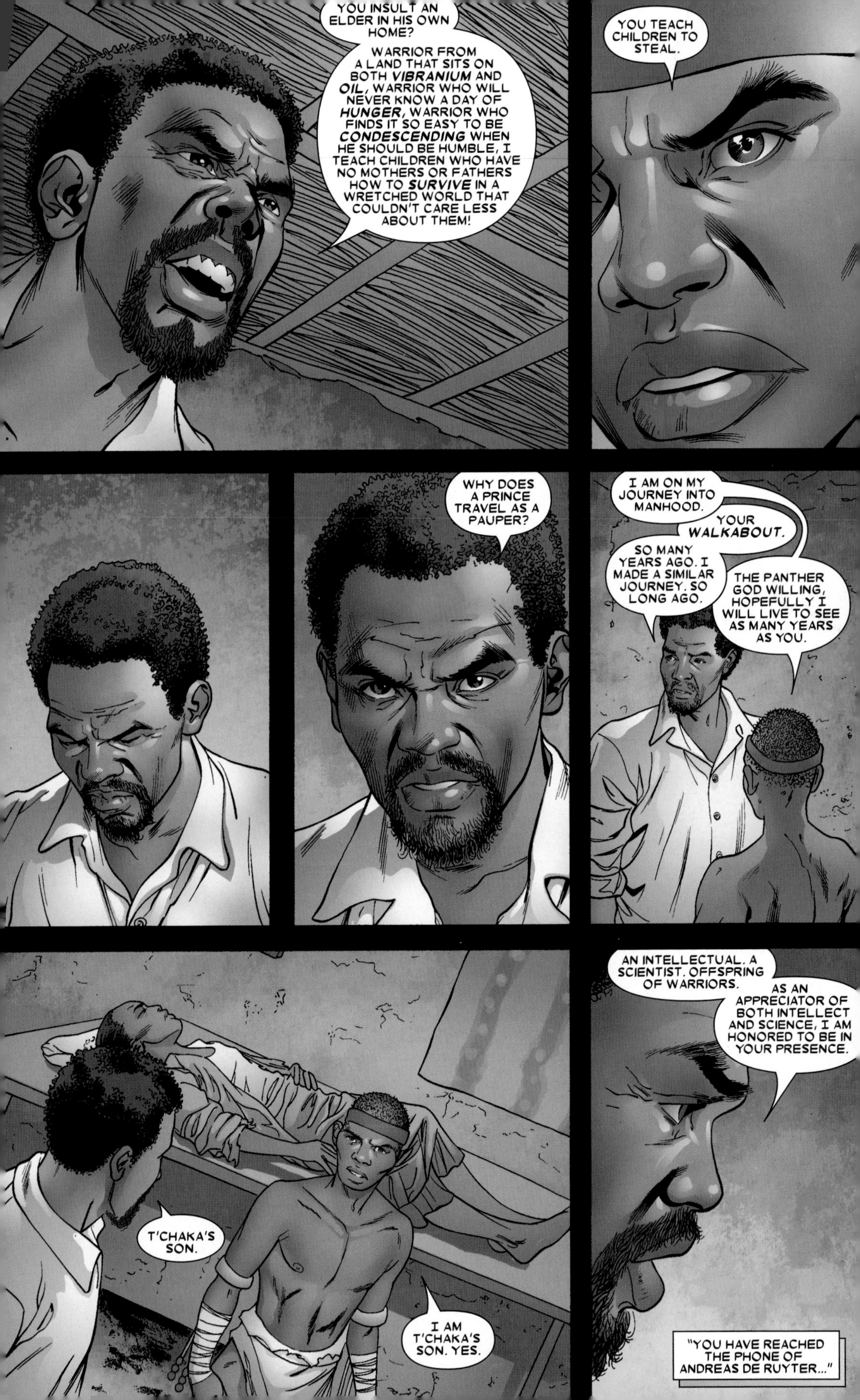

YOU INSULT AN ELDER IN HIS OWN HOME?
WARRIOR FROM A LAND THAT SITS ON BOTH VIBRANIUM AND OIL, WARRIOR WHO WILL NEVER KNOW A DAY OF HUNGER, WARRIOR WHO FINDS IT SO EASY TO BE CONDESCENDING WHEN HE SHOULD BE HUMBLE, I TEACH CHILDREN WHO HAVE NO MOTHERS OR FATHERS HOW TO SURVIVE IN A WRETCHED WORLD THAT COULDN'T CARE LESS ABOUT THEM!
YOU TEACH CHILDREN TO STEAL.
WHY DOES A PRINCE TRAVEL AS A PAUPER?
I AM ON MY JOURNEY INTO MANHOOD.
YOUR WALKABOUT.
SO MANY YEARS AGO. I MADE A SIMILAR JOURNEY. SO LONG AGO.
THE PANTHER GOD WILLING, HOPEFULLY I WILL LIVE TO SEE AS MANY YEARS AS YOU.
T'CHAKA'S SON.
I AM T'CHAKA'S SON. YES.
AN INTELLECTUAL. A SCIENTIST. OFFSPRING OF WARRIORS.
AS AN APPRECIATOR OF BOTH INTELLECT AND SCIENCE, I AM HONORED TO BE IN YOUR PRESENCE.
"YOU HAVE REACHED THE PHONE OF ANDREAS DE RUYTER..."

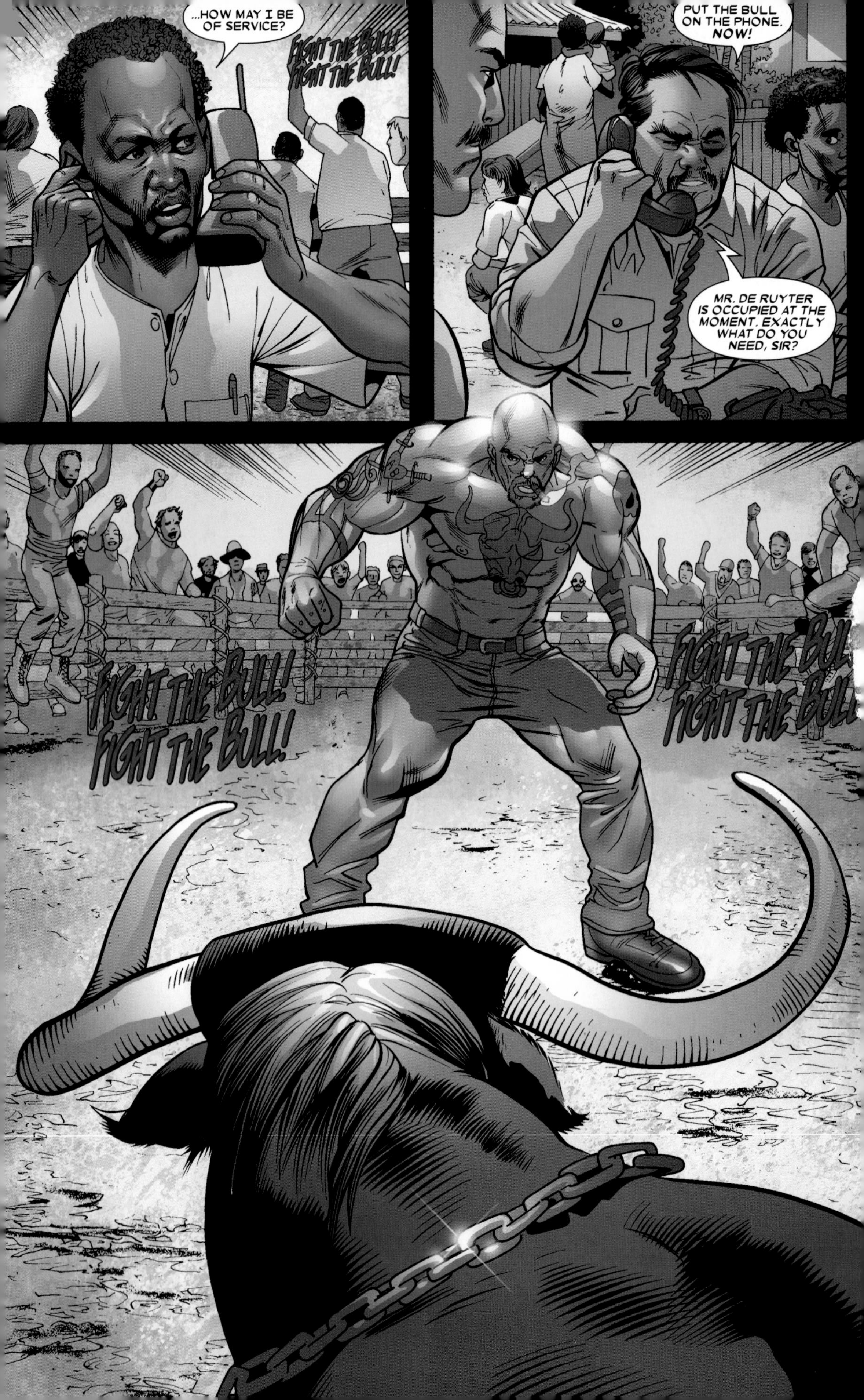
...HOW MAY I BE OF SERVICE?
FIGHT THE BULL! FIGHT THE BULL!
PUT THE BULL ON THE PHONE. NOW!
MR. DE RUYTER IS OCCUPIED AT THE MOMENT. EXACTLY WHAT DO YOU NEED, SIR?
FIGHT THE BULL! FIGHT THE BULL!
FIGHT THE BULL! FIGHT THE BULL!

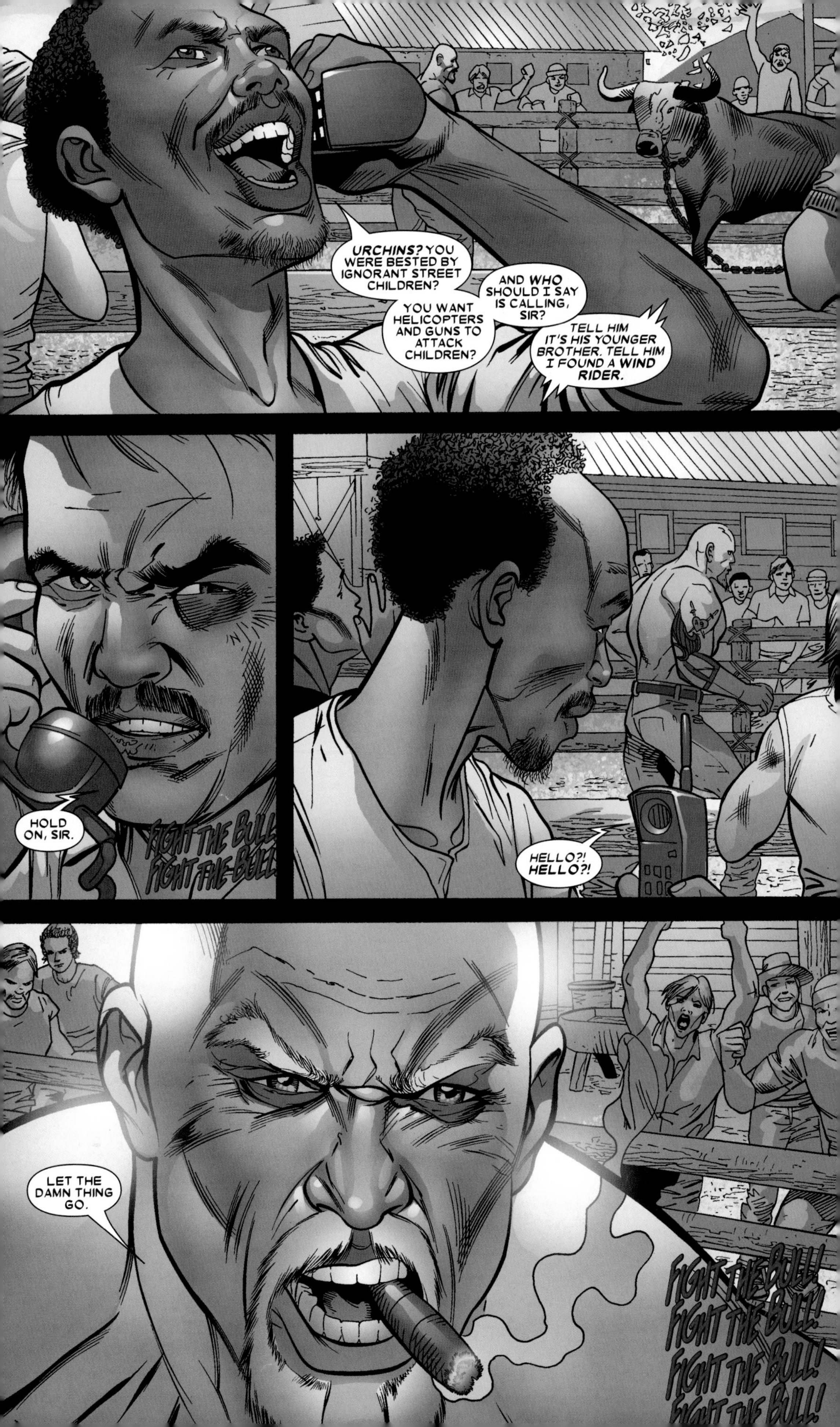
URCHINS? YOU WERE BESTED BY IGNORANT STREET CHILDREN?
YOU WANT HELICOPTERS AND GUNS TO ATTACK CHILDREN?
AND WHO SHOULD I SAY IS CALLING, SIR?
TELL HIM IT'S HIS YOUNGER BROTHER. TELL HIM I FOUND A WIND RIDER.
HOLD ON, SIR.
FIGHT THE BULL! FIGHT THE BULL!
HELLO?! HELLO?!
LET THE DAMN THING GO.
FIGHT THE BULL! FIGHT THE BULL! FIGHT THE BULL! FIGHT THE BULL!

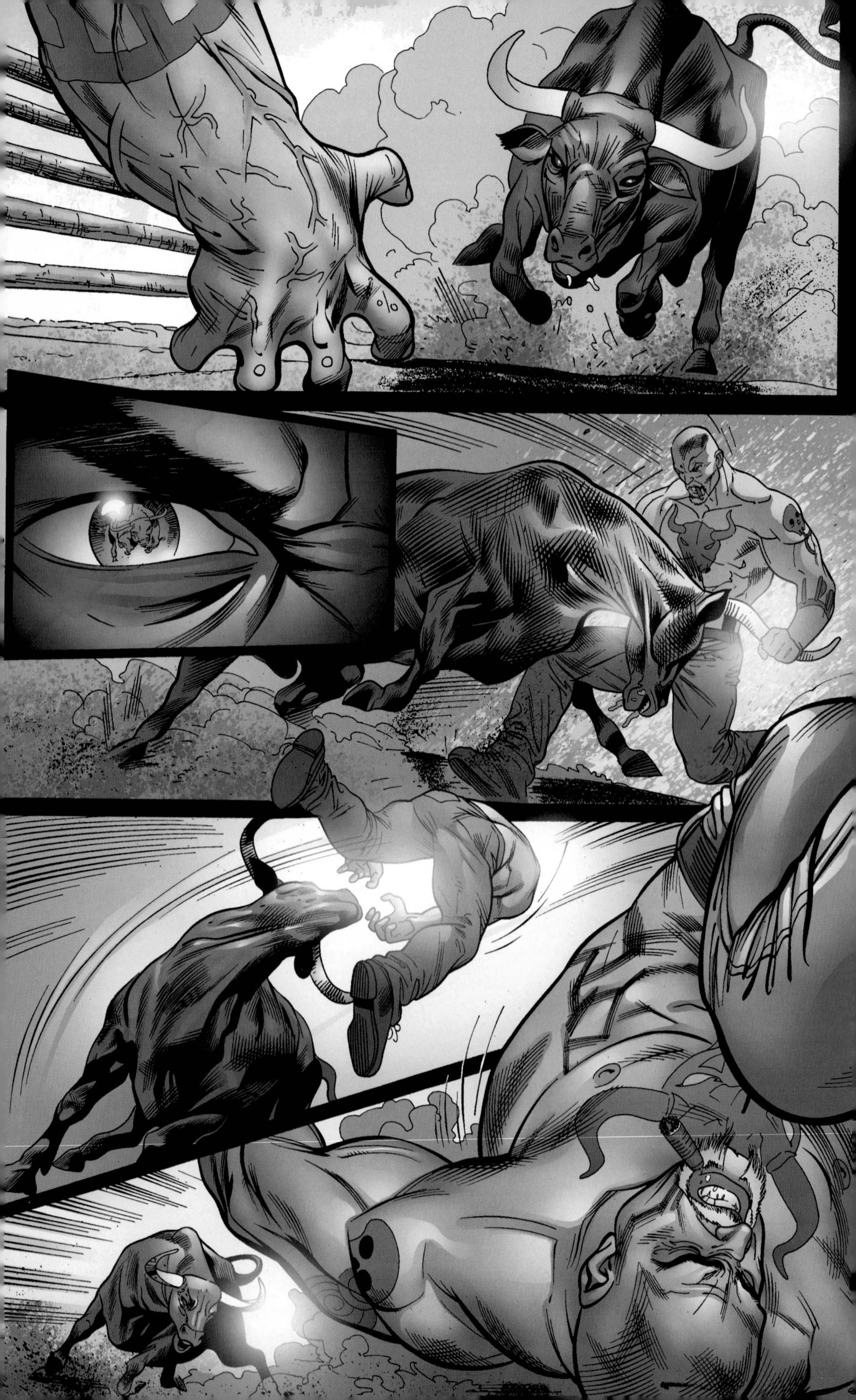

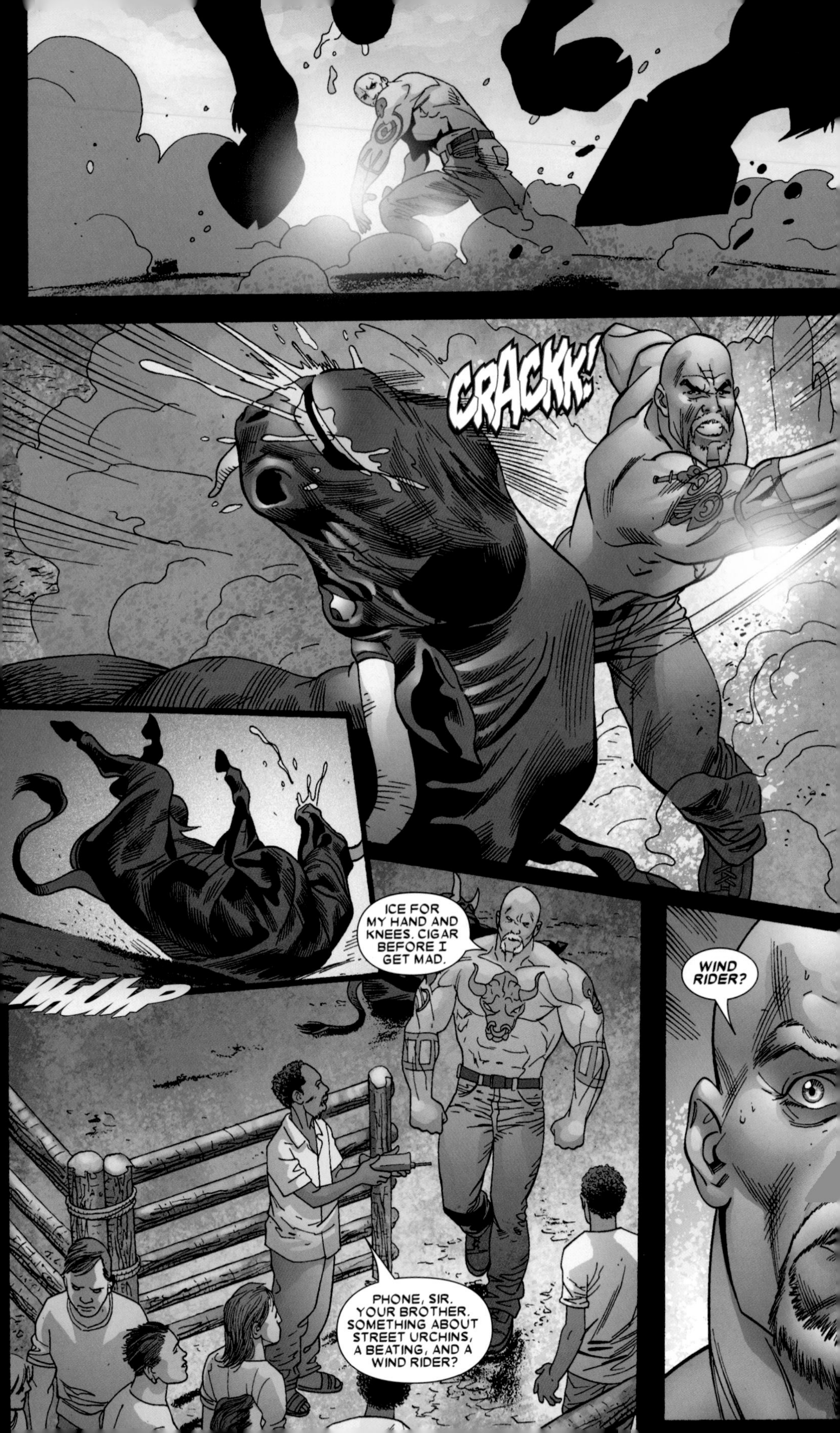
CRACKK!
WHUMP
ICE FOR MY HAND AND KNEES. CIGAR BEFORE I GET MAD.
PHONE, SIR. YOUR BROTHER. SOMETHING ABOUT STREET URCHINS, A BEATING, AND A WIND RIDER?
WIND RIDER?

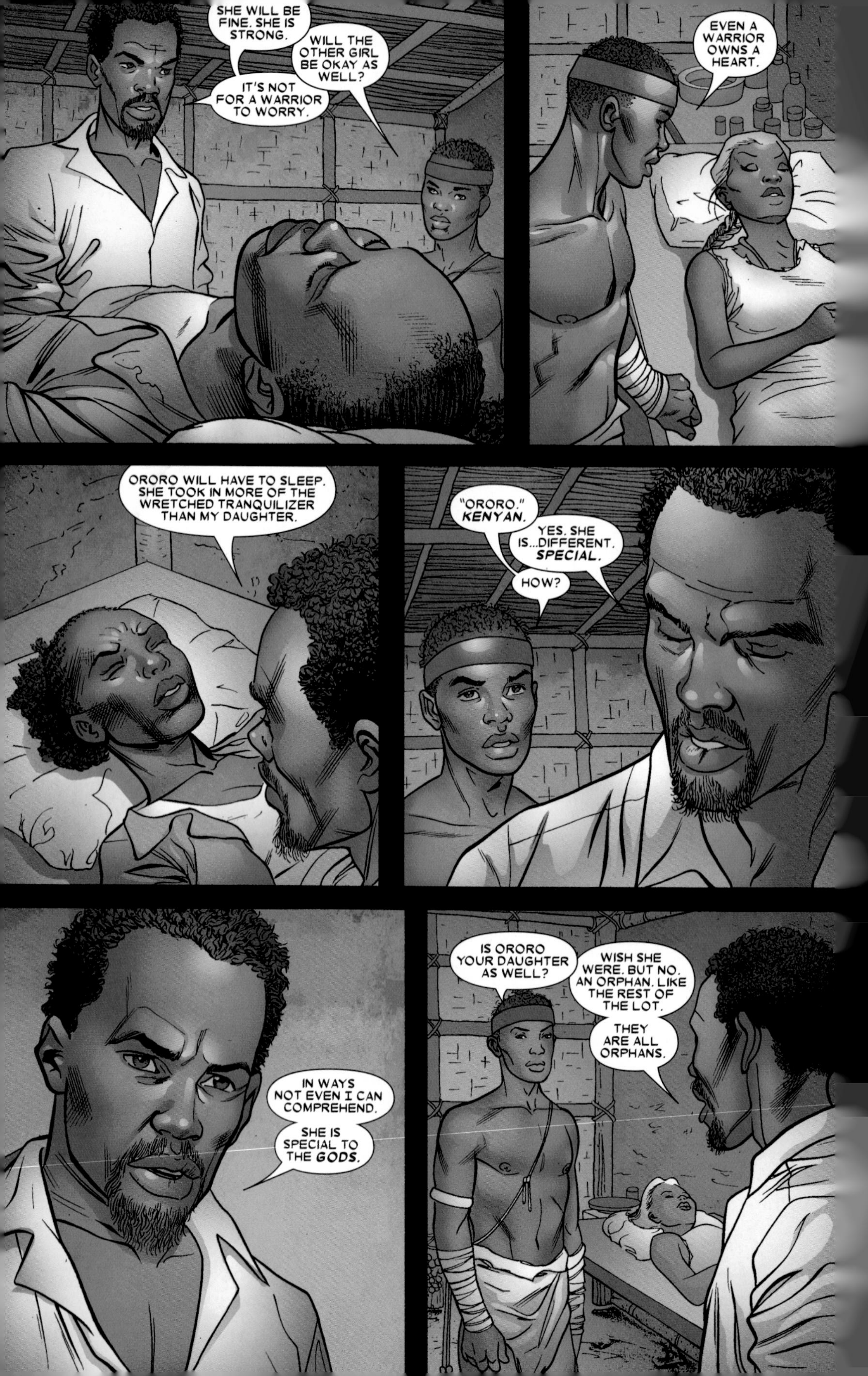
SHE WILL BE FINE. SHE IS STRONG.
WILL THE OTHER GIRL BE OKAY AS WELL?
IT'S NOT FOR A WARRIOR TO WORRY.
EVEN A WARRIOR OWNS A HEART.
ORORO WILL HAVE TO SLEEP. SHE TOOK IN MORE OF THE WRETCHED TRANQUILIZER THAN MY DAUGHTER.
"ORORO." KENYAN.
YES. SHE IS...DIFFERENT. SPECIAL.
HOW?
IN WAYS NOT EVEN I CAN COMPREHEND.
SHE IS SPECIAL TO THE GODS.
IS ORORO YOUR DAUGHTER AS WELL?
WISH SHE WERE. BUT NO. AN ORPHAN. LIKE THE REST OF THE LOT.
THEY ARE ALL ORPHANS.

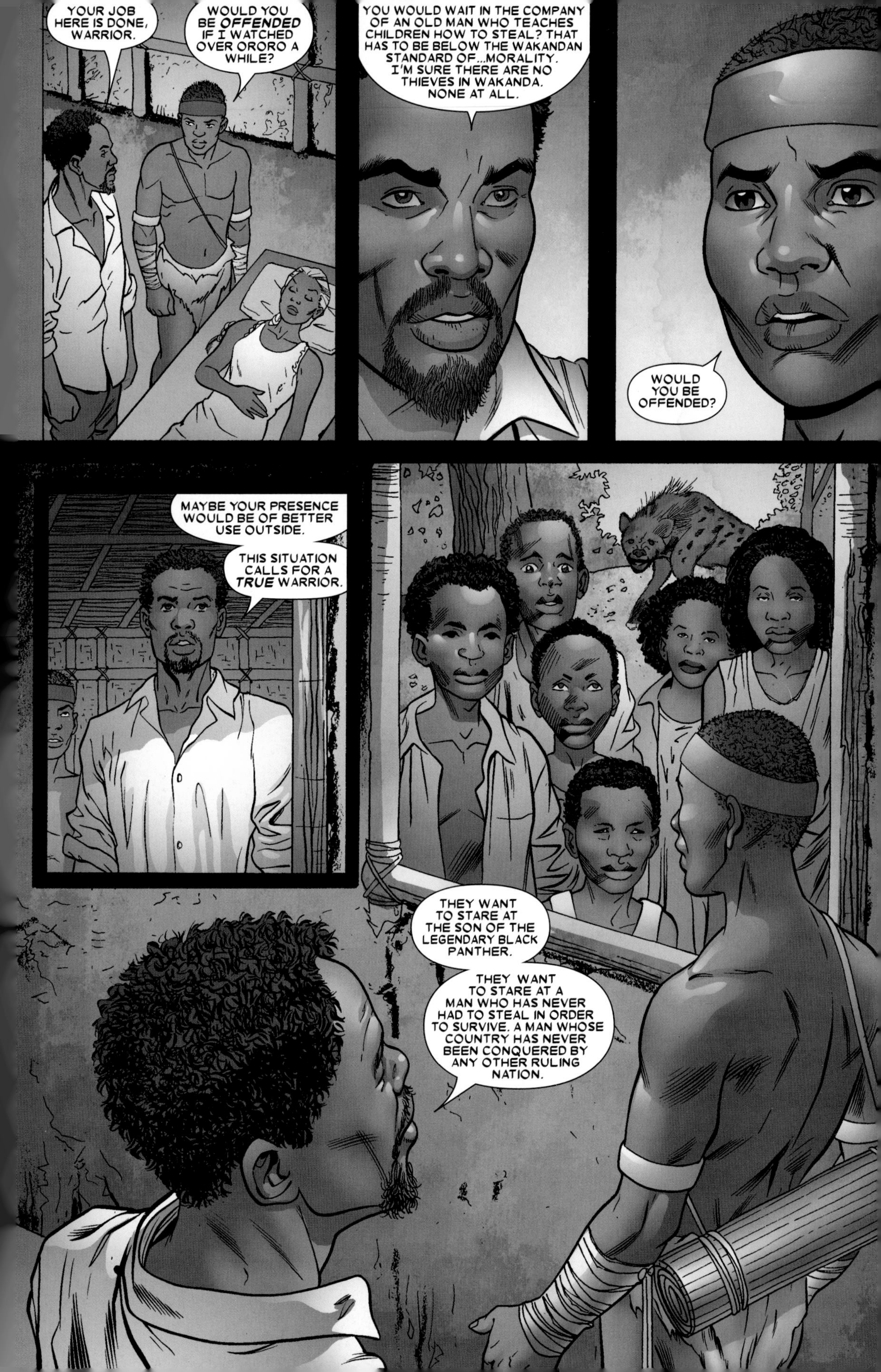
YOUR JOB HERE IS DONE, WARRIOR.
WOULD YOU BE *OFFENDED* IF I WATCHED OVER ORORO A WHILE?
YOU WOULD WAIT IN THE COMPANY OF AN OLD MAN WHO TEACHES CHILDREN HOW TO STEAL? THAT HAS TO BE BELOW THE WAKANDAN STANDARD OF...MORALITY. I'M SURE THERE ARE NO THIEVES IN WAKANDA. NONE AT ALL.
WOULD YOU BE OFFENDED?
MAYBE YOUR PRESENCE WOULD BE OF BETTER USE OUTSIDE.
THIS SITUATION CALLS FOR A *TRUE* WARRIOR.
THEY WANT TO STARE AT THE SON OF THE LEGENDARY BLACK PANTHER.
THEY WANT TO STARE AT A MAN WHO HAS NEVER HAD TO STEAL IN ORDER TO SURVIVE. A MAN WHOSE COUNTRY HAS NEVER BEEN CONQUERED BY ANY OTHER RULING NATION.

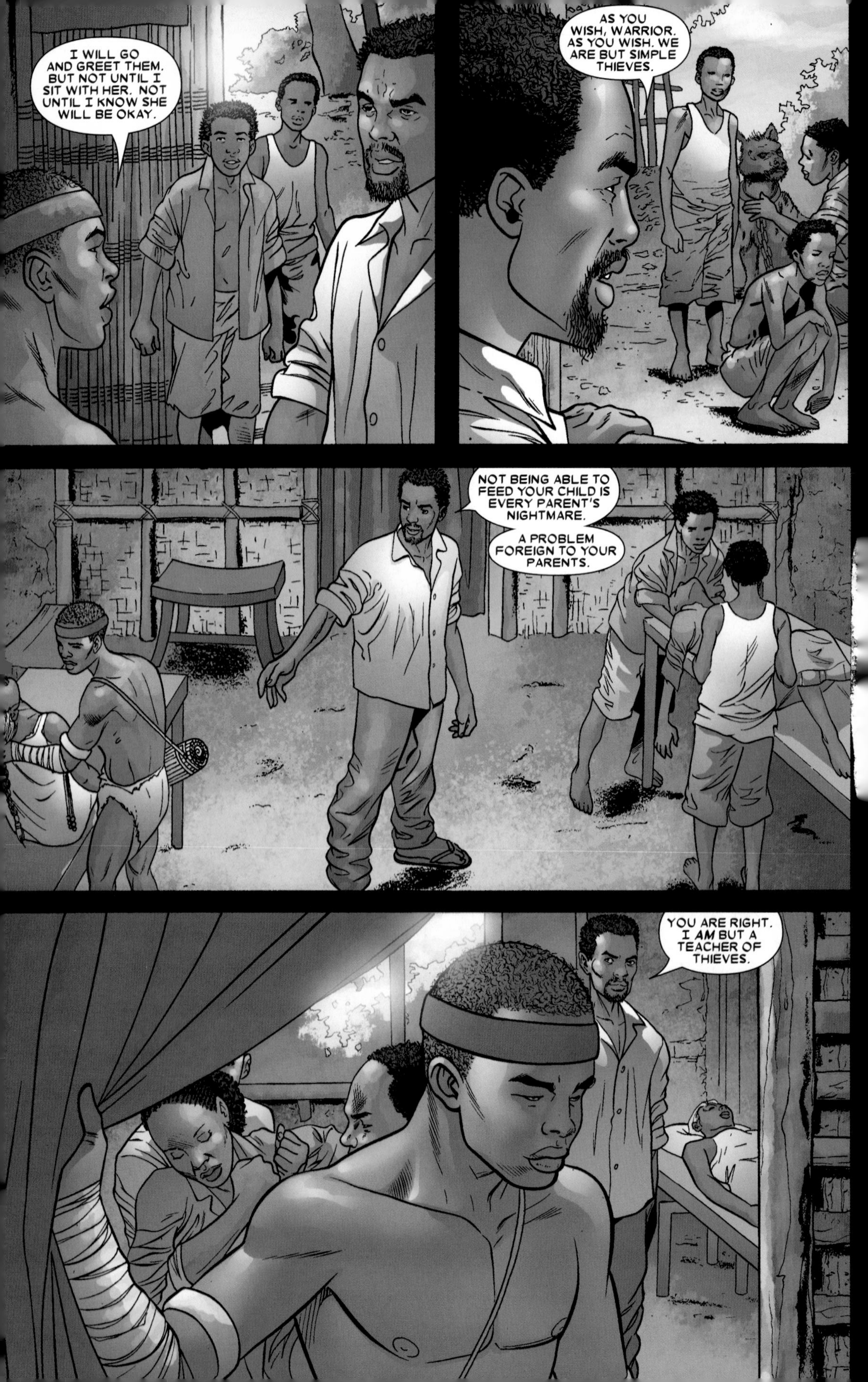
I WILL GO AND GREET THEM. BUT NOT UNTIL I SIT WITH HER. NOT UNTIL I KNOW SHE WILL BE OKAY.
AS YOU WISH, WARRIOR. AS YOU WISH. WE ARE BUT SIMPLE THIEVES.
NOT BEING ABLE TO FEED YOUR CHILD IS EVERY PARENT'S NIGHTMARE.
A PROBLEM FOREIGN TO YOUR PARENTS.
YOU ARE RIGHT. I *AM* BUT A TEACHER OF THIEVES.

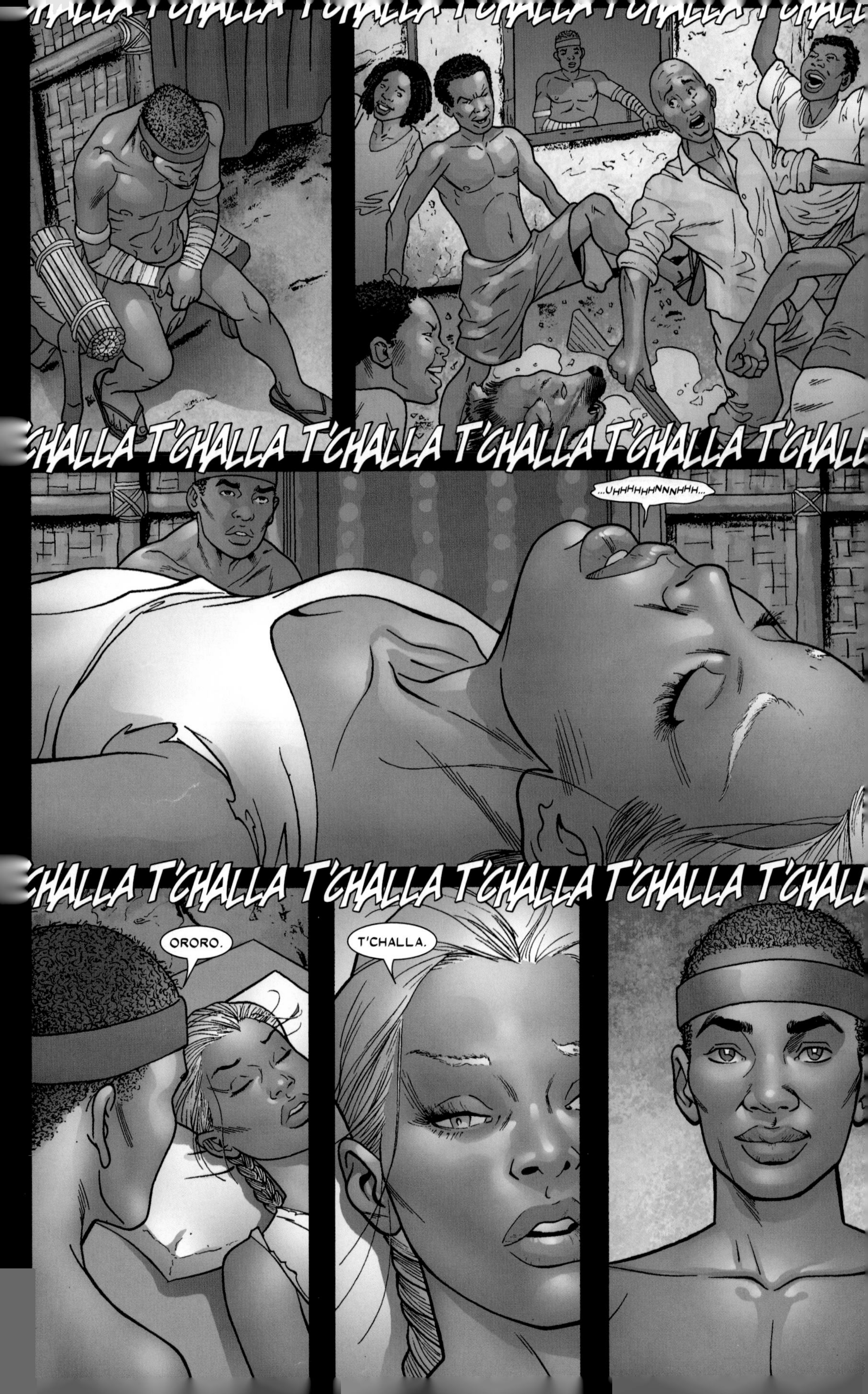
T'CHALLA T'CHALLA T'CHALLA T'CHALLA
...UHHHHHHNNNHHH...
T'CHALLA T'CHALLA T'CHALLA T'CHALLA
ORORO.
T'CHALLA.

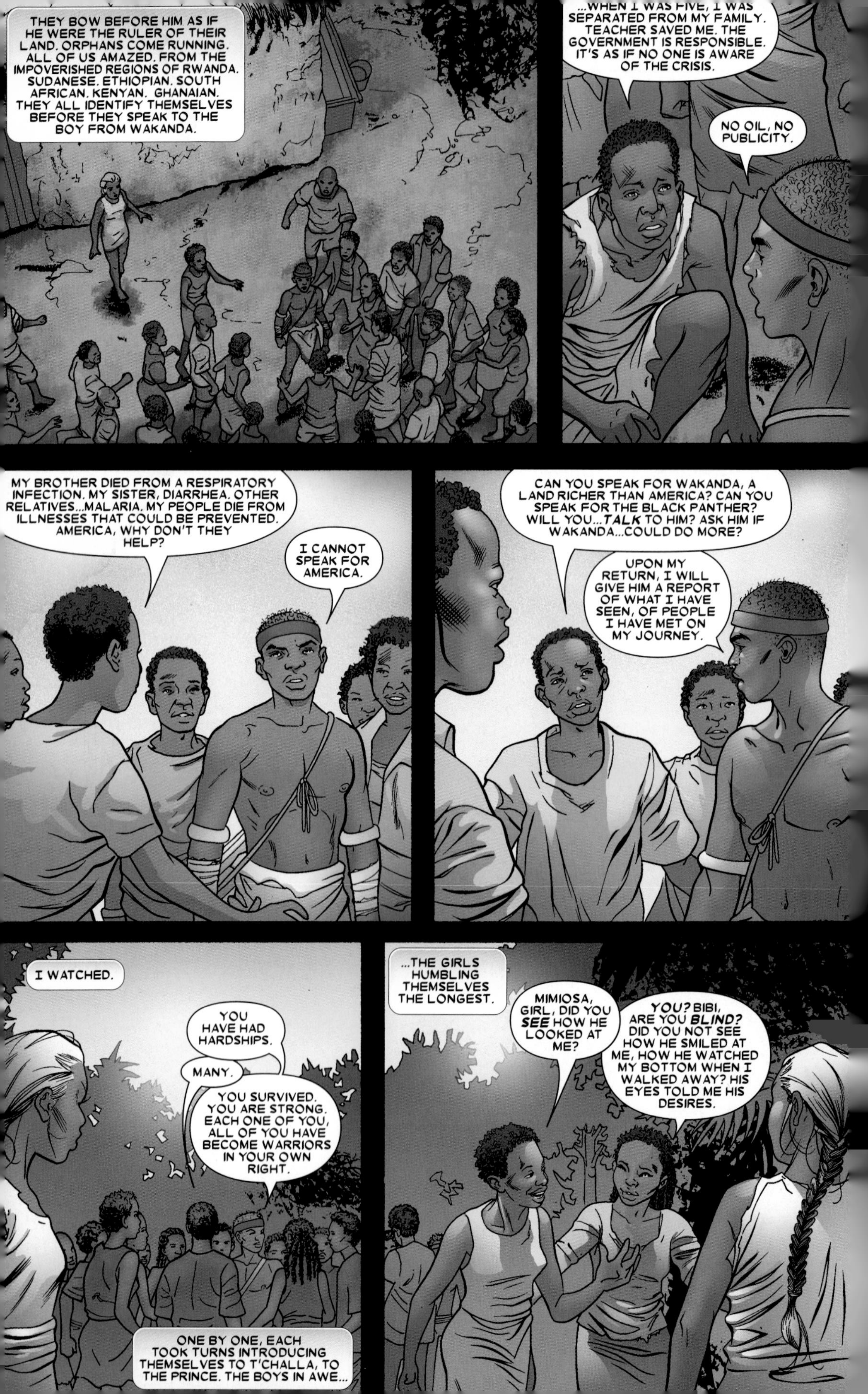
THEY BOW BEFORE HIM AS IF HE WERE THE RULER OF THEIR LAND. ORPHANS COME RUNNING. ALL OF US AMAZED. FROM THE IMPOVERISHED REGIONS OF RWANDA. SUDANESE. ETHIOPIAN. SOUTH AFRICAN. KENYAN. GHANAIAN. THEY ALL IDENTIFY THEMSELVES BEFORE THEY SPEAK TO THE BOY FROM WAKANDA.
...WHEN I WAS FIVE, I WAS SEPARATED FROM MY FAMILY. TEACHER SAVED ME. THE GOVERNMENT IS RESPONSIBLE. IT'S AS IF NO ONE IS AWARE OF THE CRISIS.
NO OIL, NO PUBLICITY.
MY BROTHER DIED FROM A RESPIRATORY INFECTION. MY SISTER, DIARRHEA. OTHER RELATIVES...MALARIA. MY PEOPLE DIE FROM ILLNESSES THAT COULD BE PREVENTED. AMERICA, WHY DON'T THEY HELP?
I CANNOT SPEAK FOR AMERICA.
CAN YOU SPEAK FOR WAKANDA, A LAND RICHER THAN AMERICA? CAN YOU SPEAK FOR THE BLACK PANTHER? WILL YOU...*TALK* TO HIM? ASK HIM IF WAKANDA...COULD DO MORE?
UPON MY RETURN, I WILL GIVE HIM A REPORT OF WHAT I HAVE SEEN, OF PEOPLE I HAVE MET ON MY JOURNEY.
I WATCHED.
YOU HAVE HAD HARDSHIPS.
MANY.
YOU SURVIVED. YOU ARE STRONG. EACH ONE OF YOU, ALL OF YOU HAVE BECOME WARRIORS IN YOUR OWN RIGHT.
ONE BY ONE, EACH TOOK TURNS INTRODUCING THEMSELVES TO T'CHALLA, TO THE PRINCE. THE BOYS IN AWE...
...THE GIRLS HUMBLING THEMSELVES THE LONGEST.
MIMIOSA, GIRL, DID YOU *SEE* HOW HE LOOKED AT ME?
YOU? BIBI, ARE YOU *BLIND?* DID YOU NOT SEE HOW HE SMILED AT ME, HOW HE WATCHED MY BOTTOM WHEN I WALKED AWAY? HIS EYES TOLD ME HIS DESIRES.

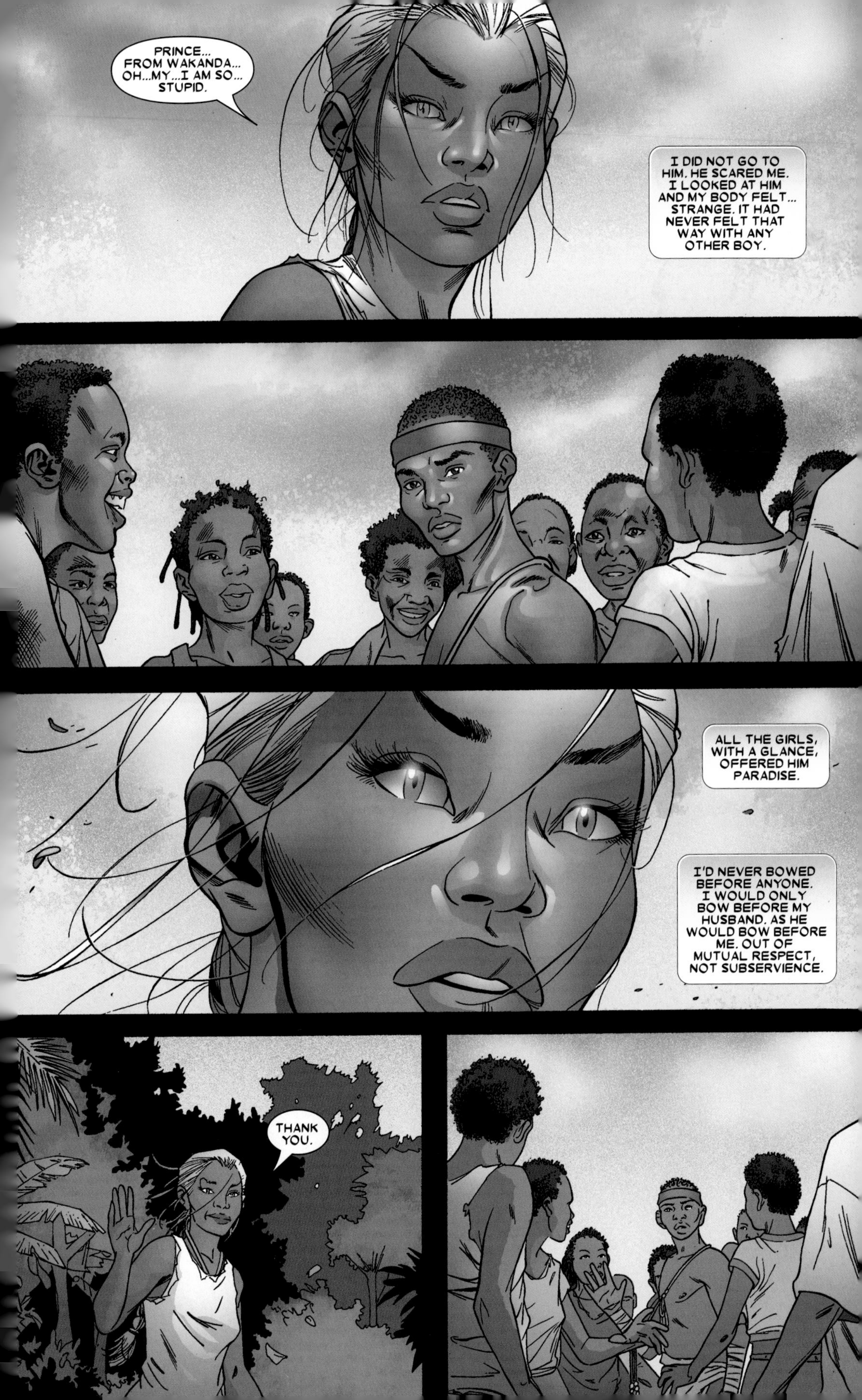
PRINCE... FROM WAKANDA... OH...MY...I AM SO... STUPID.
I DID NOT GO TO HIM. HE SCARED ME. I LOOKED AT HIM AND MY BODY FELT... STRANGE. IT HAD NEVER FELT THAT WAY WITH ANY OTHER BOY.
ALL THE GIRLS, WITH A GLANCE, OFFERED HIM PARADISE.
I'D NEVER BOWED BEFORE ANYONE. I WOULD ONLY BOW BEFORE MY HUSBAND. AS HE WOULD BOW BEFORE ME. OUT OF MUTUAL RESPECT, NOT SUBSERVIENCE.
THANK YOU.

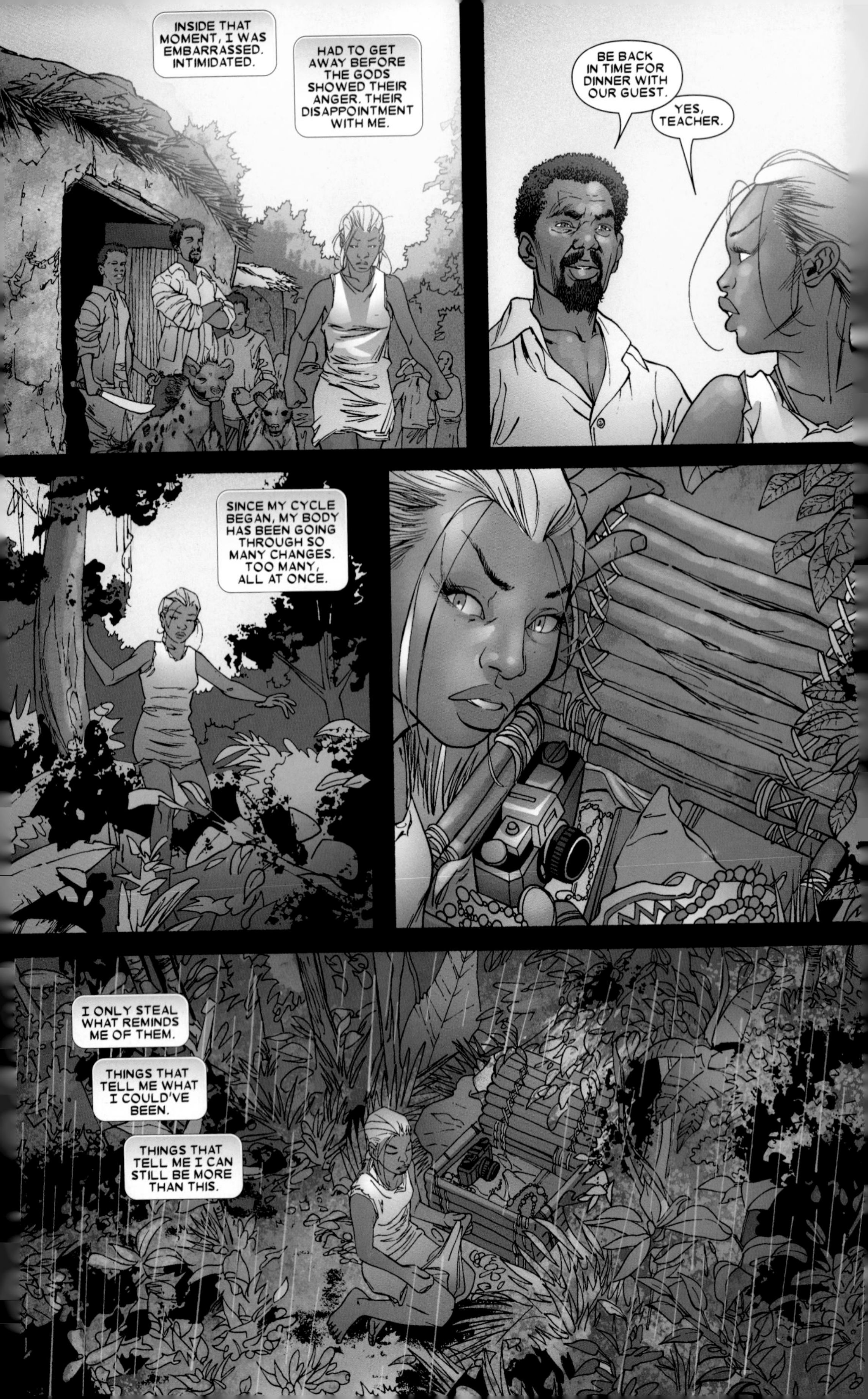
INSIDE THAT MOMENT, I WAS EMBARRASSED. INTIMIDATED.
HAD TO GET AWAY BEFORE THE GODS SHOWED THEIR ANGER. THEIR DISAPPOINTMENT WITH ME.
BE BACK IN TIME FOR DINNER WITH OUR GUEST.
YES, TEACHER.
SINCE MY CYCLE BEGAN, MY BODY HAS BEEN GOING THROUGH SO MANY CHANGES. TOO MANY, ALL AT ONCE.
I ONLY STEAL WHAT REMINDS ME OF THEM.
THINGS THAT TELL ME WHAT I COULD'VE BEEN.
THINGS THAT TELL ME I CAN STILL BE MORE THAN THIS.

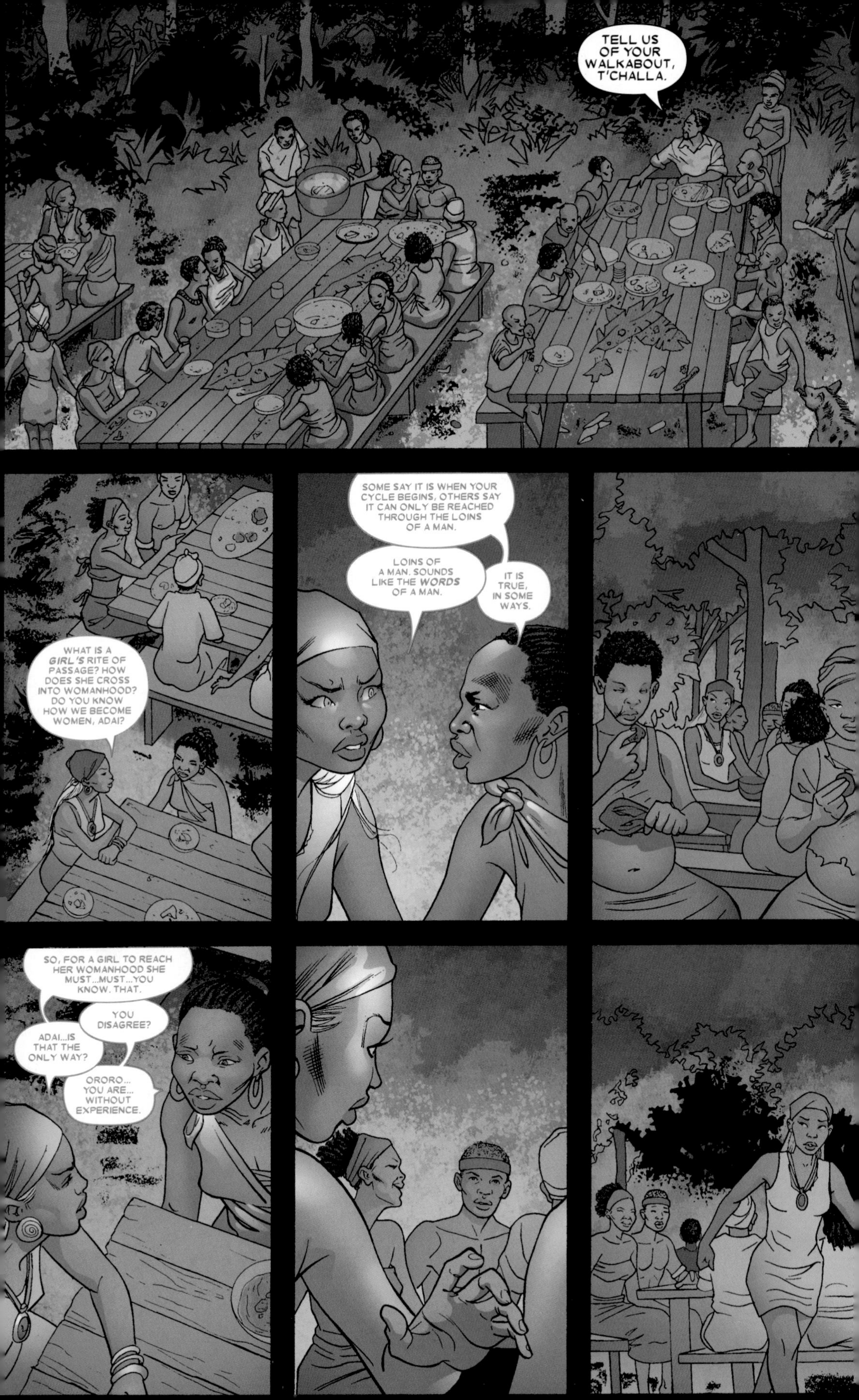
TELL US OF YOUR WALKABOUT, T'CHALLA.
WHAT IS A GIRL'S RITE OF PASSAGE? HOW DOES SHE CROSS INTO WOMANHOOD? DO YOU KNOW HOW WE BECOME WOMEN, ADAI?
SOME SAY IT IS WHEN YOUR CYCLE BEGINS, OTHERS SAY IT CAN ONLY BE REACHED THROUGH THE LOINS OF A MAN.
LOINS OF A MAN. SOUNDS LIKE THE WORDS OF A MAN.
IT IS TRUE, IN SOME WAYS.
SO, FOR A GIRL TO REACH HER WOMANHOOD SHE MUST...MUST...YOU KNOW. THAT.
YOU DISAGREE?
ADAI...IS THAT THE ONLY WAY?
ORORO... YOU ARE... WITHOUT EXPERIENCE.

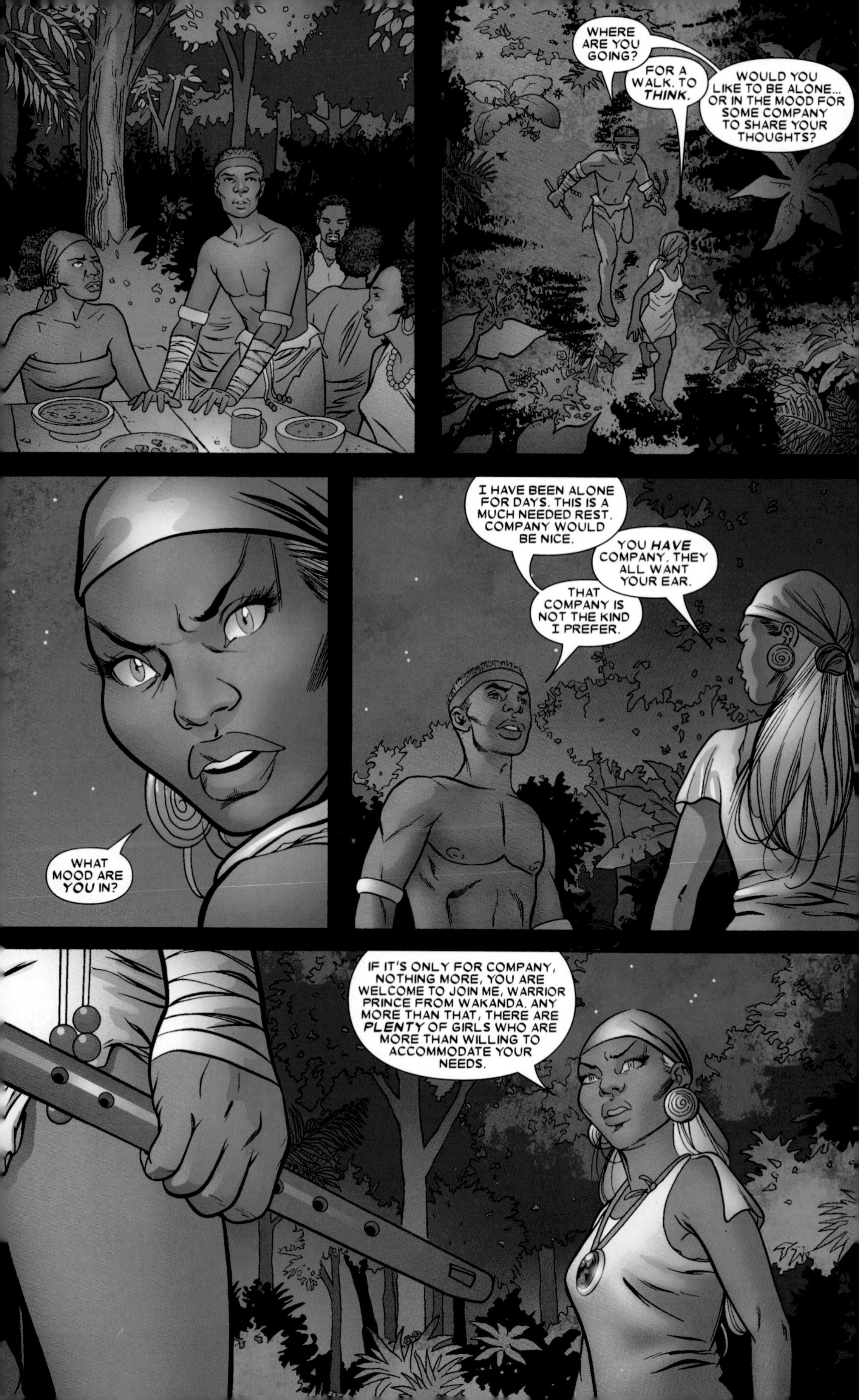
WHERE ARE YOU GOING?
FOR A WALK. TO THINK.
WOULD YOU LIKE TO BE ALONE... OR IN THE MOOD FOR SOME COMPANY TO SHARE YOUR THOUGHTS?
WHAT MOOD ARE YOU IN?
I HAVE BEEN ALONE FOR DAYS. THIS IS A MUCH NEEDED REST. COMPANY WOULD BE NICE.
YOU HAVE COMPANY. THEY ALL WANT YOUR EAR.
THAT COMPANY IS NOT THE KIND I PREFER.
IF IT'S ONLY FOR COMPANY, NOTHING MORE, YOU ARE WELCOME TO JOIN ME, WARRIOR PRINCE FROM WAKANDA. ANY MORE THAN THAT, THERE ARE PLENTY OF GIRLS WHO ARE MORE THAN WILLING TO ACCOMMODATE YOUR NEEDS.

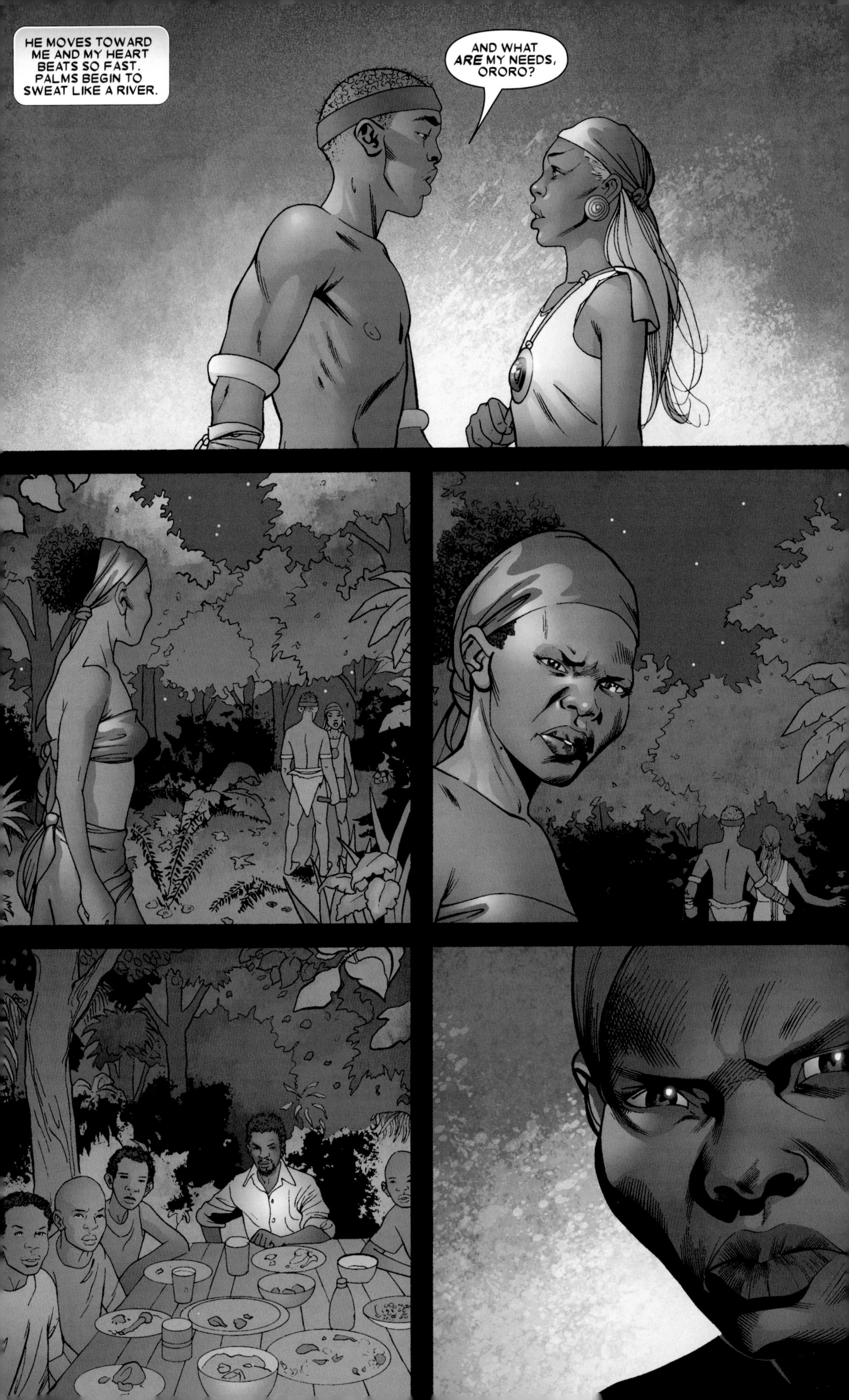
HE MOVES TOWARD ME AND MY HEART BEATS SO FAST. PALMS BEGIN TO SWEAT LIKE A RIVER.
AND WHAT *ARE* MY NEEDS, ORORO?

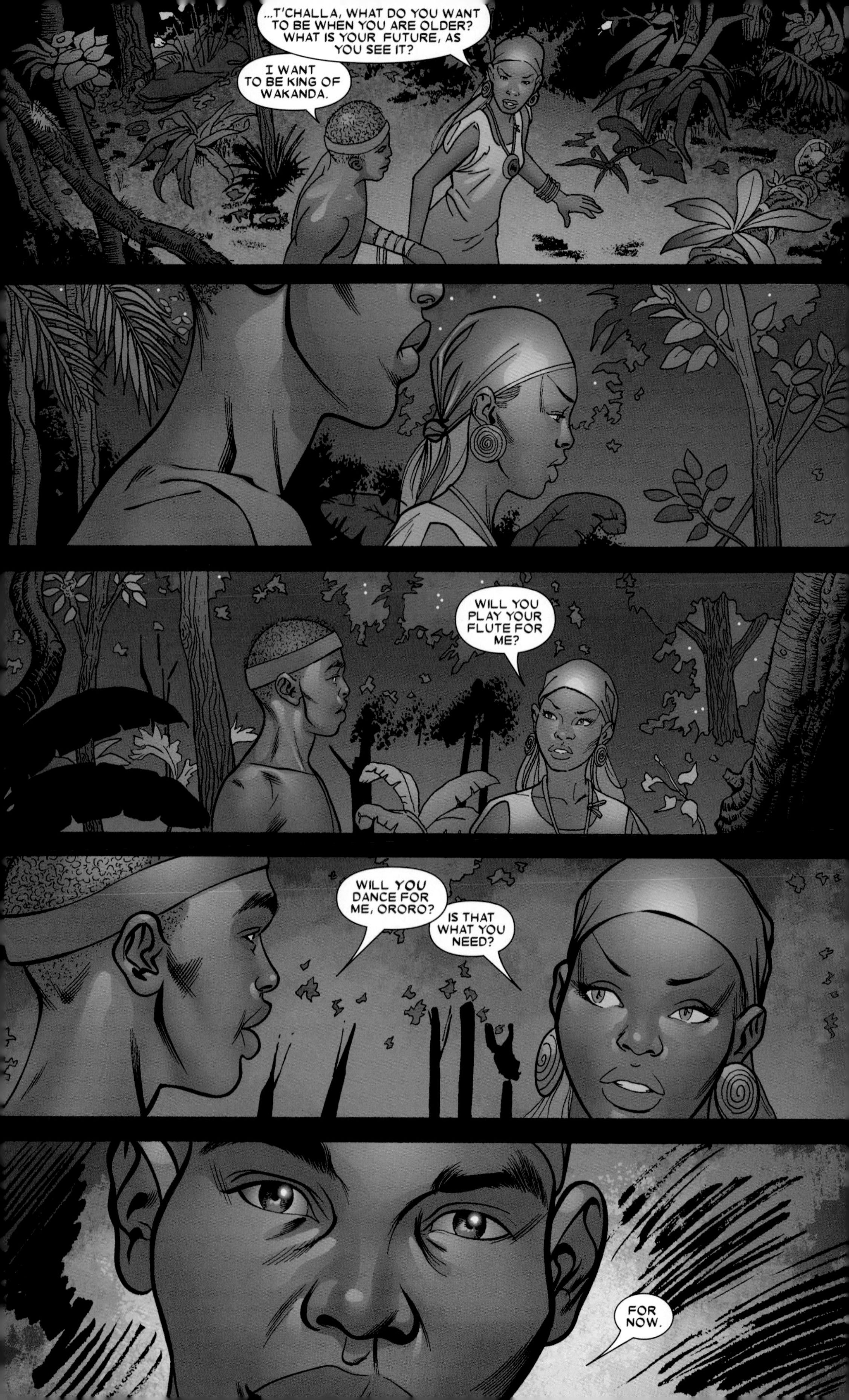

...T'CHALLA, WHAT DO YOU WANT TO BE WHEN YOU ARE OLDER? WHAT IS YOUR FUTURE, AS YOU SEE IT?
I WANT TO BE KING OF WAKANDA.
WILL YOU PLAY YOUR FLUTE FOR ME?
WILL YOU DANCE FOR ME, ORORO?
IS THAT WHAT YOU NEED?
FOR NOW.

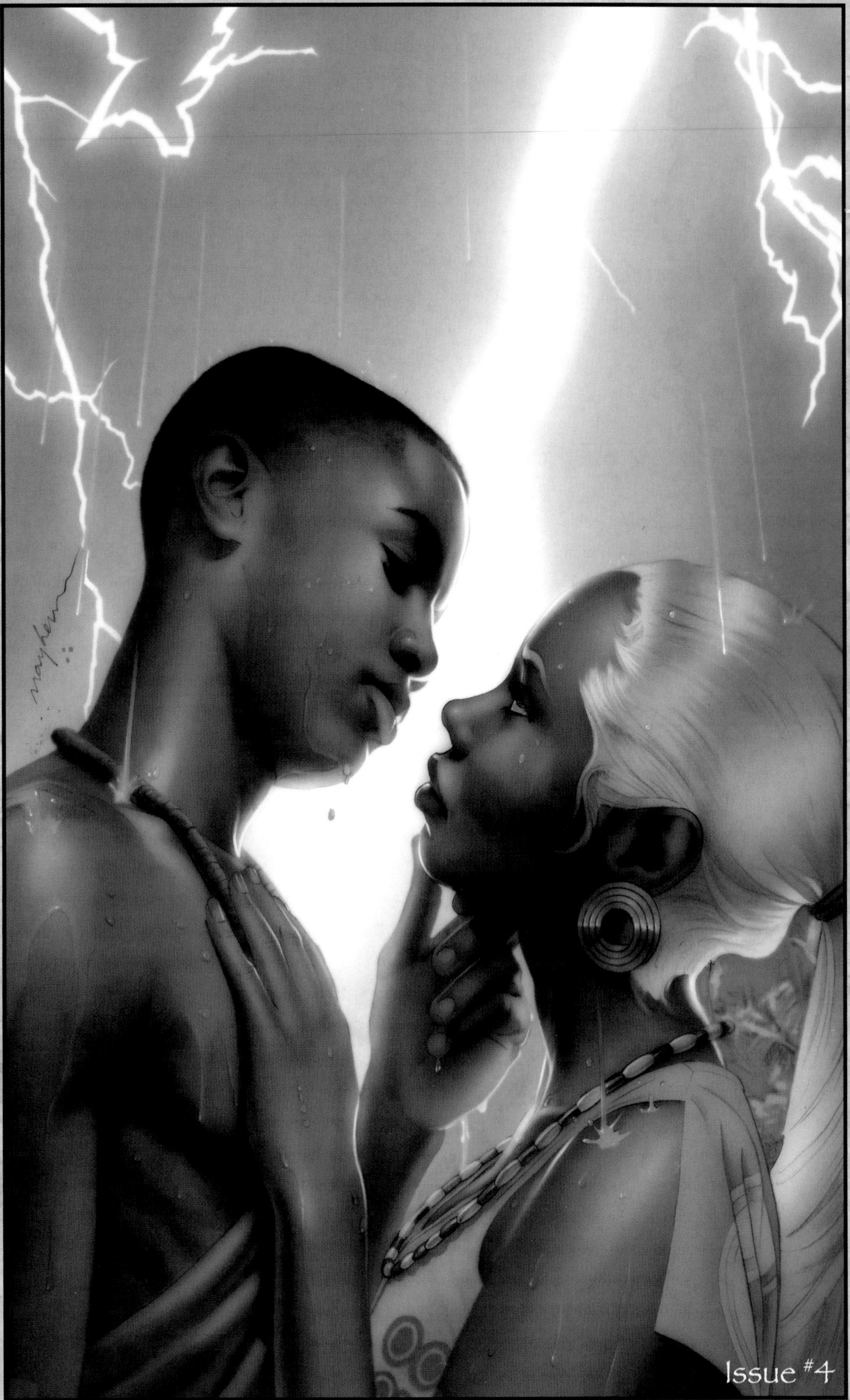
mayhew
Issue #4

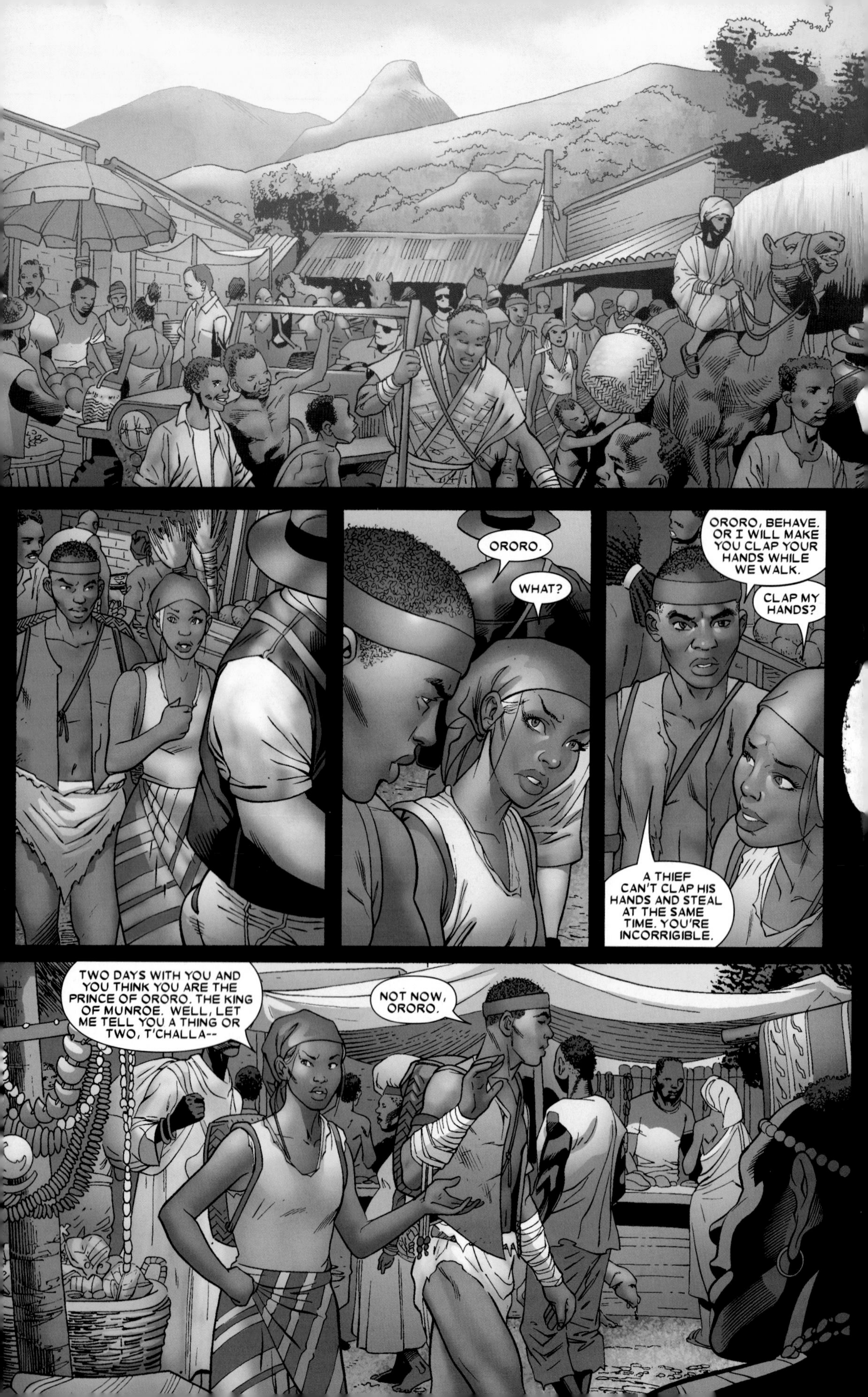
ORORO.
WHAT?
ORORO, BEHAVE. OR I WILL MAKE YOU CLAP YOUR HANDS WHILE WE WALK.
CLAP MY HANDS?
A THIEF CAN'T CLAP HIS HANDS AND STEAL AT THE SAME TIME. YOU'RE INCORRIGIBLE.
TWO DAYS WITH YOU AND YOU THINK YOU ARE THE PRINCE OF ORORO. THE KING OF MUNROE. WELL, LET ME TELL YOU A THING OR TWO, T'CHALLA--
NOT NOW, ORORO.

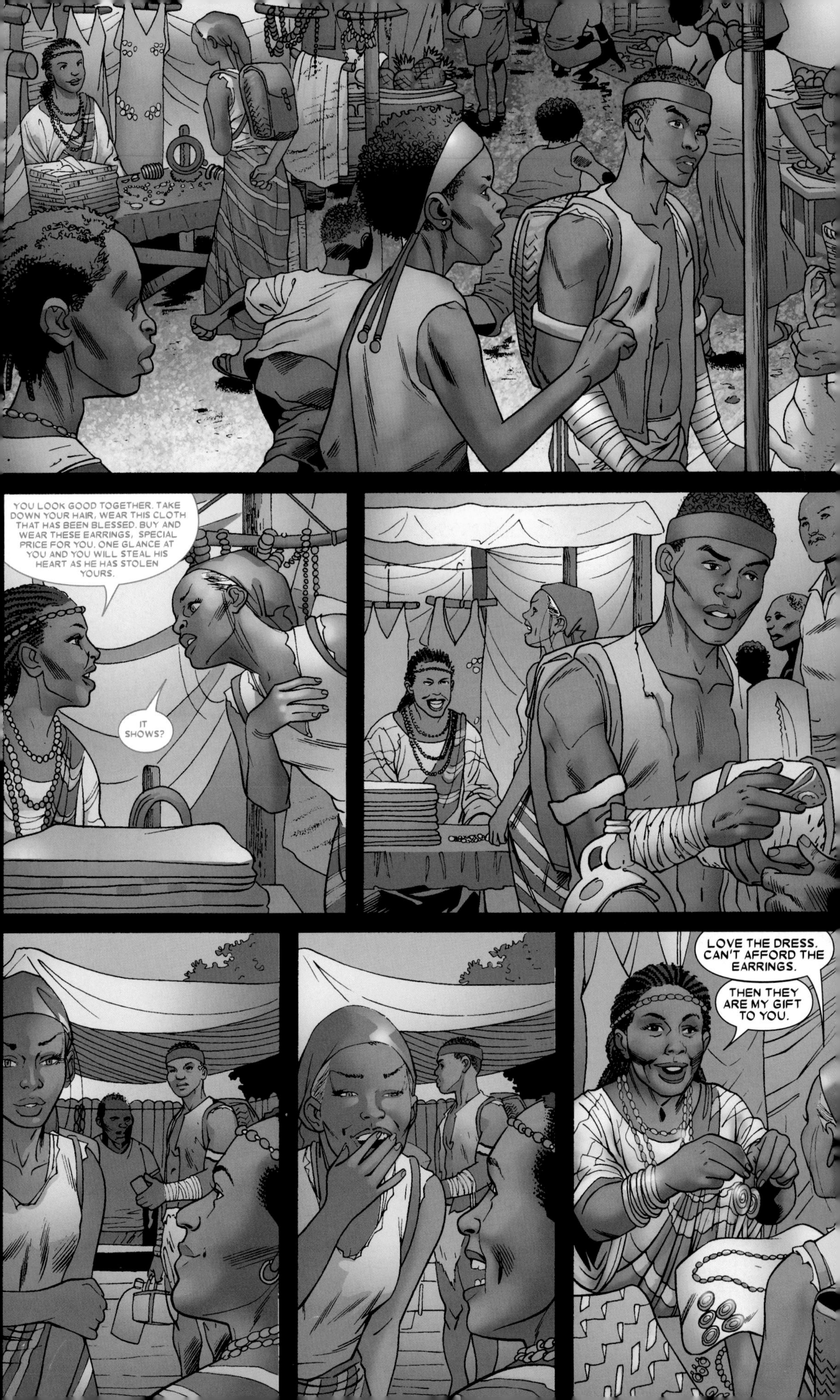
YOU LOOK GOOD TOGETHER. TAKE DOWN YOUR HAIR, WEAR THIS CLOTH THAT HAS BEEN BLESSED. BUY AND WEAR THESE EARRINGS, SPECIAL PRICE FOR YOU. ONE GLANCE AT YOU AND YOU WILL STEAL HIS HEART AS HE HAS STOLEN YOURS.
IT SHOWS?
LOVE THE DRESS. CAN'T AFFORD THE EARRINGS.
THEN THEY ARE MY GIFT TO YOU.

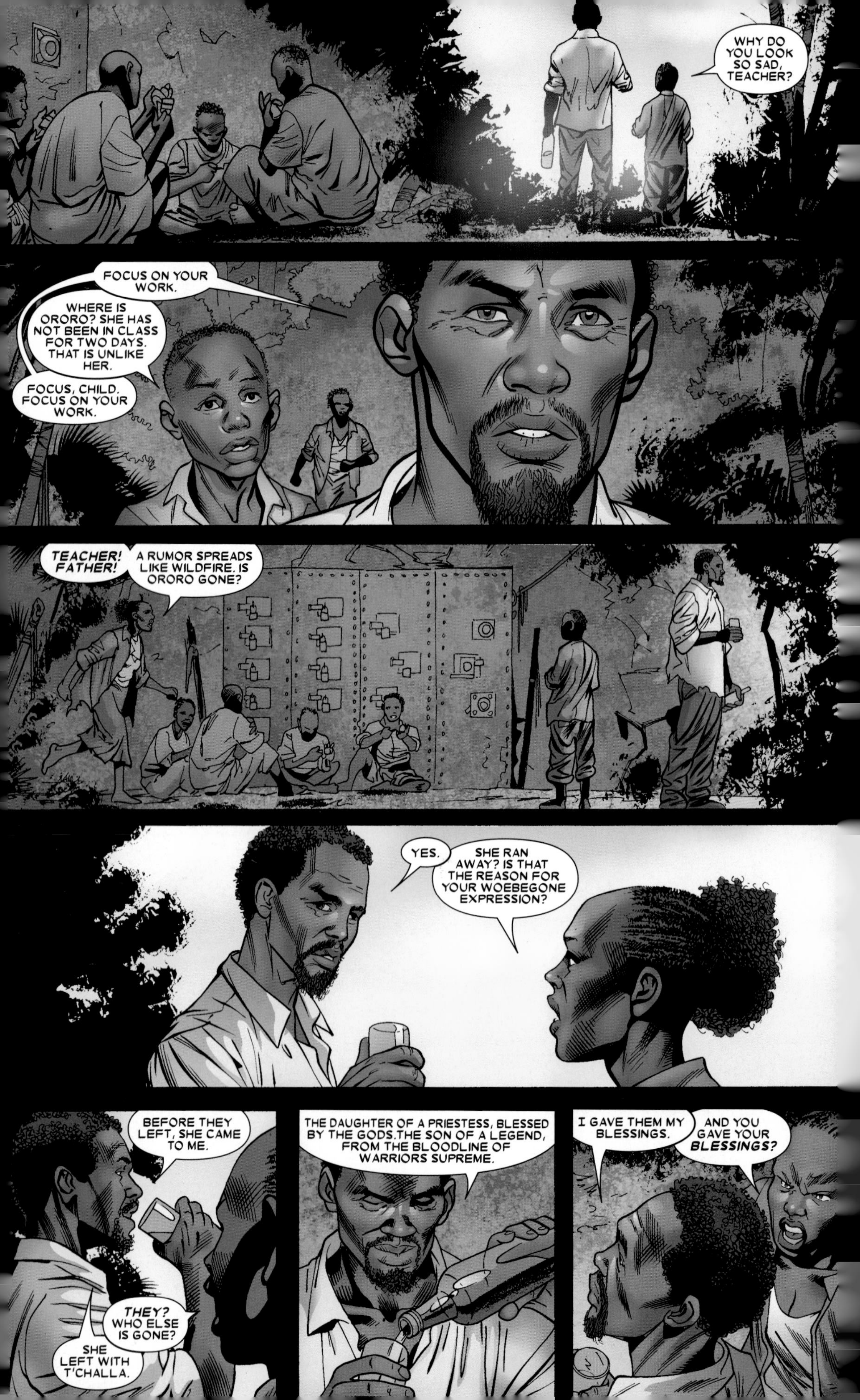
WHY DO YOU LOOK SO SAD, TEACHER?
FOCUS ON YOUR WORK.
WHERE IS ORORO? SHE HAS NOT BEEN IN CLASS FOR TWO DAYS. THAT IS UNLIKE HER.
FOCUS, CHILD. FOCUS ON YOUR WORK.
TEACHER! FATHER!
A RUMOR SPREADS LIKE WILDFIRE. IS ORORO GONE?
YES.
SHE RAN AWAY? IS THAT THE REASON FOR YOUR WOEBEGONE EXPRESSION?
BEFORE THEY LEFT, SHE CAME TO ME.
THEY? WHO ELSE IS GONE?
SHE LEFT WITH T'CHALLA.
THE DAUGHTER OF A PRIESTESS, BLESSED BY THE GODS. THE SON OF A LEGEND, FROM THE BLOODLINE OF WARRIORS SUPREME.
I GAVE THEM MY BLESSINGS.
AND YOU GAVE YOUR BLESSINGS?

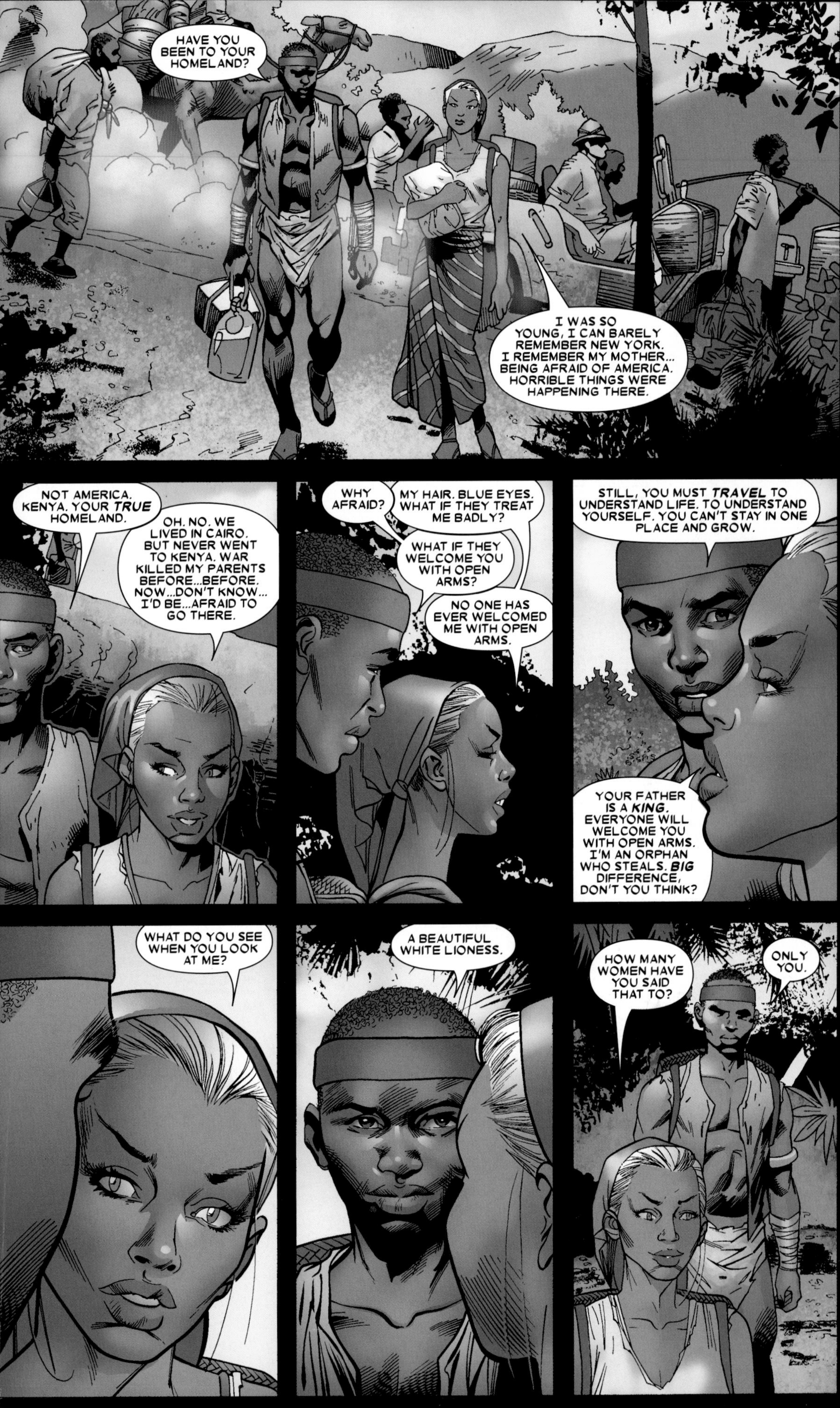
HAVE YOU BEEN TO YOUR HOMELAND?
I WAS SO YOUNG, I CAN BARELY REMEMBER NEW YORK. I REMEMBER MY MOTHER... BEING AFRAID OF AMERICA. HORRIBLE THINGS WERE HAPPENING THERE.
NOT AMERICA. KENYA. YOUR *TRUE* HOMELAND.
OH. NO. WE LIVED IN CAIRO. BUT NEVER WENT TO KENYA. WAR KILLED MY PARENTS BEFORE...BEFORE. NOW...DON'T KNOW... I'D BE...AFRAID TO GO THERE.
WHY AFRAID?
MY HAIR. BLUE EYES. WHAT IF THEY TREAT ME BADLY?
WHAT IF THEY WELCOME YOU WITH OPEN ARMS?
NO ONE HAS EVER WELCOMED ME WITH OPEN ARMS.
STILL, YOU MUST *TRAVEL* TO UNDERSTAND LIFE. TO UNDERSTAND YOURSELF. YOU CAN'T STAY IN ONE PLACE AND GROW.
YOUR FATHER IS A *KING*. EVERYONE WILL WELCOME YOU WITH OPEN ARMS. I'M AN ORPHAN WHO STEALS. *BIG* DIFFERENCE, DON'T YOU THINK?
WHAT DO YOU SEE WHEN YOU LOOK AT ME?
A BEAUTIFUL WHITE LIONESS.
HOW MANY WOMEN HAVE YOU SAID THAT TO?
ONLY YOU.

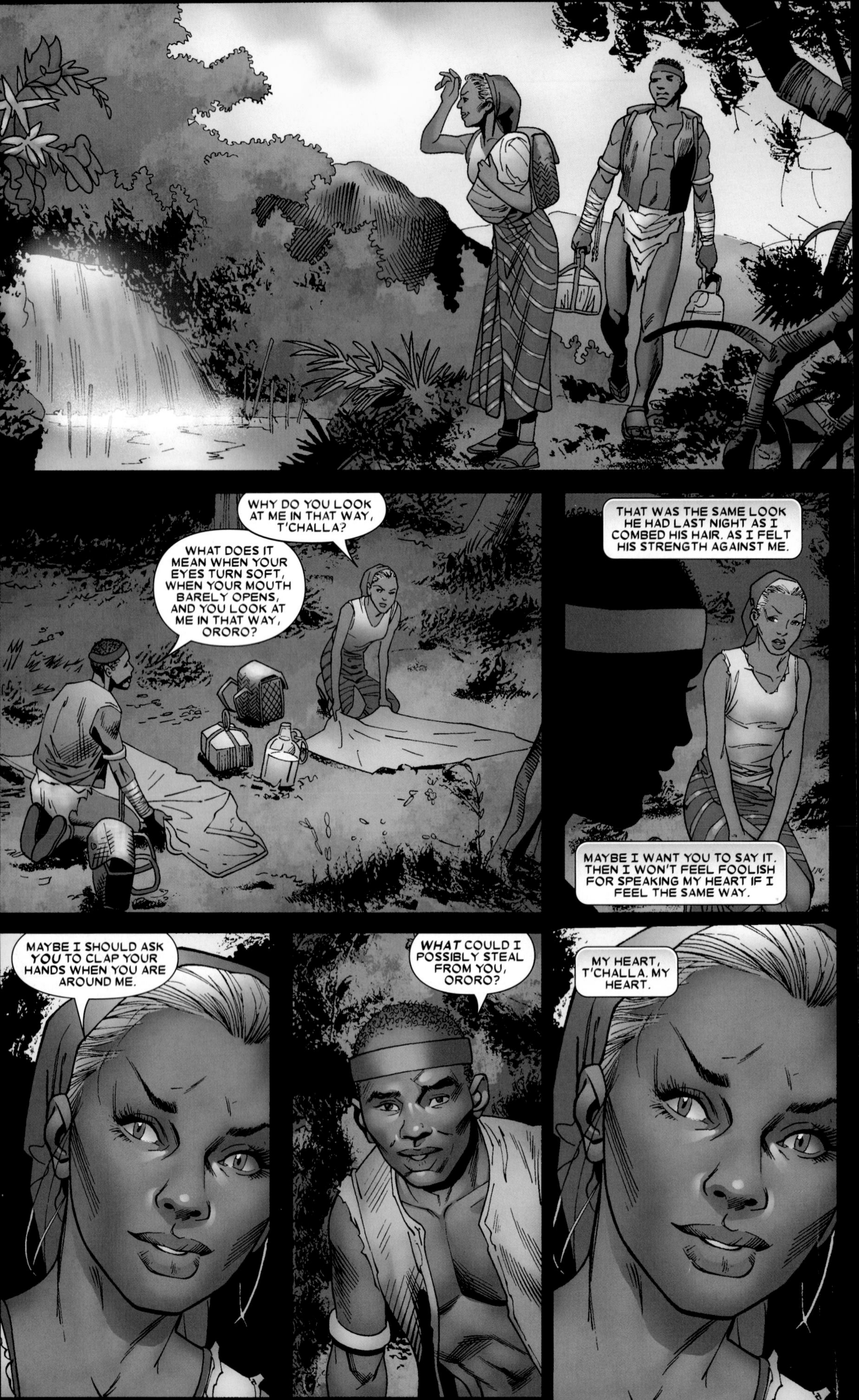
WHY DO YOU LOOK AT ME IN THAT WAY, T'CHALLA?
WHAT DOES IT MEAN WHEN YOUR EYES TURN SOFT, WHEN YOUR MOUTH BARELY OPENS, AND YOU LOOK AT ME IN THAT WAY, ORORO?
THAT WAS THE SAME LOOK HE HAD LAST NIGHT AS I COMBED HIS HAIR. AS I FELT HIS STRENGTH AGAINST ME.
MAYBE I WANT YOU TO SAY IT. THEN I WON'T FEEL FOOLISH FOR SPEAKING MY HEART IF I FEEL THE SAME WAY.
MAYBE I SHOULD ASK *YOU* TO CLAP YOUR HANDS WHEN YOU ARE AROUND ME.
WHAT COULD I POSSIBLY STEAL FROM YOU, ORORO?
MY HEART, T'CHALLA. MY HEART.

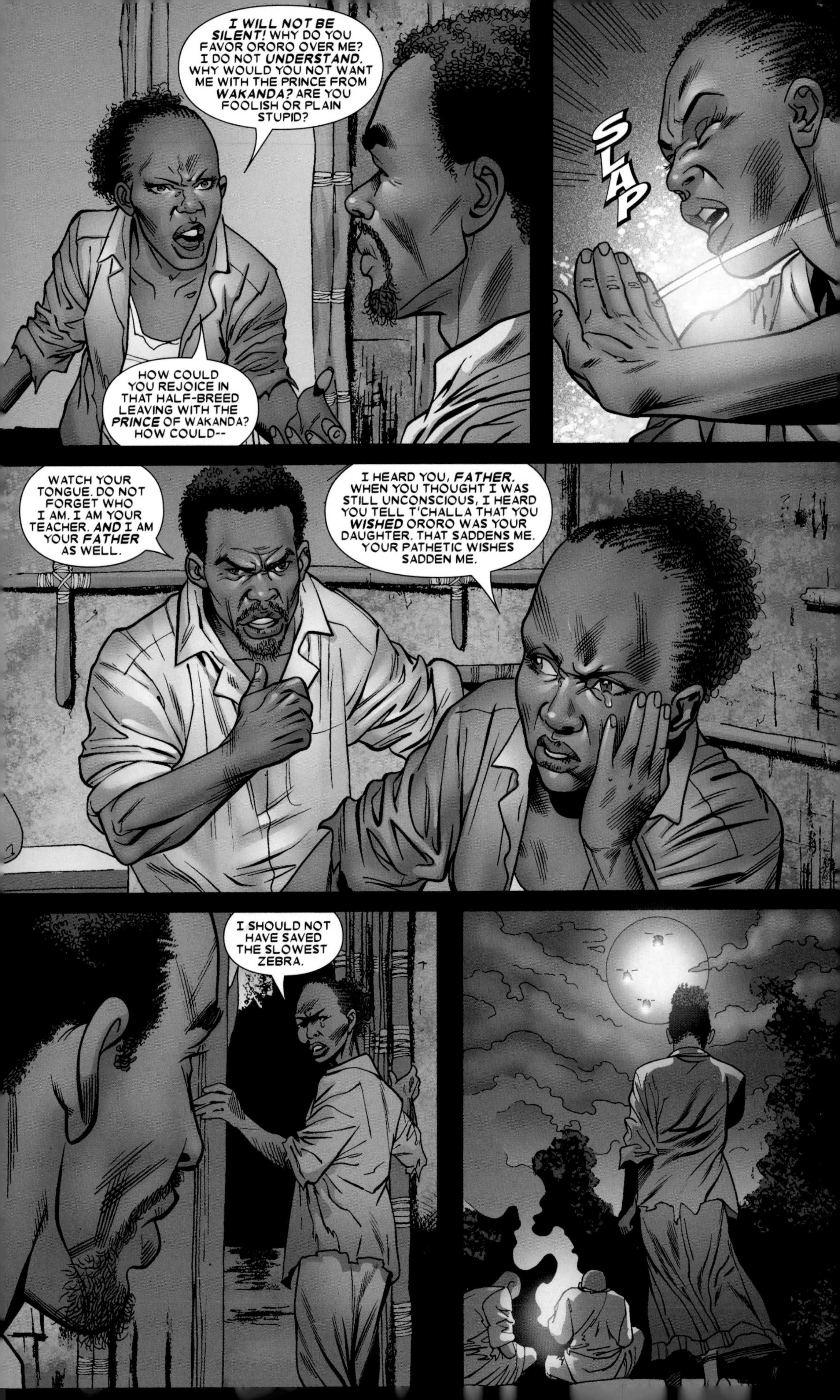
I WILL NOT BE SILENT! WHY DO YOU FAVOR ORORO OVER ME? I DO NOT UNDERSTAND. WHY WOULD YOU NOT WANT ME WITH THE PRINCE FROM WAKANDA? ARE YOU FOOLISH OR PLAIN STUPID?
HOW COULD YOU REJOICE IN THAT HALF-BREED LEAVING WITH THE PRINCE OF WAKANDA? HOW COULD--
SLAP
WATCH YOUR TONGUE. DO NOT FORGET WHO I AM. I AM YOUR TEACHER. AND I AM YOUR FATHER AS WELL.
I HEARD YOU, FATHER. WHEN YOU THOUGHT I WAS STILL UNCONSCIOUS, I HEARD YOU TELL T'CHALLA THAT YOU WISHED ORORO WAS YOUR DAUGHTER. THAT SADDENS ME. YOUR PATHETIC WISHES SADDEN ME.
I SHOULD NOT HAVE SAVED THE SLOWEST ZEBRA.

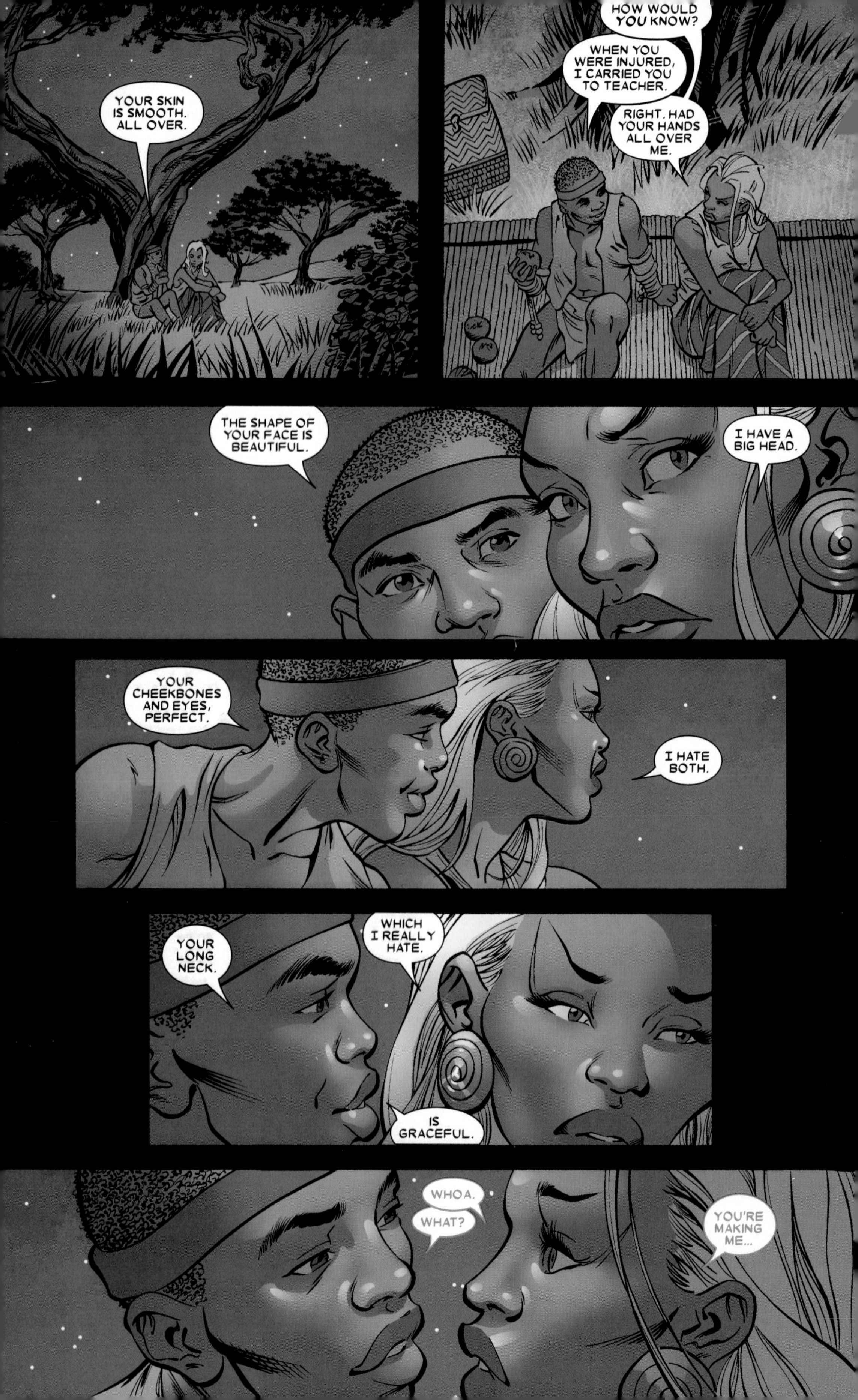
YOUR SKIN IS SMOOTH. ALL OVER.
HOW WOULD YOU KNOW?
WHEN YOU WERE INJURED, I CARRIED YOU TO TEACHER.
RIGHT. HAD YOUR HANDS ALL OVER ME.
THE SHAPE OF YOUR FACE IS BEAUTIFUL.
I HAVE A BIG HEAD.
YOUR CHEEKBONES AND EYES, PERFECT.
I HATE BOTH.
YOUR LONG NECK.
WHICH I REALLY HATE.
IS GRACEFUL.
WHOA.
WHAT?
YOU'RE MAKING ME...

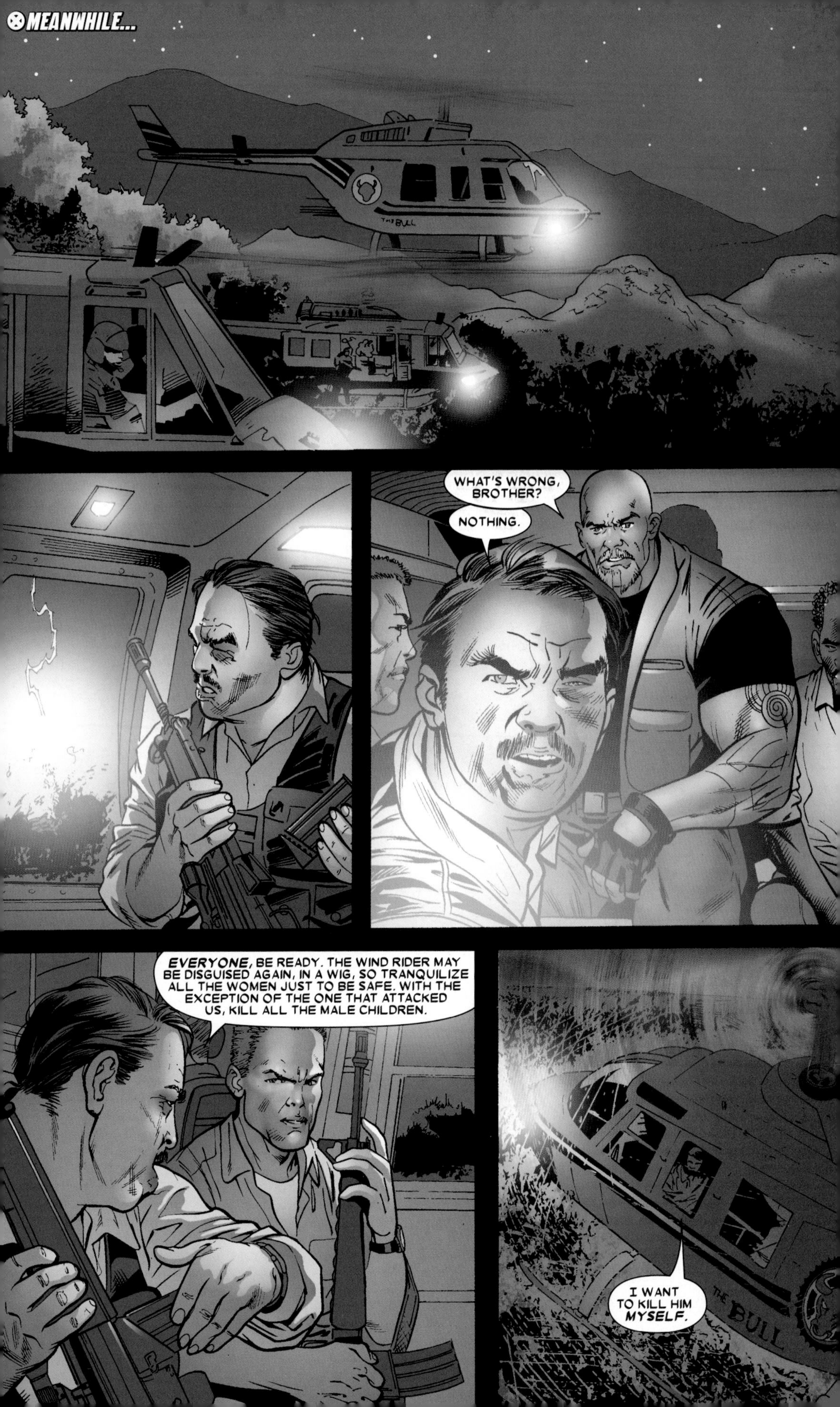
MEANWHILE...
THE BULL
WHAT'S WRONG, BROTHER?
NOTHING.
EVERYONE, BE READY. THE WIND RIDER MAY BE DISGUISED AGAIN, IN A WIG, SO TRANQUILIZE ALL THE WOMEN JUST TO BE SAFE. WITH THE EXCEPTION OF THE ONE THAT ATTACKED US, KILL ALL THE MALE CHILDREN.
I WANT TO KILL HIM MYSELF.
THE BULL

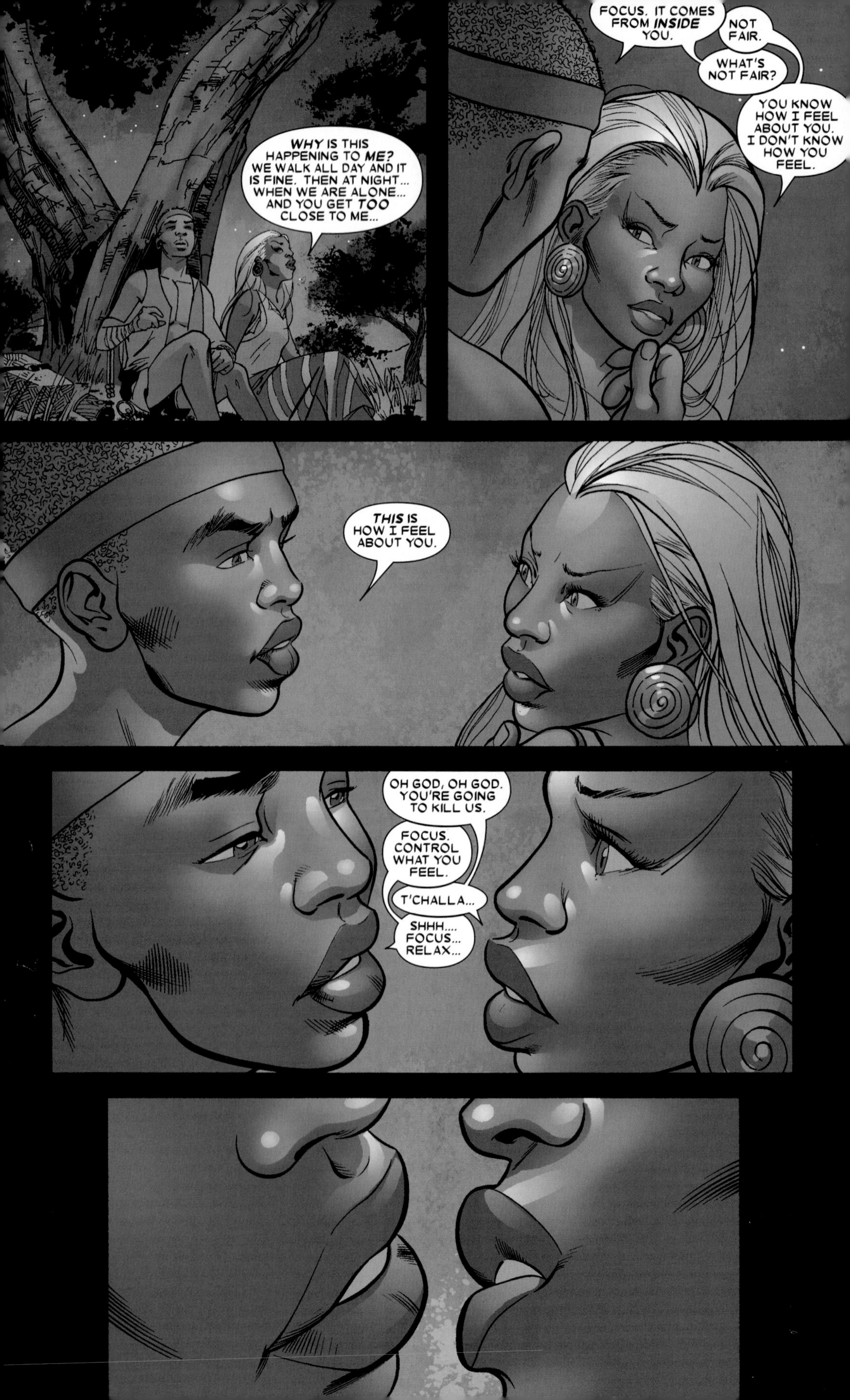
WHY IS THIS HAPPENING TO ME? WE WALK ALL DAY AND IT IS FINE. THEN AT NIGHT... WHEN WE ARE ALONE... AND YOU GET TOO CLOSE TO ME...
FOCUS. IT COMES FROM INSIDE YOU.
NOT FAIR.
WHAT'S NOT FAIR?
YOU KNOW HOW I FEEL ABOUT YOU. I DON'T KNOW HOW YOU FEEL.
THIS IS HOW I FEEL ABOUT YOU.
OH GOD, OH GOD. YOU'RE GOING TO KILL US.
FOCUS. CONTROL WHAT YOU FEEL.
T'CHALLA...
SHHH.... FOCUS... RELAX...

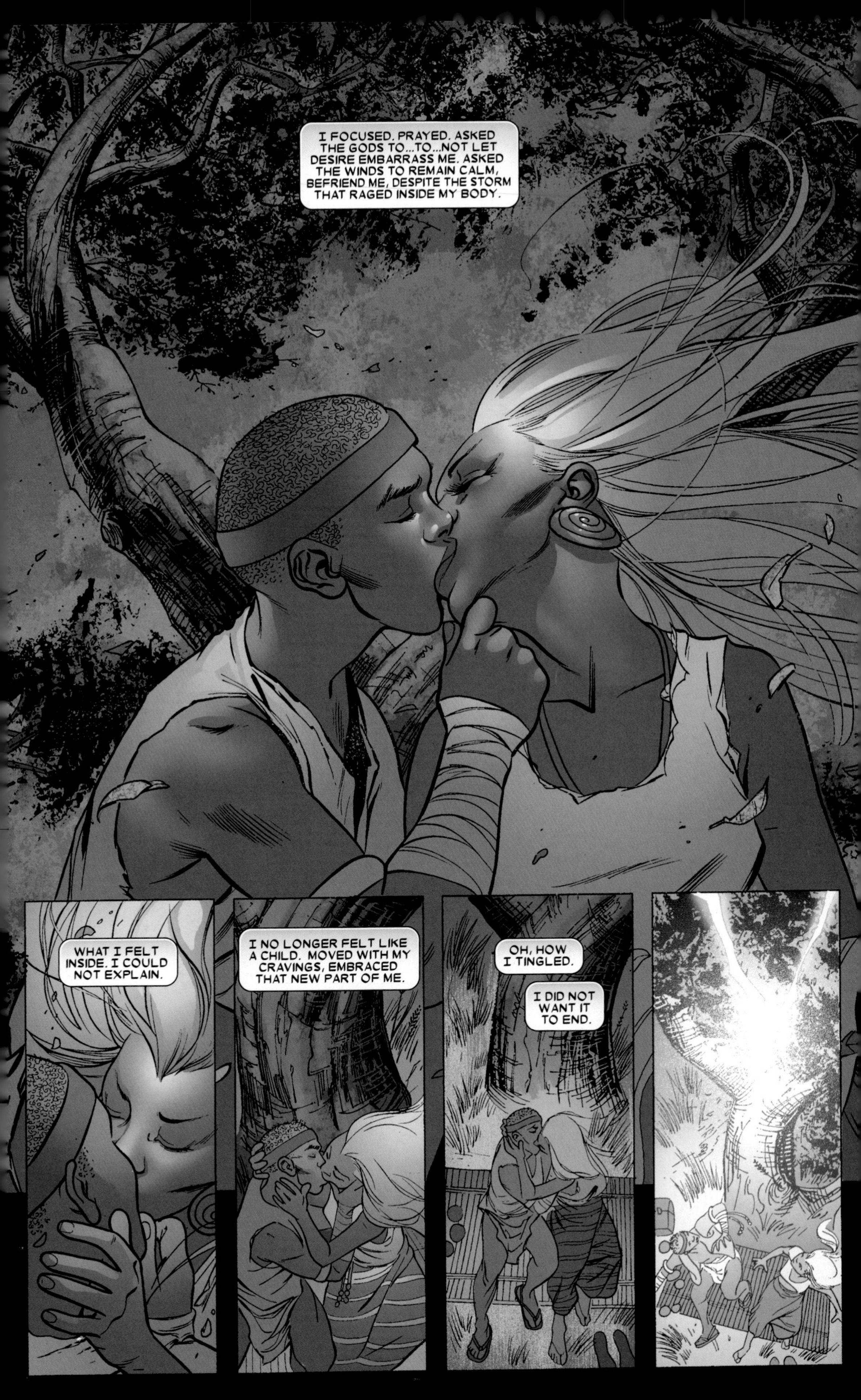
I FOCUSED. PRAYED. ASKED THE GODS TO...TO...NOT LET DESIRE EMBARRASS ME. ASKED THE WINDS TO REMAIN CALM, BEFRIEND ME, DESPITE THE STORM THAT RAGED INSIDE MY BODY.
WHAT I FELT INSIDE. I COULD NOT EXPLAIN.
I NO LONGER FELT LIKE A CHILD. MOVED WITH MY CRAVINGS, EMBRACED THAT NEW PART OF ME.
OH, HOW I TINGLED.
I DID NOT WANT IT TO END.

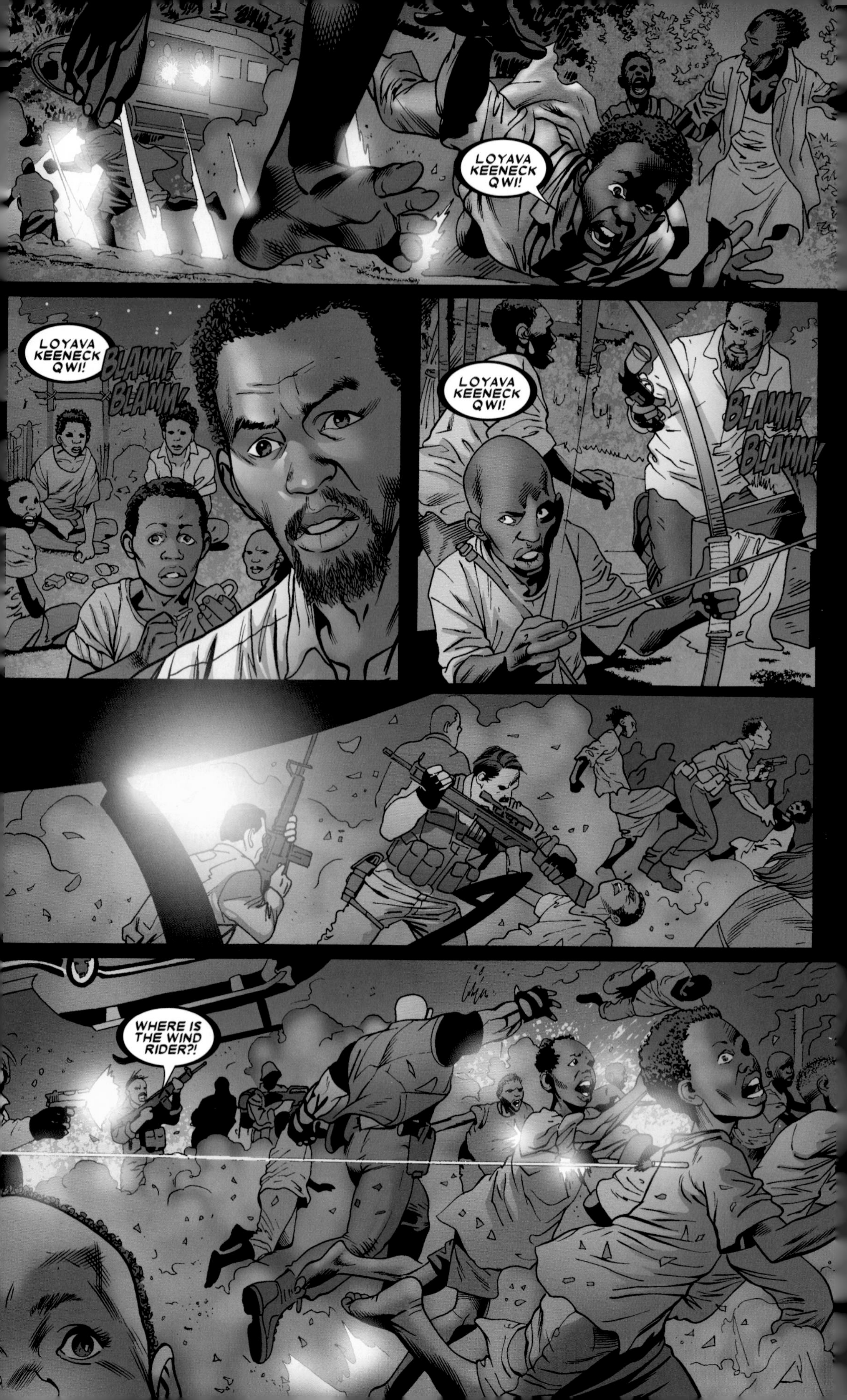
LOYAVA KEENECK QWI!
LOYAVA KEENECK QWI!
BLAMM! BLAMM!
LOYAVA KEENECK QWI!
BLAMM! BLAMM!
WHERE IS THE WIND RIDER?!

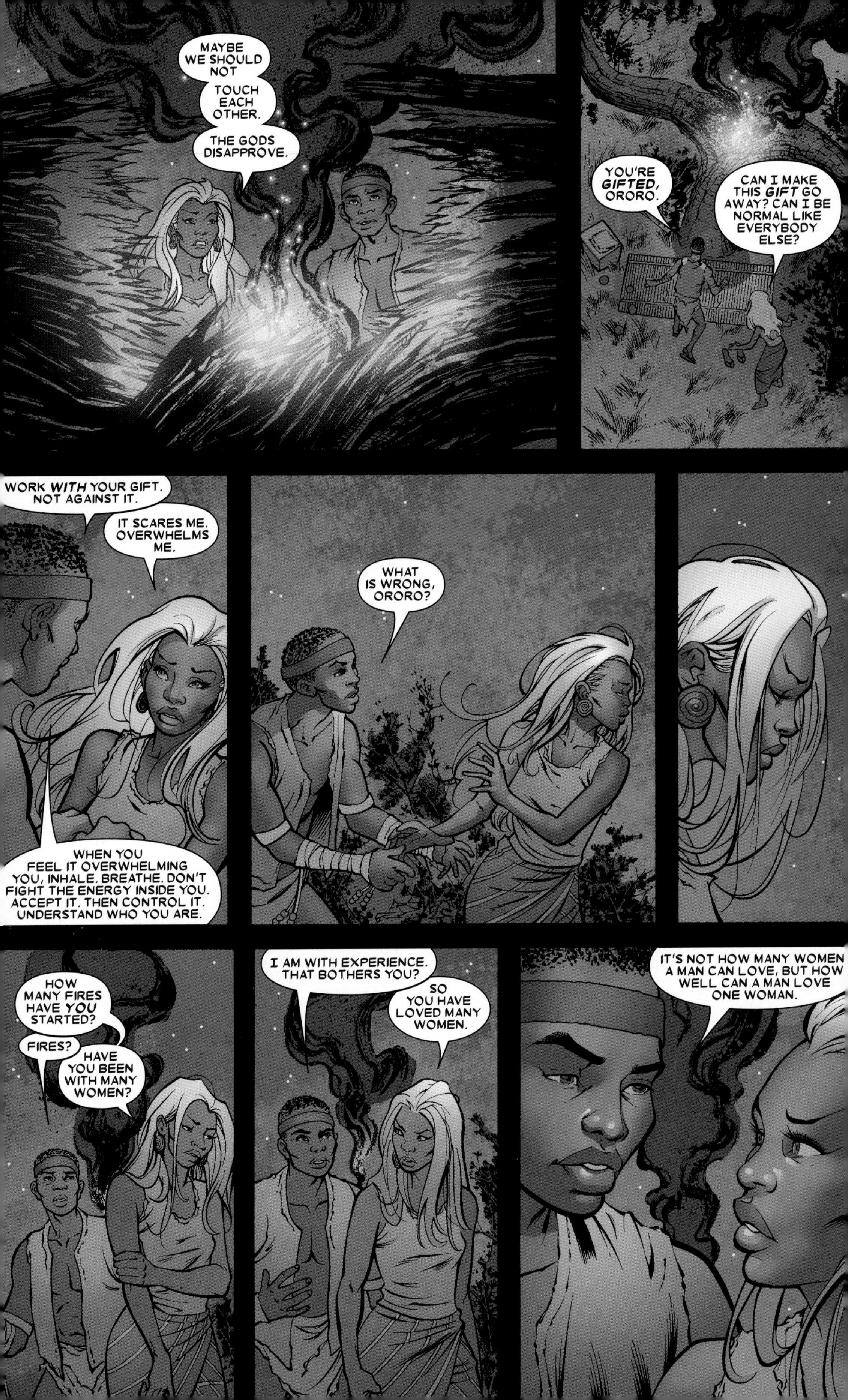
MAYBE WE SHOULD NOT
TOUCH EACH OTHER.
THE GODS DISAPPROVE.
YOU'RE GIFTED, ORORO.
CAN I MAKE THIS GIFT GO AWAY? CAN I BE NORMAL LIKE EVERYBODY ELSE?
WORK WITH YOUR GIFT. NOT AGAINST IT.
IT SCARES ME. OVERWHELMS ME.
WHEN YOU FEEL IT OVERWHELMING YOU, INHALE. BREATHE. DON'T FIGHT THE ENERGY INSIDE YOU. ACCEPT IT. THEN CONTROL IT. UNDERSTAND WHO YOU ARE.
WHAT IS WRONG, ORORO?
HOW MANY FIRES HAVE YOU STARTED?
FIRES?
HAVE YOU BEEN WITH MANY WOMEN?
I AM WITH EXPERIENCE. THAT BOTHERS YOU?
SO YOU HAVE LOVED MANY WOMEN.
IT'S NOT HOW MANY WOMEN A MAN CAN LOVE, BUT HOW WELL CAN A MAN LOVE ONE WOMAN.

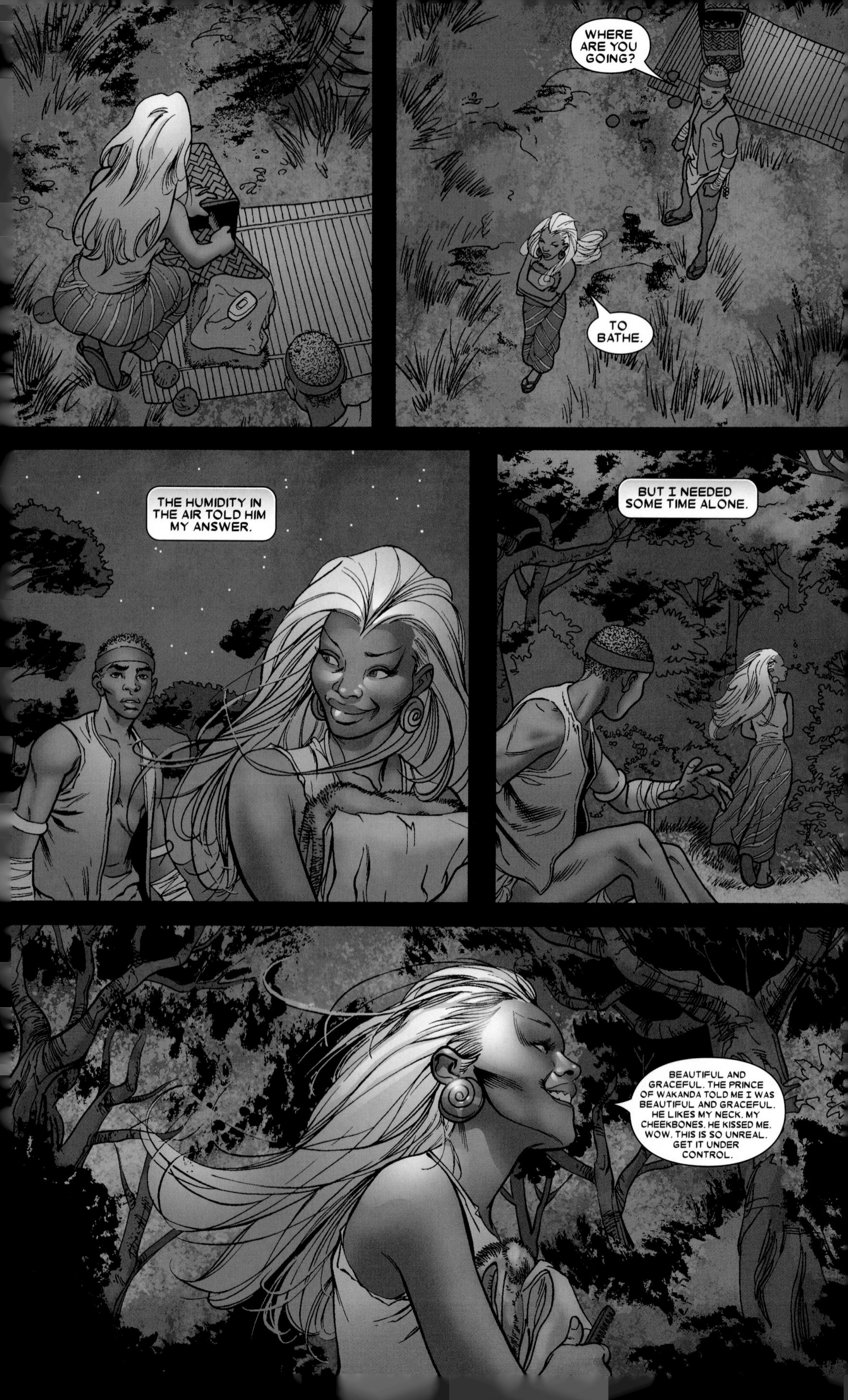
WHERE ARE YOU GOING?
TO BATHE.
THE HUMIDITY IN THE AIR TOLD HIM MY ANSWER.
BUT I NEEDED SOME TIME ALONE.
BEAUTIFUL AND GRACEFUL. THE PRINCE OF WAKANDA TOLD ME I WAS BEAUTIFUL AND GRACEFUL. HE LIKES MY NECK. MY CHEEKBONES. HE KISSED ME. WOW. THIS IS SO UNREAL. GET IT UNDER CONTROL.

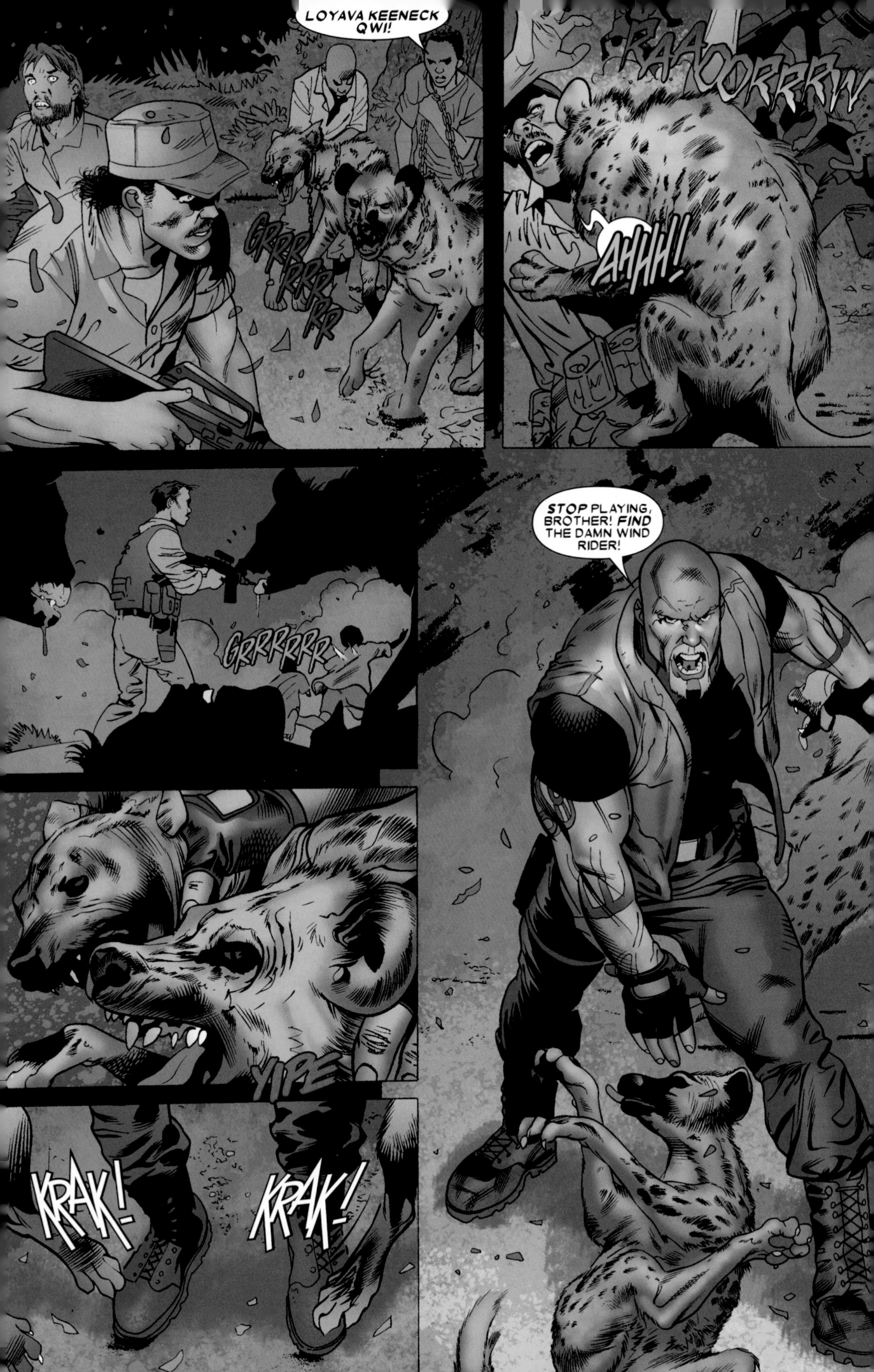
LOYAVA KEENECK QWI!
GRRRRRRRR
RAAOORRRRW
AHHH!
GRRRRRR
STOP PLAYING, BROTHER! FIND THE DAMN WIND RIDER!
YIPE
KRAK!
KRAK!

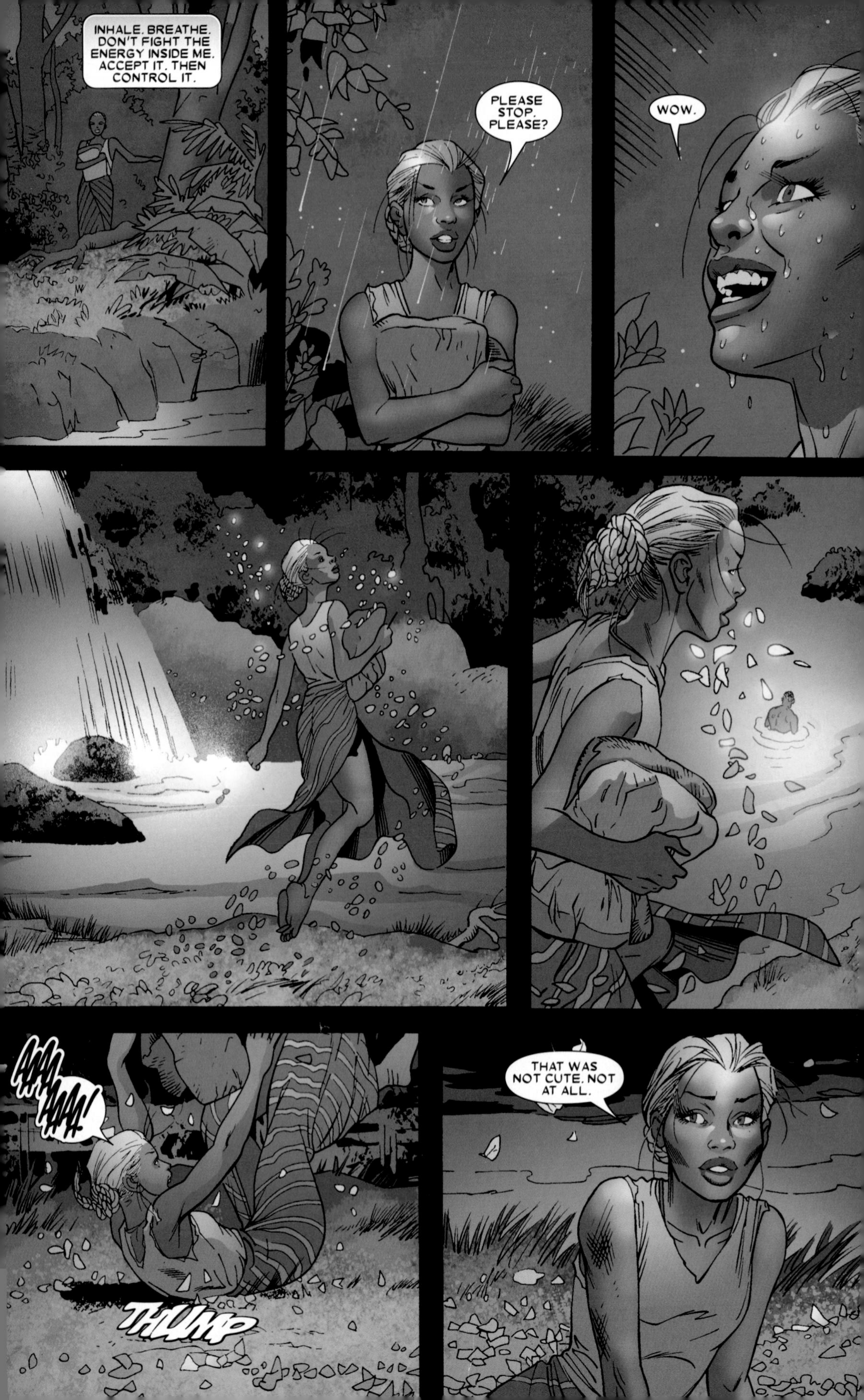
INHALE. BREATHE. DON'T FIGHT THE ENERGY INSIDE ME. ACCEPT IT. THEN CONTROL IT.
PLEASE STOP. PLEASE?
WOW.
AAAAAAA!
THUMP
THAT WAS NOT CUTE. NOT AT ALL.

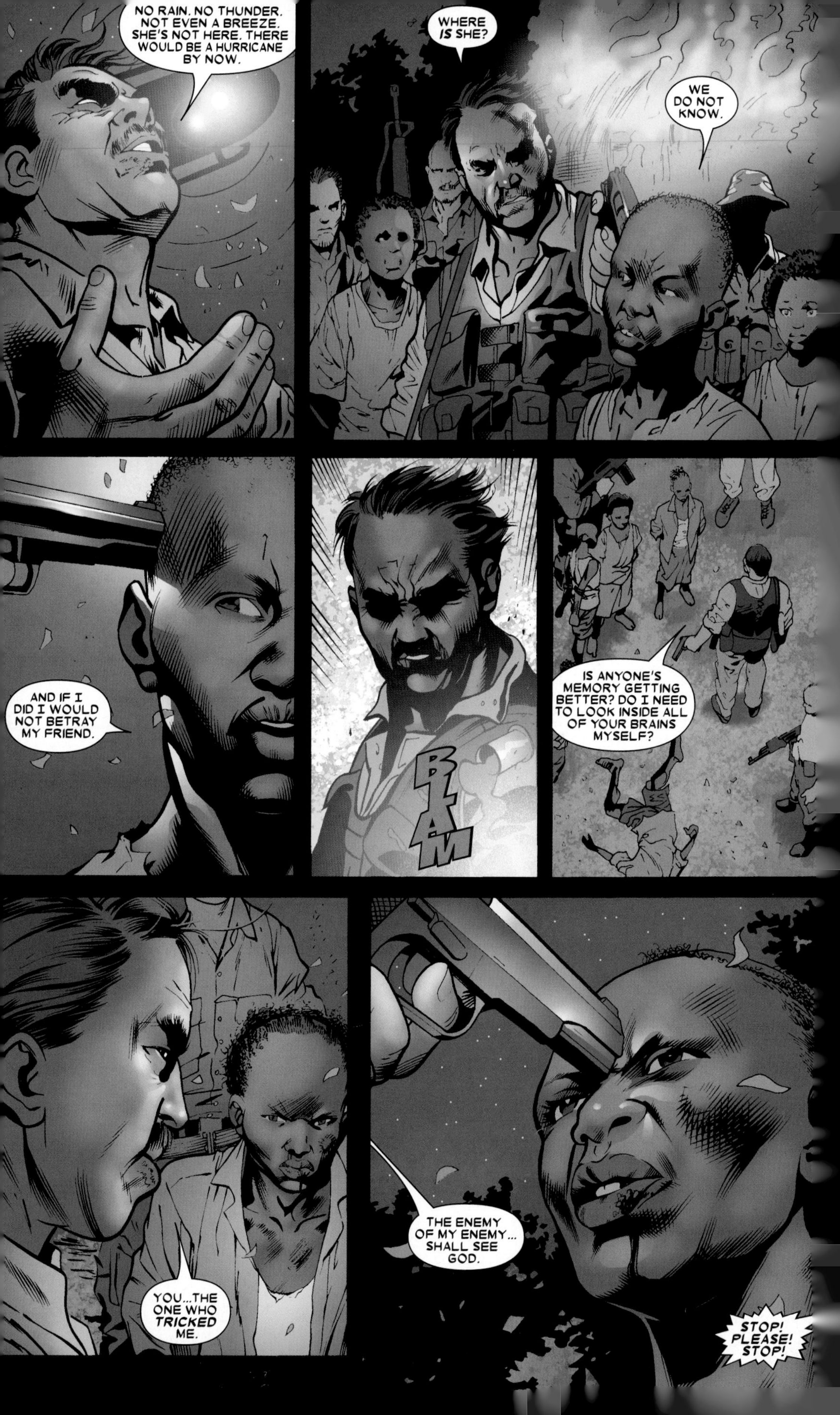
NO RAIN. NO THUNDER. NOT EVEN A BREEZE. SHE'S NOT HERE. THERE WOULD BE A HURRICANE BY NOW.
WHERE *IS* SHE?
WE DO NOT KNOW.
AND IF I DID I WOULD NOT BETRAY MY FRIEND.
BLAM
IS ANYONE'S MEMORY GETTING BETTER? DO I NEED TO LOOK INSIDE ALL OF YOUR BRAINS MYSELF?
YOU...THE ONE WHO *TRICKED* ME.
THE ENEMY OF MY ENEMY... SHALL SEE GOD.
STOP! PLEASE! STOP!

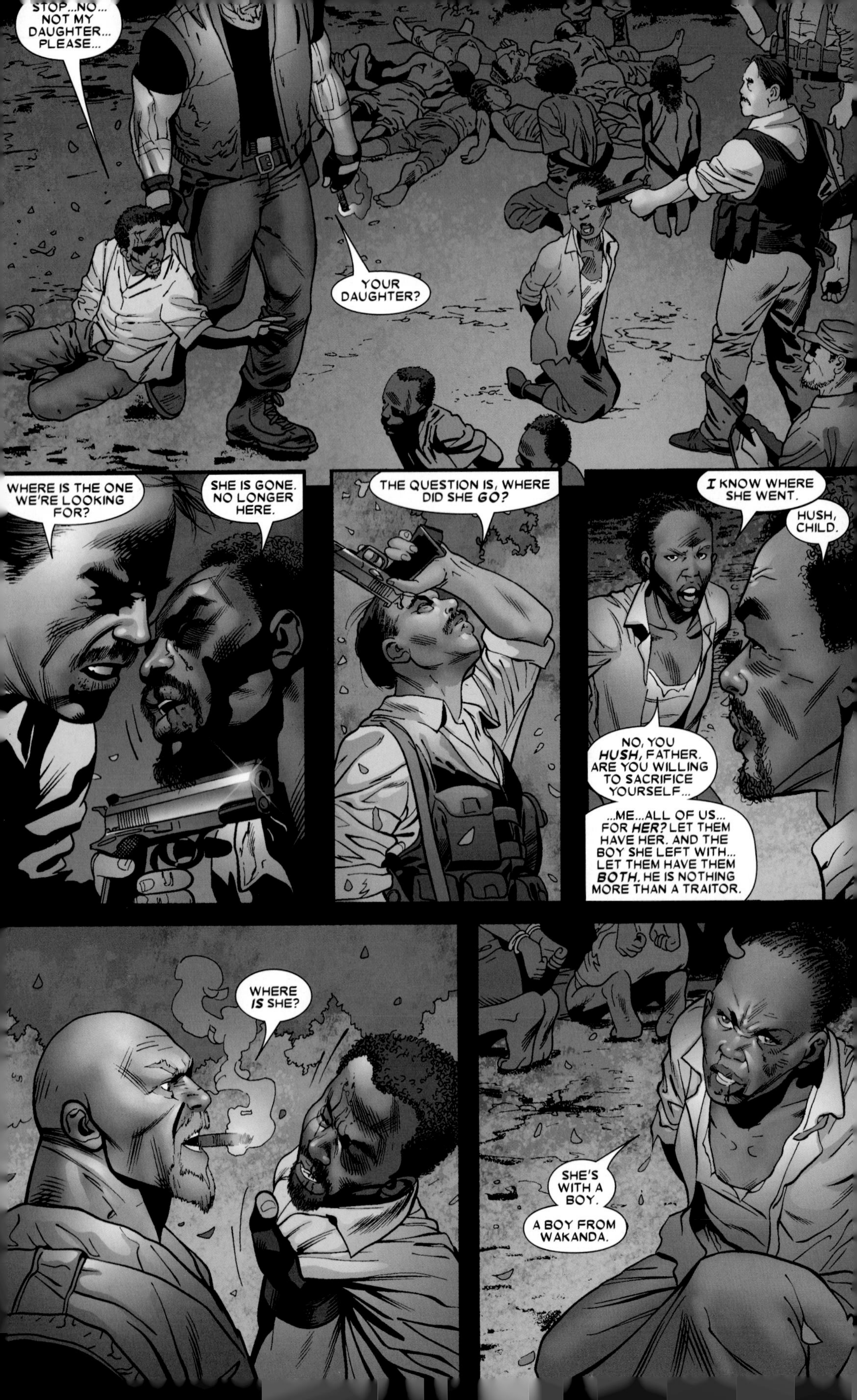
STOP...NO... NOT MY DAUGHTER... PLEASE...
YOUR DAUGHTER?
WHERE IS THE ONE WE'RE LOOKING FOR?
SHE IS GONE. NO LONGER HERE.
THE QUESTION IS, WHERE DID SHE *GO?*
I KNOW WHERE SHE WENT.
HUSH, CHILD.
NO, YOU *HUSH*, FATHER. ARE YOU WILLING TO SACRIFICE YOURSELF...
...ME...ALL OF US... FOR *HER?* LET THEM HAVE HER. AND THE BOY SHE LEFT WITH... LET THEM HAVE THEM *BOTH*. HE IS NOTHING MORE THAN A TRAITOR.
WHERE *IS* SHE?
SHE'S WITH A BOY.
A BOY FROM WAKANDA.

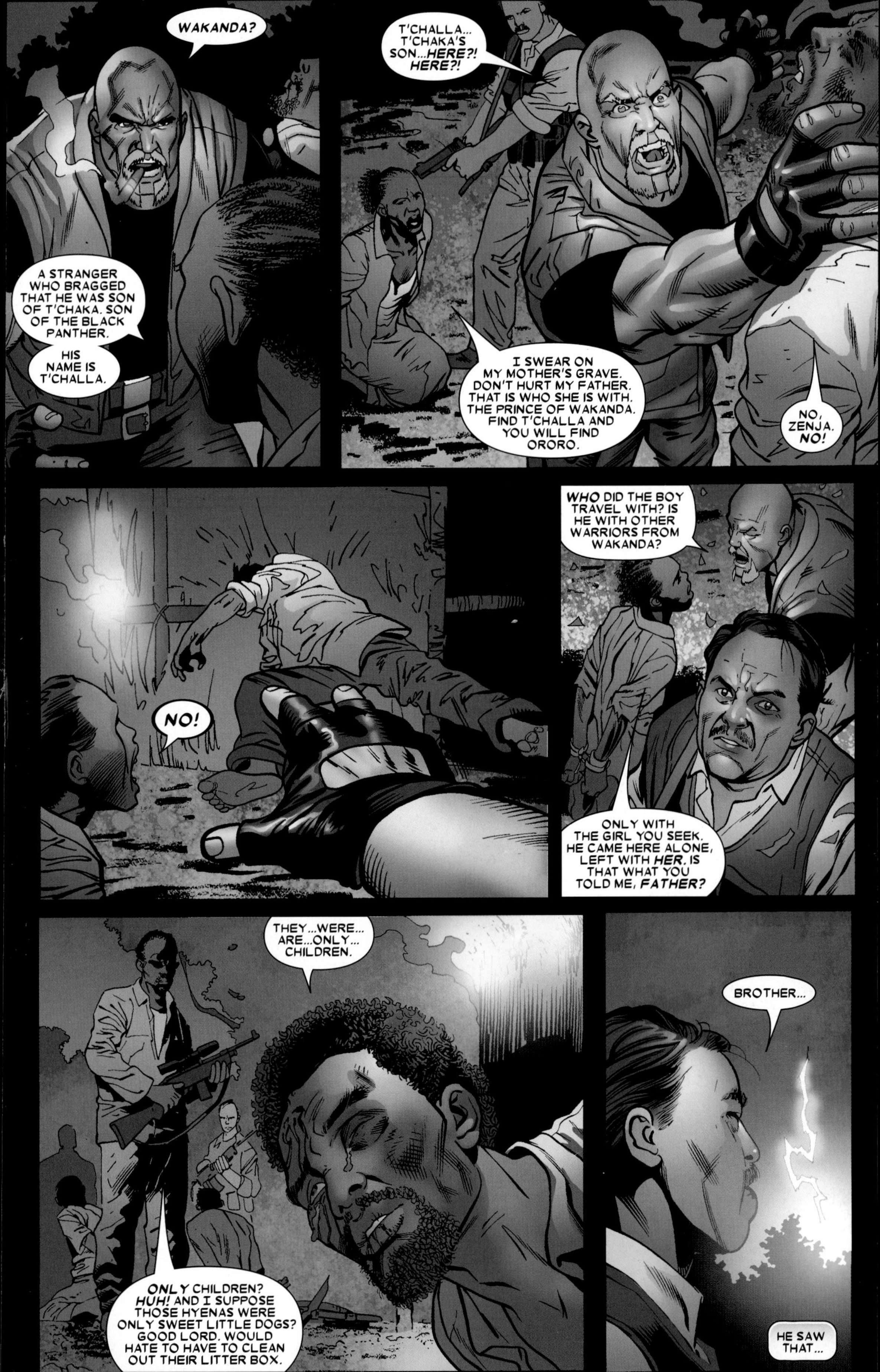
WAKANDA?
A STRANGER WHO BRAGGED THAT HE WAS SON OF T'CHAKA. SON OF THE BLACK PANTHER.
HIS NAME IS T'CHALLA.
T'CHALLA... T'CHAKA'S SON...HERE?! HERE?!
I SWEAR ON MY MOTHER'S GRAVE. DON'T HURT MY FATHER. THAT IS WHO SHE IS WITH. THE PRINCE OF WAKANDA. FIND T'CHALLA AND YOU WILL FIND ORORO.
NO, ZENJA. NO!
NO!
WHO DID THE BOY TRAVEL WITH? IS HE WITH OTHER WARRIORS FROM WAKANDA?
ONLY WITH THE GIRL YOU SEEK. HE CAME HERE ALONE, LEFT WITH HER. IS THAT WHAT YOU TOLD ME, FATHER?
THEY...WERE... ARE...ONLY... CHILDREN.
ONLY CHILDREN? HUH! AND I SUPPOSE THOSE HYENAS WERE ONLY SWEET LITTLE DOGS? GOOD LORD. WOULD HATE TO HAVE TO CLEAN OUT THEIR LITTER BOX.
BROTHER...
HE SAW THAT...

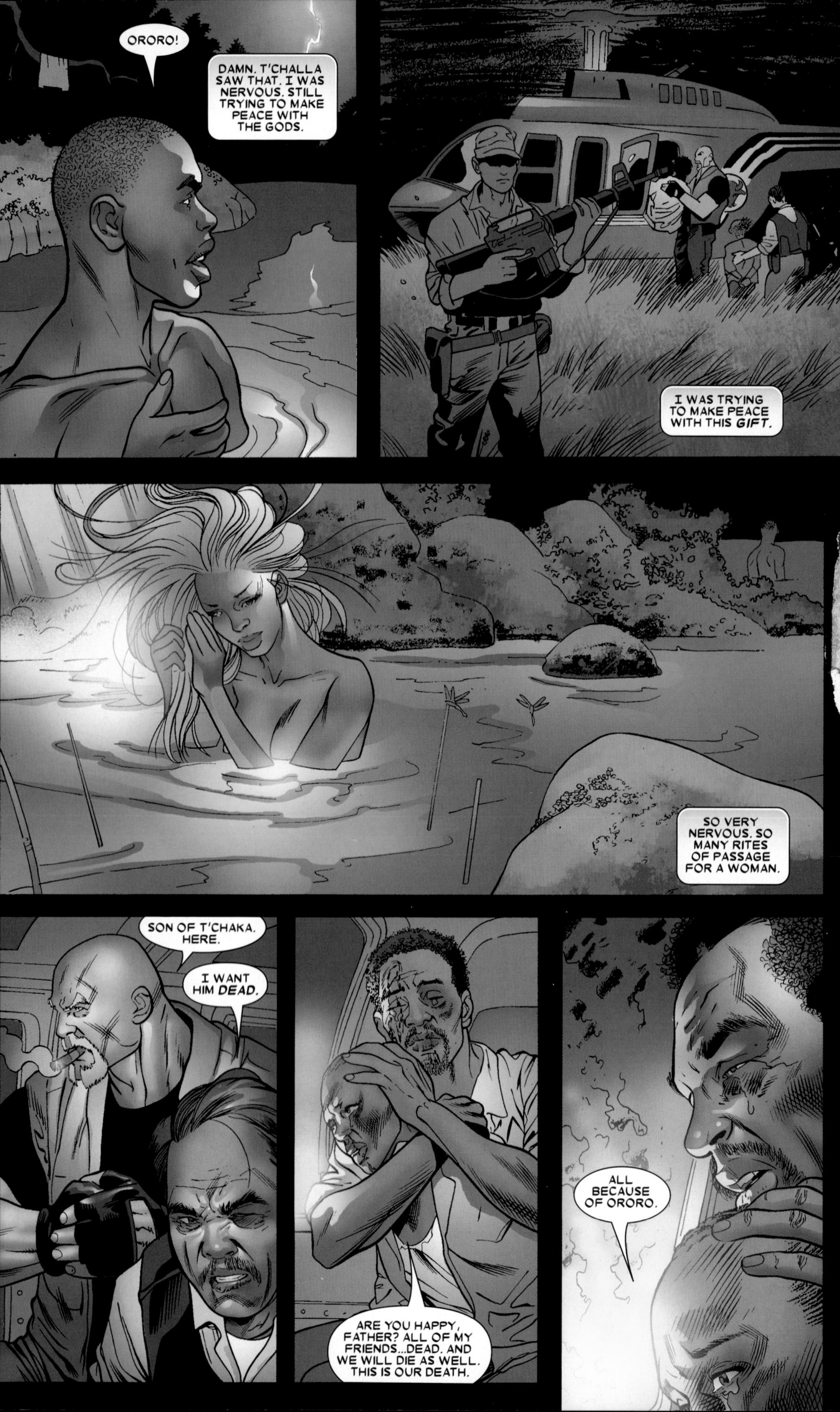
ORORO!
DAMN. T'CHALLA SAW THAT. I WAS NERVOUS. STILL TRYING TO MAKE PEACE WITH THE GODS.
I WAS TRYING TO MAKE PEACE WITH THIS *GIFT*.
SO VERY NERVOUS. SO MANY RITES OF PASSAGE FOR A WOMAN.
SON OF T'CHAKA. HERE.
I WANT HIM *DEAD*.
ARE YOU HAPPY, FATHER? ALL OF MY FRIENDS...DEAD. AND WE WILL DIE AS WELL. THIS IS OUR DEATH.
ALL BECAUSE OF ORORO.

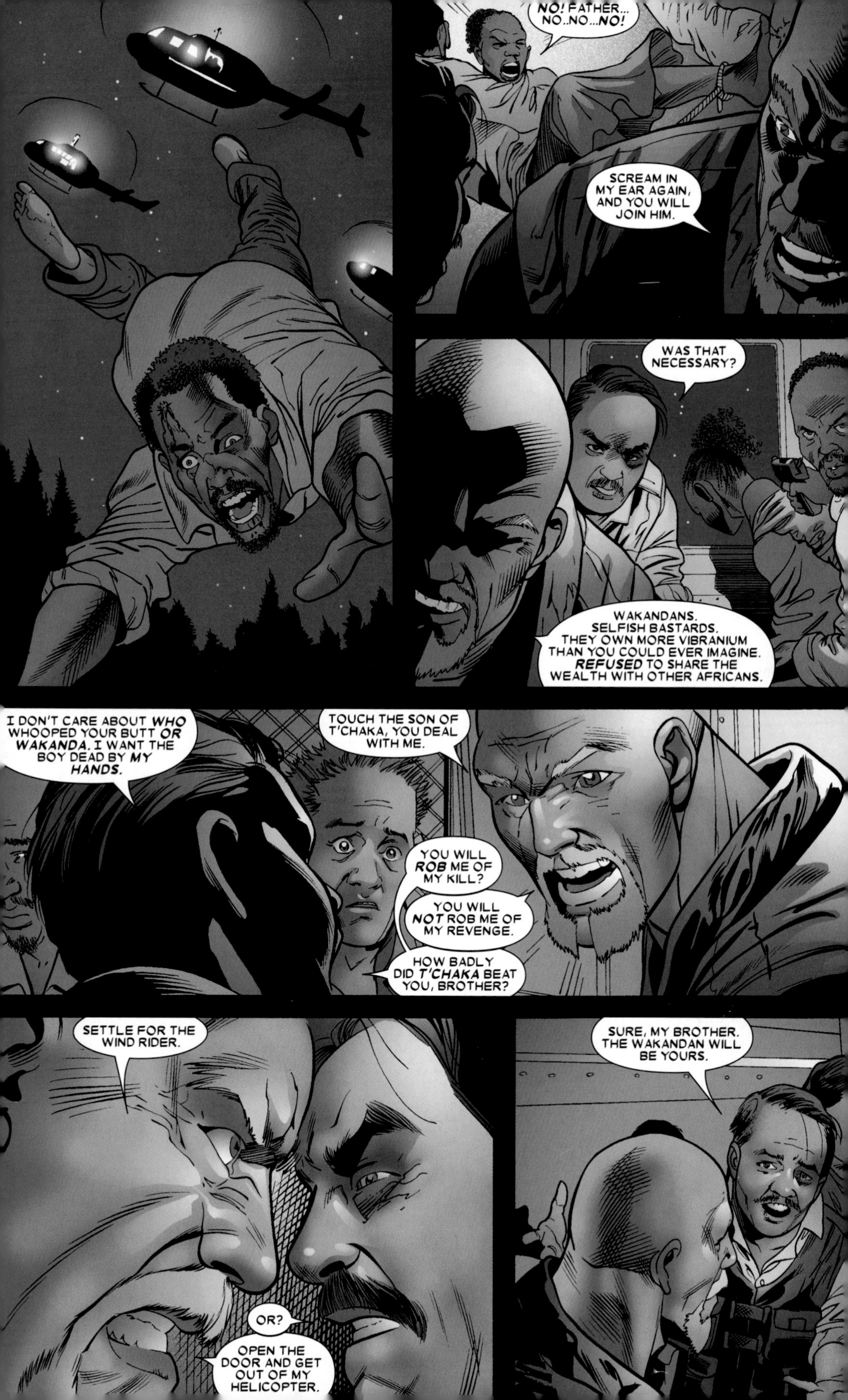
NO! FATHER... NO..NO...NO!
SCREAM IN MY EAR AGAIN, AND YOU WILL JOIN HIM.
WAS THAT NECESSARY?
WAKANDANS. SELFISH BASTARDS. THEY OWN MORE VIBRANIUM THAN YOU COULD EVER IMAGINE. REFUSED TO SHARE THE WEALTH WITH OTHER AFRICANS.
I DON'T CARE ABOUT WHO WHOOPED YOUR BUTT OR WAKANDA. I WANT THE BOY DEAD BY MY HANDS.
TOUCH THE SON OF T'CHAKA, YOU DEAL WITH ME.
YOU WILL ROB ME OF MY KILL?
YOU WILL NOT ROB ME OF MY REVENGE.
HOW BADLY DID T'CHAKA BEAT YOU, BROTHER?
SETTLE FOR THE WIND RIDER.
OR?
OPEN THE DOOR AND GET OUT OF MY HELICOPTER.
SURE, MY BROTHER. THE WAKANDAN WILL BE YOURS.

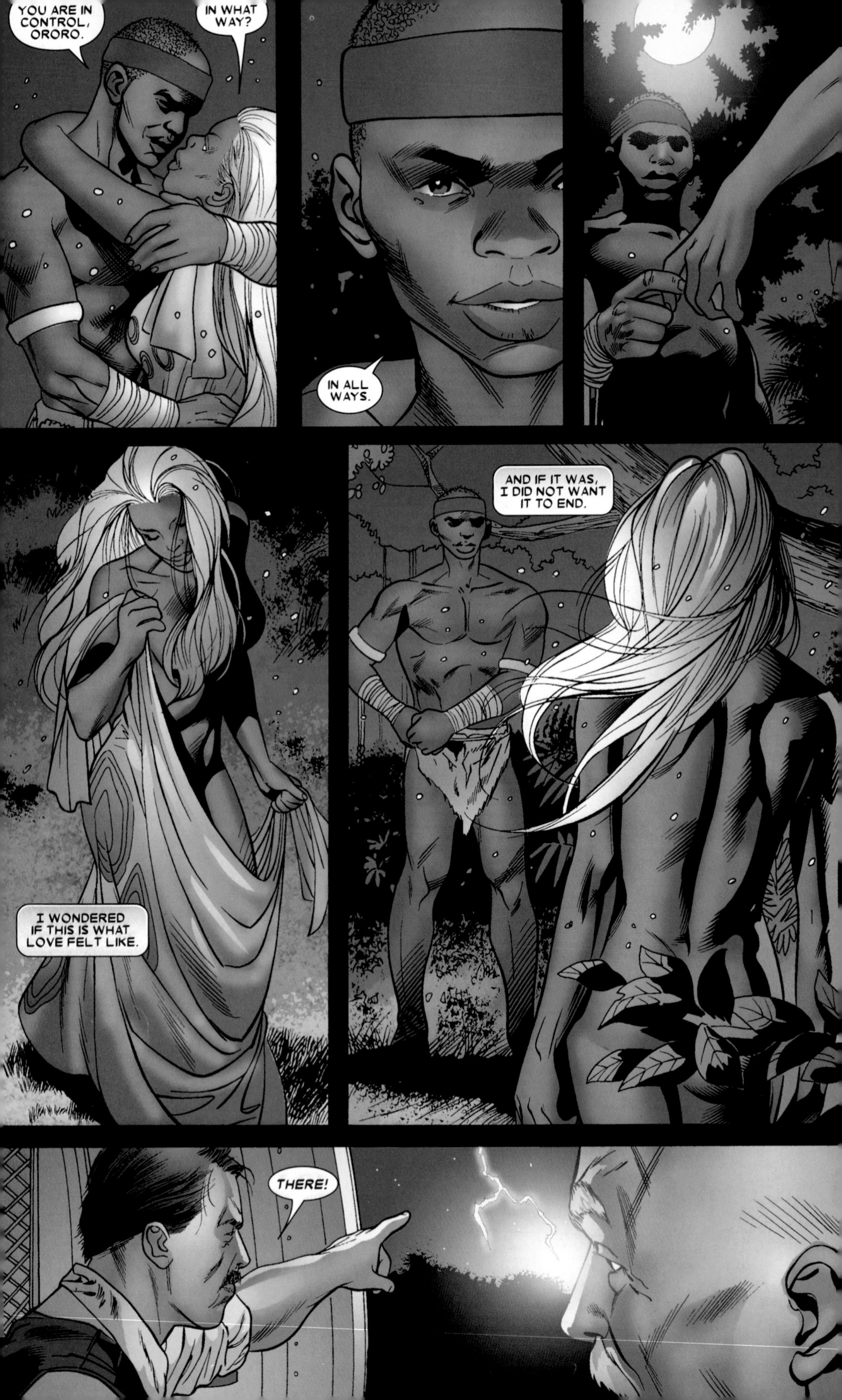
YOU ARE IN CONTROL, ORORO.
IN WHAT WAY?
IN ALL WAYS.
I WONDERED IF THIS IS WHAT LOVE FELT LIKE.
AND IF IT WAS, I DID NOT WANT IT TO END.
THERE!

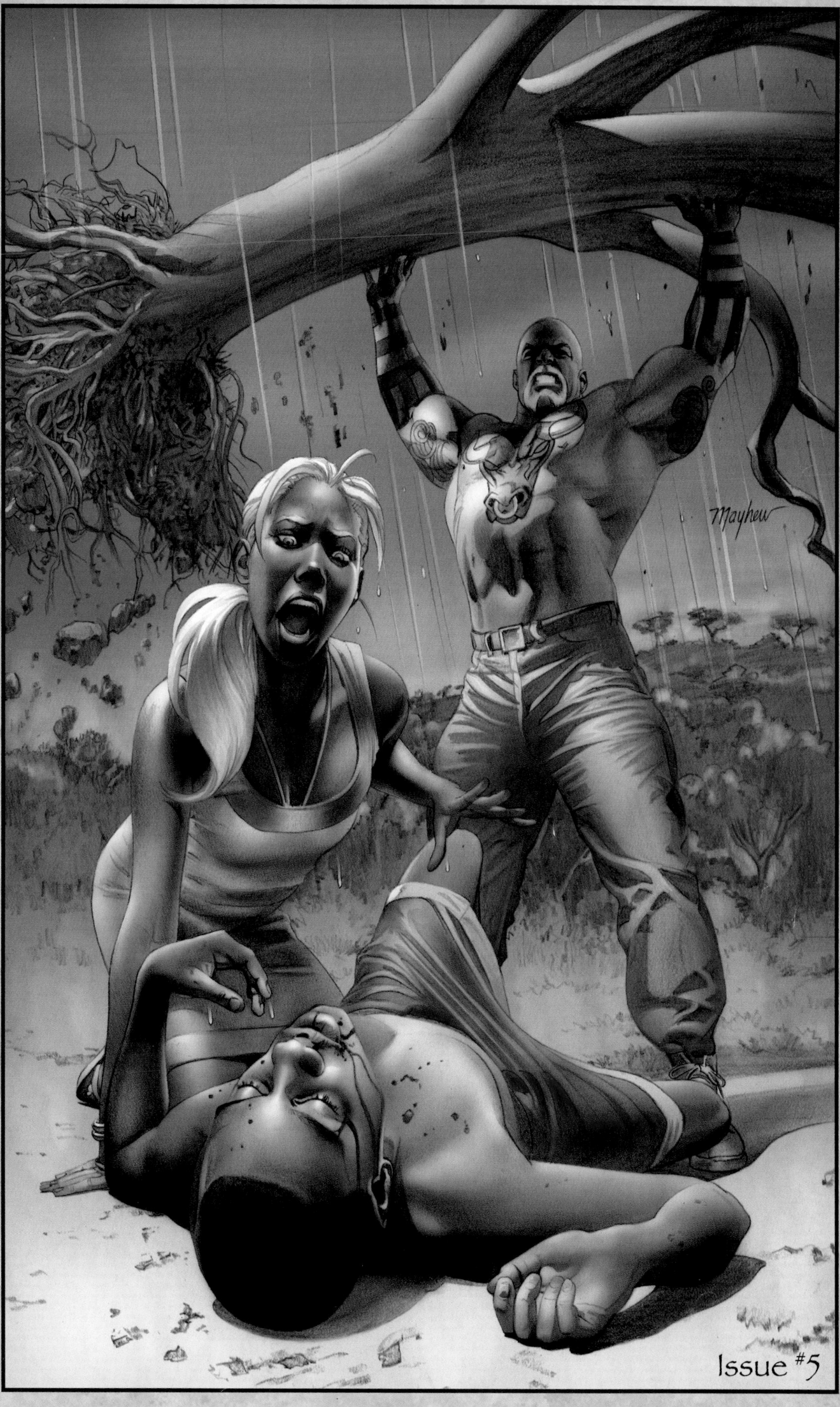
Mayhew
Issue #5

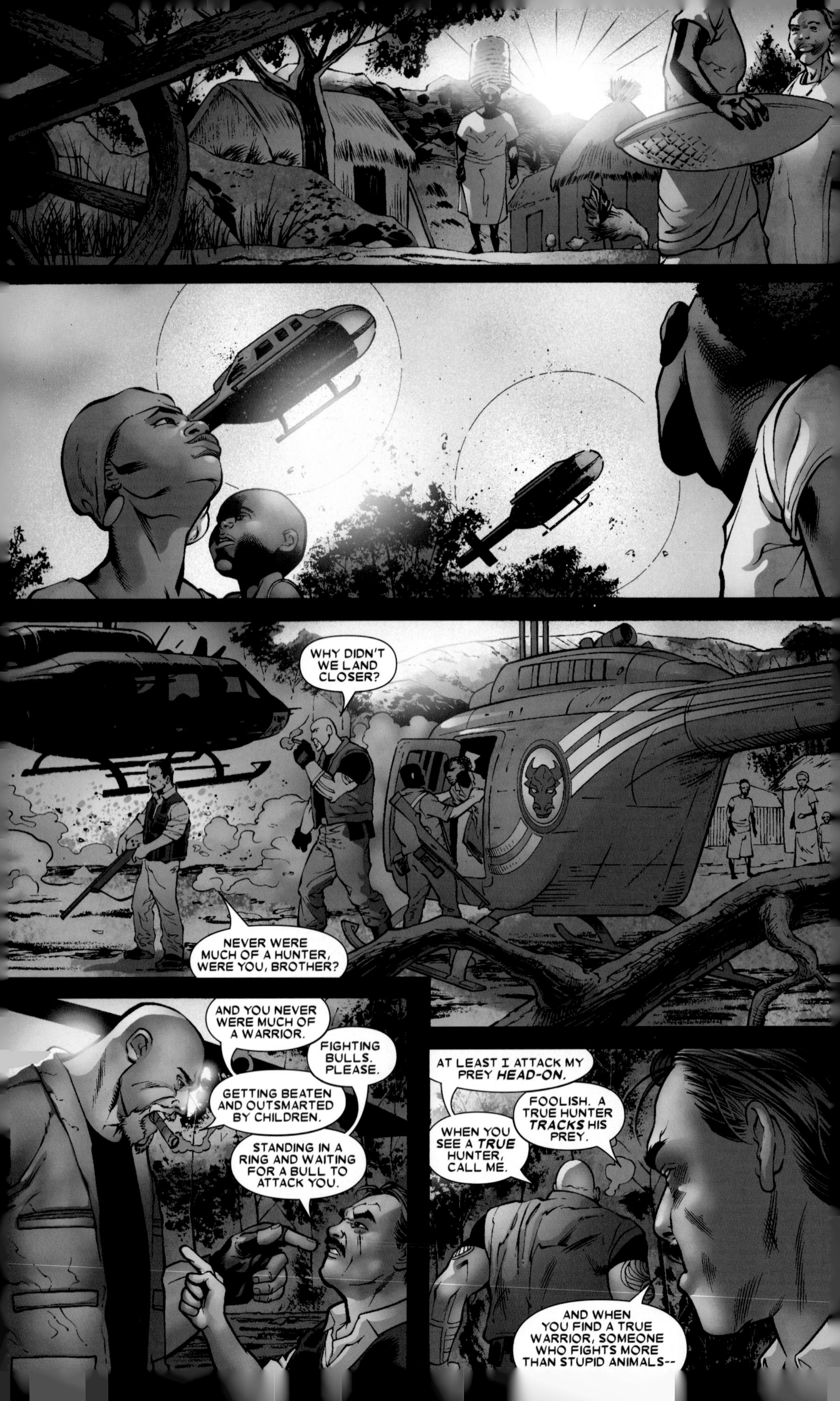
WHY DIDN'T WE LAND CLOSER?
NEVER WERE MUCH OF A HUNTER, WERE YOU, BROTHER?
AND YOU NEVER WERE MUCH OF A WARRIOR.
FIGHTING BULLS. PLEASE.
GETTING BEATEN AND OUTSMARTED BY CHILDREN.
STANDING IN A RING AND WAITING FOR A BULL TO ATTACK YOU.
AT LEAST I ATTACK MY PREY *HEAD-ON.*
FOOLISH. A TRUE HUNTER *TRACKS* HIS PREY.
WHEN YOU SEE A *TRUE* HUNTER, CALL ME.
AND WHEN YOU FIND A TRUE WARRIOR, SOMEONE WHO FIGHTS MORE THAN STUPID ANIMALS--

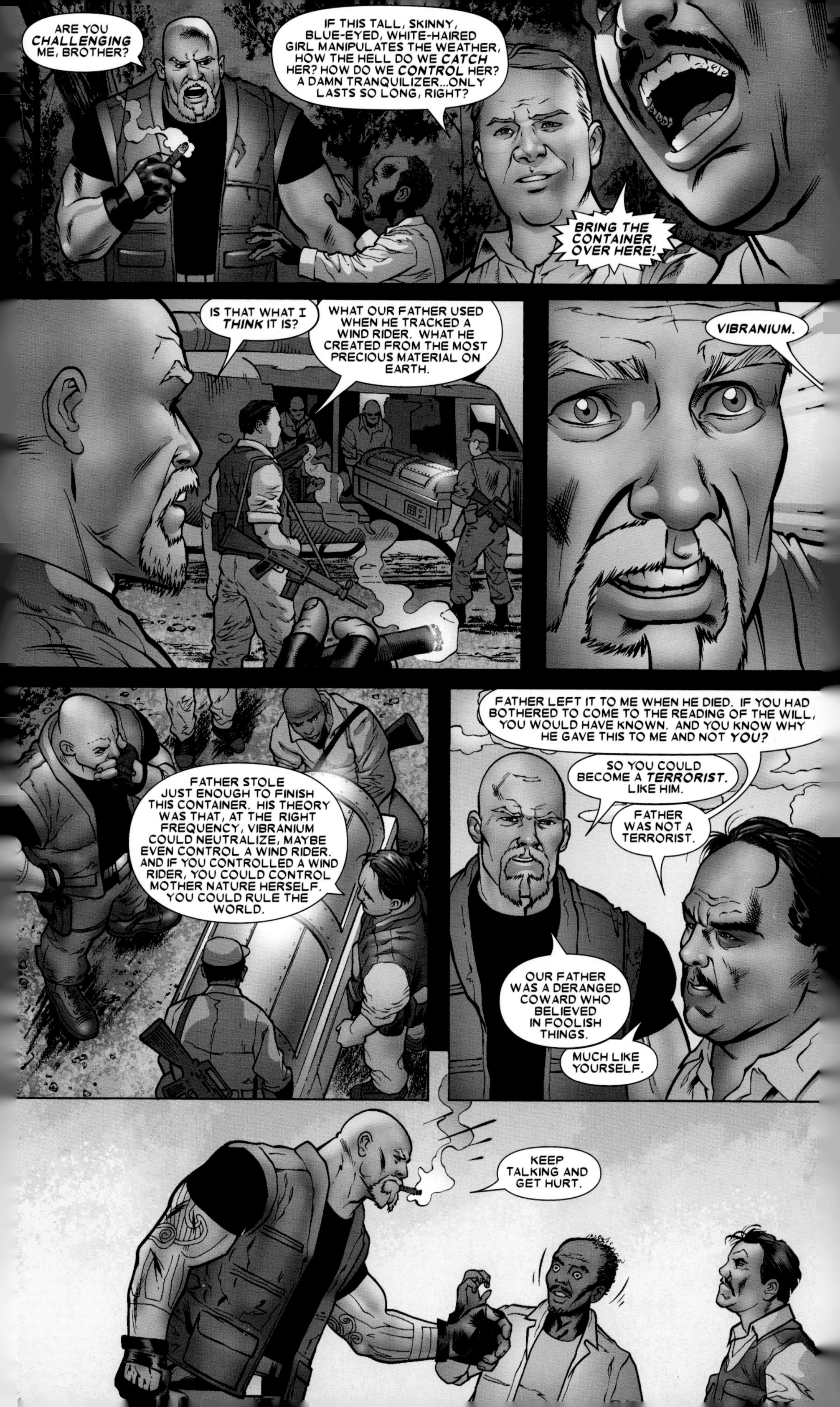

ARE YOU CHALLENGING ME, BROTHER?
IF THIS TALL, SKINNY, BLUE-EYED, WHITE-HAIRED GIRL MANIPULATES THE WEATHER, HOW THE HELL DO WE CATCH HER? HOW DO WE CONTROL HER? A DAMN TRANQUILIZER...ONLY LASTS SO LONG, RIGHT?
BRING THE CONTAINER OVER HERE!
IS THAT WHAT I THINK IT IS?
WHAT OUR FATHER USED WHEN HE TRACKED A WIND RIDER. WHAT HE CREATED FROM THE MOST PRECIOUS MATERIAL ON EARTH.
VIBRANIUM.
FATHER STOLE JUST ENOUGH TO FINISH THIS CONTAINER. HIS THEORY WAS THAT, AT THE RIGHT FREQUENCY, VIBRANIUM COULD NEUTRALIZE, MAYBE EVEN CONTROL A WIND RIDER. AND IF YOU CONTROLLED A WIND RIDER, YOU COULD CONTROL MOTHER NATURE HERSELF. YOU COULD RULE THE WORLD.
FATHER LEFT IT TO ME WHEN HE DIED. IF YOU HAD BOTHERED TO COME TO THE READING OF THE WILL, YOU WOULD HAVE KNOWN. AND YOU KNOW WHY HE GAVE THIS TO ME AND NOT YOU?
SO YOU COULD BECOME A TERRORIST. LIKE HIM.
FATHER WAS NOT A TERRORIST.
OUR FATHER WAS A DERANGED COWARD WHO BELIEVED IN FOOLISH THINGS.
MUCH LIKE YOURSELF.
KEEP TALKING AND GET HURT.

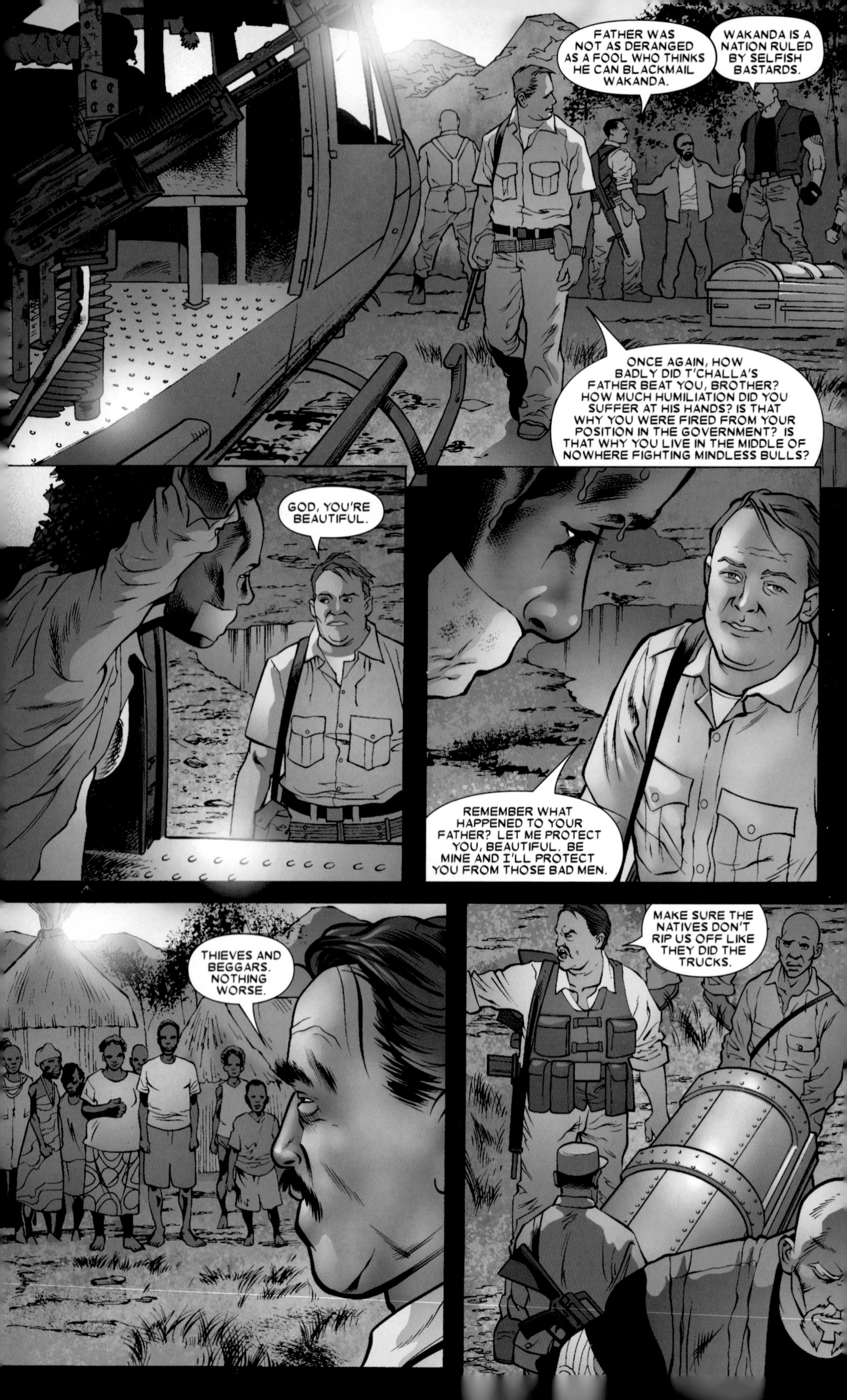
FATHER WAS NOT AS DERANGED AS A FOOL WHO THINKS HE CAN BLACKMAIL WAKANDA.
WAKANDA IS A NATION RULED BY SELFISH BASTARDS.
ONCE AGAIN, HOW BADLY DID T'CHALLA'S FATHER BEAT YOU, BROTHER? HOW MUCH HUMILIATION DID YOU SUFFER AT HIS HANDS? IS THAT WHY YOU WERE FIRED FROM YOUR POSITION IN THE GOVERNMENT? IS THAT WHY YOU LIVE IN THE MIDDLE OF NOWHERE FIGHTING MINDLESS BULLS?
GOD, YOU'RE BEAUTIFUL.
REMEMBER WHAT HAPPENED TO YOUR FATHER? LET ME PROTECT YOU, BEAUTIFUL. BE MINE AND I'LL PROTECT YOU FROM THOSE BAD MEN.
THIEVES AND BEGGARS. NOTHING WORSE.
MAKE SURE THE NATIVES DON'T RIP US OFF LIKE THEY DID THE TRUCKS.

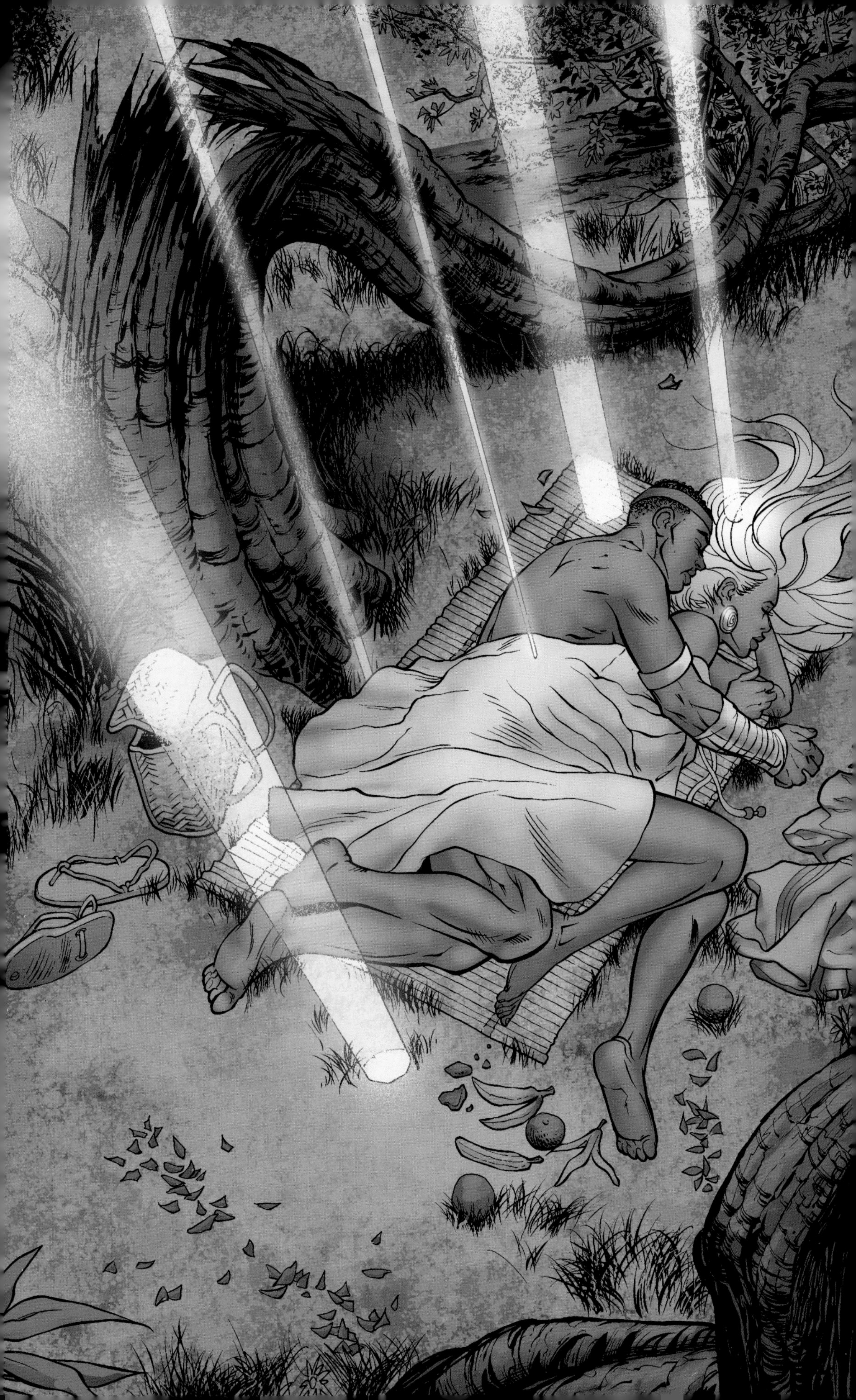

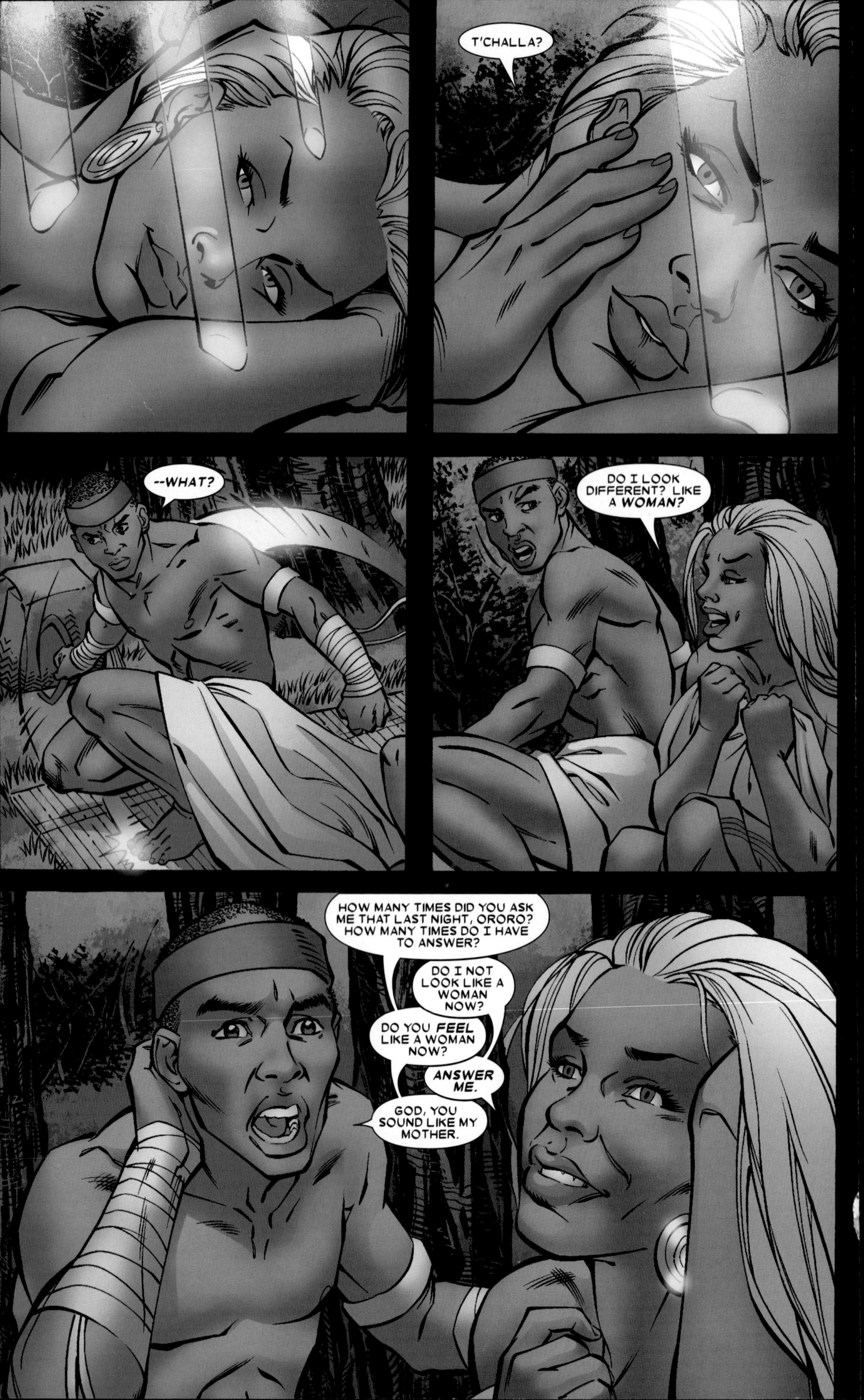
T'CHALLA?
--WHAT?
DO I LOOK DIFFERENT? LIKE A *WOMAN?*
HOW MANY TIMES DID YOU ASK ME THAT LAST NIGHT, ORORO? HOW MANY TIMES DO I HAVE TO ANSWER?
DO I NOT LOOK LIKE A WOMAN NOW?
DO YOU *FEEL* LIKE A WOMAN NOW?
ANSWER ME.
GOD, YOU SOUND LIKE MY MOTHER.

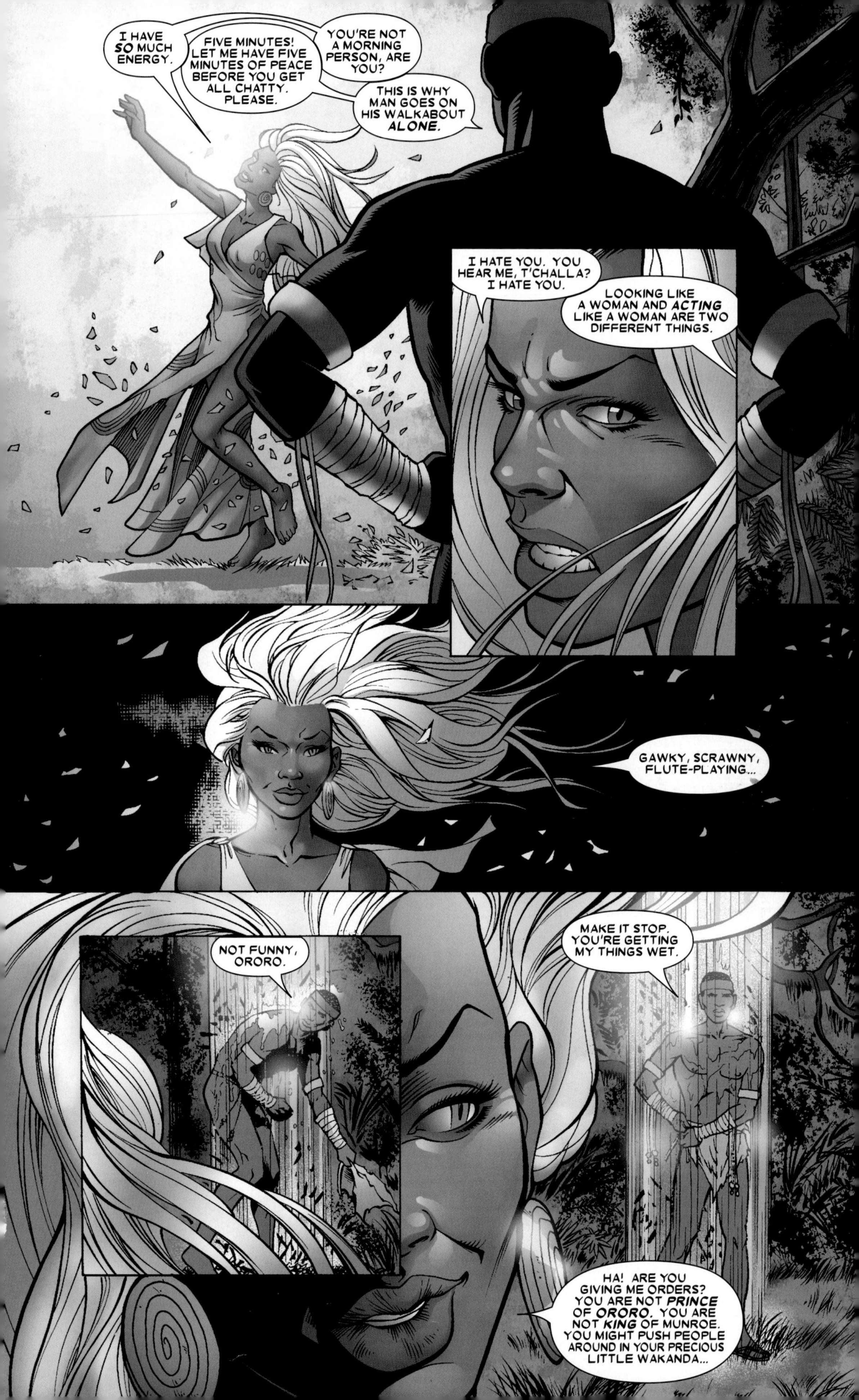
I HAVE SO MUCH ENERGY.
FIVE MINUTES! LET ME HAVE FIVE MINUTES OF PEACE BEFORE YOU GET ALL CHATTY. PLEASE.
YOU'RE NOT A MORNING PERSON, ARE YOU?
THIS IS WHY MAN GOES ON HIS WALKABOUT ALONE.
I HATE YOU. YOU HEAR ME, T'CHALLA? I HATE YOU.
LOOKING LIKE A WOMAN AND ACTING LIKE A WOMAN ARE TWO DIFFERENT THINGS.
GAWKY, SCRAWNY, FLUTE-PLAYING...
NOT FUNNY, ORORO.
MAKE IT STOP. YOU'RE GETTING MY THINGS WET.
HA! ARE YOU GIVING ME ORDERS? YOU ARE NOT PRINCE OF ORORO. YOU ARE NOT KING OF MUNROE. YOU MIGHT PUSH PEOPLE AROUND IN YOUR PRECIOUS LITTLE WAKANDA...

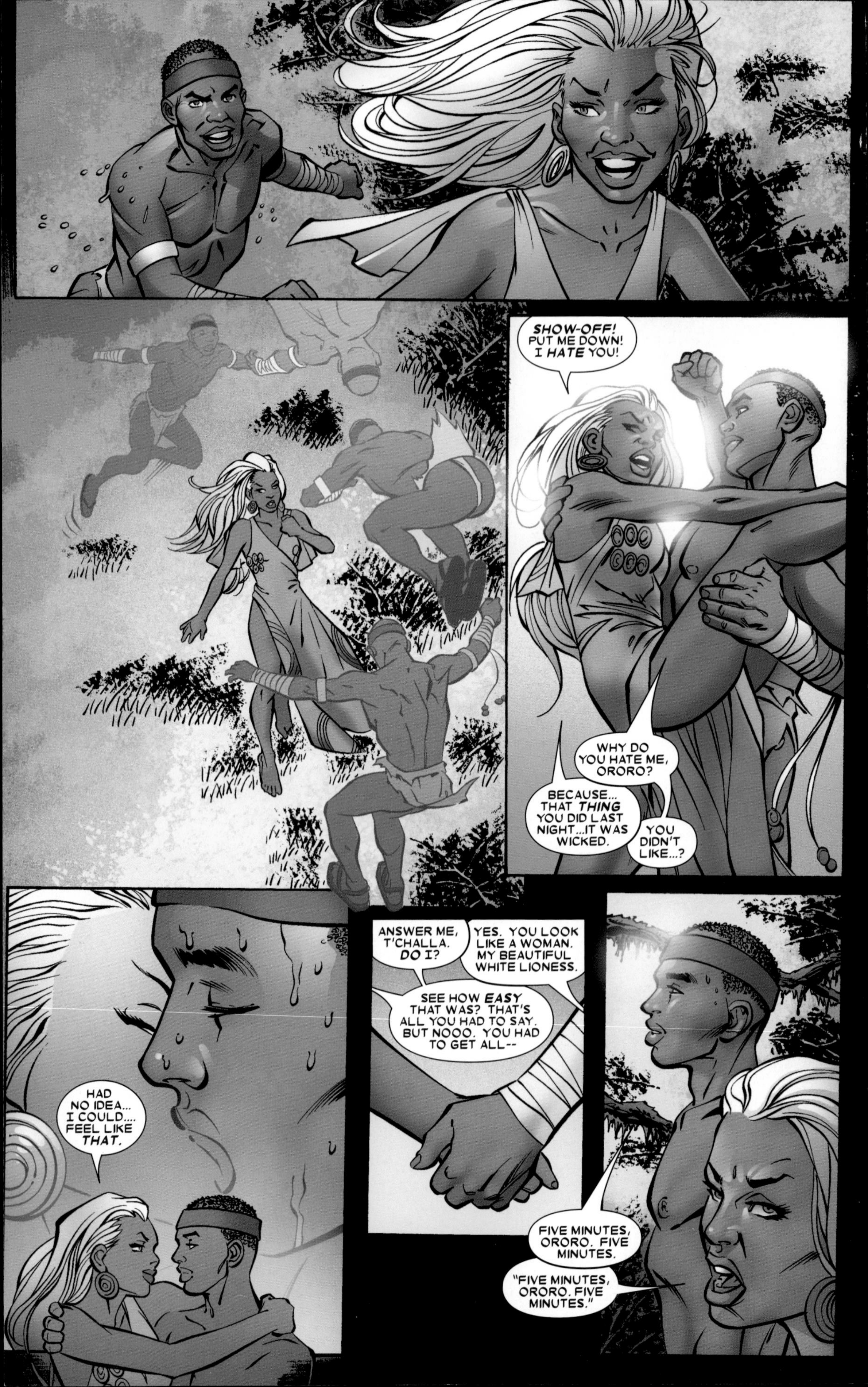

SHOW-OFF! PUT ME DOWN! I *HATE* YOU!
WHY DO YOU HATE ME, ORORO?
BECAUSE... THAT *THING* YOU DID LAST NIGHT...IT WAS WICKED.
YOU DIDN'T LIKE...?
HAD NO IDEA... I COULD.... FEEL LIKE *THAT.*
ANSWER ME, T'CHALLA. *DO* I?
YES. YOU LOOK LIKE A WOMAN. MY BEAUTIFUL WHITE LIONESS.
SEE HOW *EASY* THAT WAS? THAT'S ALL YOU HAD TO SAY. BUT NOOO. YOU HAD TO GET ALL--
FIVE MINUTES, ORORO. FIVE MINUTES.
"FIVE MINUTES, ORORO. FIVE MINUTES."

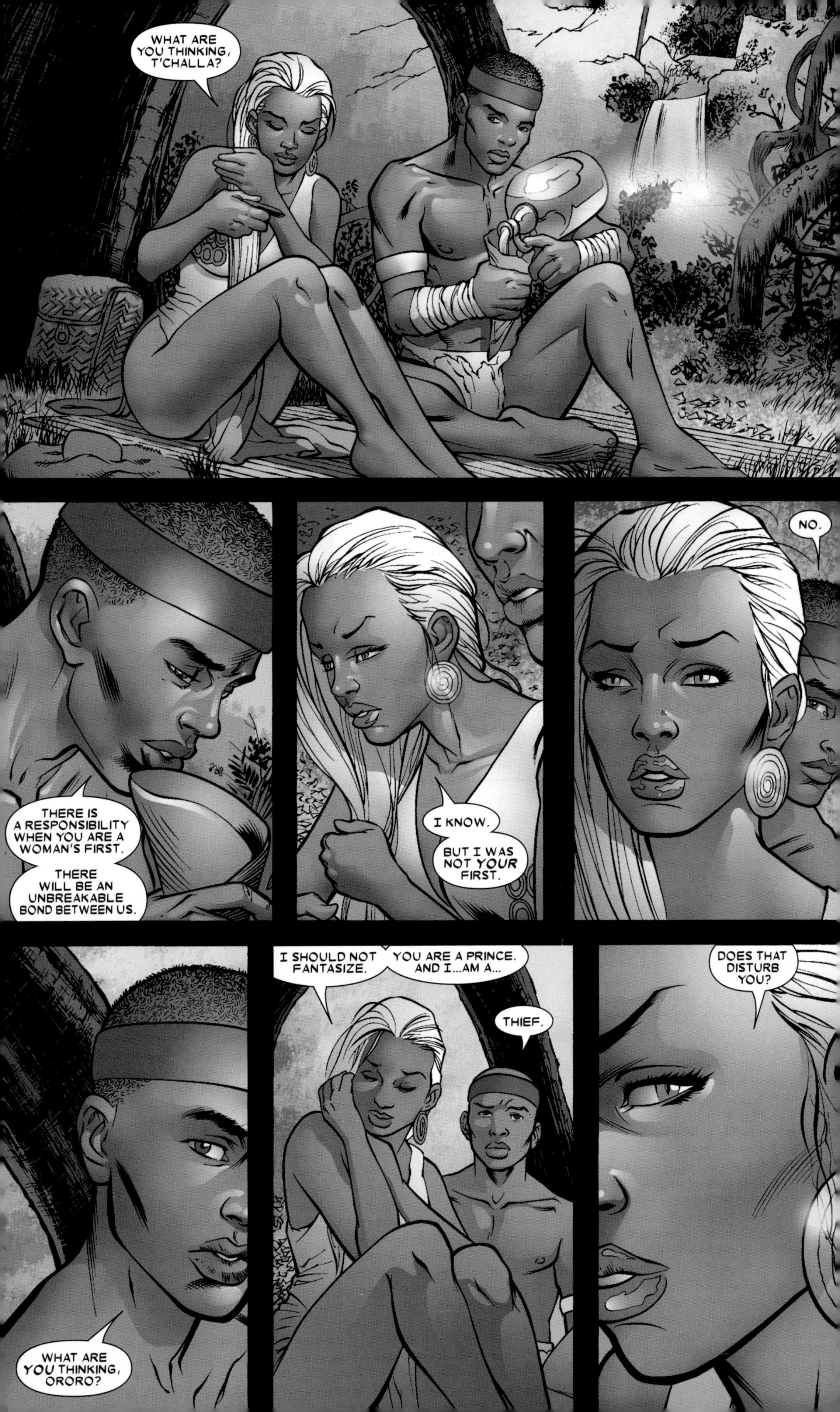
WHAT ARE YOU THINKING, T'CHALLA?
THERE IS A RESPONSIBILITY WHEN YOU ARE A WOMAN'S FIRST.
THERE WILL BE AN UNBREAKABLE BOND BETWEEN US.
I KNOW.
BUT I WAS NOT YOUR FIRST.
NO.
WHAT ARE YOU THINKING, ORORO?
I SHOULD NOT FANTASIZE.
YOU ARE A PRINCE. AND I...AM A...
THIEF.
DOES THAT DISTURB YOU?

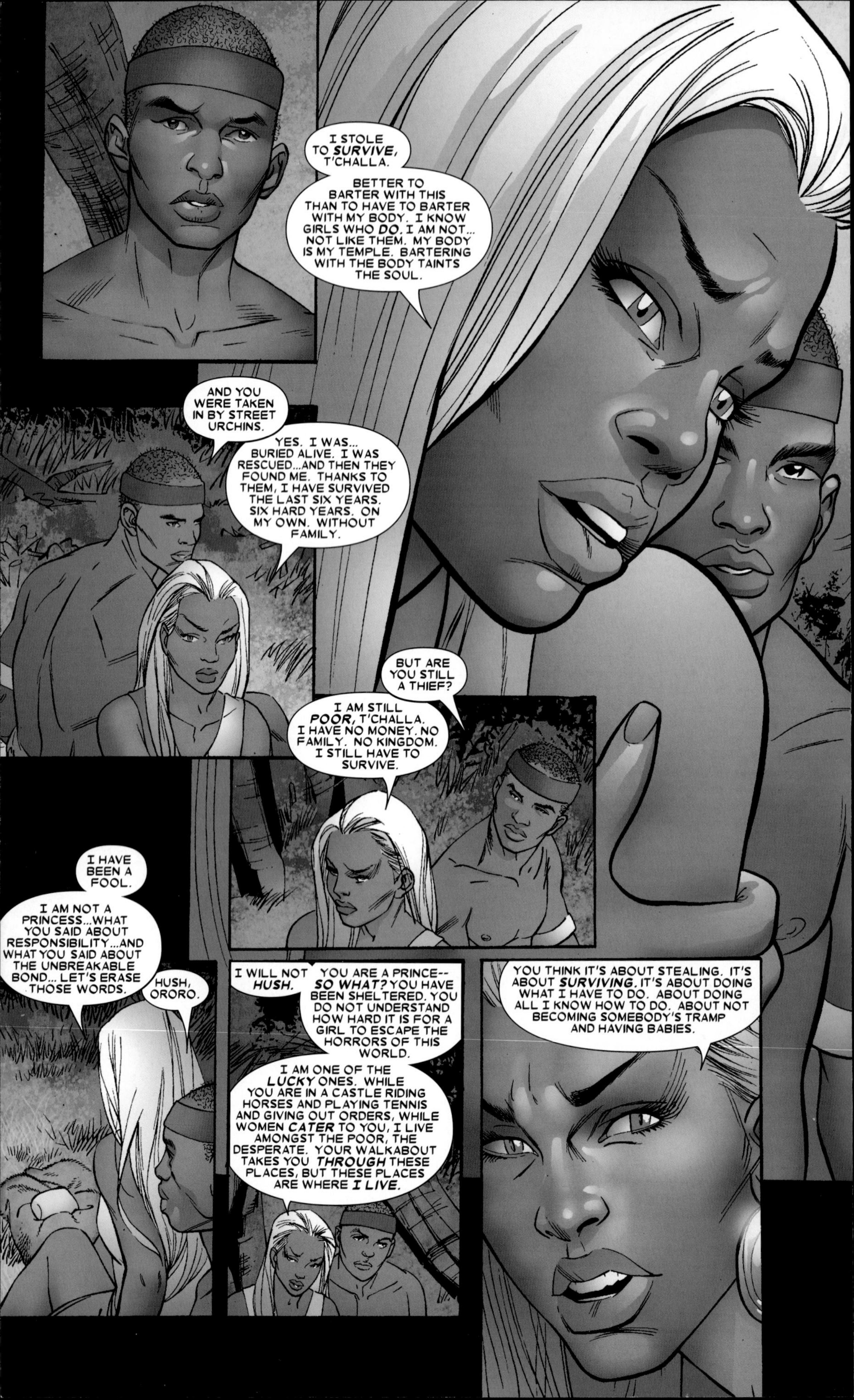
I STOLE TO SURVIVE, T'CHALLA.
BETTER TO BARTER WITH THIS THAN TO HAVE TO BARTER WITH MY BODY. I KNOW GIRLS WHO DO. I AM NOT... NOT LIKE THEM. MY BODY IS MY TEMPLE. BARTERING WITH THE BODY TAINTS THE SOUL.
AND YOU WERE TAKEN IN BY STREET URCHINS.
YES. I WAS... BURIED ALIVE. I WAS RESCUED...AND THEN THEY FOUND ME. THANKS TO THEM, I HAVE SURVIVED THE LAST SIX YEARS. SIX HARD YEARS. ON MY OWN. WITHOUT FAMILY.
BUT ARE YOU STILL A THIEF?
I AM STILL POOR, T'CHALLA. I HAVE NO MONEY. NO FAMILY. NO KINGDOM. I STILL HAVE TO SURVIVE.
I HAVE BEEN A FOOL.
I AM NOT A PRINCESS...WHAT YOU SAID ABOUT RESPONSIBILITY...AND WHAT YOU SAID ABOUT THE UNBREAKABLE BOND... LET'S ERASE THOSE WORDS.
HUSH, ORORO.
I WILL NOT HUSH.
YOU ARE A PRINCE-- SO WHAT? YOU HAVE BEEN SHELTERED. YOU DO NOT UNDERSTAND HOW HARD IT IS FOR A GIRL TO ESCAPE THE HORRORS OF THIS WORLD.
I AM ONE OF THE LUCKY ONES. WHILE YOU ARE IN A CASTLE RIDING HORSES AND PLAYING TENNIS AND GIVING OUT ORDERS, WHILE WOMEN CATER TO YOU, I LIVE AMONGST THE POOR, THE DESPERATE. YOUR WALKABOUT TAKES YOU THROUGH THESE PLACES, BUT THESE PLACES ARE WHERE I LIVE.
YOU THINK IT'S ABOUT STEALING. IT'S ABOUT SURVIVING. IT'S ABOUT DOING WHAT I HAVE TO DO. ABOUT DOING ALL I KNOW HOW TO DO. ABOUT NOT BECOMING SOMEBODY'S TRAMP AND HAVING BABIES.

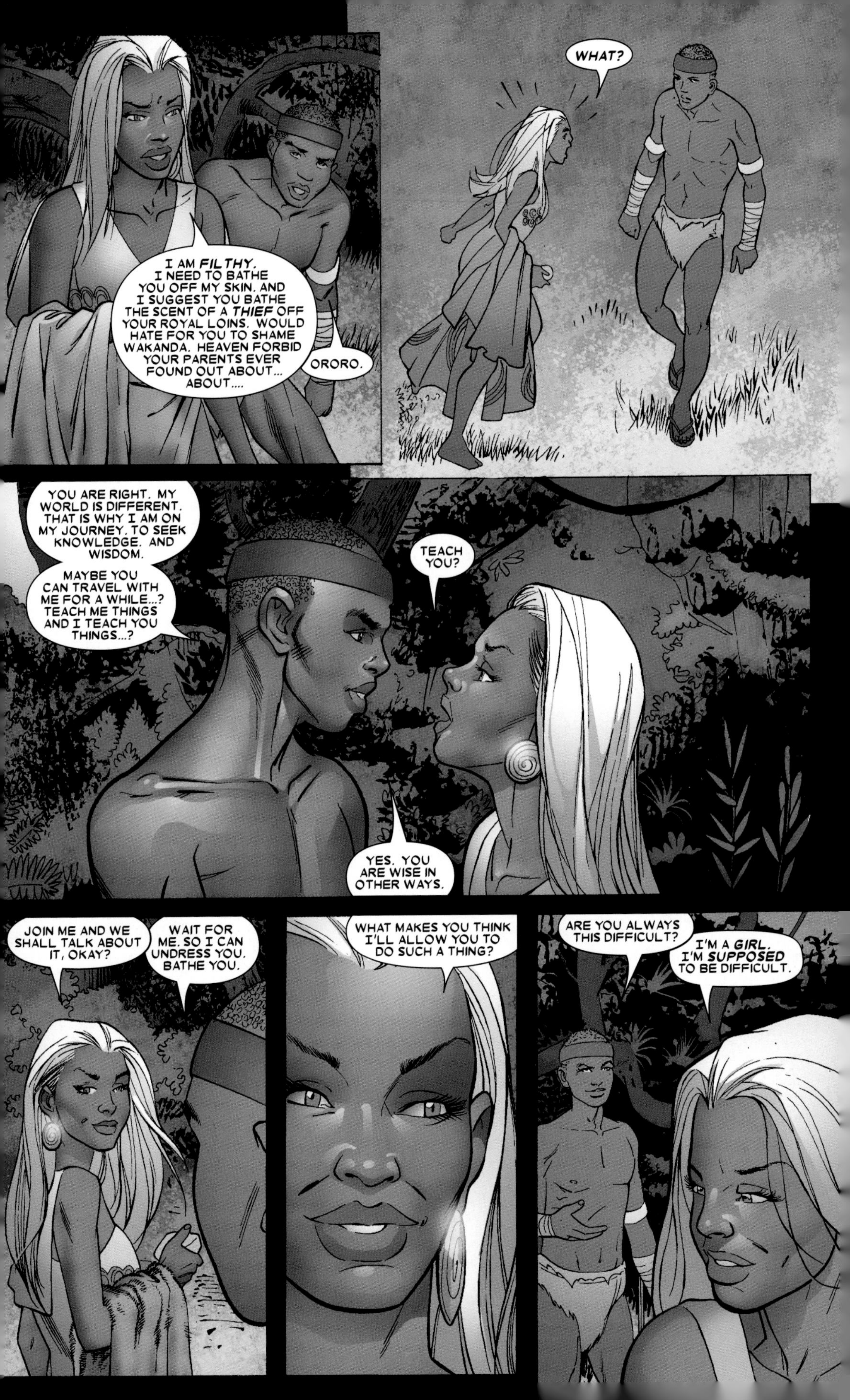
I AM FILTHY. I NEED TO BATHE YOU OFF MY SKIN. AND I SUGGEST YOU BATHE THE SCENT OF A THIEF OFF YOUR ROYAL LOINS. WOULD HATE FOR YOU TO SHAME WAKANDA. HEAVEN FORBID YOUR PARENTS EVER FOUND OUT ABOUT... ABOUT....
ORORO.
WHAT?
YOU ARE RIGHT. MY WORLD IS DIFFERENT. THAT IS WHY I AM ON MY JOURNEY. TO SEEK KNOWLEDGE. AND WISDOM.
MAYBE YOU CAN TRAVEL WITH ME FOR A WHILE...? TEACH ME THINGS AND I TEACH YOU THINGS...?
TEACH YOU?
YES. YOU ARE WISE IN OTHER WAYS.
JOIN ME AND WE SHALL TALK ABOUT IT, OKAY?
WAIT FOR ME. SO I CAN UNDRESS YOU. BATHE YOU.
WHAT MAKES YOU THINK I'LL ALLOW YOU TO DO SUCH A THING?
ARE YOU ALWAYS THIS DIFFICULT?
I'M A GIRL. I'M SUPPOSED TO BE DIFFICULT.

AS THE SUN RISES ON A NEW DAY, INSIDE THIS MOMENT, SO MUCH HAPPINESS RESIDES WITHIN ME. I WANT TO SCREAM, TELL THE WORLD.

WANT MY EMOTIONS, NEED MY THOUGHTS TO REACH HEAVEN, LET MY MOTHER KNOW I AM HAPPY, ASK HER TO WHISPER IN MY FATHER'S EAR, LET HIM KNOW THAT FOR THE FIRST TIME SINCE THAT DAY THEY LEFT ME, THEIR LITTLE GIRL IS OKAY. THAT SHE HAS SURVIVED AND SHE IS A WOMAN NOW. THAT SHE WILL SURVIVE ON THE WINGS OF THEIR LOVE.

I CRY. AND THERE IS NO RAIN. NO THUNDER. NO CHAOS IN THE SKIES. T'CHALLA WILL NOT KNOW.

I LOVE THIS MOMENT.

WARRIOR, I *HEAR* YOU COMING UP BEHIND ME.

MAYBE, IF YOU ARE NICE TO ME, I WILL ASK THE GODS TO RAIN ON US. WE CAN TAKE A NICE SHOWER TOGETHER. WHAT DO YOU THINK ABOUT *THAT*, T'CHALLA?

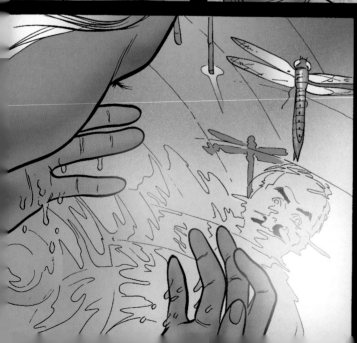

SFFFFFFT

NO...

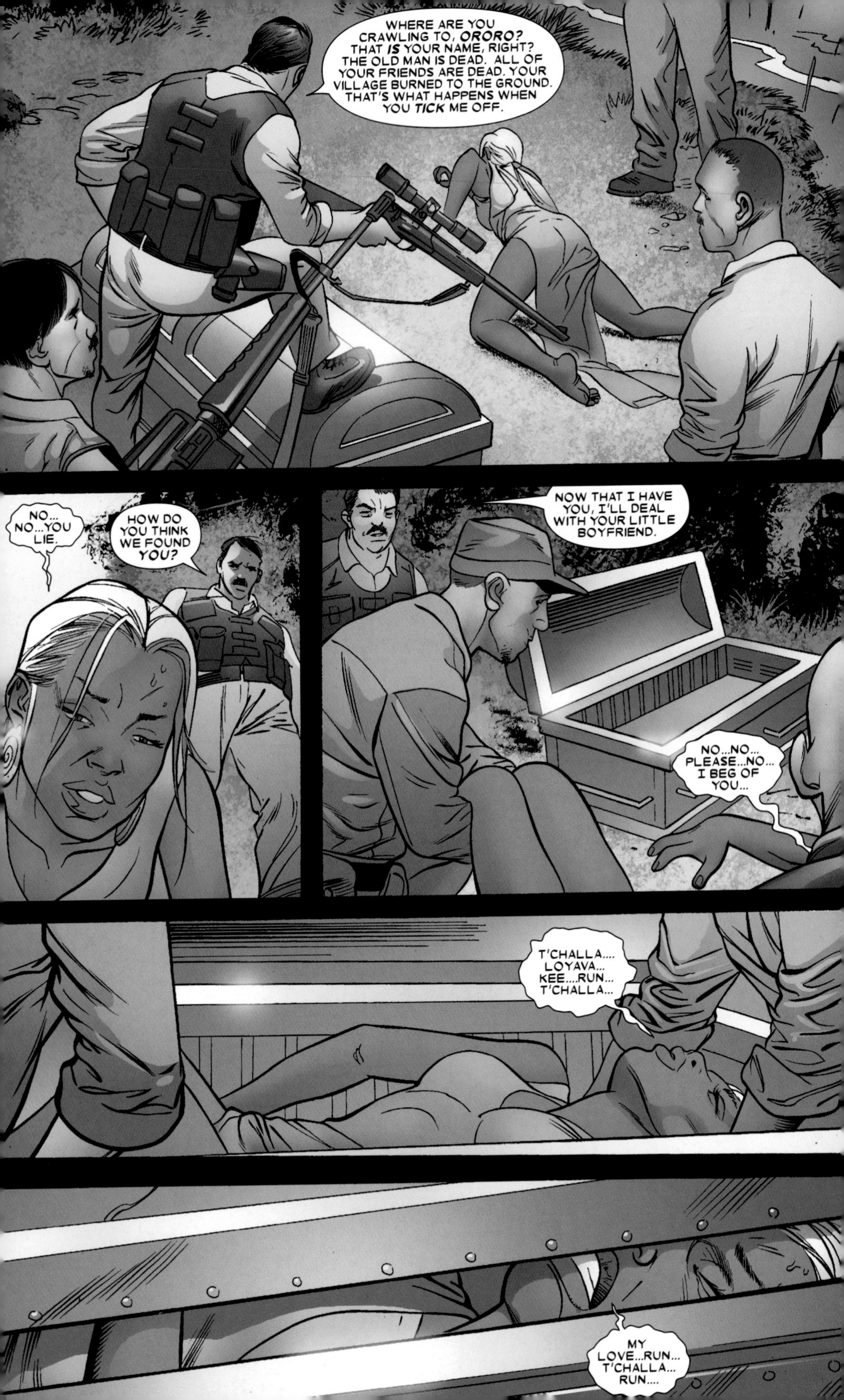
WHERE ARE YOU CRAWLING TO, ORORO? THAT IS YOUR NAME, RIGHT? THE OLD MAN IS DEAD. ALL OF YOUR FRIENDS ARE DEAD. YOUR VILLAGE BURNED TO THE GROUND. THAT'S WHAT HAPPENS WHEN YOU TICK ME OFF.
NO... NO...YOU LIE.
HOW DO YOU THINK WE FOUND YOU?
NOW THAT I HAVE YOU, I'LL DEAL WITH YOUR LITTLE BOYFRIEND.
NO...NO... PLEASE...NO... I BEG OF YOU...
T'CHALLA.... LOYAVA... KEE....RUN... T'CHALLA...
MY LOVE...RUN... T'CHALLA... RUN....

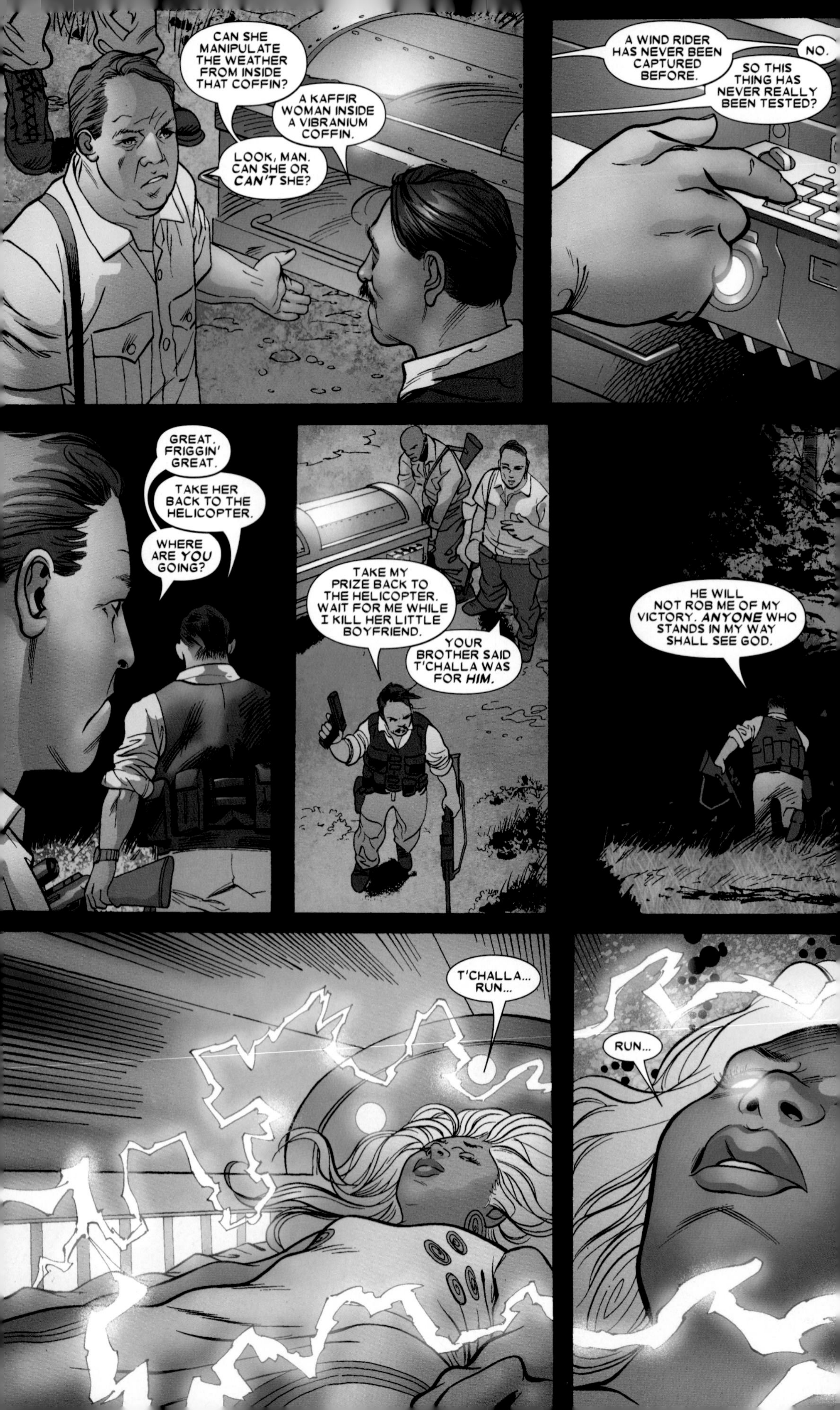
CAN SHE MANIPULATE THE WEATHER FROM INSIDE THAT COFFIN?
A KAFFIR WOMAN INSIDE A VIBRANIUM COFFIN.
LOOK, MAN. CAN SHE OR *CAN'T* SHE?
A WIND RIDER HAS NEVER BEEN CAPTURED BEFORE.
NO.
SO THIS THING HAS NEVER REALLY BEEN TESTED?
GREAT. FRIGGIN' GREAT.
TAKE HER BACK TO THE HELICOPTER.
WHERE ARE *YOU* GOING?
TAKE MY PRIZE BACK TO THE HELICOPTER. WAIT FOR ME WHILE I KILL HER LITTLE BOYFRIEND.
YOUR BROTHER SAID T'CHALLA WAS FOR *HIM.*
HE WILL NOT ROB ME OF MY VICTORY. *ANYONE* WHO STANDS IN MY WAY SHALL SEE GOD.
T'CHALLA... RUN...
RUN...

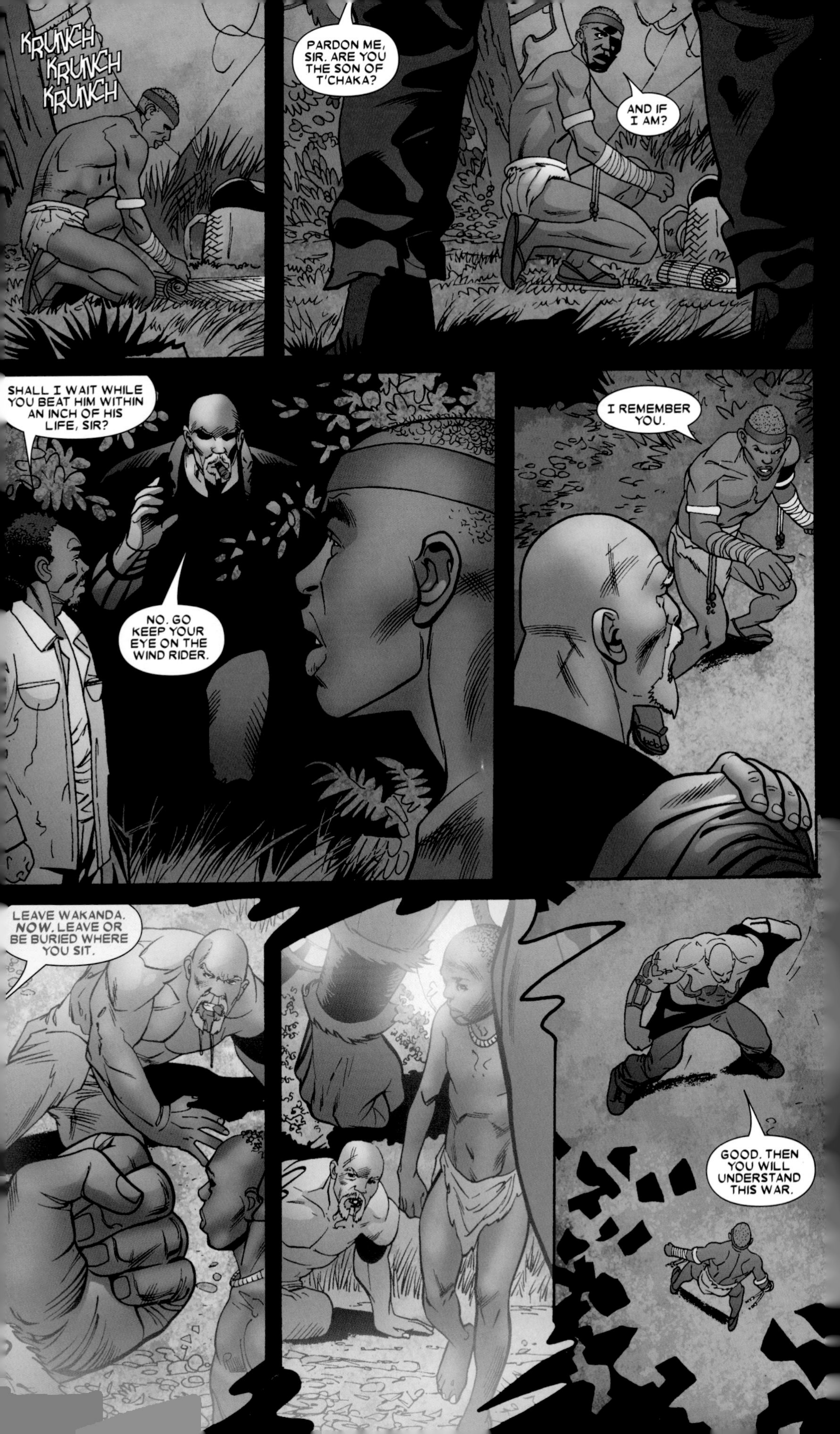
KRUNCH
KRUNCH
KRUNCH
PARDON ME, SIR. ARE YOU THE SON OF T'CHAKA?
AND IF I AM?
SHALL I WAIT WHILE YOU BEAT HIM WITHIN AN INCH OF HIS LIFE, SIR?
NO. GO KEEP YOUR EYE ON THE WIND RIDER.
I REMEMBER YOU.
LEAVE WAKANDA. NOW. LEAVE OR BE BURIED WHERE YOU SIT.
GOOD. THEN YOU WILL UNDERSTAND THIS WAR.

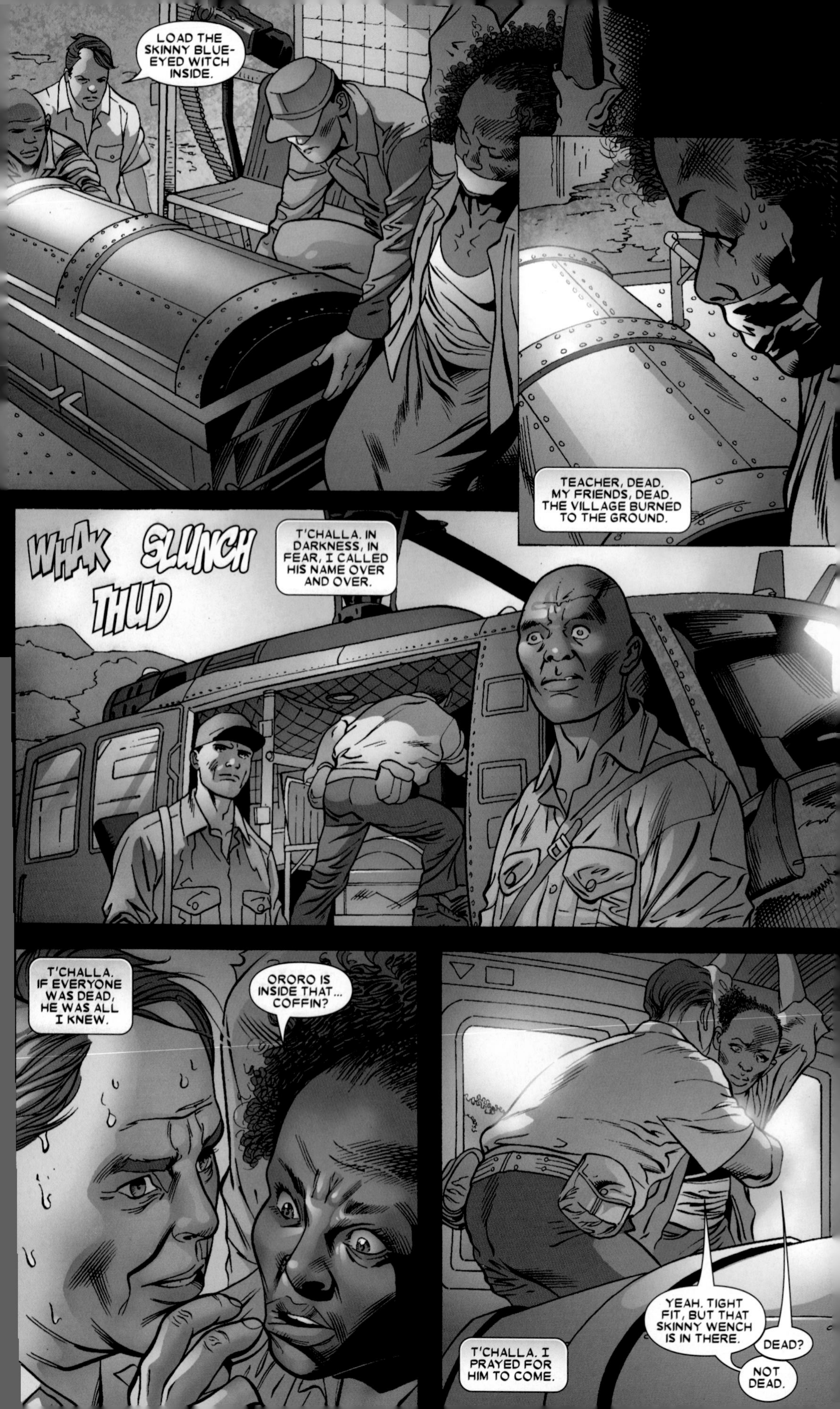
LOAD THE SKINNY BLUE-EYED WITCH INSIDE.
TEACHER, DEAD. MY FRIENDS, DEAD. THE VILLAGE BURNED TO THE GROUND.
WHAK
SLUNCH
THUD
T'CHALLA. IN DARKNESS, IN FEAR, I CALLED HIS NAME OVER AND OVER.
T'CHALLA. IF EVERYONE WAS DEAD, HE WAS ALL I KNEW.
ORORO IS INSIDE THAT... COFFIN?
YEAH. TIGHT FIT, BUT THAT SKINNY WENCH IS IN THERE.
DEAD?
NOT DEAD.
T'CHALLA. I PRAYED FOR HIM TO COME.

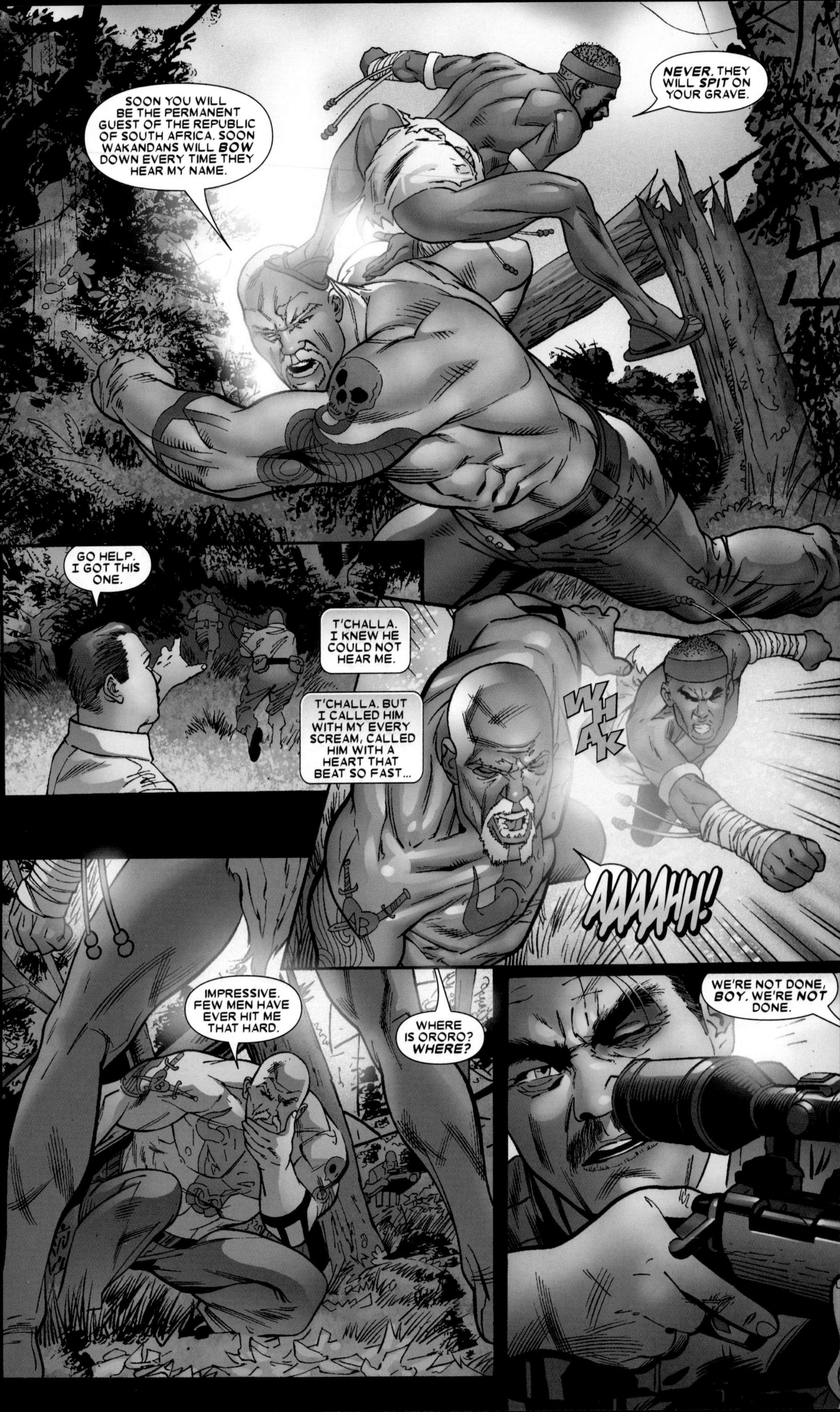
SOON YOU WILL BE THE PERMANENT GUEST OF THE REPUBLIC OF SOUTH AFRICA. SOON WAKANDANS WILL BOW DOWN EVERY TIME THEY HEAR MY NAME.
NEVER. THEY WILL SPIT ON YOUR GRAVE.
GO HELP. I GOT THIS ONE.
T'CHALLA. I KNEW HE COULD NOT HEAR ME.
T'CHALLA. BUT I CALLED HIM WITH MY EVERY SCREAM, CALLED HIM WITH A HEART THAT BEAT SO FAST...
WHAK
AAAAHH!
IMPRESSIVE. FEW MEN HAVE EVER HIT ME THAT HARD.
WHERE IS ORORO? WHERE?
WE'RE NOT DONE, BOY. WE'RE NOT DONE.

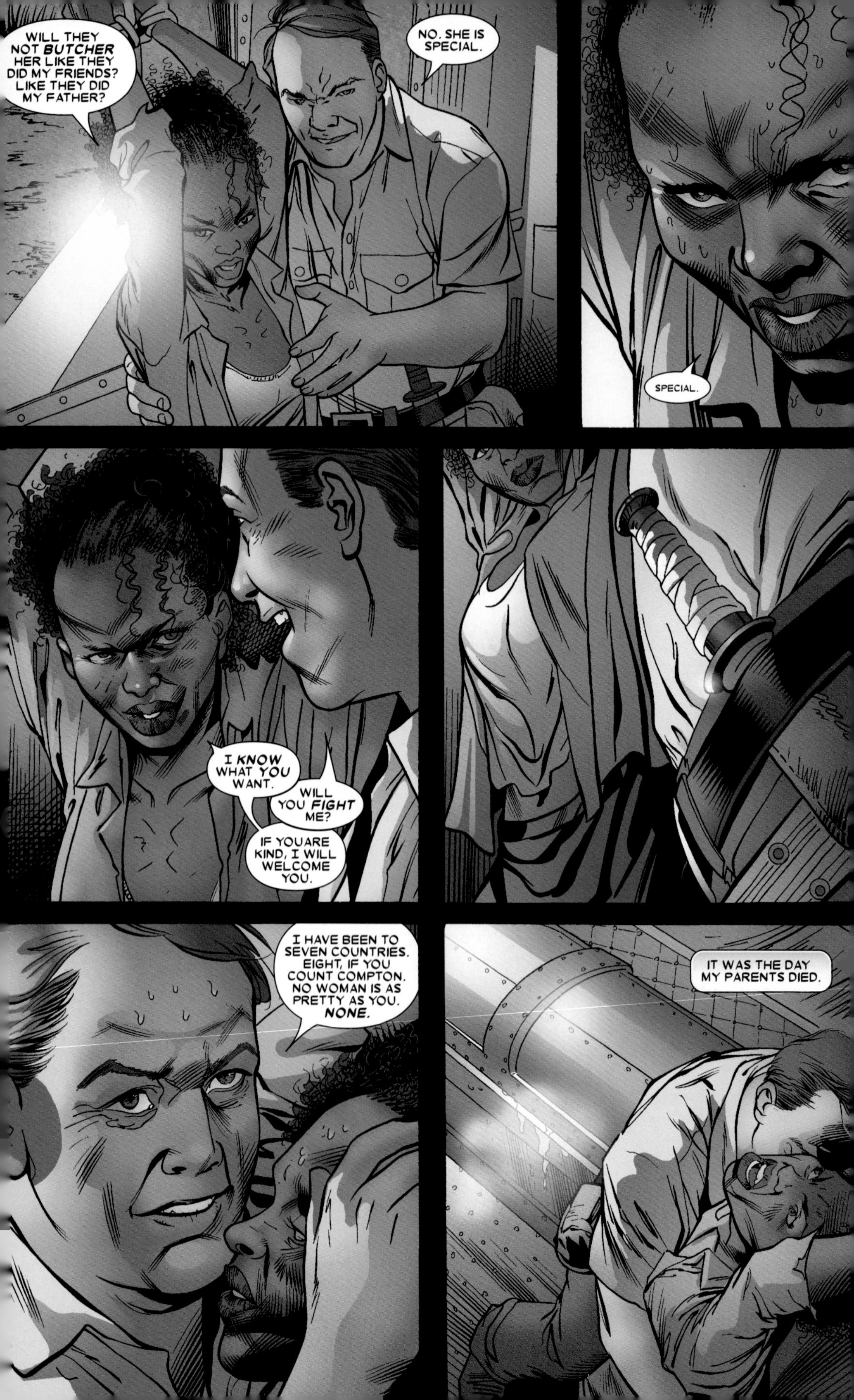

WILL THEY NOT *BUTCHER* HER LIKE THEY DID MY FRIENDS? LIKE THEY DID MY FATHER?
NO. SHE IS SPECIAL.
SPECIAL.
I *KNOW* WHAT *YOU* WANT.
WILL YOU *FIGHT* ME?
IF YOUARE KIND, I WILL WELCOME YOU.
I HAVE BEEN TO SEVEN COUNTRIES. EIGHT, IF YOU COUNT COMPTON. NO WOMAN IS AS PRETTY AS YOU. *NONE.*
IT WAS THE DAY MY PARENTS DIED.

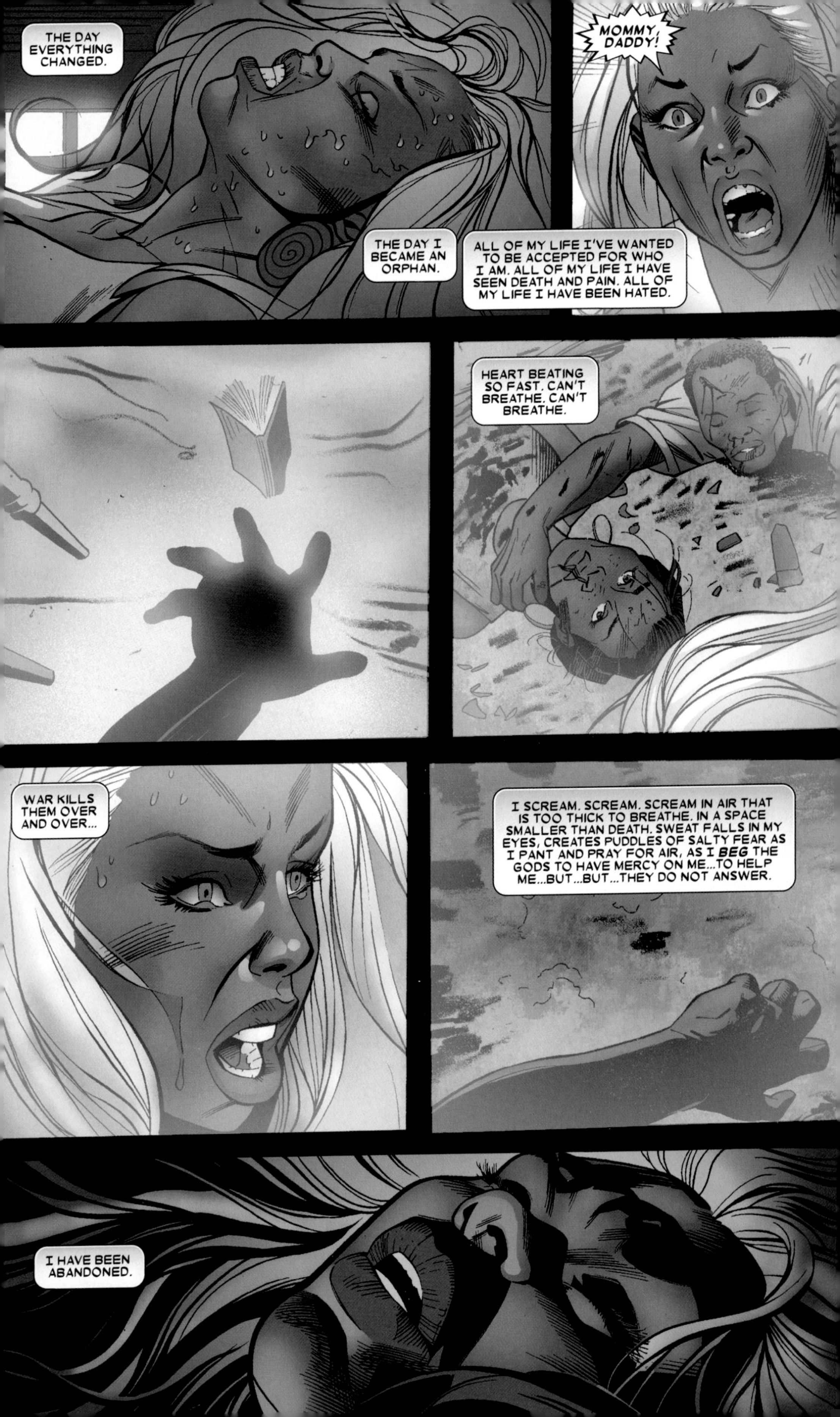
THE DAY EVERYTHING CHANGED.
MOMMY, DADDY!
THE DAY I BECAME AN ORPHAN.
ALL OF MY LIFE I'VE WANTED TO BE ACCEPTED FOR WHO I AM. ALL OF MY LIFE I HAVE SEEN DEATH AND PAIN. ALL OF MY LIFE I HAVE BEEN HATED.
HEART BEATING SO FAST. CAN'T BREATHE. CAN'T BREATHE.
WAR KILLS THEM OVER AND OVER...
I SCREAM. SCREAM. SCREAM IN AIR THAT IS TOO THICK TO BREATHE. IN A SPACE SMALLER THAN DEATH. SWEAT FALLS IN MY EYES, CREATES PUDDLES OF SALTY FEAR AS I PANT AND PRAY FOR AIR, AS I *BEG* THE GODS TO HAVE MERCY ON ME...TO HELP ME...BUT...BUT...THEY DO NOT ANSWER.
I HAVE BEEN ABANDONED.

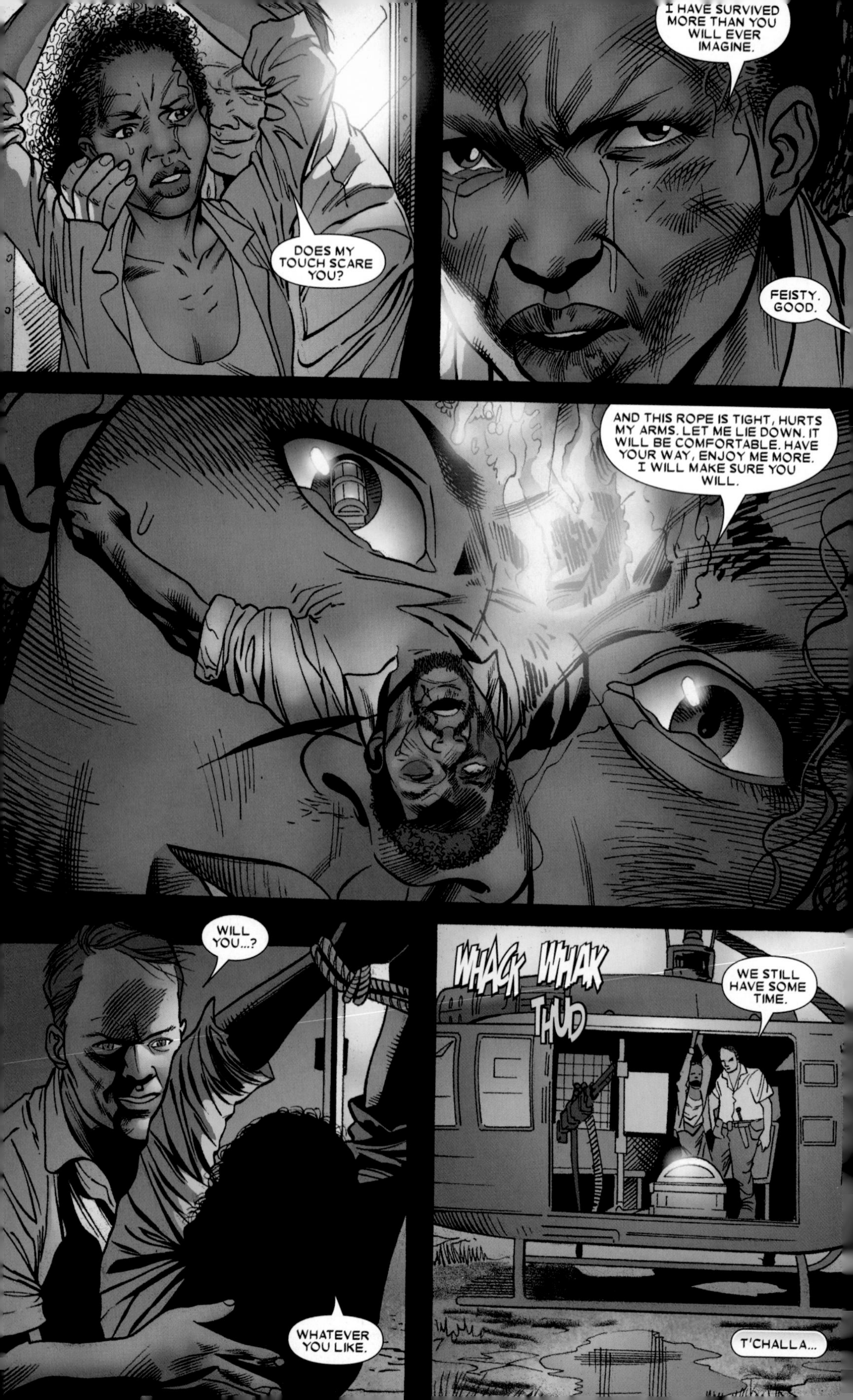
DOES MY TOUCH SCARE YOU?
I HAVE SURVIVED MORE THAN YOU WILL EVER IMAGINE.
FEISTY. GOOD.
AND THIS ROPE IS TIGHT, HURTS MY ARMS. LET ME LIE DOWN. IT WILL BE COMFORTABLE. HAVE YOUR WAY, ENJOY ME MORE. I WILL MAKE SURE YOU WILL.
WILL YOU...?
WHATEVER YOU LIKE.
WHACK WHAK
THUD
WE STILL HAVE SOME TIME.
T'CHALLA...

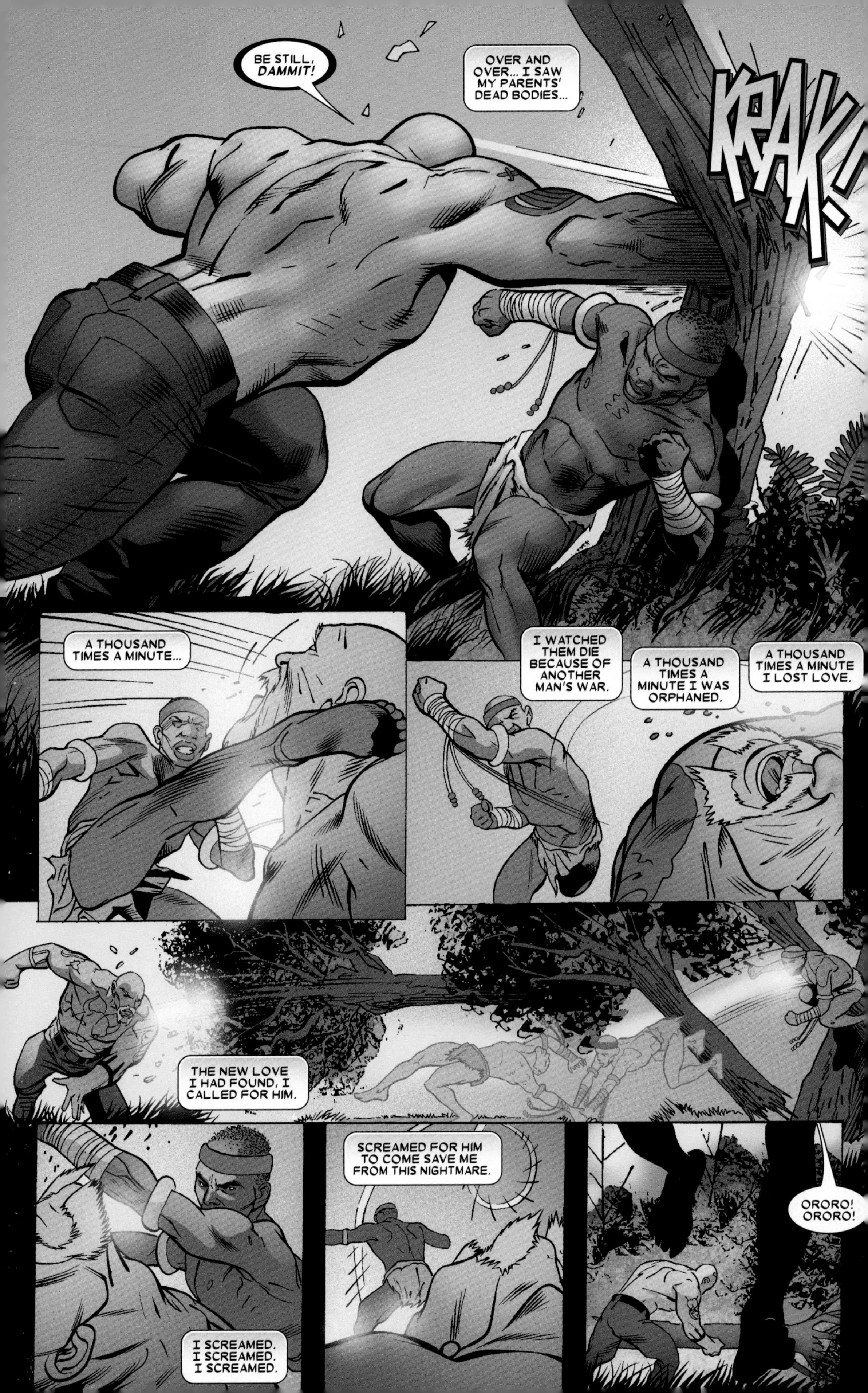
BE STILL, DAMMIT!
OVER AND OVER... I SAW MY PARENTS' DEAD BODIES...
KRAK!!
A THOUSAND TIMES A MINUTE...
I WATCHED THEM DIE BECAUSE OF ANOTHER MAN'S WAR.
A THOUSAND TIMES A MINUTE I WAS ORPHANED.
A THOUSAND TIMES A MINUTE I LOST LOVE.
THE NEW LOVE I HAD FOUND, I CALLED FOR HIM.
I SCREAMED. I SCREAMED. I SCREAMED.
SCREAMED FOR HIM TO COME SAVE ME FROM THIS NIGHTMARE.
ORORO! ORORO!

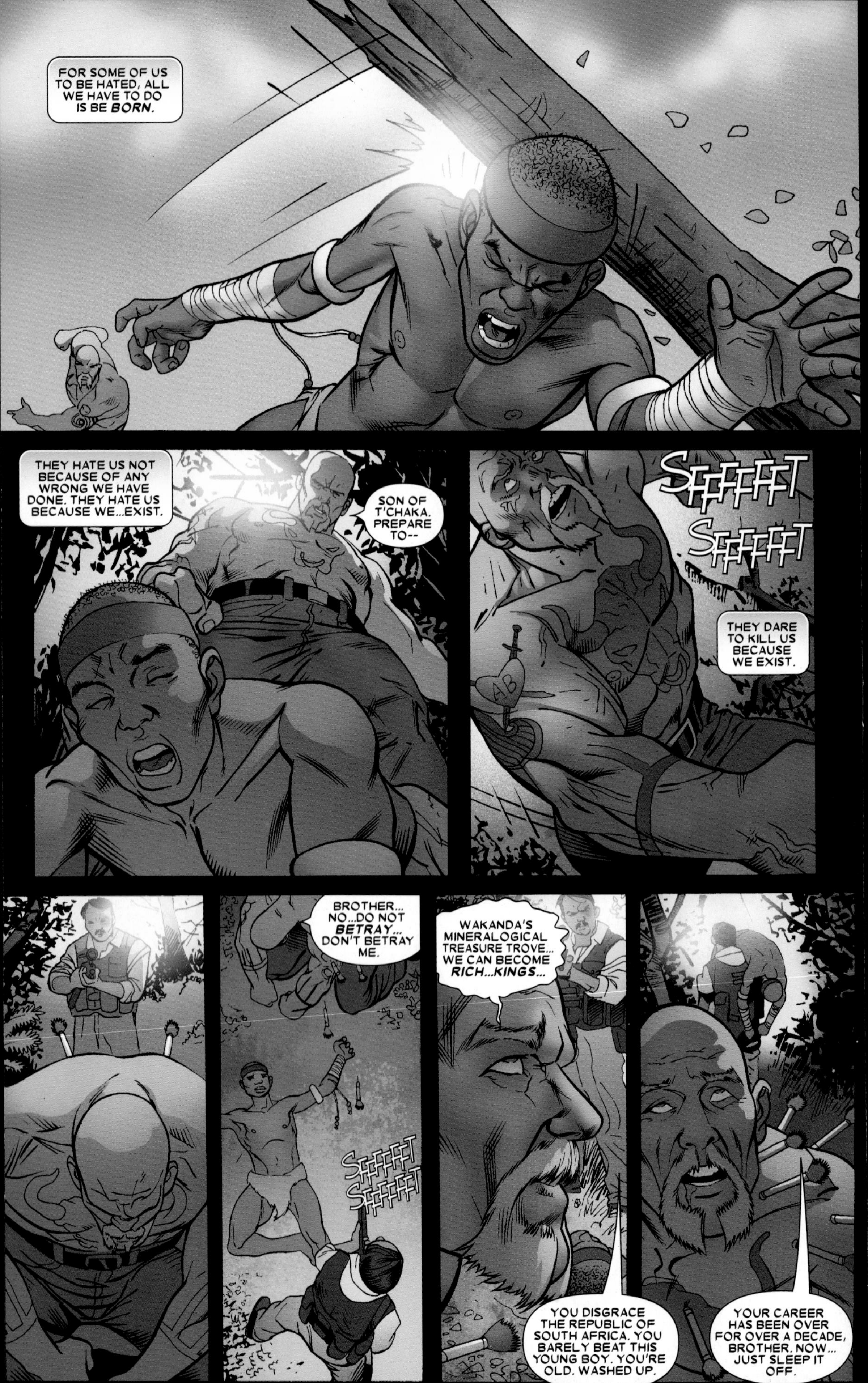
FOR SOME OF US TO BE HATED, ALL WE HAVE TO DO IS BE BORN.
THEY HATE US NOT BECAUSE OF ANY WRONG WE HAVE DONE. THEY HATE US BECAUSE WE...EXIST.
SON OF T'CHAKA. PREPARE TO--
SFFFFFFT
SFFFFFFT
THEY DARE TO KILL US BECAUSE WE EXIST.
BROTHER... NO...DO NOT BETRAY... DON'T BETRAY ME.
SFFFFFT
SFFFFFT
WAKANDA'S MINERALOGICAL TREASURE TROVE... WE CAN BECOME RICH...KINGS...
YOU DISGRACE THE REPUBLIC OF SOUTH AFRICA. YOU BARELY BEAT THIS YOUNG BOY. YOU'RE OLD. WASHED UP.
YOUR CAREER HAS BEEN OVER FOR OVER A DECADE, BROTHER. NOW... JUST SLEEP IT OFF.

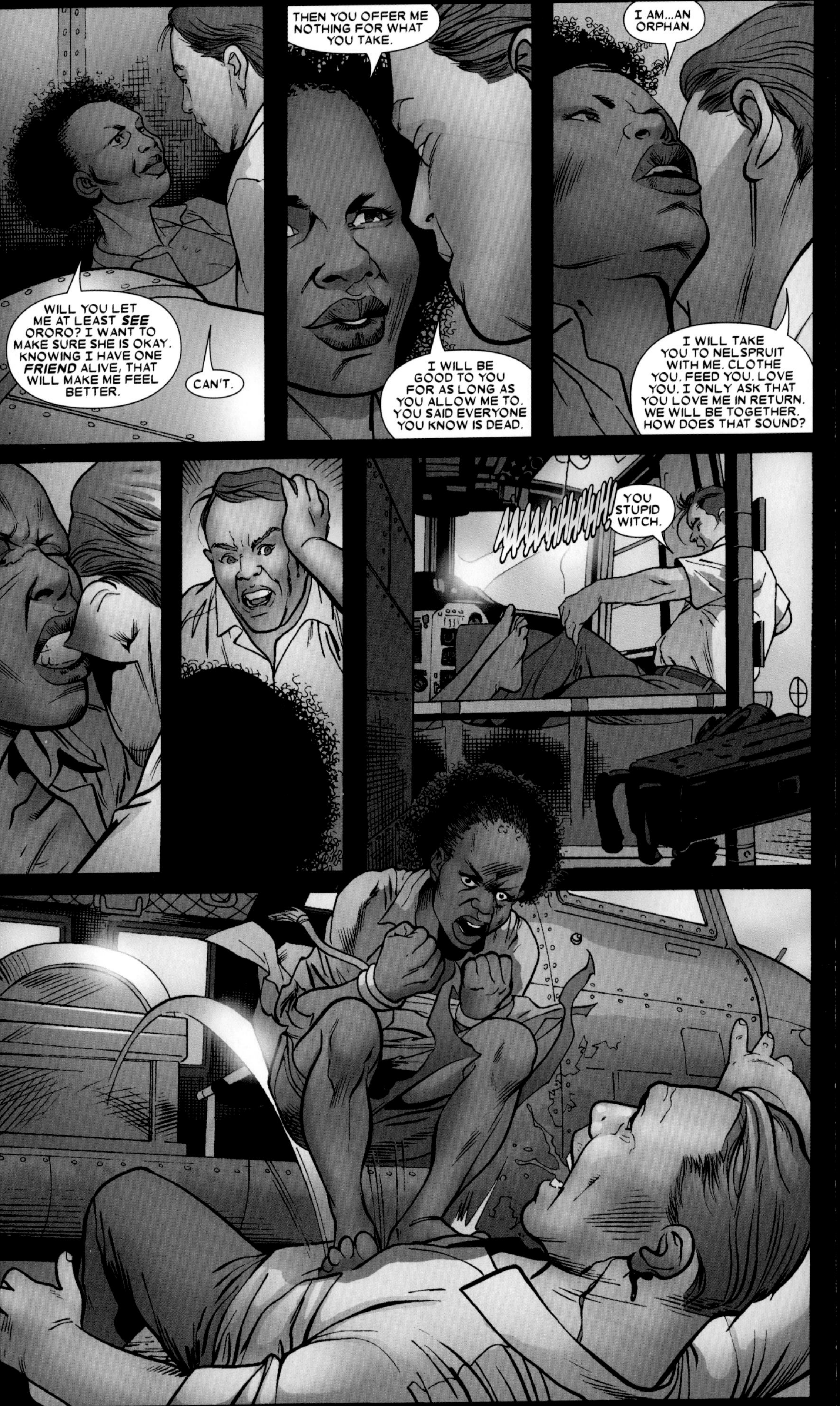
WILL YOU LET ME AT LEAST SEE ORORO? I WANT TO MAKE SURE SHE IS OKAY. KNOWING I HAVE ONE FRIEND ALIVE, THAT WILL MAKE ME FEEL BETTER.
CAN'T.
THEN YOU OFFER ME NOTHING FOR WHAT YOU TAKE.
I WILL BE GOOD TO YOU FOR AS LONG AS YOU ALLOW ME TO. YOU SAID EVERYONE YOU KNOW IS DEAD.
I AM...AN ORPHAN.
I WILL TAKE YOU TO NELSPRUIT WITH ME. CLOTHE YOU. FEED YOU. LOVE YOU. I ONLY ASK THAT YOU LOVE ME IN RETURN. WE WILL BE TOGETHER. HOW DOES THAT SOUND?
AAAAAHHHHH!
YOU STUPID WITCH.

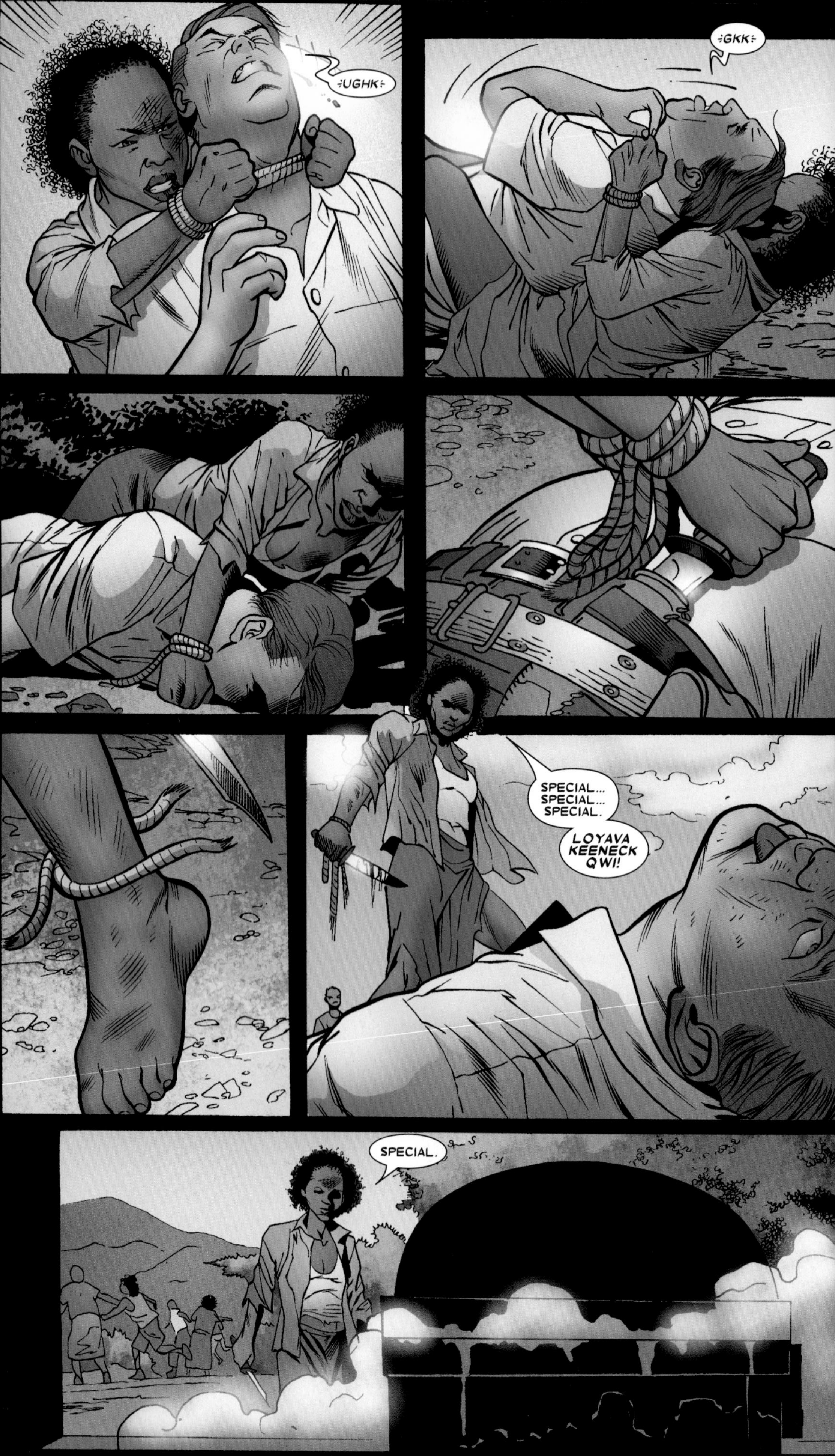
UGHK
GKK
SPECIAL... SPECIAL... SPECIAL.
LOYAVA KEENECK QWI!
SPECIAL.

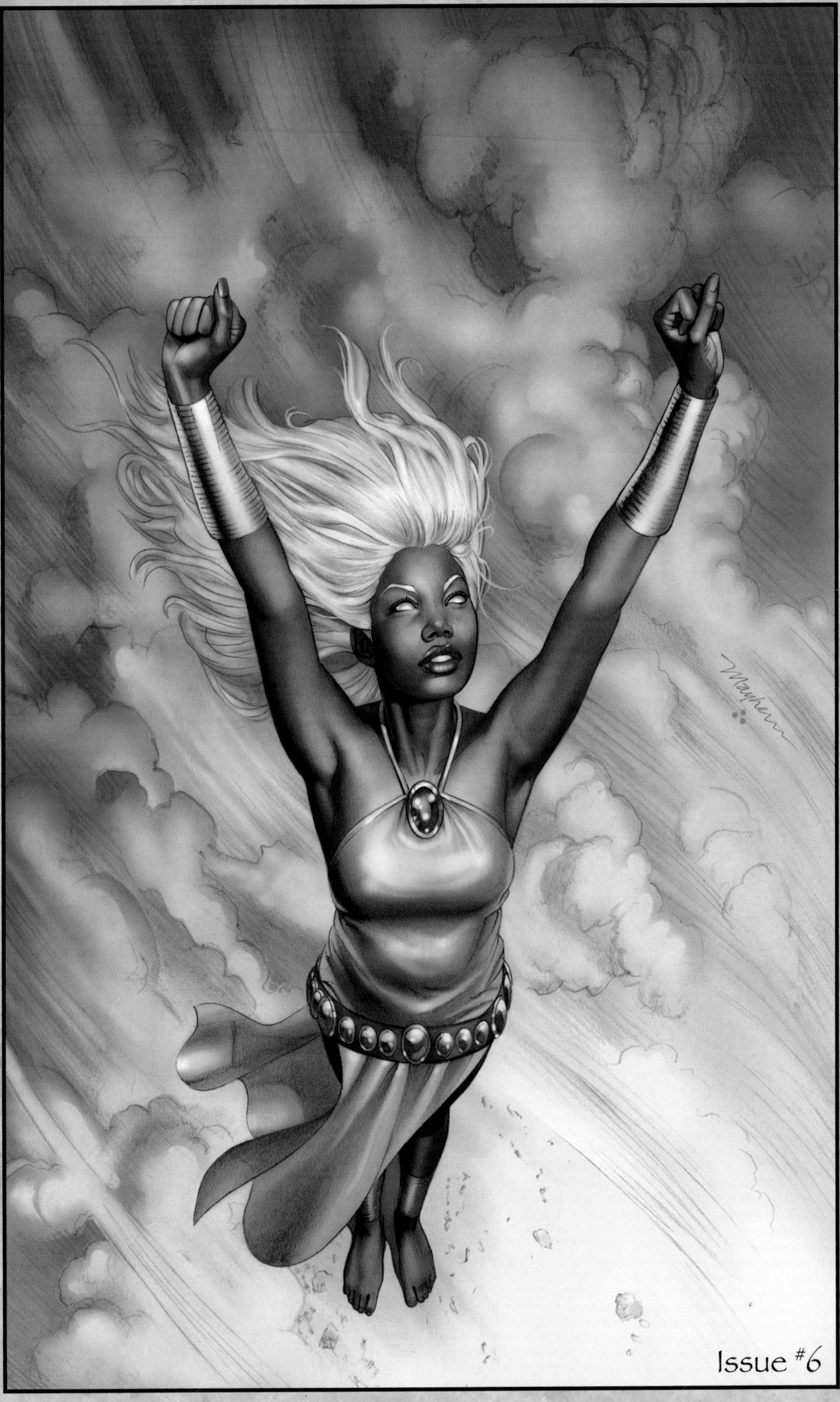
Issue #6

I WILL GET TO YOU. YOU WILL FEEL MY PAIN.

LIKE YOU, ORORO, I CAN OPEN *ANY* LOCK.

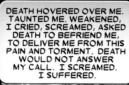

DEATH HOVERED OVER ME. TAUNTED ME. WEAKENED, I CRIED, SCREAMED, ASKED DEATH TO BEFRIEND ME, TO DELIVER ME FROM THIS PAIN AND TORMENT. DEATH WOULD NOT ANSWER MY CALL. I SCREAMED. I SUFFERED.

CLICK
WHRRRRR

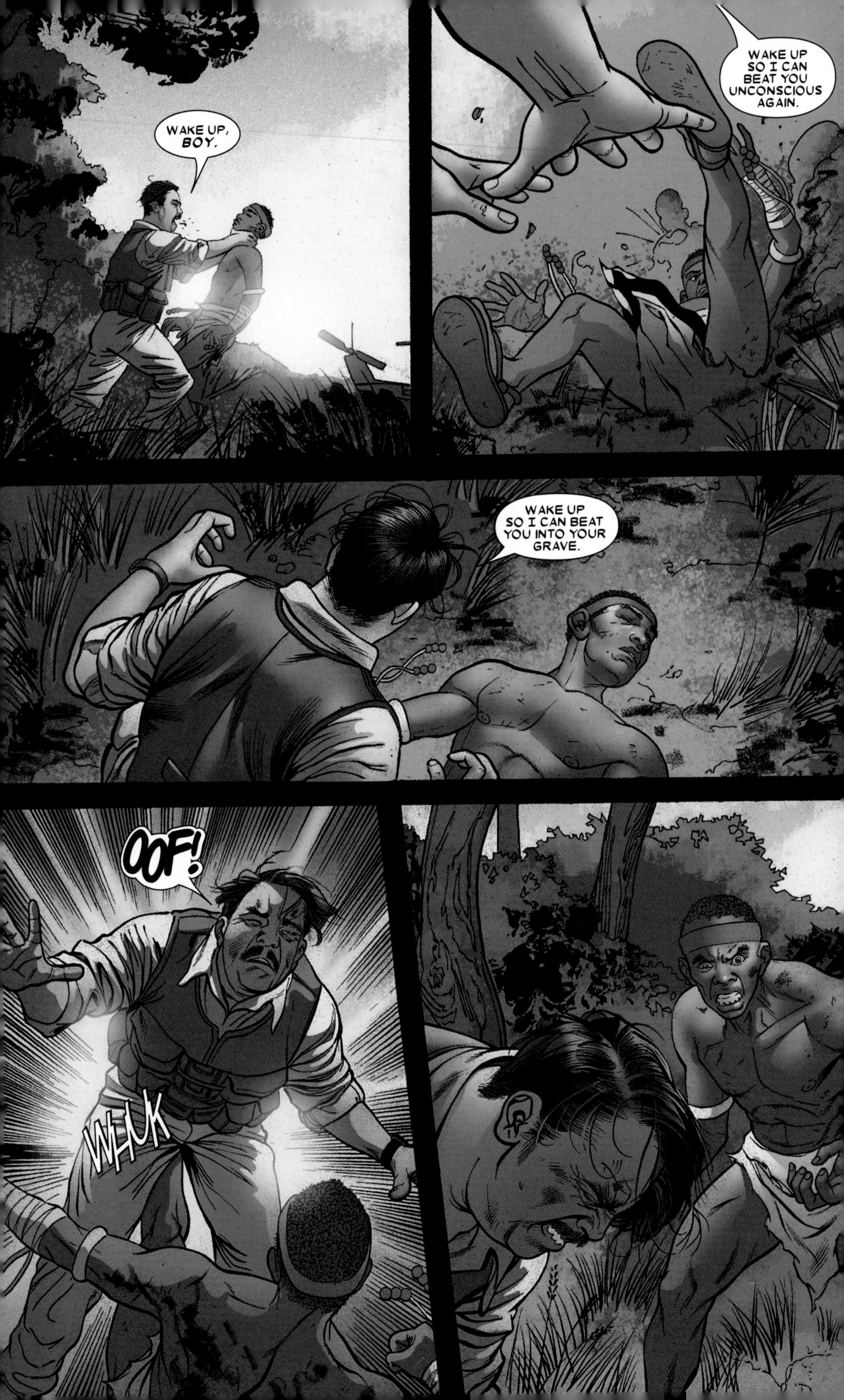
WAKE UP, BOY.
WAKE UP SO I CAN BEAT YOU UNCONSCIOUS AGAIN.
WAKE UP SO I CAN BEAT YOU INTO YOUR GRAVE.
OOF!
WHUK

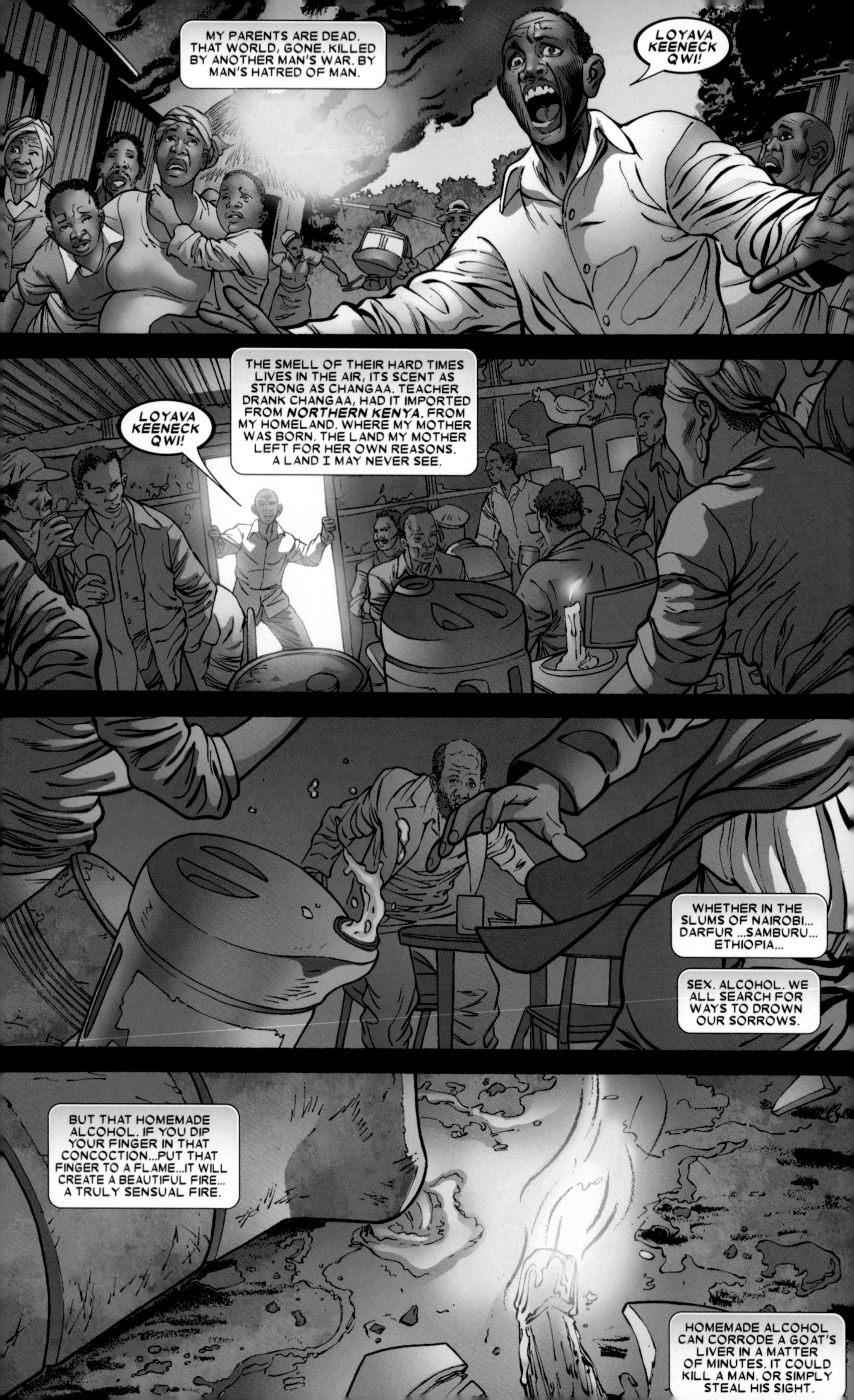
MY PARENTS ARE DEAD. THAT WORLD, GONE. KILLED BY ANOTHER MAN'S WAR. BY MAN'S HATRED OF MAN.
LOYAVA KEENECK QWI!
THE SMELL OF THEIR HARD TIMES LIVES IN THE AIR, ITS SCENT AS STRONG AS CHANGAA. TEACHER DRANK CHANGAA, HAD IT IMPORTED FROM NORTHERN KENYA. FROM MY HOMELAND. WHERE MY MOTHER WAS BORN. THE LAND MY MOTHER LEFT FOR HER OWN REASONS. A LAND I MAY NEVER SEE.
LOYAVA KEENECK QWI!
WHETHER IN THE SLUMS OF NAIROBI... DARFUR ...SAMBURU... ETHIOPIA...
SEX. ALCOHOL. WE ALL SEARCH FOR WAYS TO DROWN OUR SORROWS.
BUT THAT HOMEMADE ALCOHOL. IF YOU DIP YOUR FINGER IN THAT CONCOCTION...PUT THAT FINGER TO A FLAME...IT WILL CREATE A BEAUTIFUL FIRE... A TRULY SENSUAL FIRE.
HOMEMADE ALCOHOL CAN CORRODE A GOAT'S LIVER IN A MATTER OF MINUTES. IT COULD KILL A MAN. OR SIMPLY STEAL HIS SIGHT.

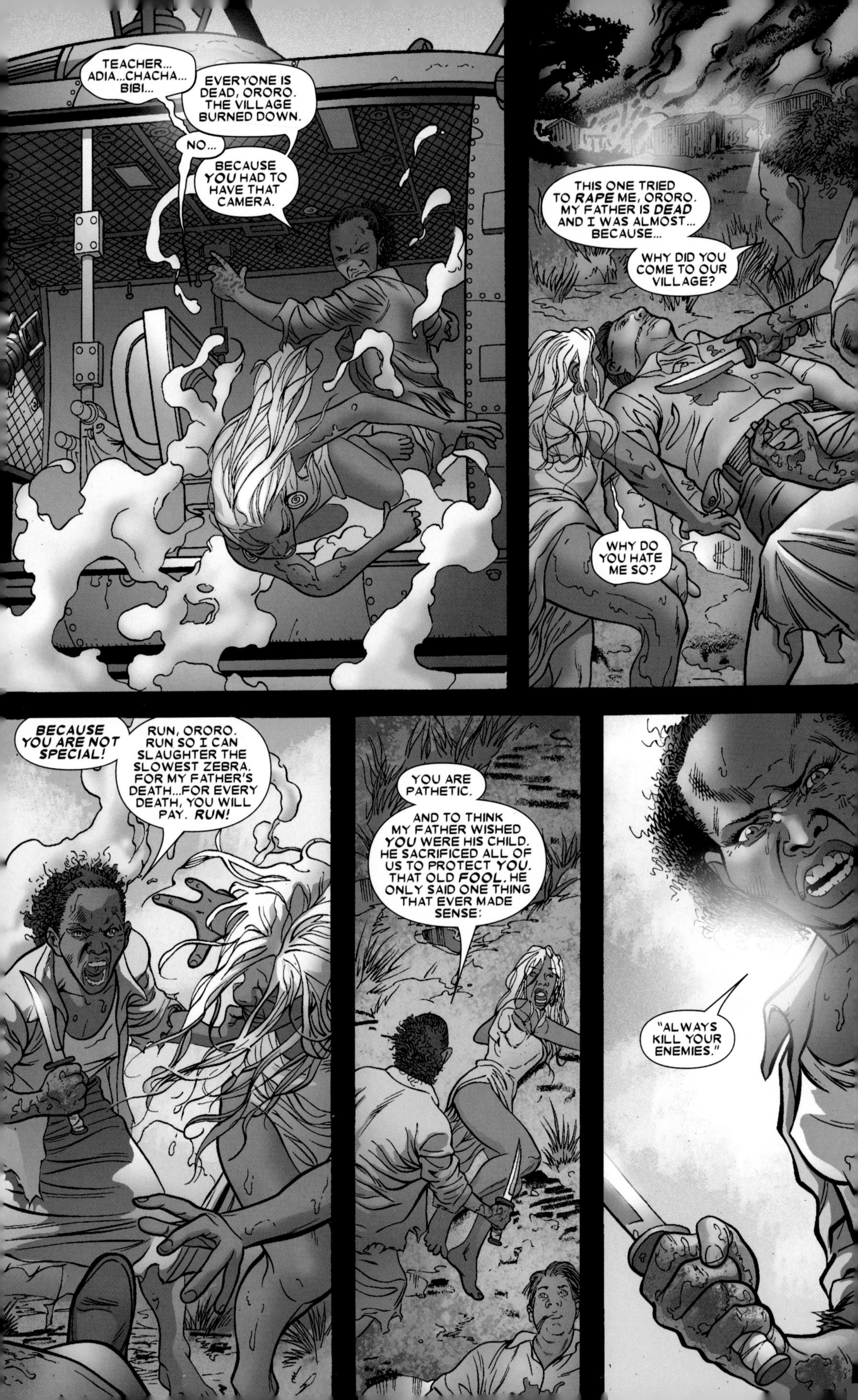
TEACHER... ADIA...CHACHA... BIBI...
EVERYONE IS DEAD, ORORO. THE VILLAGE BURNED DOWN.
NO...
BECAUSE YOU HAD TO HAVE THAT CAMERA.
THIS ONE TRIED TO RAPE ME, ORORO. MY FATHER IS DEAD AND I WAS ALMOST... BECAUSE...
WHY DID YOU COME TO OUR VILLAGE?
WHY DO YOU HATE ME SO?
BECAUSE YOU ARE NOT SPECIAL!
RUN, ORORO. RUN SO I CAN SLAUGHTER THE SLOWEST ZEBRA. FOR MY FATHER'S DEATH...FOR EVERY DEATH, YOU WILL PAY. RUN!
YOU ARE PATHETIC.
AND TO THINK MY FATHER WISHED YOU WERE HIS CHILD. HE SACRIFICED ALL OF US TO PROTECT YOU, THAT OLD FOOL. HE ONLY SAID ONE THING THAT EVER MADE SENSE:
"ALWAYS KILL YOUR ENEMIES."

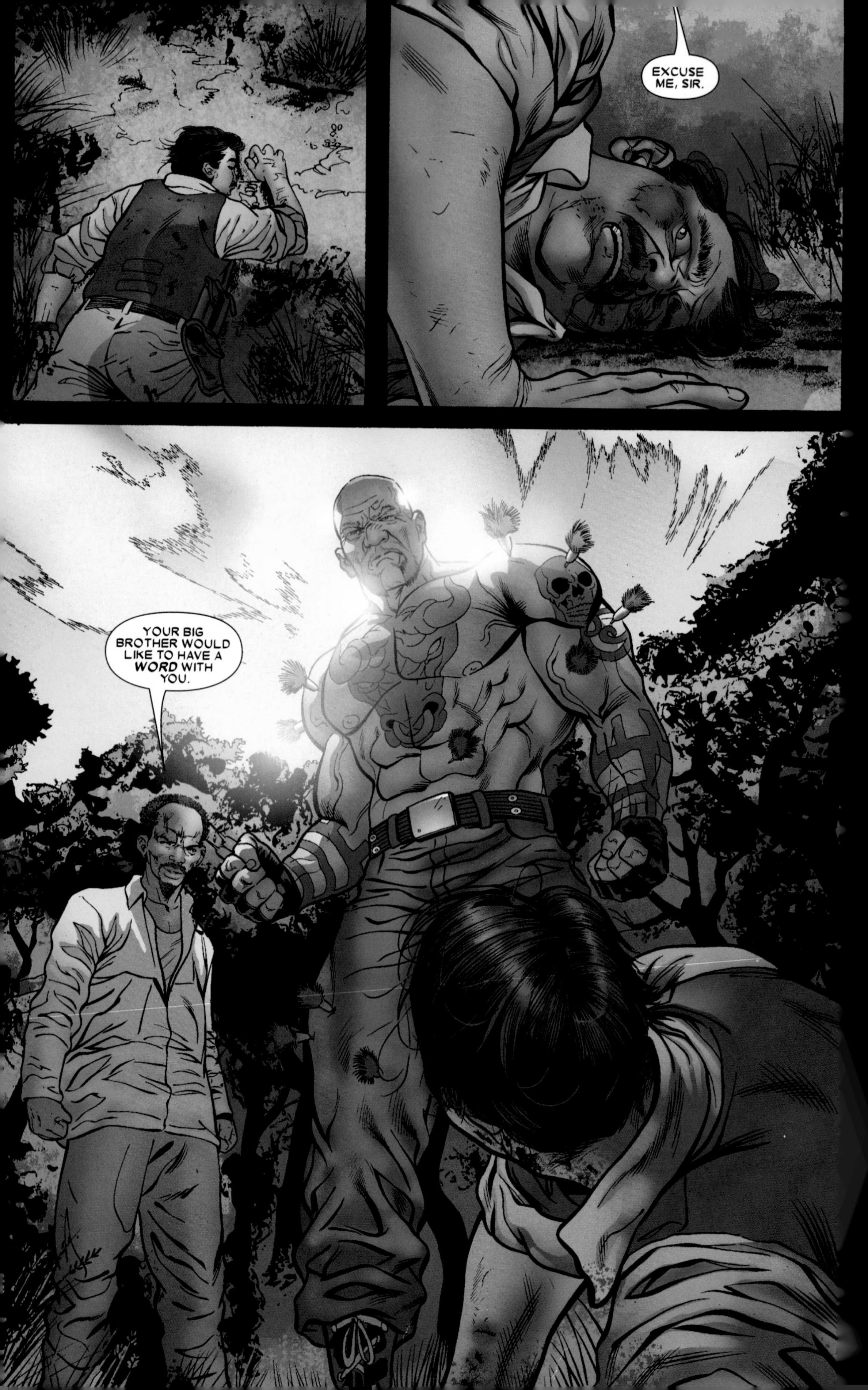
EXCUSE ME, SIR.
YOUR BIG BROTHER WOULD LIKE TO HAVE A WORD WITH YOU.

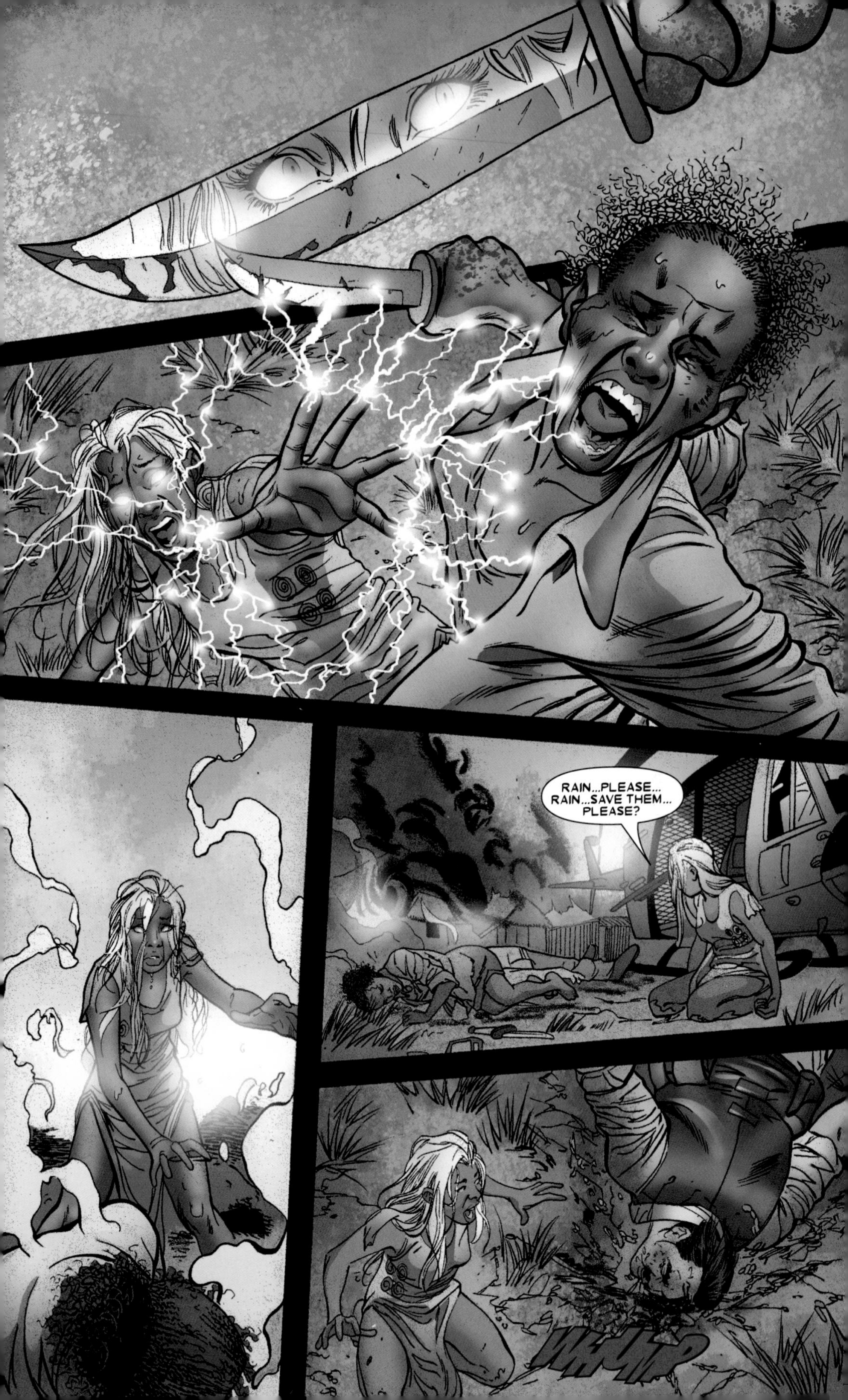
RAIN...PLEASE...
RAIN...SAVE THEM...
PLEASE?

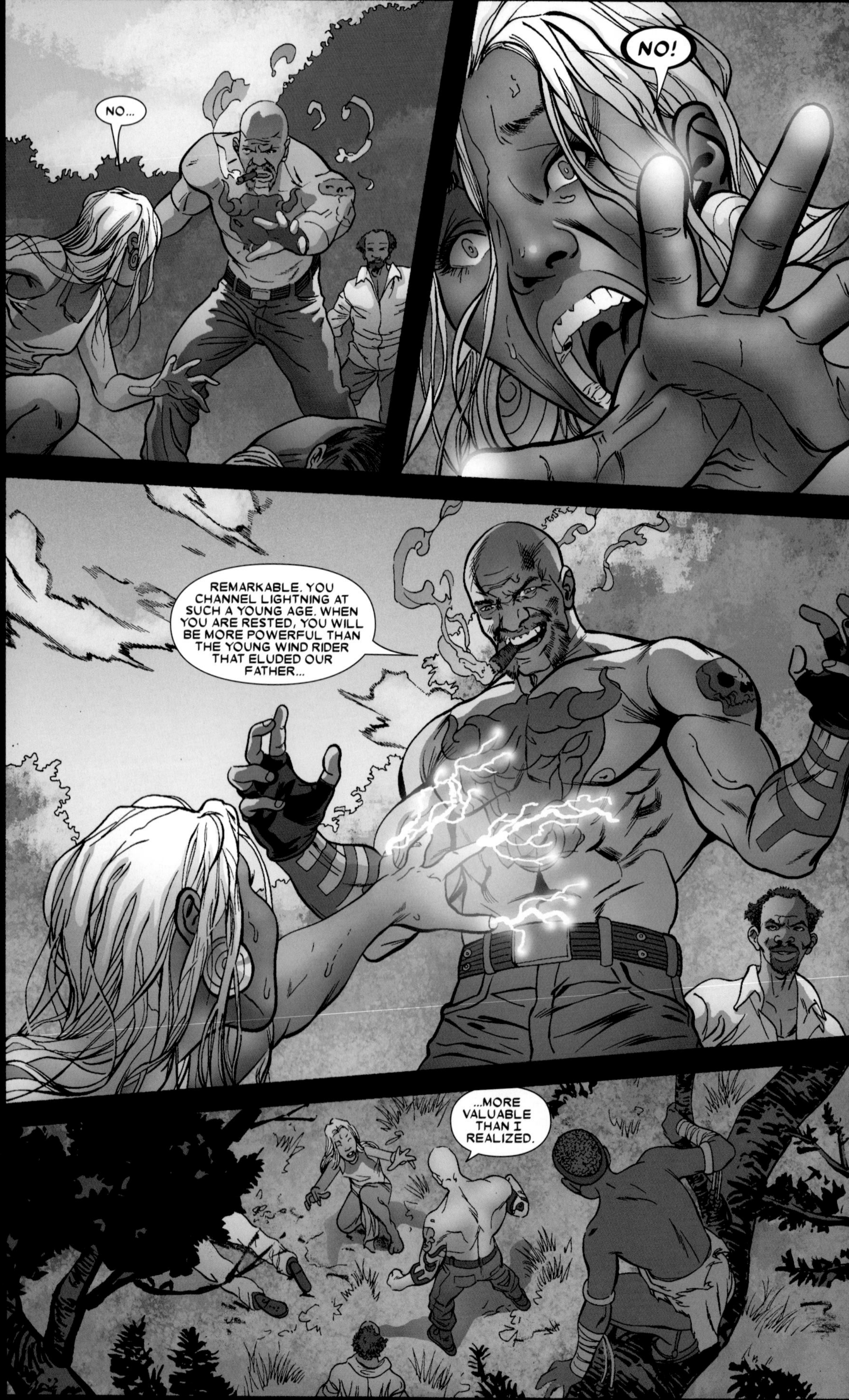
NO...
NO!
REMARKABLE. YOU CHANNEL LIGHTNING AT SUCH A YOUNG AGE. WHEN YOU ARE RESTED, YOU WILL BE MORE POWERFUL THAN THE YOUNG WIND RIDER THAT ELUDED OUR FATHER...
...MORE VALUABLE THAN I REALIZED.

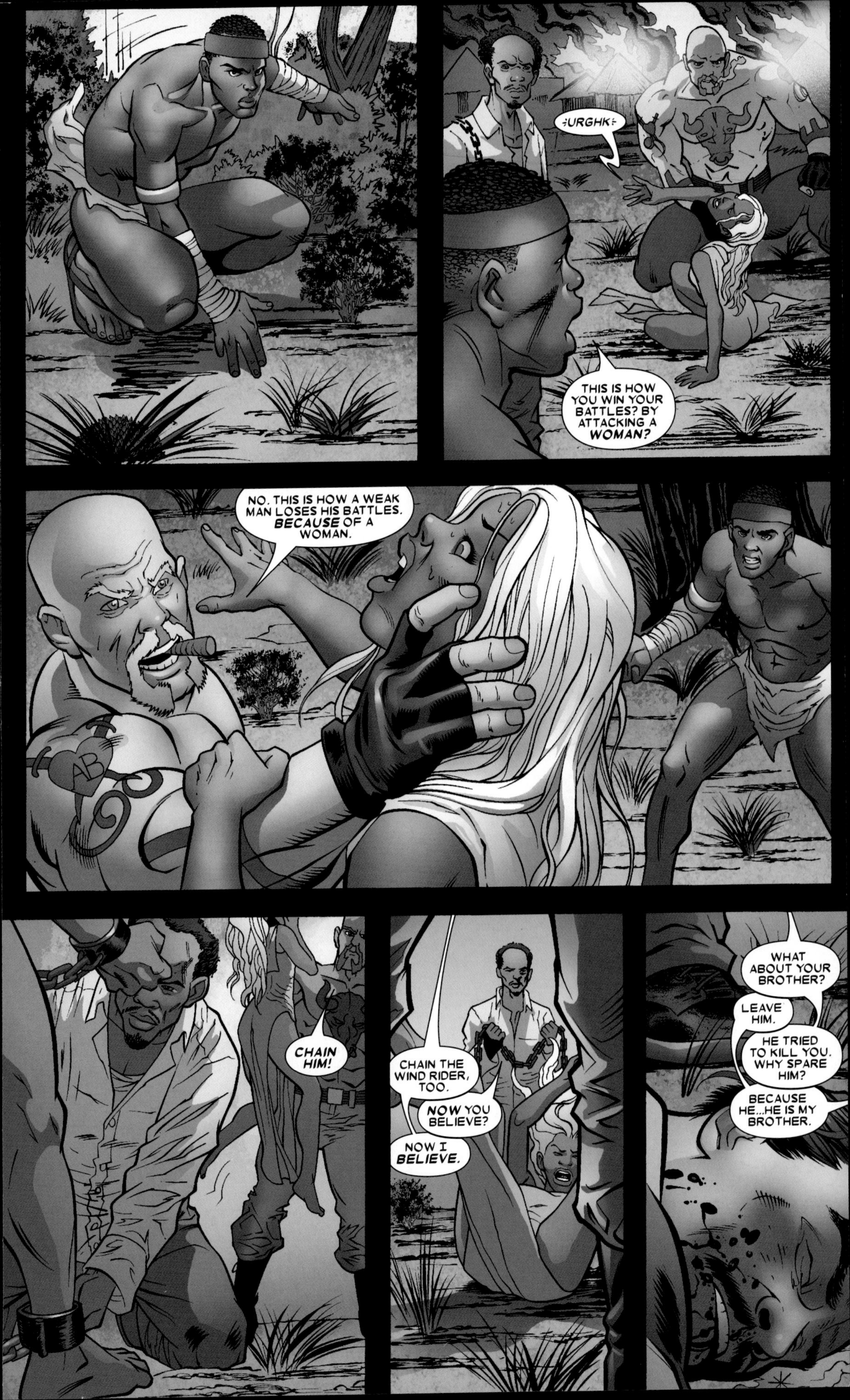

URGHK
THIS IS HOW YOU WIN YOUR BATTLES? BY ATTACKING A WOMAN?
NO. THIS IS HOW A WEAK MAN LOSES HIS BATTLES. BECAUSE OF A WOMAN.
CHAIN HIM!
CHAIN THE WIND RIDER, TOO.
NOW YOU BELIEVE?
NOW I BELIEVE.
WHAT ABOUT YOUR BROTHER?
LEAVE HIM.
HE TRIED TO KILL YOU. WHY SPARE HIM?
BECAUSE HE...HE IS MY BROTHER.

WHAT HAVE WE *DONE* TO YOU? WHY ARE YOU DOING THIS TO US?

YOUR BOYFRIEND IS THE *KEY* TO WAKANDA. THE KEY TO VIBRANIUM. MONEY. WEALTH. POWER.

AND *YOU*, YOUNG LADY, APPEAR TO HAVE THE ABILITY TO CONTROL THE WEATHER.

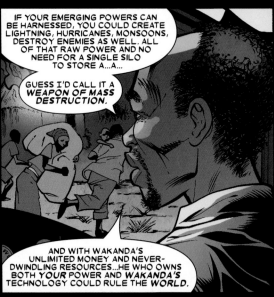

IF YOUR EMERGING POWERS CAN BE HARNESSED, YOU COULD CREATE LIGHTNING, HURRICANES, MONSOONS, DESTROY ENEMIES AS WELL. ALL OF THAT RAW POWER AND NO NEED FOR A SINGLE SILO TO STORE A...A...

GUESS I'D CALL IT A *WEAPON OF MASS DESTRUCTION.*

AND WITH WAKANDA'S UNLIMITED MONEY AND NEVER-DWINDLING RESOURCES...HE WHO OWNS BOTH *YOUR* POWER AND *WAKANDA'S* TECHNOLOGY COULD RULE THE *WORLD.*

AROUND THREE DECADES AGO, THERE WAS RUMORED TO BE ANOTHER LIKE YOU IN THIS COUNTRY, ONLY THAT WIND RIDER VANISHED AFTER MY EMPLOYER'S FATHER ATTEMPTED TO CAP--

HUSH. DON'T TALK TO THEM.

SHE *ASKED.* DIDN'T WANT TO BE RUDE.

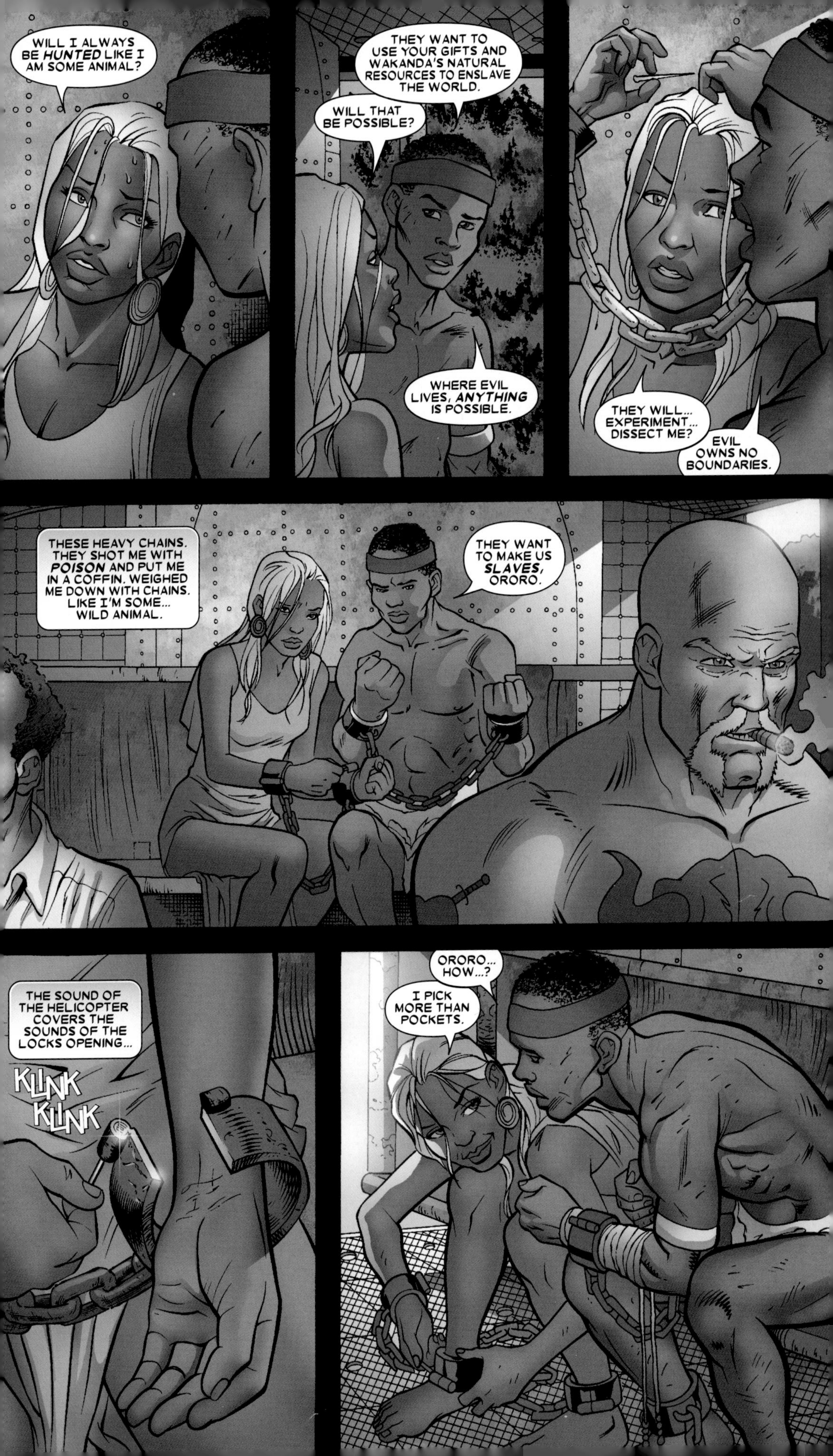

WILL I ALWAYS BE *HUNTED* LIKE I AM SOME ANIMAL?
THEY WANT TO USE YOUR GIFTS AND WAKANDA'S NATURAL RESOURCES TO ENSLAVE THE WORLD.
WILL THAT BE POSSIBLE?
WHERE EVIL LIVES, *ANYTHING* IS POSSIBLE.
THEY WILL... EXPERIMENT... DISSECT ME?
EVIL OWNS NO BOUNDARIES.
THESE HEAVY CHAINS. THEY SHOT ME WITH *POISON* AND PUT ME IN A COFFIN. WEIGHED ME DOWN WITH CHAINS. LIKE I'M SOME... WILD ANIMAL.
THEY WANT TO MAKE US *SLAVES*, ORORO.
THE SOUND OF THE HELICOPTER COVERS THE SOUNDS OF THE LOCKS OPENING...
KLINK
KLINK
ORORO... HOW...?
I PICK MORE THAN POCKETS.

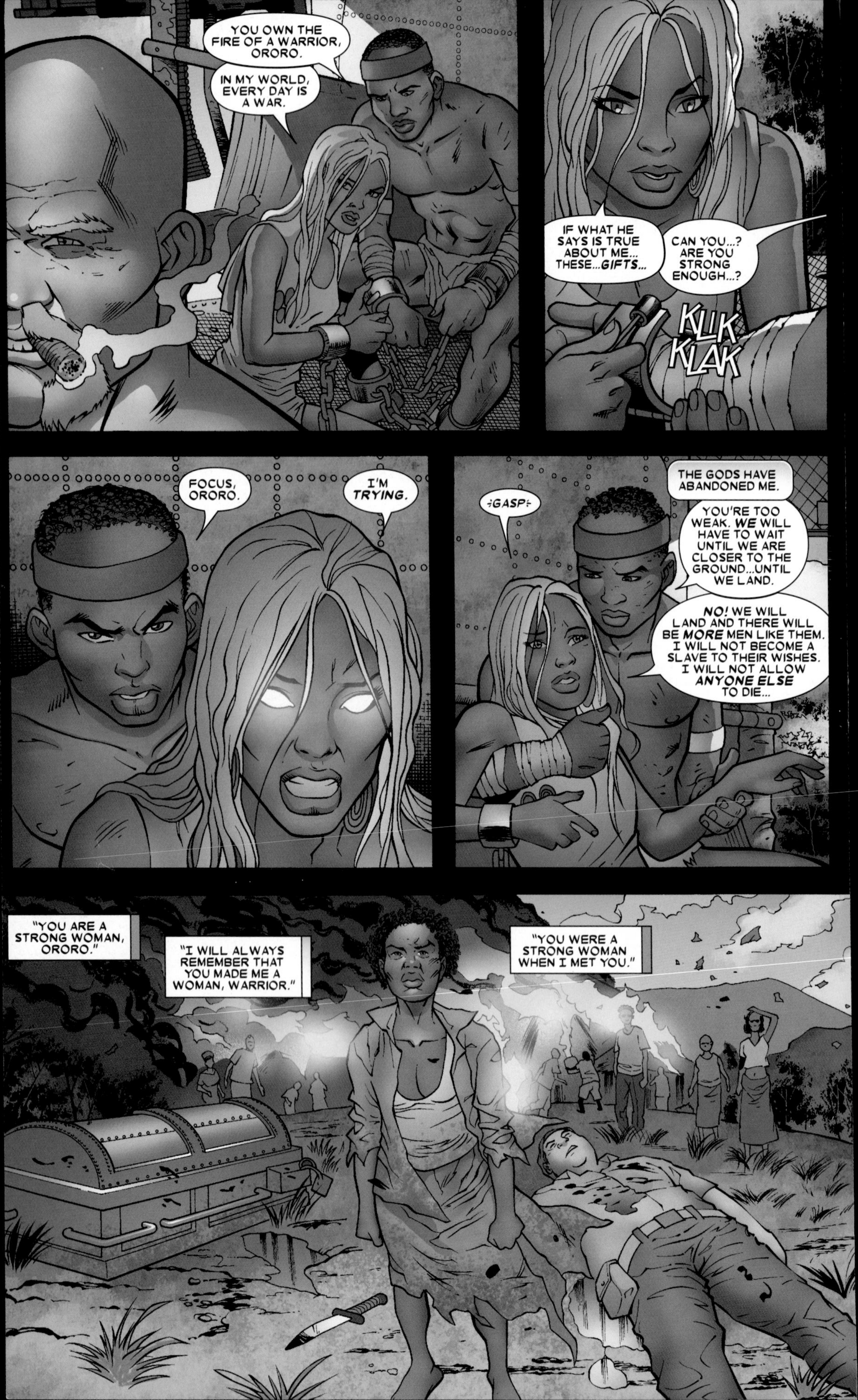
YOU OWN THE FIRE OF A WARRIOR, ORORO.
IN MY WORLD, EVERY DAY IS A WAR.
IF WHAT HE SAYS IS TRUE ABOUT ME... THESE...GIFTS...
CAN YOU...? ARE YOU STRONG ENOUGH...?
KLIK KLAK
FOCUS, ORORO.
I'M TRYING.
GASP
THE GODS HAVE ABANDONED ME.
YOU'RE TOO WEAK. WE WILL HAVE TO WAIT UNTIL WE ARE CLOSER TO THE GROUND...UNTIL WE LAND.
NO! WE WILL LAND AND THERE WILL BE MORE MEN LIKE THEM. I WILL NOT BECOME A SLAVE TO THEIR WISHES. I WILL NOT ALLOW ANYONE ELSE TO DIE...
"YOU ARE A STRONG WOMAN, ORORO."
"I WILL ALWAYS REMEMBER THAT YOU MADE ME A WOMAN, WARRIOR."
"YOU WERE A STRONG WOMAN WHEN I MET YOU."

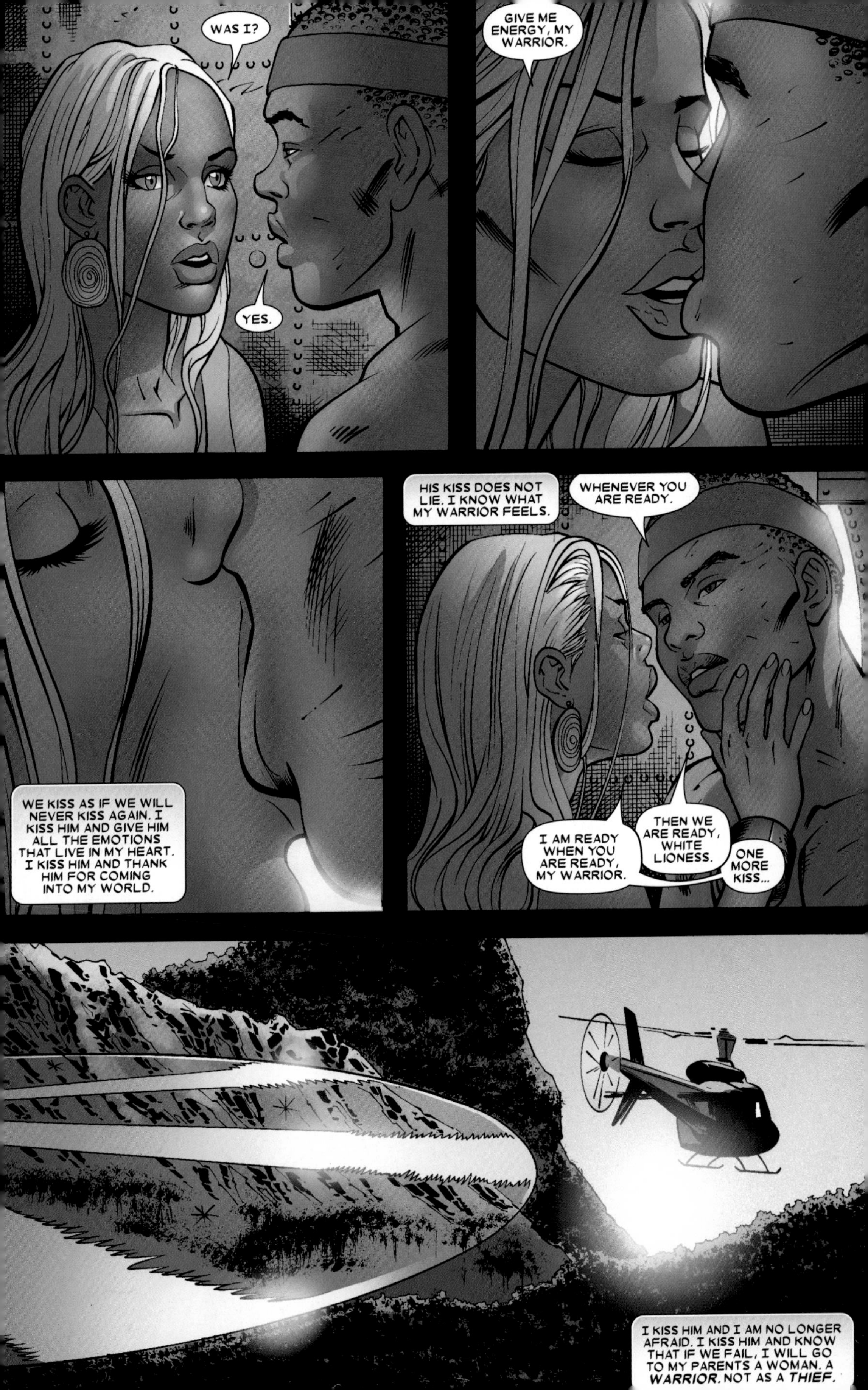
WAS I?
YES.
GIVE ME ENERGY, MY WARRIOR.
WE KISS AS IF WE WILL NEVER KISS AGAIN. I KISS HIM AND GIVE HIM ALL THE EMOTIONS THAT LIVE IN MY HEART. I KISS HIM AND THANK HIM FOR COMING INTO MY WORLD.
HIS KISS DOES NOT LIE. I KNOW WHAT MY WARRIOR FEELS.
WHENEVER YOU ARE READY.
I AM READY WHEN YOU ARE READY, MY WARRIOR.
THEN WE ARE READY, WHITE LIONESS.
ONE MORE KISS...
I KISS HIM AND I AM NO LONGER AFRAID. I KISS HIM AND KNOW THAT IF WE FAIL, I WILL GO TO MY PARENTS A WOMAN. A *WARRIOR*. NOT AS A *THIEF*.

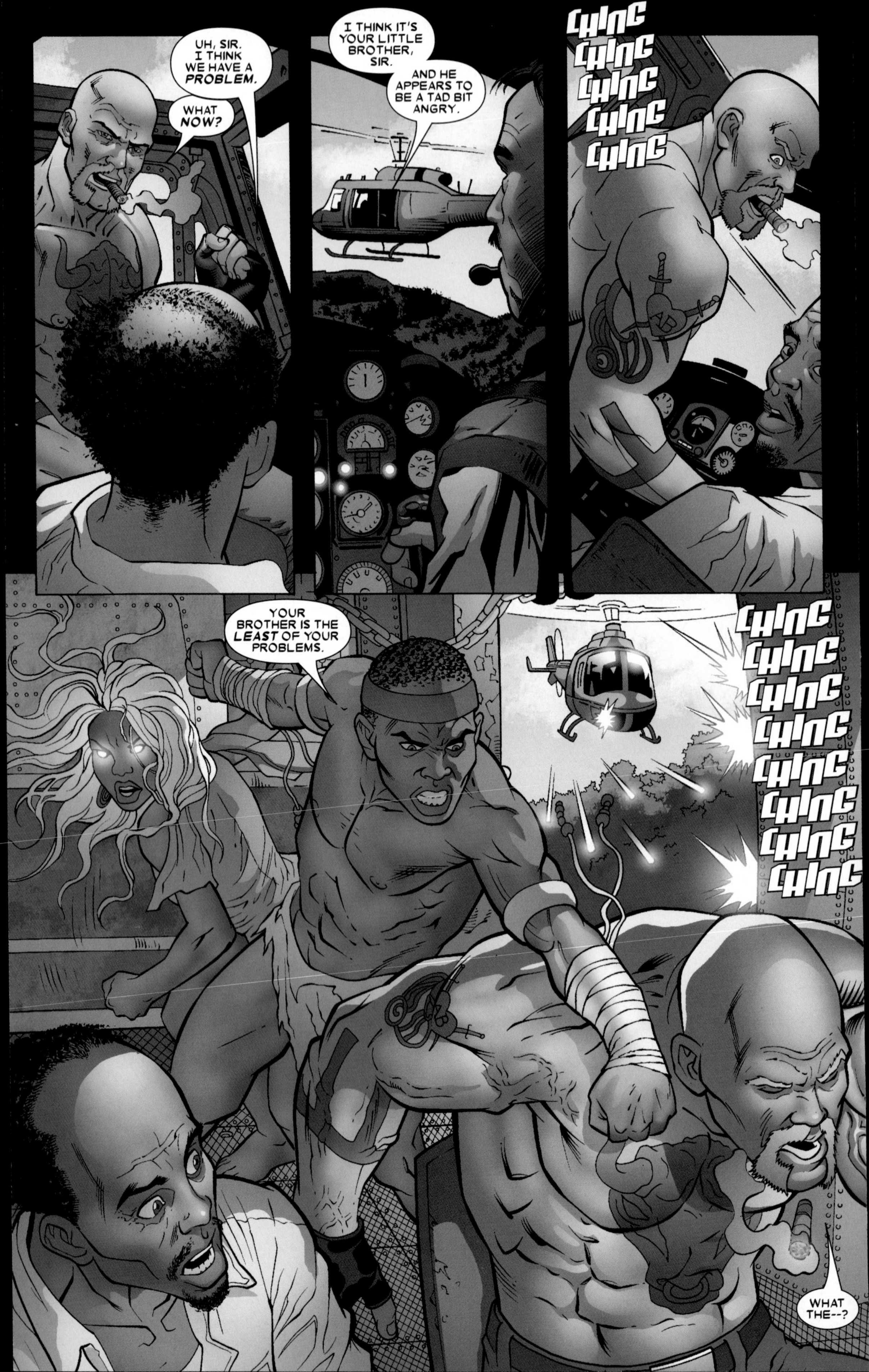
UH, SIR. I THINK WE HAVE A PROBLEM.
WHAT NOW?
I THINK IT'S YOUR LITTLE BROTHER, SIR.
AND HE APPEARS TO BE A TAD BIT ANGRY.
CHING CHING CHING CHING CHING
YOUR BROTHER IS THE LEAST OF YOUR PROBLEMS.
CHING CHING CHING CHING CHING CHING CHING CHING
WHAT THE--?

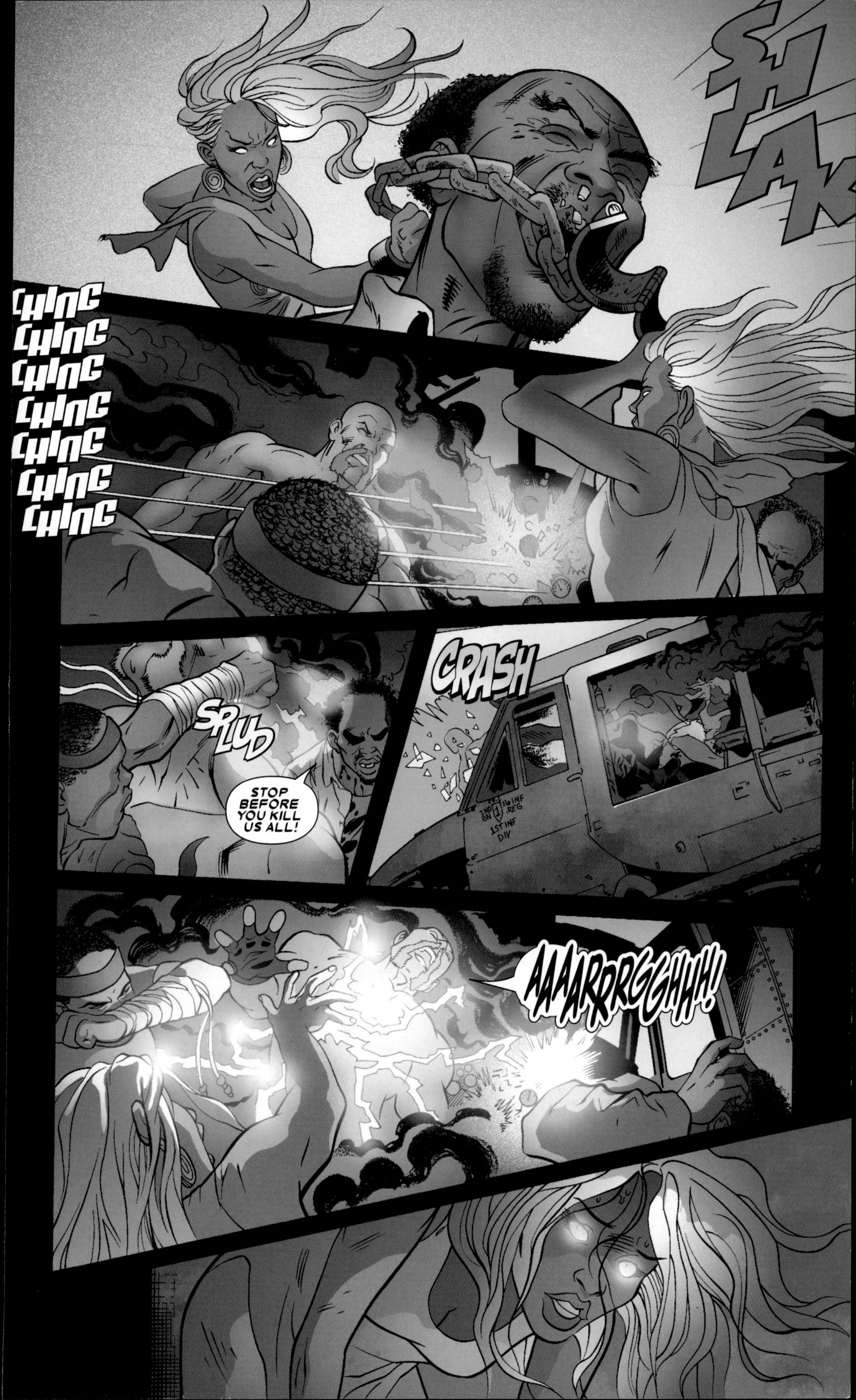
SHLAK
CHING
CHING
CHING
CHING
CHING
CHING
CHING
SPLUD
STOP BEFORE YOU KILL US ALL!
CRASH
2ND BN 1 16 INF REG
1ST INF DIV
AAAARRRGGHHH!

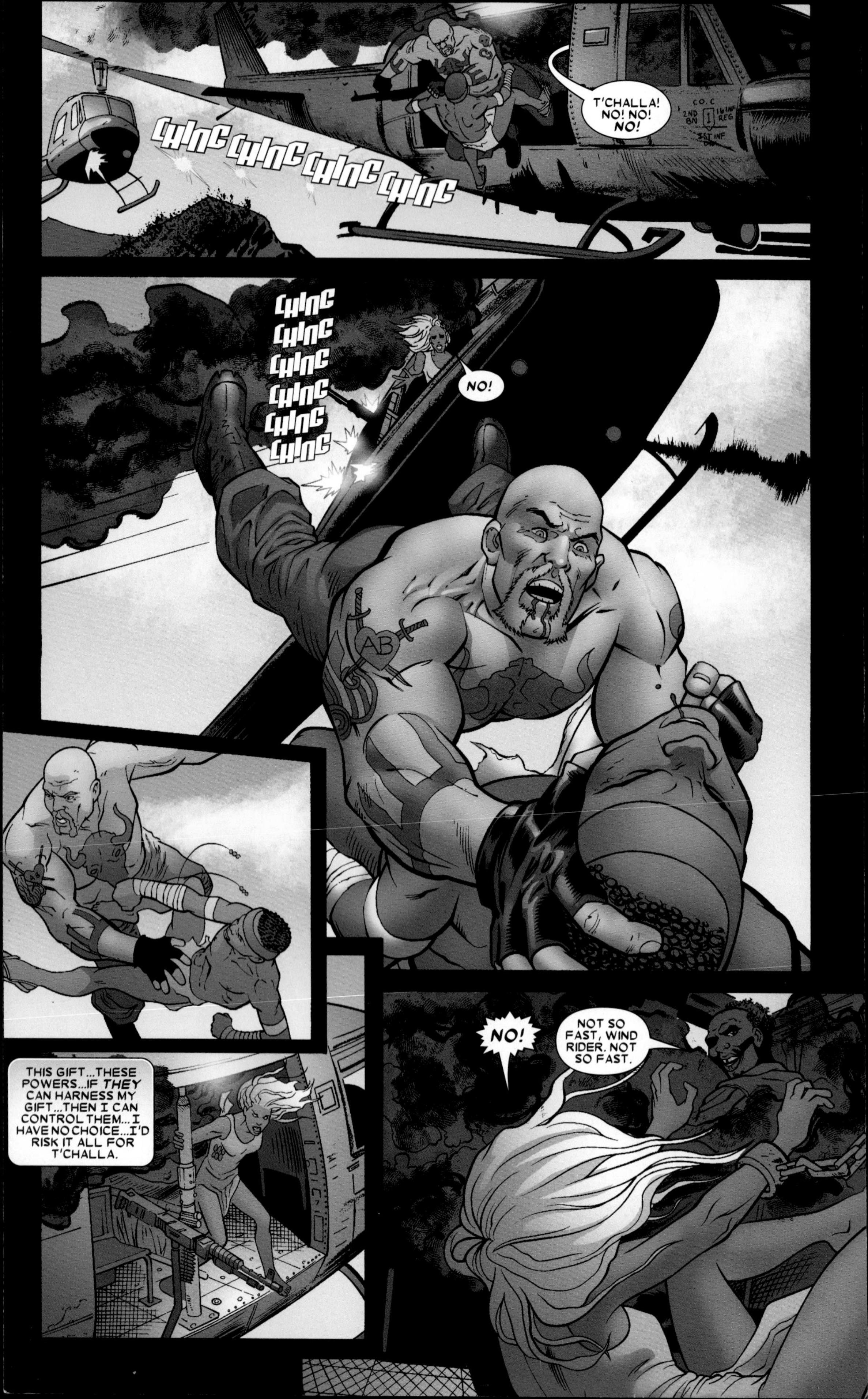
CHINC CHINC CHINC CHINC
T'CHALLA! NO! NO! NO!
CHINC CHINC CHINC CHINC CHINC CHINC
NO!
THIS GIFT...THESE POWERS...IF THEY CAN HARNESS MY GIFT...THEN I CAN CONTROL THEM...I HAVE NO CHOICE...I'D RISK IT ALL FOR T'CHALLA.
NO!
NOT SO FAST, WIND RIDER. NOT SO FAST.

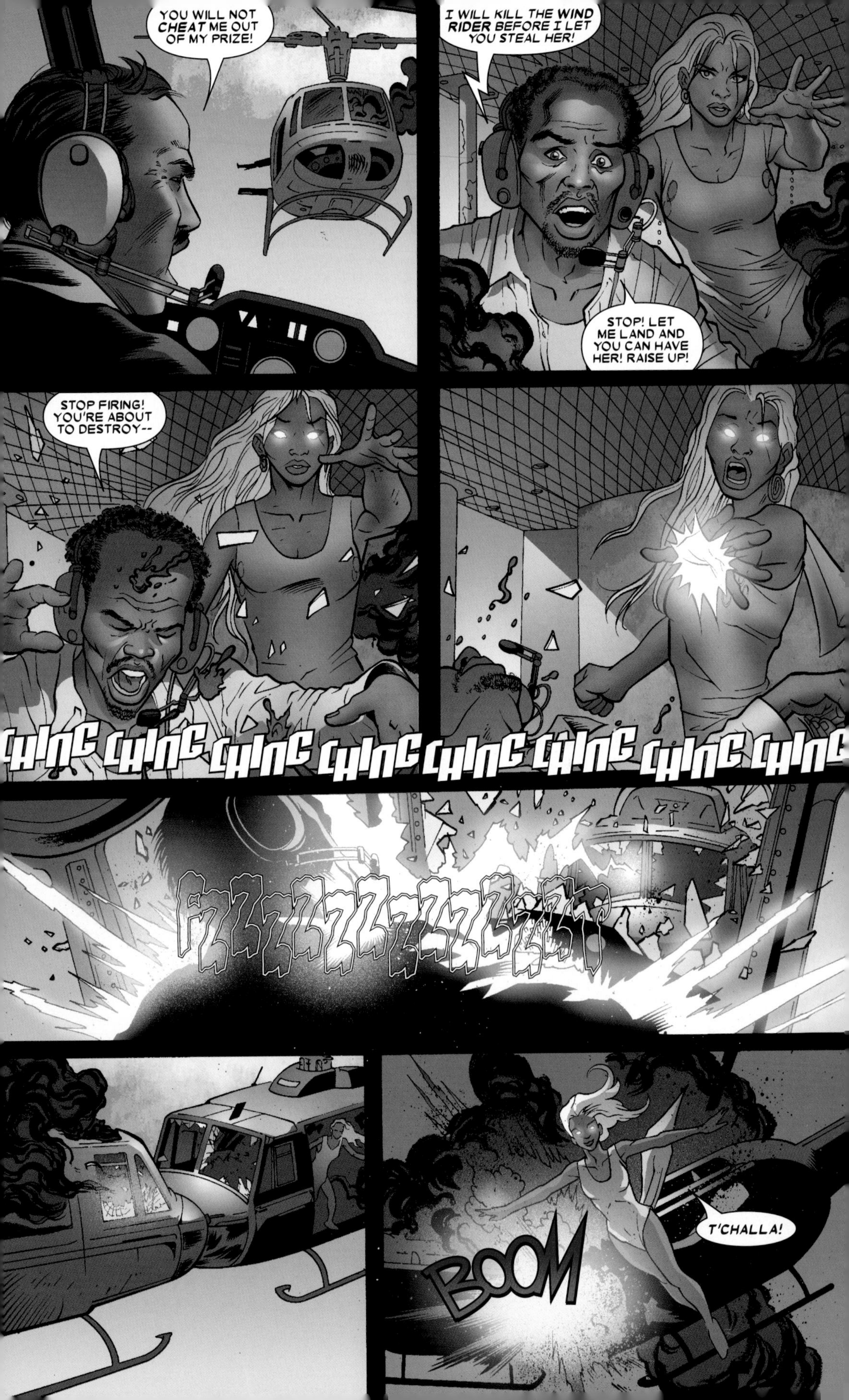
YOU WILL NOT CHEAT ME OUT OF MY PRIZE!
I WILL KILL THE WIND RIDER BEFORE I LET YOU STEAL HER!
STOP! LET ME LAND AND YOU CAN HAVE HER! RAISE UP!
STOP FIRING! YOU'RE ABOUT TO DESTROY--
CHING CHING CHING CHING CHING CHING CHING CHING
BOOM
T'CHALLA!

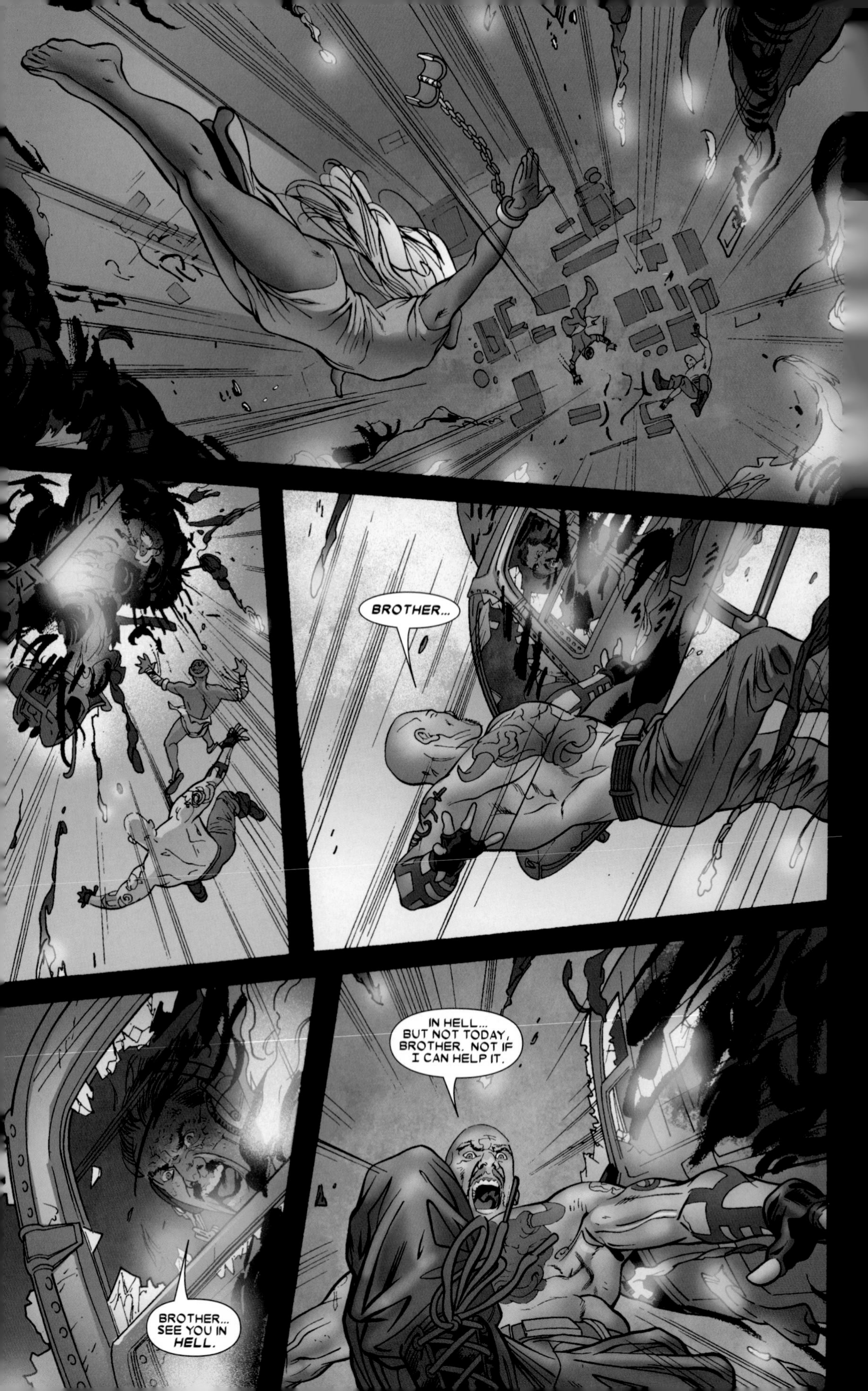
BROTHER...
BROTHER... SEE YOU IN HELL.
IN HELL... BUT NOT TODAY, BROTHER. NOT IF I CAN HELP IT.

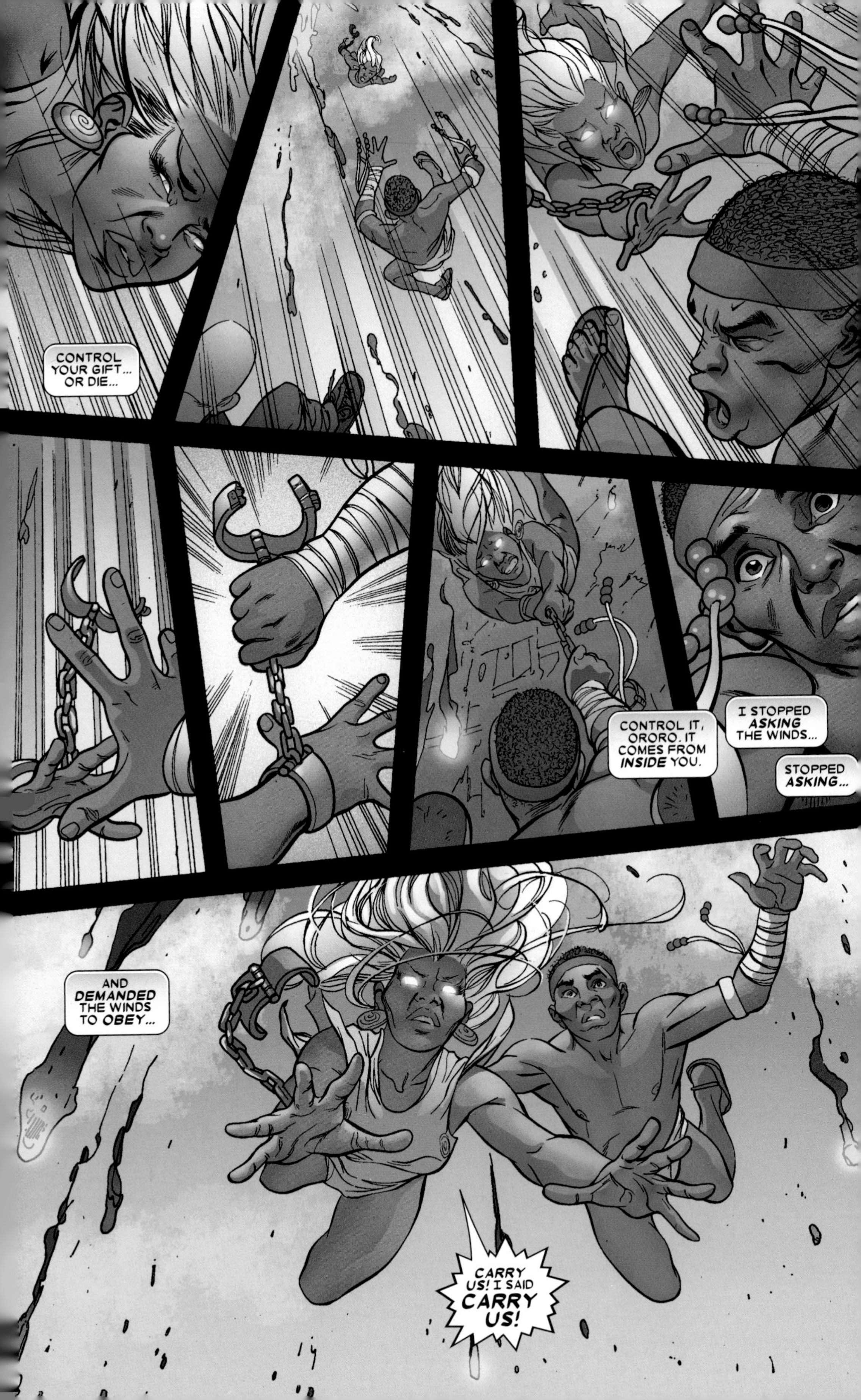
CONTROL YOUR GIFT... OR DIE...
CONTROL IT, ORORO. IT COMES FROM INSIDE YOU.
I STOPPED ASKING THE WINDS...
STOPPED ASKING...
AND DEMANDED THE WINDS TO OBEY...
CARRY US! I SAID CARRY US!

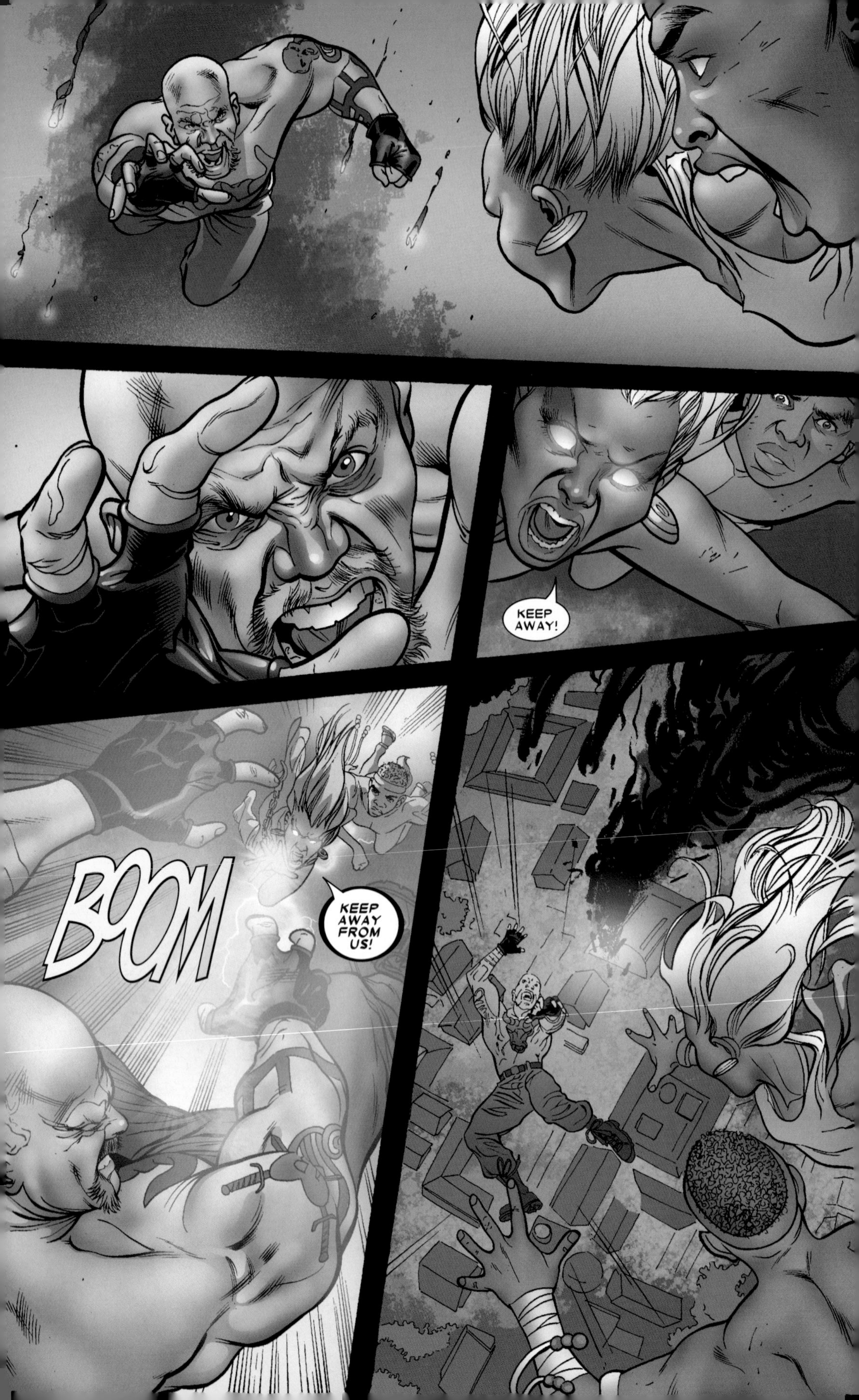
KEEP AWAY!
BOOM
KEEP AWAY FROM US!

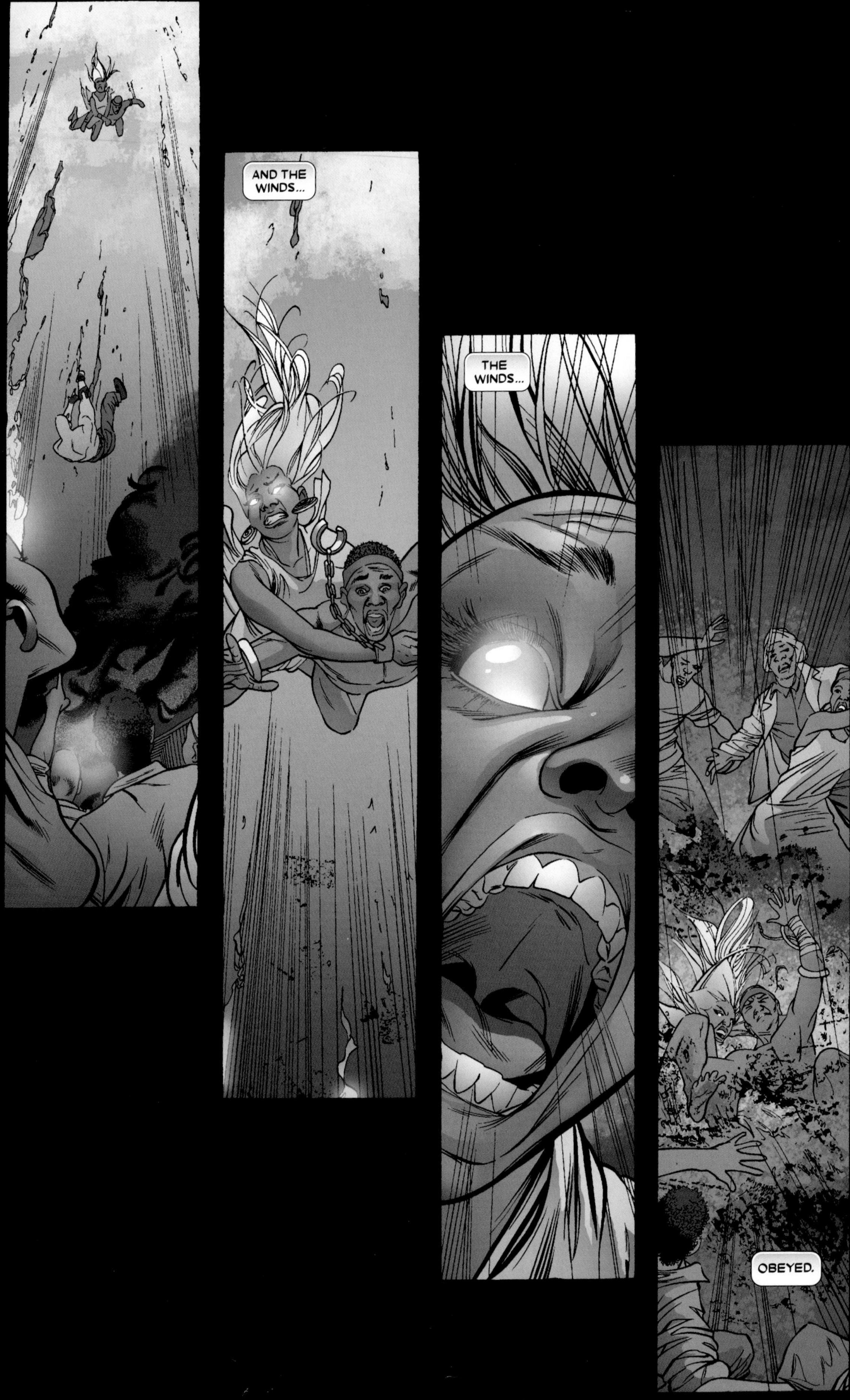
AND THE WINDS...
THE WINDS...
OBEYED.

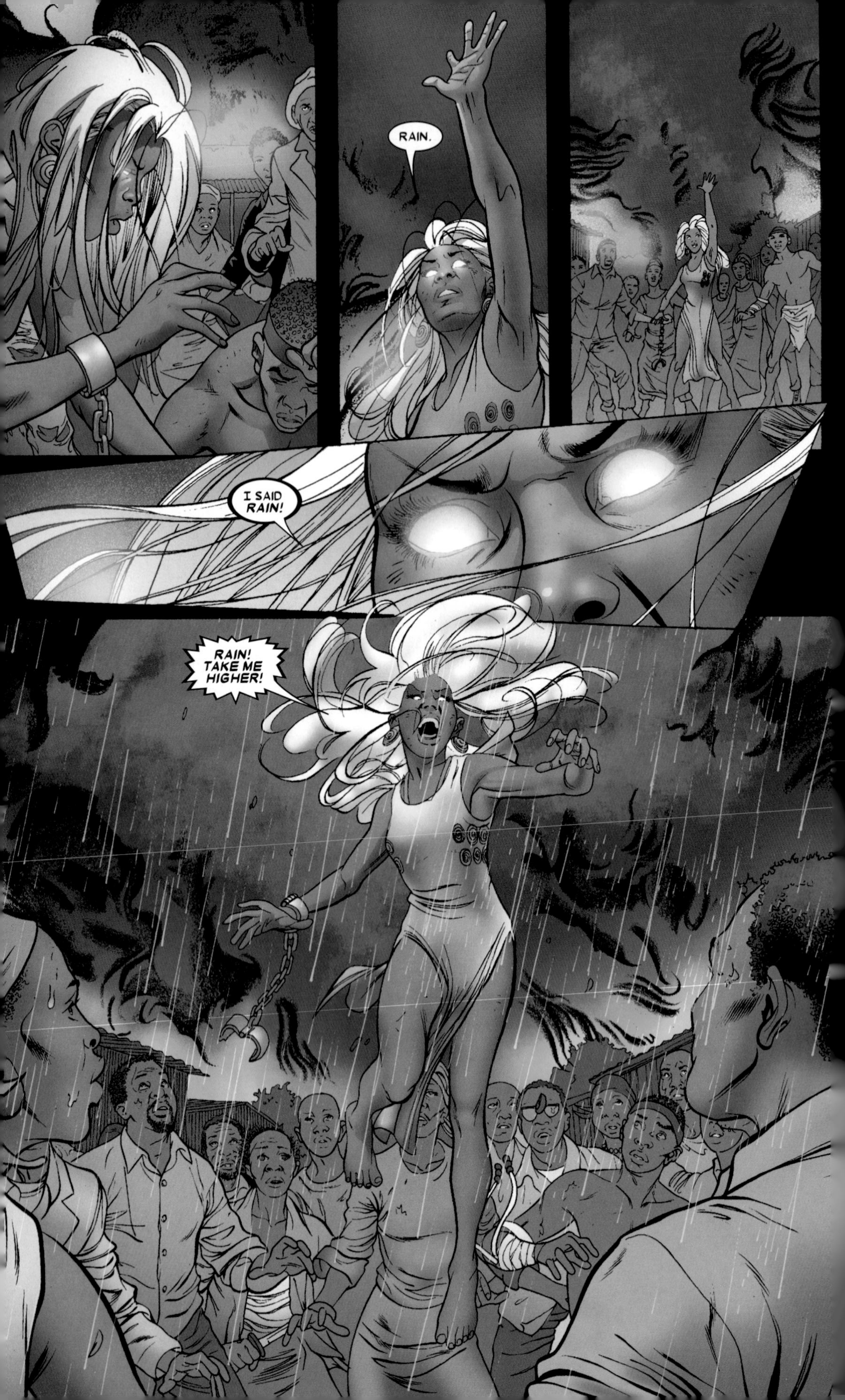
RAIN.
I SAID RAIN!
RAIN! TAKE ME HIGHER!

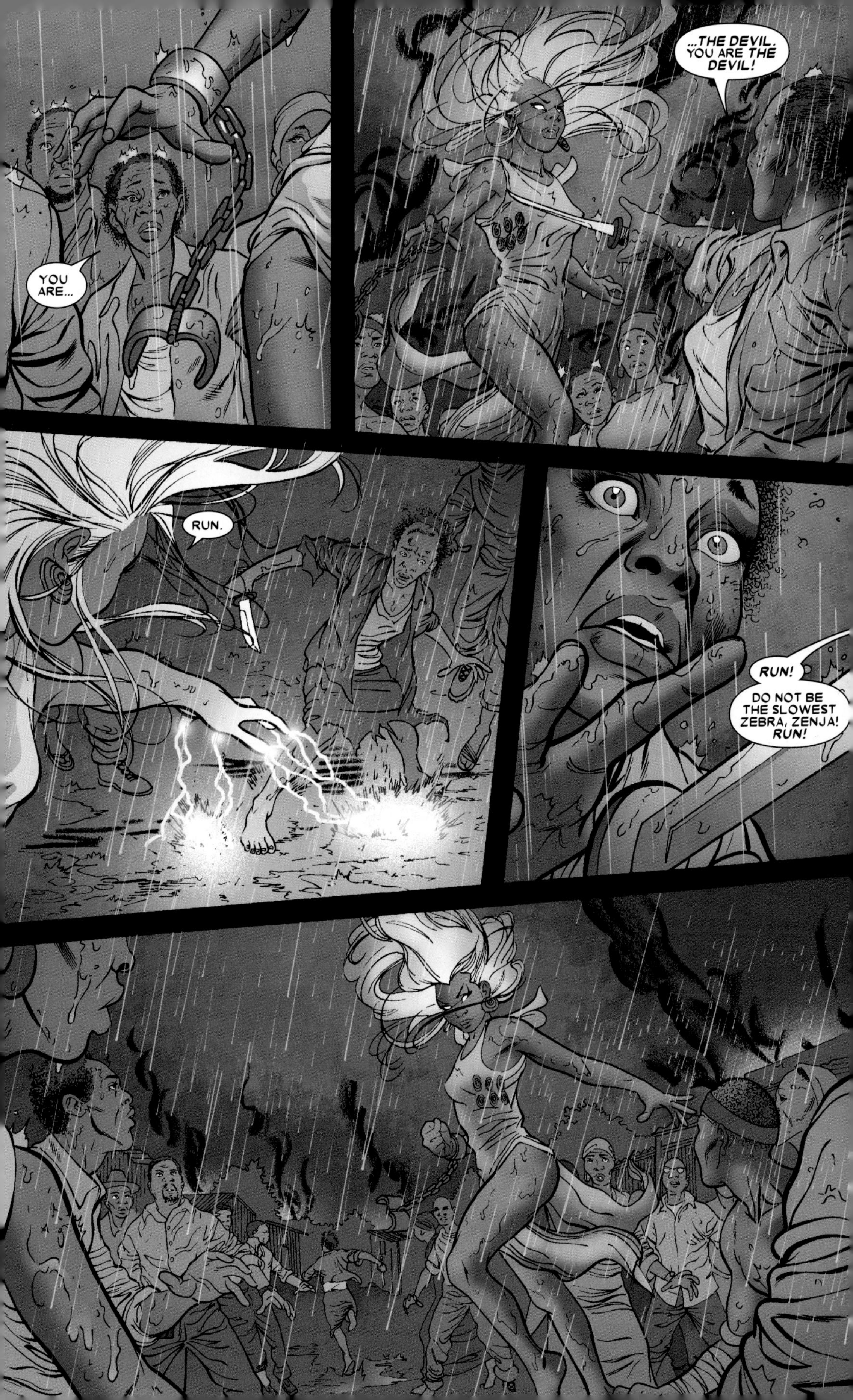
YOU ARE...
...THE DEVIL. YOU ARE THE DEVIL!
RUN.
RUN!
DO NOT BE THE SLOWEST ZEBRA, ZENJA! RUN!

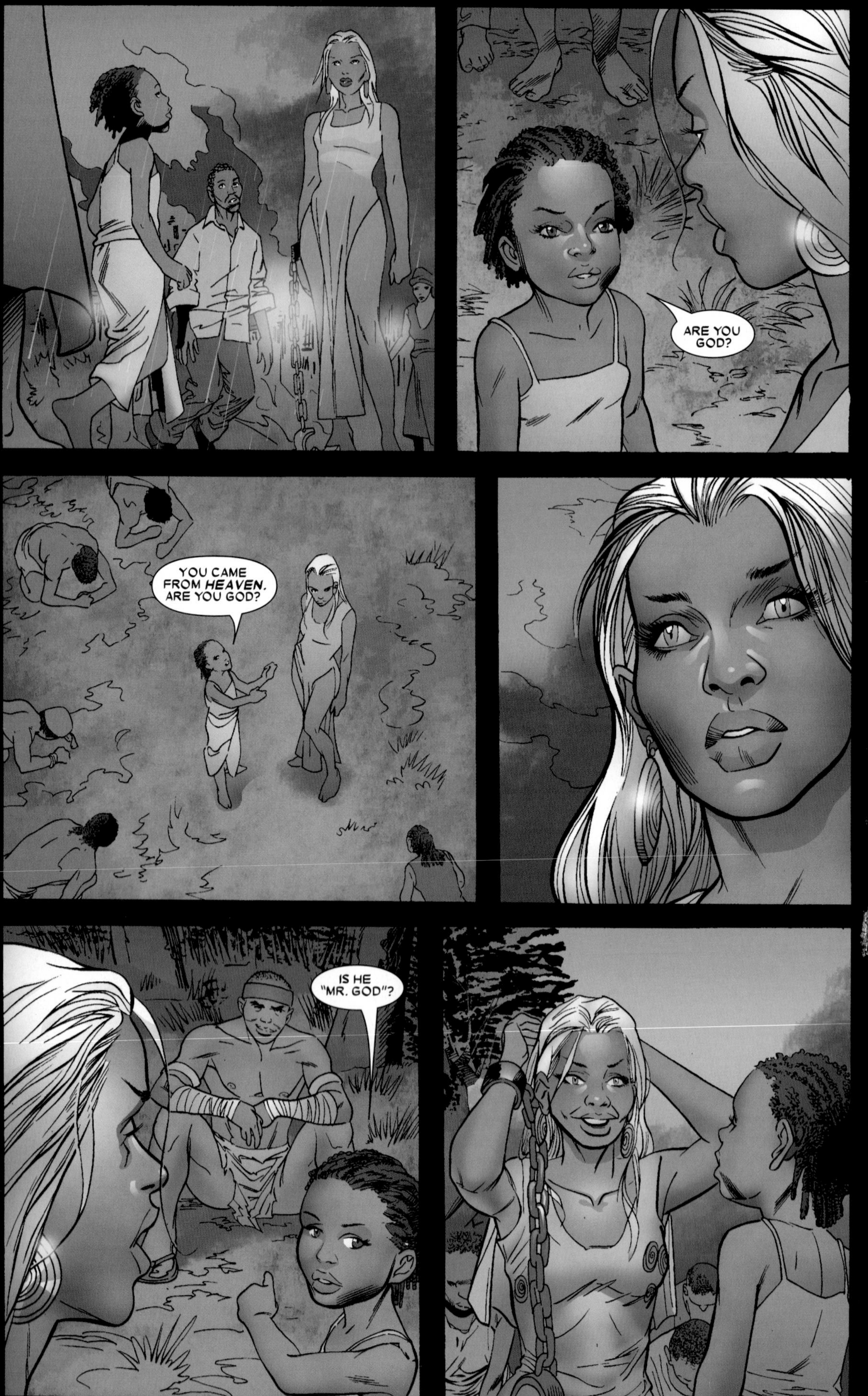
ARE YOU GOD?
YOU CAME FROM *HEAVEN.* ARE YOU GOD?
IS HE "MR. GOD"?

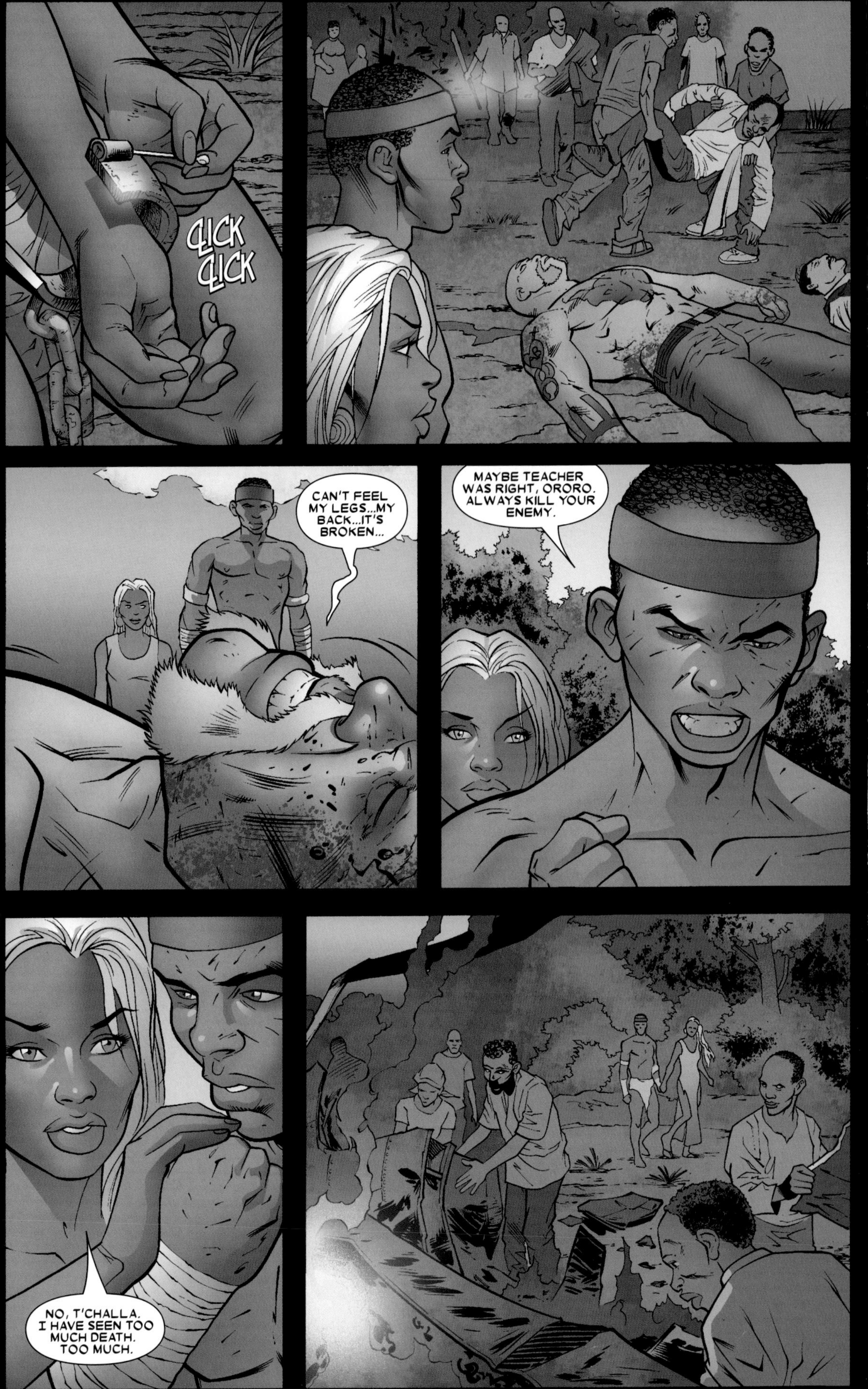
CLICK CLICK
CAN'T FEEL MY LEGS...MY BACK...IT'S BROKEN...
MAYBE TEACHER WAS RIGHT, ORORO. ALWAYS KILL YOUR ENEMY.
NO, T'CHALLA. I HAVE SEEN TOO MUCH DEATH. TOO MUCH.

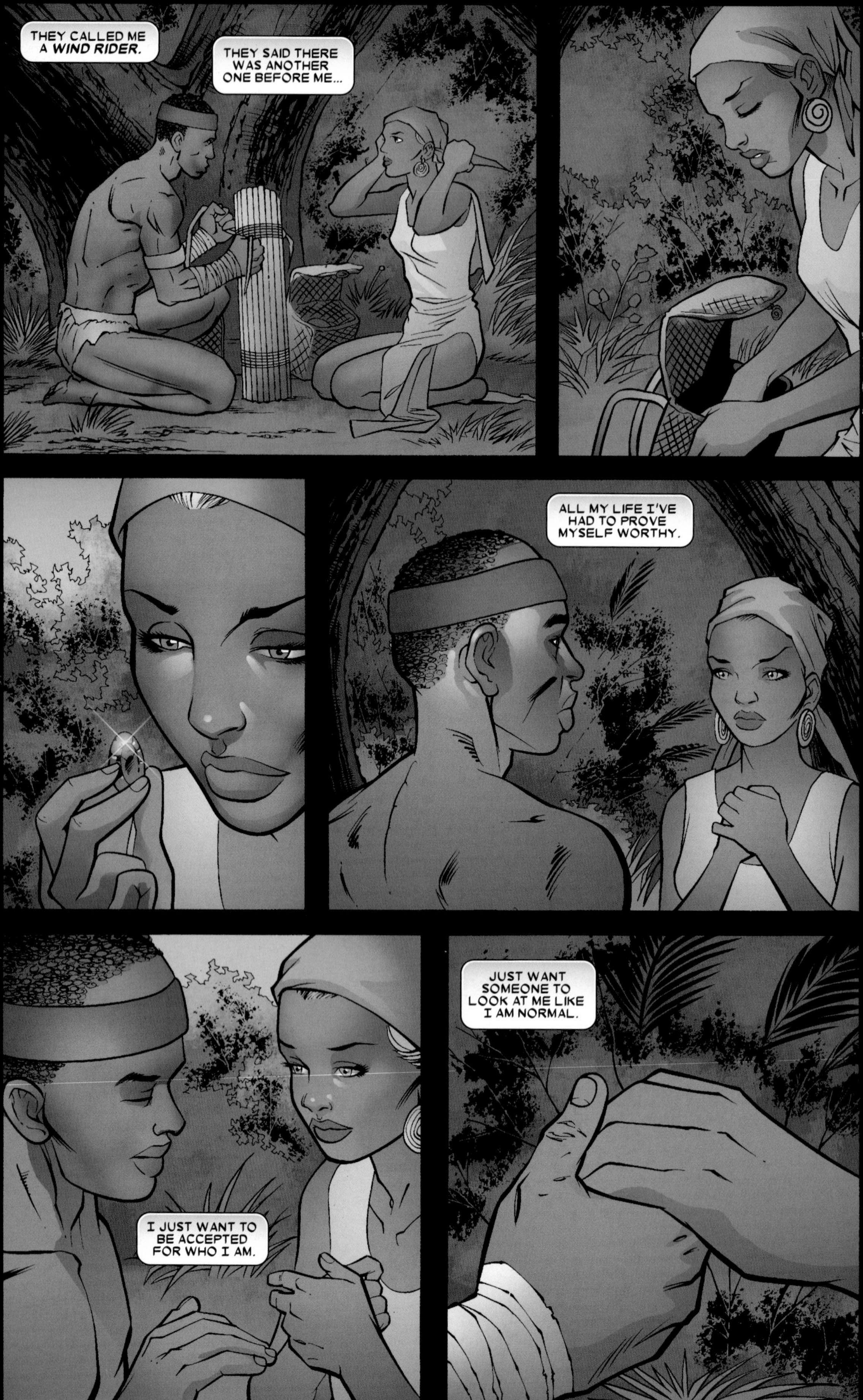
THEY CALLED ME A ***WIND RIDER.***
THEY SAID THERE WAS ANOTHER ONE BEFORE ME...
ALL MY LIFE I'VE HAD TO PROVE MYSELF WORTHY.
I JUST WANT TO BE ACCEPTED FOR WHO I AM.
JUST WANT SOMEONE TO LOOK AT ME LIKE I AM NORMAL.

I WAS
A THIEF.

AN ORPHAN.

BEHAVE.

WHAT DID I TELL
YOU ABOUT TALKING
TO ME LIKE I'M A CHILD?
I AM A WOMAN,
T'CHALLA.

THEN
BEHAVE,
WOMAN.

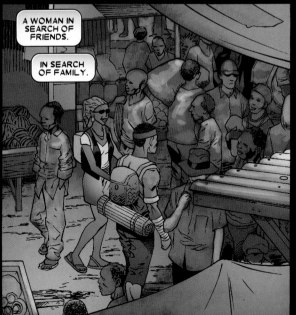

A WOMAN IN
SEARCH OF
FRIENDS.

IN SEARCH
OF FAMILY.

ARE YOU TRYING
TO START A FIRE,
T'CHALLA?

BEHAVE.

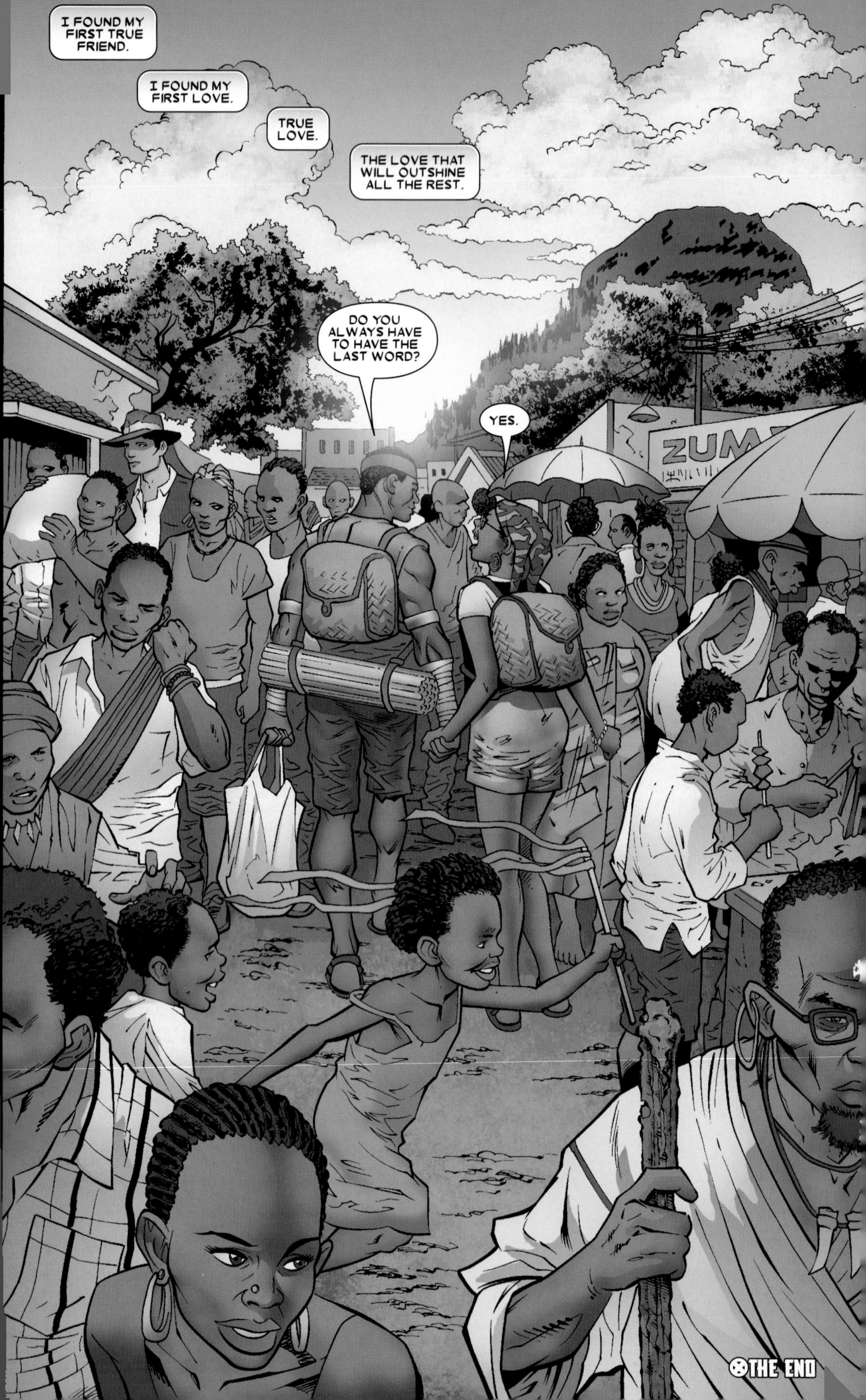
I FOUND MY FIRST TRUE FRIEND.
I FOUND MY FIRST LOVE.
TRUE LOVE.
THE LOVE THAT WILL OUTSHINE ALL THE REST.
DO YOU ALWAYS HAVE TO HAVE THE LAST WORD?
YES.
ZUM
THE END